# China Joins the World: Progress and Prospects

### Edited by
### Elizabeth Economy     Michel Oksenberg

COUNCIL ON FOREIGN RELATIONS PRESS
NEW YORK

The Council on Foreign Relations, Inc., a nonprofit, nonpartisan national membership organization founded in 1921, is dedicated to promoting understanding of international affairs through the free and civil exchange of ideas. The Council's members are dedicated to the belief that America's peace and prosperity are firmly linked to that of the world. From this flows the mission of the Council: to foster America's understanding of its fellow members of the international community, near and far, their peoples, cultures, histories, hopes, quarrels, and ambitions; and thus to serve, protect, and advance America's own global interests through study and debate, private and public.

From time to time books, monographs, and reports written by members of the Council's research staff or others are published as a "Council on Foreign Relations Book." Any work bearing that designation is, in the judgment of the Committee on Studies of the Council's Board of Directors, a responsible treatment of a significant international topic.

THE COUNCIL TAKES NO INSTITUTIONAL POSITION ON POLICY ISSUES AND HAS NO AFFILIATION WITH THE U.S. GOVERNMENT. ALL STATEMENTS OF FACT AND EXPRESSIONS OF OPINION CONTAINED IN ALL ITS PUBLICATIONS ARE THE SOLE RESPONSIBILITY OF THE AUTHOR OR AUTHORS.

*Council on Foreign Relations Books are distributed by Brookings Institution Press (1-800-275-1447). For further information on Council publications, please write the Council on Foreign Relations, 58 East 68th Street, New York, NY 10021, or call the Director of Communications at (212) 434-9400. Or visit our web site at www.foreignrelations.org.*

Library of Congress Cataloging-in-Publication Data

China Joins the World: Progress and Prospects / edited by Elizabeth
   Economy and Michel Oksenberg.
        p.      cm.
   Includes bibliographical references and index.
   ISBN 0-87609-225-3
   1. China.   2. China–Foreign Relations.
   3. United States—Foreign relations.
KZ6373.E28   1999
327.1'17—DC21

# Contents

# Contents

# Foreword

CHINA began to redress its international isolation only 25 years ago. The changes have transformed every aspect of China's relationship with the outside world: from exclusion from the United Nations to participation in over 150 international organizations; from a U.S. trade embargo to $300 billion in foreign trade; from a handful of Chinese students studying abroad to over 100,000 participants in educational exchange programs; from one China Cable Office dispatching telegrams to over 2,000 circuit links between China and the United States alone; from a policy of self-reliance and suspicion to one of openness and integration.

What does the future hold for China and the world? Will a resilient economy combined with foreign policy restraint bring a leadership position in the international community? Or will a growing defense budget, expansive territorial claims, arms sales, and weapons technology transfers intensify concerns about China's future course? Will China's new generation of leaders make the compromise necessary to sustain forward momentum on such major issues as Taiwan and accession to the World Trade Organization?

Elizabeth Economy and Michel Oksenberg's volume examines the record of the last quarter century for clues about China's future orientation. Authoritative contributors to this volume analyze China's participation in eight international regimes: the United Nations, arms control, human rights, trade, banking and finance, telecommunications, energy, and the environment. The chapters explore the evolution of China's behavior and provide insights for U.S. policymakers and practitioners seeking Beijing's cooperation in each of these regimes.

*Lawrence J. Korb*
Maurice R. Greenberg Chair, Director of Studies
Council on Foreign Relations

# Preface

Secretary of State Madeleine Albright has stated that the United States has multifaceted interests with regard to China and that none of these prevails over all the others. The findings of this volume underline her observation. At the same time, we conclude that American policy must go beyond the slogan of "constructive engagement" and recognition that American interests are multifaceted. Even though no single interest is overriding, American policy must display a sense of priorities and an understanding of the interrelationship among its many interests. A workable and sustainable China policy must answer three fundamental questions: What are the priorities? What strategic mix of enticements and pressures should be pursued to encourage China to participate constructively in world affairs? What precautionary measures should be built into this strategy in case these efforts fail?

Our case studies of Chinese participation in eight international regimes—human rights, arms control, the United Nations, trade, banking, the environment, energy, and telecommunications—suggest that U.S. priorities should be on enhancing mutual security, developing economic relations that benefit both partners more equally, and encouraging the rule of law. China has yet to acknowledge the interdependent nature of security. Its leaders pursue Chinese security while engendering a sense of insecurity among its neighbors. The United States has to do far better at gaining Chinese cooperation in deterring nuclear proliferation and an arms race in the Asia-Pacific and South Asian regions. In the economic domain, China has taken only the first steps on some major domestic economic reforms, particularly in phasing out state-owned enterprises, that are vital to its continued progress in abiding by global trade and financial norms. Beijing seeks unfettered access to American markets, but remains protective of its own; it seems unconcerned about the negative effects of its growing trade surplus with the United States. Finally, Chinese officials claim to seek the rule of law while resisting establishment of the basic conditions for it. Without the rule of law, China's commerce will continue to rest on poorly regulated and insecure ground; corruption will flourish; and human rights abuses will continue. Moreover, unconstrained by law at home, rulers are more able to behave arbitrarily abroad.

How do we advance these U.S. priorities? The case studies in this volume also illuminate those strategies most likely to elicit cooperative behavior on the part of the Chinese. These strategies require that U.S. policymakers adopt a long-term approach to advancing the Sino-American relationship. Multilateralism, engaging in strategic dialogue, promoting institutional development, behaving credibly and avoiding hypocrisy and working in tandem with nongovernmental organizations and the private sector, and providing incentives have all yielded positive change in Chinese behavior over the past two decades in our eight cases. At the same time, careful targeting or threatening of sanctions in the realms of trade, the environment, and arms proliferation, has also proved a highly valuable strategy in ensuring Chinese compliance with its international agreements.

Finally, we stress that a forthcoming posture toward China cannot be a guaranteed success: China could emerge as an assertive and disruptive force or it could disintegrate. The United States must therefore take precautionary measures. First and foremost, as we have outlined above, we must ensure that our policies flow from a sense of American priorities; each American initiative must stand on its own merits. China will seize generous offers of cooperation that only serve Chinese interests, but it will give little in return. In addition, the United States must retain a robust military presence in Asia and maintain strong relations with other nations in the Asia-Pacific region. This includes a full range of unofficial relations with Taiwan. We must also ensure that China enters international regimes on terms that protect the core purpose of the regime—this is particularly true for China's current negotiations to join the World Trade Organization. Finally, the United States must retain an independent capacity to understand Chinese domestic and foreign affairs by cultivating and rewarding its foreign service officers, commercial counselors, military officers, and intelligence analysts who have expertise on China. We cannot allow our national analytical capabilities to become dependent on funding from China or Taiwan.

*Elizabeth Economy*
Deputy Director, Asia Studies;
Senior Fellow, China Studies
Council on Foreign Relations

*Michel Oksenberg*
Senior Fellow and Professor
Asia-Pacific Research Center, Stanford University

# Acknowledgments

THE GENESIS of this volume was a Council on Foreign Relations study group during 1996-1997 to understand better the implications of the dramatic changes that had taken place in the People's Republic of China over the past 25 years for China's participation in the international community. During the course of six sessions, the group discussed, debated, and challenged the findings of our chapter writers thereby enriching greatly the quality of the final product. While the following participants do not necessarily agree with the conclusions that we and our chapter authors have reached, we are greatly indebted to them. They include: Charles N. Andreae, Lisa B. Barry, Robert L. Bernstein, Jan Berris, David J. Biggs, Carroll Bogert, Mary Brown Bullock, Richard Bush, Laura B. Campbell, Karl W. Eikenberry, Hart Fessenden, Wendy Frieman, Harry Harding, Robert M. Hathaway, Mikkal E. Herberg, Richard Herold, Merit E. Janow, Robert A. Kapp, Andrew Byongsoo Kim, James Klurfeld, Dinah Lee Kung, David M. Lampton, John D. Langlois, Terrill E. Lautz, Kenneth Lieberthal, Eric P. Liu, Daniel C. Lynch, Douglas P. Murray, Stephen Orlins, Susan Williams O'Sullivan, Maynard Parker, Margaret M. Pearson, Linda J. Perkin, Alexander Platt, Robert S. Price, Jr., Arthur H. Rosen, Enid C.B. Shoettle, Daniel A. Sharp, Ann B. Sloane, Richard J. Smith, Allan Y. Song, Maynard Toll, James T. B. Tripp, Ko-Yung Tung, Casimir A. Yost, Alice Young, and David Zweig.

Of course, the project would never have gotten so far without the intellectual leadership and energy provided by our chapter authors—Samuel S. Kim, Michael D. Swaine, Alastair Iain Johnston, Andrew J. Nathan, Margaret M. Pearson, Nicholas Lardy, Frederick S. Tipson, Todd M. Johnson, and Lester Ross. It is their expertise that provided the core of this project.

# 1

# Introduction:
# China Joins the World

## MICHEL OKSENBERG AND ELIZABETH ECONOMY

POPULAR American images cast China in a different light every two to three years. The alluring, reforming China of the mid-1980s—particularly in comparison to the Soviet Union of the time—yielded, in the post-1989 Tiananmen era, to the repulsive, harshly oppressive communist regime headed for imminent collapse. Soon thereafter came the rapidly modernizing China of 1993 to 1995, which in turn was replaced by the China menace of 1996–1997, America's next enemy. More recently, in the wake of the Asian economic disaster of 1997–1998, China has become a responsible partner in promoting regional growth and stability—the country that swiftly contributed to the Thai bailout package, backed the Hong Kong currency in 1998, and hastened to stimulate the domestic economy through increased government infrastructure and accelerated enterprise and banking reforms.

The recommended American posture for this seemingly ever-changing China morphs with equally dizzying rapidity: cooperate with the mid-1980s reformers; sanction the late 1980s oppressors; profit from the early 1990s economic juggernaut; prepare for the Armageddon with the mid-1990s rising power; engage the late 1990s responsible China.

This description of the past decade only slightly caricatures the continually shifting portrayal of China and the recommended policy toward it that American media have presented. Each view was rooted in a more complex reality. Obviously China gyrated less than the media portrayals, and American policy exhibited greater continuity than the pundits preferred in their sound bites and on the op-ed pages.

The challenge for the United States today, as for the past century, is to develop an accurate sense of the Chinese domestic scene and its foreign policy and to avoid the oscillations between romantic attraction and venomous rejection that have tended to characterize American policy toward China.

Ever since China's opening to the outside world and the rapprochement between China and the United States in the early 1970s, China's economic growth rate has hovered around 10 percent per year. Indeed, except for the disastrous Great Leap Forward and its aftermath (1957–1962) and the early years of the Cultural Revolution (1966–1971), the economy has demonstrated robustness for nearly 50 years. It is increasingly evident that China's rapid industrialization and urbanization is one of the major developments of the late 20th and early 21st century.

For that reason, strategic thinkers increasingly are focusing on the implications of China's rise in world affairs. Will its growing presence cause major disruptions and conflict, especially between it and the United States, with America's chosen responsibility to help bring order to world affairs? And how can the United States best cooperate with China to bring about its peaceful inclusion into the international community on mutually acceptable terms?

These two questions are explored in this and eight subsequent chapters that explore China's behavior during the past 25 years through eight pivotal international "regimes." By "regime" we mean the arrangements, institutions, norms, and practices that bring some order to those eight spheres of activity. These chapters examine China's record in the United Nations, arms control and disarmament, human rights, international trade, international finance, telecommunications, energy, and environment. They examine the accomplishments and failures, and they measure the progress and chart the terrain that has yet to be covered. In so doing, they help provide the basis for a coherent, consistent, and realistic U.S. policy toward China.

This chapter begins with a brief description of China's extreme isolation in the early 1970s, in order to recall the remarkable progress since then. Next it maps the current debate over China policy in the United States. The debate is fueled by contrasting assessments of American strengths and vulnerabilities as well as of the nature of the post–cold war world. The chapter then summarizes the findings of the eight case studies. The studies reveal differing Chinese behavior within the eight regimes: resistant to some and cooperative with others; active in some while quiescent in others. Next this chapter identifies the factors that explain the variance in Chinese behavior: the objectives of the leaders; the nature of the regime; Chinese domestic politics; and deeply rooted Chinese strategies and tactics. Finally the introduction traces the implications of the findings for American policy toward China.

## Recalling an Isolated China

Twenty-five years ago China was in the midst of the chaotic and violent Cultural Revolution. To an extent then unrecognized in the outside world, its people lived in fear and poverty. Tens of millions suffered from political terror and persecution. Political prisoners, their names unknown to the outside world, toiled in labor camps.

The nation was largely isolated in world affairs. Its leaders vilified international arms control agreements and the international economic system. Despite the February 1972 visit by President Richard Nixon, government rhetoric militantly defied both the United States and the Soviet Union. The Chinese army recently had clashed with Soviet forces, and the Sino-Soviet border was tense. And in Indochina, China was assisting North Vietnam, the Khmer Rouge, and Laotian communists, while the United States was too bogged down in the Vietnam war to halt communism's advance into the region. Sino-American rivalry brought tension to the entire region.

Over the opposition of the United States, the People's Republic of China (PRC) had just acquired the China seat in the United Nations previously held by the Republic of China on Taiwan. The Beijing government had not yet become a member of the principal U.N. organizations. Foreign trade accounted for less than 5 percent of gross national product, and the U.S. trade embargo had just been lifted. Only a handful of Chinese students studied abroad. The nation's isolation resulted primarily from the choices of its leaders, who championed a policy of extreme self-reliance, but also from the efforts of the industrialized democracies—compelled by the United States—to isolate and contain China.

To be sure, the regime had relations with various revolutionary and splinter Marxist-Leninist parties around the world, and it had diplomatic relations with most of the developing countries in Africa and Asia. It had formed alliances and working relations with several of its neighbors, especially North Korea, North Vietnam, Pakistan, and Burma. The trade embargo on China was not totally successful; some seepage of high technology and banned equipment did occur. And millions of ethnic Chinese residing abroad did retain surreptitious contact with their relatives on the mainland.

But these linkages to the outside world were marginal. In essence, China was isolated and contained. It is difficult to recall how remote China was but a generation ago. Most people entered and departed China via Hong Kong. No "through trains" carried passengers to Canton and Beijing. Rather, the arduous journey began with an early-morning train trip from the old station located at the tip of Kowloon, adjacent to the Star Ferry pier, to the end of the line at the Hong Kong–China border. Baggage in hand, China travelers then trudged northward across the Lowu Bridge over the Shenzhen River. They saw rural villages, water buffalo, and rice paddies where today over 2 million people reside in the towering apartments of the Shenzhen Special Economic Zone. After clearing Chinese passport control and eating lunch in the Chinese station, passengers next boarded a slow train to Canton. Then, picked up by a black Hongqi limousine or green Shanghai sedan (a Chinese copy of a 1947 Plymouth), travelers roared through the bicycle-filled streets of the city. Cultural Revolution slogans and blaring horns assaulted eyes and ears until arrival at the sleepy airport for the late-afternoon flight to Beijing. Visitors were thankful for a safe arrival in Beijing aboard an aging Soviet turboprop or Ilyushin jet of the variety that had taken Mao's anointed successor, Lin Piao, to his mysterious death a few months earlier.

In the early 1970s no direct air flights linked the capital of China to any major city of Asia. Most parts of the country, including most provincial capitals, were closed to travel by foreigners. So few foreigners traveled to China that foreign governments recorded and disseminated a monthly list of all foreign delegations and individuals who visited the country as well as of all Chinese delegations traveling abroad. Only five largely empty hotels accommodated foreigners in the Chinese capital—the Beijing, the Xinjiao, the Minzu, the Friendship, and the Huaqiao, which was limited to overseas Chinese. The west wing of the Beijing Hotel had yet to be built. No foreign publications were available, and the British Broadcasting Corporation and Voice of America radio frequencies were jammed. Travelers learned of developments abroad via a daily, mimeographed English-language bulletin of foreign news that the New China News Agency edited and distributed. Telecommunications facilities to the outside world were few and indirect. Long-distance telephone service was unreliable. Few foreign businessmen made it to the capital; most were confined to the semiannual Canton trade fair. If they made it to Beijing, they had to go to the China

Cable Office to dispatch a telegram. Not until later did it become possible for them to communicate by telex.

To Americans, at least, it seemed as if the then 800 million Chinese lived on another planet. And the overwhelming majority of the Chinese had little notion about the outside world. Even their leaders were captives of the propaganda they had disseminated.

A generation later all this had changed dramatically. China has rejoined the world. No significant aspect of world affairs is exempt from its influence, and ordinary Chinese have much greater access to the outside world. Hong Kong has become part of China, and Taiwan has developed extensive economic and cultural contacts with the mainland. The nation's total foreign trade has risen from $21 billion in 1978 to $73.8 billion in 1986, to over $300 billion in 1997. By late 1997 China had accumulated over $130 billion in foreign currency reserves and had an external indebtedness of over $120 billion. It is the largest recipient of World Bank loans. In the early and mid-1990s China ranked with the United States as one of the two largest recipients of foreign direct investment. It has become a member of over 50 international governmental organizations and well over 1,000 international nongovernmental organizations. Fiber-optic cables now link Shanghai to Japan and beyond, and AT&T and the Ministry of Post and Telecommunications (MPT) now have over 2,000 circuits linking China and the United States. Direct flights now connect Beijing to cities throughout the Northern Hemisphere: Chicago, Detroit, Tokyo, Helsinki, Moscow, Warsaw, Frankfurt, Paris, Zurich, London, and all major capitals of Southeast Asia. Well over 100,000 Chinese scholars and graduate students have studied and are studying in the West and Japan, and several tens of thousands have returned to China after long and short periods of study abroad. Through television, pirated videotapes, and CDs, Michael Jackson, Michael Jordan, Madonna, and Hong Kong and Taiwanese pop stars are well-known figures.

China's opening to the outside world occurred because both its leaders and the industrial democracies concluded the nation's isolation was costly and dangerous for China, the region, and the world. In the 1970s Mao Zedong, Zhou Enlai, and Deng Xiaoping on the Chinese side and such Western leaders as Presidents Richard Nixon and Jimmy Carter, Germany's Helmut Schmidt and Franz Joseph Strauss, and Japan's Kakuei Tanaka and Takeo Fukuda—political foes within their own country—had reached the same conclusion: The weak and divided China of the late 1960s and early 1970s invited foreign aggression from the Soviet Union and was a source of global and regional instability. But a modernizing and stable China could be a bulwark for regional peace and prosperity.

## An Altered Strategic Context

The decisions of those leaders to nurture China's participation in world affairs, coupled with China's domestic reforms, have prompted remarkable economic growth. China's gross national product has more than quadrupled in the past 25 years. Never in history has the economy of so many people grown as rapidly, as extensively, and for as sustained a time as has the economy of China's now nearly 1.3 billion citizens. Moreover, economists both within and outside China believe that, with inevitable fluctuations, rapid growth could continue for the foreseeable future as a result of the favorable underlying fundamentals: a high rate of savings; an entrepreneurial and increasingly well-educated populace; the dissemination of technology; generally sound economic policies; and a propitious international environment. Economists also caution, however, that China confronts severe constraints on its ability to sustain high growth rates and that the Asian economic crisis will also adversely affect it. Nevertheless, even with somewhat slower growth rates, within another generation China could have one of the world's largest economies and one of the world's largest central government budgets. Under those circumstances, its political leaders—no matter who they might be and no matter what the nature of their political system—easily could devote a substantial portion of increased government revenue in pursuit of modern military might. This possibility is appropriately beginning to worry strategists and military planners in many countries throughout the Asia-Pacific region.

Aspects of Chinese behavior have intensified concerns: an increasing defense budget, efforts to intimidate Taiwan through military exercises, expansive territorial claims in the South and East China seas, arms sales and technology transfers to Pakistan and Iran (especially nuclear and missile technology), and only reluctant acceptance of various U.N. international peacekeeping efforts. Much also can be said positively about the Chinese record of the past 25 years, as is done in subsequent chapters, but Chinese assertiveness on many international issues has raised apprehensions about its future course.

Moreover, China's leaders did incalculable damage to their image through their brutal suppression of the spring 1989 demonstrations. The tragedy that unfolded in Beijing demonstrated to the entire world that a vast chasm separated China's leaders from the leaders of the industrial democracies concerning human rights and the rule of law. In the United States the event helped to forge an anti-China coalition drawn from various parts of the political spectrum, including Americans concerned with China's policies on human rights, forced abortion, prison labor, child labor, Taiwan, Tibet, trade deficits, nuclear proliferation, protection of intellectual property, and environmental practices. Uniting its disparate members is the belief that leaders who deprive their own people of basic human and civil rights guaranteed in the United Nations' Universal Declaration of Human Rights should not be allowed the benefits derived from participation in world affairs until they change their method of rule. They argue that China's repressive authoritarian political system precludes it from creating a genuine market economy and makes it a capricious partner in world affairs.

In addition, some strategists believe that the collapse of the Soviet Union spelled the end of China's strategic utility to the industrial democracies. China was useful as a partner in the effort to halt Soviet expansionism, but the disappearance of the Soviet Union has transformed Chinese military might from an asset to a long-term threat to Western and especially American interests.

Finally, China's domestic situation has changed. Not only has its phenomenal economic growth made the nation stronger, but a generational succession has occurred among the leaders. The prior generation of Mao Zedong, Zhou Enlai, and Deng Xiaoping thought in global strategic terms. Their accomplishments as revolutionary leaders yielded them considerable self-confidence. At least in the earliest stages of their ascent, their successors seemed more constrained, less capable of pursuing grand designs and historic accommodations, such as Mao's opening to the United States or Deng's one-country, two-systems solution for the Hong Kong reversion. They appeared to lack the strength to make the necessary compromises to sustain forward momentum on such major issues as Taiwan and the terms of China's entry into the World Trade Organization. However, the successes they achieved in 1997 over the smooth transfer of Hong Kong to Chinese rule, the enunciation of a bold economic reform program at the fifteenth Party Congress, and the restoration of progress in Sino-American relations in 1997–1998 may have signaled a greater capacity to address thorny issues in the years ahead.

## Mapping the National Debate

As a result of these considerations, foreign policy experts in the United States have become embroiled in a national debate over American China policy. Many strategic thinkers have ceased to worry about the dangers posed by a potentially weak and unstable China. They slight the successes encountered in drawing China out of its isolation. They neglect that China's involvement in regional affairs has contributed significantly to the unprecedented peace and stability that East Asia has enjoyed since the mid-1970s. American strategists worry instead about the future. They ponder the potential dangers posed by China's likely emergence as a global power in the decades ahead and wonder how best to cope with the altered context. And in light of the altered context, they tend to dismiss the record of the past 25 years as irrelevant.

Instead, the debate is largely informed by differing theoretical perspectives on world affairs that suggest differing priorities for American policy. To oversimplify, the different schools can be mapped along two dimensions. Along one dimension are the accommodationalists versus the confrontationalists. The accommodationalists believe it is better to recognize some Chinese interests now, while preserving core American interests, so that China can acquire a stake in an evolving status quo. The confrontationalists believe the United States should use its superior strength to compel China to adjust to the existing international system; better to wage that struggle now than later, while the United States can still extract maximum concessions and affect China internally. Accommodationalists tend to believe a future, hostile Sino-American relationship can be prevented, while confrontationalists believe an animosity-ridden relationship, particularly with this communist regime, is inevitable.

The other dimension involves the classic debate among those who believe that the military strength and power of a state continues to be the basic building blocks of the international system; those who believe that economic and technological might are the primary forces driving world affairs; and those who believe that the power of ideas and the capacity to shape the way people think are the crucial ingredients affecting international affairs. The three perspectives lead their adherents to emphasize different aspects of Sino-American relations.

This mapping of the China policy debate yields a two-by-three matrix, with six cells, and identifies six schools in the China policy debate: accommodational realists, confrontational realists, accommodational neoliberals, economic nationalists, accommodational ideationalists, and confrontational ideationalists. (See Table 1–1.) To be sure, this classification scheme is too simple. Most analysts advocate an eclectic combination of accommodation and confrontation. They believe that military, economic, and idea power are all relevant in today's world. Nonetheless, analysts differ over the priority they assign to each of these dimensions of a China policy.

Table 1–1.  The China Debate and Policy Preferences

| | Posture | |
|---|---|---|
| Perspective | Accommodationalists | Confrontationalists |
| Realists | Cooperate with China to maintain regional balance of power; support Chinese membership in various arms control regimes | Protect Taiwan; maintain alliances with Japan and Korea; discourage China's sale of missiles and nuclear technology |
| Economic Primacy | Secure Chinese entry into the World Trade Organization; encourage World Bank lending; cooperate in the environmental sphere | Threaten and use economic sanctions; support the rights of Chinese workers |
| Ideationalists | Maintain constant high-level dialogue with Chinese leaders; educate next generation of China's leaders; facilitate institutional development | Condition other aspects of relationship upon China's human rights record; press for religious freedom, support Radio Free Asia |

## REALISM

The realists tend to believe that the nature of international relations has not changed fundamentally, that the nation-state remains the essential building block of the international system, that a hierarchy inevitably exists among nations, with some stronger than others, and that leaders of nations for the most part act rationally in pursuit of security, wealth, and power for themselves and their country. The dominant powers create and maintain a set of arrangements and norms that serve their interests, while rising powers inevitably seek to alter these arrangements so that their interests are taken into account. Realists attach priority to the security dimension in Sino-American relations.

### Accommodational Realists

Accommodational realists argue that China's rise is in its early stages and that there is still time to create a security framework or architecture that can embrace China and minimize future Sino-American rivalry. They believe that, if China is incorporated into a global and regional system, its strength could prove useful to balance other possibly assertive Asian powers. Some analysts of this persuasion advocate that the United States should help construct a regional "concert of nations" with agreed norms and dispute resolution mechanisms reminiscent of nineteenth-century European arrangements. Others, noting the many obstacles to creating a multilateral security architecture in Asia, focus on cultivation of constructive bilateral security relations with all of the major Asian actors including China; they envision a classic balance-of-power arrangement reminiscent of British diplomacy toward continental Europe. Most in this school support the pursuit of a combination of multilateralism and bilateralism. In any case, to such realists, it is far too early to proclaim China an enemy.

### Confrontational Realists

Confrontational realists argue that the United States must begin now to prepare for the upcoming hostile and tense relationship with China. They point to the early signs of divergent interests between the United States and China and emphasize the latter's determination to acquire military might as rapidly as financial conditions and technological capabilities permit. Their argument is buttressed by China's arms and military technology purchases from Russia and its evolving strategic doctrine that places emphasis on acquiring the capacity to wage high-technology, limited war on its periphery. They draw parallels between China's rise and that of the Soviet Union, and advocate girding for a new cold war by maintaining a robust American military presence and strong alliances in Asia. In particular, they condemn and seek to counter China's policies toward Korea and Taiwan and its sales of missiles and nuclear technology.

### ECONOMIC PRIMACY

Other analysts attach primacy to economic considerations and believe that the very nature of international relations is changing fundamentally. The prior centrality of military might is yielding to the growing importance of trade, international finance, and economic competitiveness. Further, nation-states are losing their previous autonomy and power in an increasingly interdependent world; leaders of nations are decreasingly able to control the flow of people, ideas, and money across their borders. National governments are less relevant actors than they used to be in organizing world affairs; they are losing out to multinational corporations, financial markets, international organizations especially in the economic realm (specifically the World Bank, the International Monetary Fund, and the new World Trade Organization), nongovernmental international associations or communities that exert considerable influence on national governments (i.e., environmentalists, human rights organizations, women's rights groups, or religions), and international drug cartels, crime syndicates, and terrorists intent upon subverting international order. However, those who attach priority to the economic dimension of Sino-American relations are sharply divided between the neoliberals, who embrace and wish to foster economic interdependence, and the economic nationalists, who insist, while American strength is still supreme, that the new world must be crafted carefully to protect American interests.

## Neoliberals

Neoliberals are confident that an open international trading system, with minimal constraints on trade, will promote American and international economic growth, and that the openness and growth in turn will promote liberalizing tendencies and democratic values around the world. Moreover, the telecommunications and transportation transformations make an open trading system and international financial system more feasible than in the past; foreign trade is physically easier to carry out than in the past.

To the neoliberals, China's rise cannot be compared with the rise of earlier major powers; it is occurring in a totally different international context. Neoliberals believe that unprecedented opportunities exist to integrate China into various international arrangements that will constrain its future latitude. Their preferred strategy in an increasingly interdependent world is to encourage China's openness to external influences, so that domestic Chinese constituencies linked to the outside world will influence the course of their government. Thus China's increasing involvement in international trade is to be encouraged and accommodated, since the nation's leaders then will have greater incentive to support the existing international trade regime. Chinese membership in the World Trade Organization (WTO) is therefore a priority objective, as is opening the country to foreign direct investment, assisting it to develop its capital markets, and securing foreign access to the service sector of its economy. Neoliberals also stress the importance of cooperating with China in resolving transnational problems that interdependence intensifies: environmental degradation, drug trafficking, illegal population migration, and so on.

Most neoliberals recognize that forging ties with China will proceed slowly and be vulnerable to reversal. They are prepared to be patient, in recognition of the fact that the full benefits of these policies become evident after years rather than months of persistence. Moreover, most recognize that the effort to integrate China into the world community on mutually acceptable terms may fail. Therefore, while they welcome China's desire to participate, they stress that the terms of entry must protect the purposes of the systems they seek to join. And the United States must retain an insurance policy in case the effort fails, especially through maintenance of robust bilateral alliances with its partners in the region and a credible, forward-deployed military presence in the region.

*Economic Nationalists*

Economic nationalists concur that economic strength has become central in world affairs and that trade issues are paramount in a nation's agenda. But they reject the notion that interdependence in itself is automatically beneficial to the United States or that the United States can protect its interests through a heavy reliance on multilateral fora. They are sometimes misidentified as isolationists, but in fact most recognize the value of trade. They are not in favor of economic self-sufficiency, but they believe that the terms of trade must be carefully set by the U.S. government and that American economic strength is sufficiently great that, through confrontation, tough-minded negotiations, and use of sanctions, the United States can compel other countries to comply with its demands. They argue that China needs access to the American market more than the United States needs access to the China market. They fear that unless the United States uses its economic strength now to compel changes in China's trade practices, China will retain its neomercantilist characteristics and emerge as another Japan on the world scene. They therefore emphasize that the United States should stipulate the terms of Chinese entry into the WTO in a way that clearly protects American national interests, that the United States employ trade sanctions until China meets American expectations in such areas as protection of intellectual property rights and/or working conditions of Chinese labor, and that protectionist measures should be undertaken until China addresses its trade imbalances with the United States.

THE POWER OF IDEAS

While the realists tend to focus on the military dimension of international affairs and the neoliberals and economic nationalists on the economic dimension, a third set of analysts focuses on the power of ideas and the capacity of people to learn and alter their views. To such analysts, international affairs are governed not only by an objective set of external economic and security considerations but perhaps more important by how leaders and their citizens perceive world affairs. To such analysts, culture, ideology, and knowledge matter. Analysts of this persuasion believe the United States has an opportunity to shape Chinese thinking about the major issues of the day. Efforts to influence Chinese thought should be a central dimension of policy. However, ideationalists are divided over exactly whom the United States should seek to influence and with what message.

### Accommodational Ideationalists

Some believe that the key target should be China's leaders and strategic thinkers—the elite—and the message should focus on the nature of the post–cold war world. These accommodational ideationalists seek a strategic dialogue with leading Chinese in order to develop a shared perspective on the major threats to world and regional peace and stability and on the pivotal trends shaping the direction of world affairs. They advocate lengthy and candid discussions between the two sides concerning each side's fundamental values, interests and strategies. They hope that out of such discussions, requiring many hours of patient explanations, would emerge a deeper understanding of how the two nations can best cooperate in areas where their values and interests overlap and how best to contain the areas of divergence. Only such dialogue can engender an element of mutual trust and the will by leaders on each side to prevail over their respective, recalcitrant bureaucracies to address the thorniest issues dividing the two countries.

Adherents of this view draw their inspiration in part from the dialogues that Henry Kissinger and Zbigniew Brzezinski held with Mao, Zhou, Deng, and their principal advisors in the 1970s. As those privy to the record of those conversations have concluded, they were essential to the early progress in Sino-American relations, and their cessation from 1989 to 1996 contributed significantly to the erosion in the relationship. But such discussions require treating China's leaders with respect and dignity and being open to and accommodating their ideas as well. The extraordinary public debates between Presidents Jiang Zemin and Bill Clinton during their October 1997 and June 1998 summits suggested these two leaders were continuing in that tradition, albeit extending the discussion to the realm of human rights and sharing their dialogue with their citizens. Perhaps as significant have been the extensive dialogues between Chinese economic officials and officials of the World Bank or Western academic economists. These conversations injected new ideas and a new vocabulary into Chinese economic thought, as Chapter 5 points out, which in turn led to the creation of new economic institutions. And these new structures in turn introduced profound cultural change whose political ramifications have yet to be fully felt. Dialogue, in short, alters strategic thought and induces institutional development.

### Confrontational Ideationalists

Others who believe ideas make a difference tend to scorn the top elite and rather advocate targeting the broader Chinese public in service of democratic values. The supporters of this approach phrase their purpose in diverse ways. Some, assuming that significant prodemocracy and pro–human rights constituencies already exist in China, wish to provide those Chinese with the information they need to sustain their beliefs and activities. Others, less sure that many Chinese adhere to values championed by the United States, wish to cultivate such sentiments. The confrontational ideationalists support Radio Free Asia, people-to-people diplomacy, and the exile dissident community as well as dissidents within China. They recommend confronting China's leaders with the inadequacy of their ideology and challenging them to embark on democratization. Adherents of this view draw their inspiration in part from the role they believe such activities ultimately played in the transformation of Eastern Europe.

## THE POLITICS OF THE DEBATE

The debate between accommodationalists and confrontationalists and among realists, economy firsters, and ideationalists has been waged, in fact, since the establishment of the PRC and especially since 1972 and Richard Nixon's opening to China. At that time confrontational realists warned about China's rise, while accommodational realists focused on cooperation with China against the Soviet Union. Some expressed alarm about China's sponsorship of guerilla war and its development of nuclear weapons, while others emphasized the opportunities that Mao's initiative offered. Some thought that Chinese membership in the United Nations would doom the organization; they foresaw disruptive behavior that would bring the body to a near standstill. Others thought that through dialogue and participation, China's positions on crucial issues would evolve.

Within the U.S. goverment, the strongest proponents for mutual accommodation and comprehensive engagement have existed within the executive branch, while the staunchest advocates of confrontation have been in the Congress. Not surprisingly, realists predominate at the Pentagon; economic firsters prevail at the Treasury, Commerce, and the Office of the Special Trade Representative; and the State Department tends to esteem dialogue conducted under its aegis. Policy preferences stem in part from bureaucratic missions.

From 1972 to 1989 the debate was muted. The political success of the Nixon opening created a broad consensus in favor of accommodation. Dissenters on specific dimensions of policy existed, such as on abortion, Taiwan, technology transfer, and trade deficits. The tragedy of June 4, 1989, shattered the consensus and made it much more difficult for Presidents Bush and Clinton to achieve policy coherence within the bureaucracy and between the Congress and the executive branch. Since 1989 various interest groups have solidified alliances with particular members of the Congress and portions of the bureaucracy in ways that characterize many other aspects of the American political process. To the bewilderment of Chinese officials, who are reluctant to believe policy can be made and implemented in such an undisciplined fashion, China policy is the product of disjointed decisions, only loosely and sporadically coordinated in the White House. Since 1989 the American China policy has been a collage of all six preferences described above.

## China's International Behavior since 1972

Disparate bureaucratic perspectives, narrow special interests, and abstract theories of international relations do not provide an adequate basis for a viable, coherent, and consistent China policy. The policy must be rooted in the record of the past 25 years. What does the effort to integrate China into various international regimes reveal? We now turn to our eight case studies.

Chapter 2, Samuel S. Kim's study of Chinese participation in the U.N.'s General Assembly and Security Council, illuminates the evolution of China as an actor over the past 25 years from system transformer to system reformer and system maintainer. Kim directly challenges the notion that China seeks to disrupt the status quo and argues that Beijing is most concerned with how the United Nations can best serve China's modernization effort. Chinese participation in U.N.-sponsored treaties and organizations has expanded dramatically[1] and has contributed to shifts in policy on a wide range of issues, including arms control, U.N. peacekeeping, North-South relations, human rights, science and technology, and environmental protection. At the same time Kim argues that China's participation in the United Nations continues to be shaped by its view of the world as a "statecentric system anchored in such principles as state sovereignty, state equality, state responsibility, and state rights." Moreover, China pursues a policy of maxi/mini realpolitik, in which it maximizes benefits while minimizing financial responsibilities. Nonetheless, Kim concludes that overall, China's international behavior has been a slow but steady movement from conflict to cooperation.

In Chapter 3, Michael D. Swaine and Alastair Iain Johnston's study of Chinese participation in arms control regimes, also notes the emphasis on sovereignty in shaping China's participation in the global security regime. They comment that "in the face of an increasingly intrusive international arms control agenda, Chinese arms control behavior in most instances reflects efforts to devise the most effective means to avoid placing China's capabilities on arms control tables, and is designed to preserve and improve its relative capabilities." Beijing has been reluctant to endorse cooperative concepts of security and to accept the need to place real restrictions on its military capabilities. China backs measures that cost it little and enhance its image. At the same time, Swaine and Johnston also perceive a shift in Chinese perspective over the past 10 to 15 years from one that viewed arms control as largely irrelevant to Chinese concerns to one that recognizes that the nation could benefit from greater participation in international arms control regimes. China now participates in a range of accords that condemn the proliferation of conventional arms and weapons of mass destruction, including the Comprehensive Test Ban Treaty (CTBT), the Nuclear Nonproliferation Treaty (NPT), and the chemical and biological weapons conventions. It also has become active in the full range of official and semiofficial security dialogues, such as the Association of South East Asian Nations (ASEAN) Regional Forum and the Committee on Security Cooperation in the Asia-Pacific region. Moreover, Swaine and Johnston identify the existence of a nascent community of arms control experts within China who interact extensively with their counterparts in the West and are supportive of ideas of cooperative security. They note, however, that this community represents a distinct minority of those involved in arms control decision making in China, and overall, China's growing involvement in arms control negotiations primarily has taught it to use the arms control arena more effectively for its state-centric security purposes rather than to prompt a reconsideration of how best to attain security.

Chapter 4 indicates that China remains a gross violator of basic civil and political human rights. Andrew J. Nathan argues that China, in general, has defied the efforts of international human rights organizations and individual governments—especially the United States—to judge its performance and impose international standards on its political system. At the same time, Nathan points out that China's concern over its image has led the People's Republic to pursue a mix of policies. Its response to the widespread criticism in international forums of its human rights practices has combined ideological resistance and selective substantive concessions to rally Third World support, especially in multilateral settings, to appeal to advocates of realpolitik in the West, and to construct policy dilemmas for human rights advocates. Despite China's lack of cooperation with international human rights organizations and its behavioral inadequacies, Nathan also notes that its declared policy increasingly has conformed with international standards and that the Chinese government has undertaken measures to address some of these inadequacies, such as the 1995 Judges Law and the 1996 amendments to the 1979 Criminal Procedures Law, although these have not ended the abuses.

Chapter 5, Margaret M. Pearson's case study of China's participation in the international trade regime, offers perhaps the clearest example of the extent to which China has become an active and important player in the international community. China continues to make substantive concessions to gain entry into the WTO, is a member of the Asia Pacific Economic Cooperation (APEC) process, and has joined the world intellectual property rights regime. Pearson illuminates how the Chinese government has restructured itself to attract foreign technology, capital, and trade. It has established an entirely new system to attract foreign direct investment, including copyright, trademark, and patent offices and stock exchanges in Shanghai and Shenzhen. Pearson also argues that the easiest period of Chinese economic integration with the international community has passed already. Further opening of Chinese economy has been and will prove to be increasingly difficult, given Chinese concerns to protect their infant and core industries and maintain social stability. Nonetheless, a large community of Chinese—both within the People's Republic and overseas—continues to push for further reform and deeper integration of the Chinese economy into the world market.

According to Nicholas R. Lardy in Chapter 6, China's participation in international financial regimes also evidences an important evolution in policy. Lardy points out that China has become a very active player in international financial institutions. It is the World Bank's largest borrower, is a significant commercial borrower, and is one of only three transition economies with an investment-grade credit rating on its sovereign external debt. China's major state-owned banks all seek to expand their operations overseas. In addition, Lardy notes that China has taken a number of steps over the past several years that are intended to bring it closer to international banking practices. It has configured itself in more subtle ways to meet international financial standards, including such areas as statistical reporting, accounting procedures, and bidding practices. Moreover, China has taken the first halting steps in opening its banking, insurance, and financial service industries to foreign competition by allowing select foreign firms to sell insurance in Shanghai. Undergirding these developments is the growing number of think tanks and policy research groups, which have been influential in the formulation of China's domestic and foreign economic policy. Nonetheless, Lardy, like Pearson, sees a number of areas where barriers to a more open economy remain high. He notes that China remains most recalcitrant about opening its banking sector to foreign competition and is not fully prepared to meet international equity markets' demands for competitive rates of return to foreign lenders for development projects.

Frederick S. Tipson demonstrates in Chapter 7 that protectionist impulses also have constrained China's integration into the global telecommunications system. While the International Telecommunication Union's advocacy of interoperable communications technologies has helped foreign companies gain access to the Chinese market, the Chinese have resisted the wholesale import of foreign technologies and set restrictions on levels of direct foreign investment. China's participation in the telecommunications regime also is hampered by its desire to protect its sovereignty by controlling the types of technology introduced in the country. With limited success, the authorities have attempted to control popular access to direct satellite television broadcasts and the Internet. Still, as Tipson notes, the developments in telecommunications in China have been staggering. Circuits to the United States carried by the Ministry of Post and Telecommunications and AT&T alone have increased from 220 in 1989 to 1,908 in 1995. The People's Republic has both participated in the formal regime under the International Telecommunication Union (ITU) and had extensive interaction with private-sector telecommunications equipment manufacturers and service providers outside the ITU context. Corporations such as Hughes, AT&T, Motorola, NEC, Siemens, Hong Kong Telecom, and Hitachi have become major actors in the Chinese market, with joint venture manufacturing of switching equipment and computers that together constitute the telecommunications transformation.

While China has joined a range of organizations that influence the course of its energy development—the International Atomic Energy Agency, the World Bank, and APEC—Chapter 8, by Todd M. Johnson, on Chinese participation in international energy organizations and accords, brings a unique focus to the importance that the market can play as a natural enforcer of reform. China's continued economic development hinges on its ability to secure ever greater amounts of energy. Thus the energy sector has become increasingly open to foreign involvement. China depends heavily on the international community for assistance in developing its oil and gas reserves as well as its electric power capacity.

Such multinational corporations as AMOCO, Exxon, and ARCO have played major roles in introducing Chinese leaders and bureaucrats to the norms of international petroleum development, and these norms have affected Chinese behavior significantly. In fact, Beijing has responded directly to international demands for change. Under pressure from the international financial institutions, China has opened its doors to competitive bidding and begun some price reforms. It also has been aggressive in pursuing World Bank funds for projects such as the Changchun coal mine in Shanxi Province, the development of the Sichuan natural gas fields, and a number of energy-efficiency and energy-pricing programs. It even has subjected some of its power plants to the international financial markets by listing them on the New York Stock Exchange. Still, according to Johnson, China's efforts to meet its energy demands through cooperation with the international community are constrained by both national security concerns and institutional inefficiencies. Chinese institutions are reluctant to pay for foreign personnel and experts. State-owned enterprises often refuse to yield management control over assets and personnel, while foreign enterprises cannot hold majority stakes. The coal industry, for example, presents problems due to a "lack of management, ownership, pricing and legal reforms."

Chapter 9, by Lester Ross, on Chinese participation in international environmental regimes, reflects both the progress and the problems of China's integration into the international community. China's involvement in environmental treaties and U.N. organizations that support environmental protection activities has been extensive. Furthermore, this involvement has had far-reaching implications for domestic institutional evolution in the People's Republic. For each environmental treaty China has signed, the leadership has established a complex arrangement of institutions to ensure that all relevant agencies are involved in the decision-making and implementation processes. By 1992 China had 200 research institutes employing 20,000 scientists and technicians engaged in environmental research. Most interesting, perhaps, is the birth of environmental nongovernmental organizations in China, which are playing a limited but increasingly important role in advancing environmental protection in China. Still, as Ross notes, Chinese cooperation on global environmental affairs has been hampered by concerns over sovereignty, and an aversion to monitoring, reporting demands, or transfering decision-making authority to an international body. Concerns over maintaining rapid rates of economic growth also have stymied a more proactive Chinese approach to global environmental protection. Perhaps surprisingly, one bright spot that Ross discerns is the role that the private sector is playing in advancing

Chinese environmental protection through standard setting. The International Standards Organization 9000 and 14000 processes governing product quality and environmental management standards already are having a positive impact on China's adoption of better environmental practices.

## Factors Affecting Chinese Behavior

Much has been accomplished in 25 years. China and the outside world—including the United States—have done a great deal to further their joint participation in international regimes. China's formal record of integration is extensive. The leaders have reformed governmental institutions to aid the nation's participation in world affairs and allowed considerable external involvement in its development.

The record reveals that China's behavior thus far contrasts sharply with that of earlier rising powers at similar stages in their ascent. Germany and Japan in the late 1800s and early 1900s began to compete with the established imperial powers as soon as their might permitted. And the Soviet Union created its own military, economic, and ideological bloc.

At the same time, China's behavior in the eight areas reveals that it has adapted to the norms of some regimes with ease and rapidity, but in other areas, it has been more defiant. The record reveals that four factors help to explain both the consistent elements of Chinese behavior and the variance in its conduct in different regimes: the objectives of its leaders, the nature of the international regimes themselves, Chinese domestic politics, and the tactics leaders habitually employ in the pursuit of their objectives.

### OBJECTIVES

Chinese behavior in the international system serves five objectives: protecting Chinese sovereignty, maintaining national security, eroding Taiwan's status, cultivating a favorable image, and promoting economic interests. Several categories of behavior, including an often-rigid insistence on protecting Chinese sovereignty and precluding Taiwan's independence, generally have constrained China's participation in the world community. Other categories, such as the cultivation of a favorable image, generally have fostered participation.

*Protecting Chinese Sovereignty*
In their rhetoric, Chinese leaders have adopted the Western concept of sovereignty as a sacred principle. Defense of territorial integrity and

national independence has become their rallying cry, and they use it to advance their own political interests. Chinese policies in the human rights and telecommunications regimes, for example, have reflected its leaders' resolve to guard against the influx of foreign values and ideas, "to take what is good from the outside world and filter out what is potentially harmful to them." This becomes particularly clear in the human rights, telecommunications, and environmental spheres.

*Maintaining Chinese Security*
Maintenance of national security is a second objective of Chinese behavior. In Chapter 3 Swaine and Johnston stress that China has adopted "basically a state-centered balance-of-power calculus intended to maintain China's strategic independence" rather than manifesting any deep concern for strengthening mutual security. Thus Beijing has been reluctant to endorse cooperative concepts of security and to accept the need to place real restrictions on Chinese military capabilities. Many Chinese strategic thinkers reject the notion that global interdependence has replaced national interests. For these reasons, China has been more reluctant to join international and regional security regimes than those in the economic sphere.

*Precluding Taiwan's Independence*
A third major objective of China's foreign policy is to erode Taiwan's international status and constrain its international activities. As is evidenced in virtually every area, the People's Republic expends significant diplomatic energy countering Taiwan's effort to enhance its international status by gaining entry into international organizations or participating in international accords. Moreover, it insists on setting the terms under which Taiwan is granted entry. In short, Taiwan remains a contentious issue in China's dealings with other nations in both bilateral and multilateral forums.

*Securing a Favorable International Image*
The fourth objective of China's participation in international regimes is to secure a favorable image. China has a great concern for its international image, and it wants to be viewed as a cooperative and responsible actor. This means that it is reluctant to defy an international consensus, and unlike the Soviet Union, it is reluctant to exercise veto power. Rather, China frequently either remains aloof or threatens to obstruct a course of action until the moment has arrived when it must join the consensus, abstain, or disrupt the action. This posture can be interpreted as free-riding, reaping the benefits from the U.N. action

against Iraq, for example, while bearing none of the costs. China extracts a price from the industrial democracies by forbearing to exercise its veto and enhances its stature among other countries by expressing reservations about an action. On the other hand, China's passive posture can be seen as a blessing in disguise. Its voting record in the United Nations places it among those countries most often opposed to the U.S. position. If China were more active in the United Nations, the United States might find itself in a more difficult position. China has chosen not to turn the United Nations into an arena of diplomatic conflict.

*Promoting Economic Development*
Finally, Chinese participation in international regimes is intended to promote its economic development. Increasingly, however, its leaders have constrained further integration because of perceived risks for social stability. This is most evident in China's involvement in trade, financial, energy, and telecommunications regimes. One senses in each realm that beneath the surface there is an ongoing struggle between the proponents and opponents of further integration. Chinese behavior reflects this ambivalence, and at any point in time, its policy reflects the current balance of power between these competing forces. The most recent and prominent example involves China's accession to the World Trade Organization.

## NATURE OF THE REGIME

Chinese behavior in international regimes also responds to and takes advantage of each regime's particular nature: its governance, the degree of international consensus over its norms, and its trajectory.

*The Type of Regime*
China responds more favorably to impersonal and market regimes, where the rules of the game apply equally to all countries. The international financial regime is a case in point. Regimes clearly organized and led by the industrial democracies for their benefit or enforced primarily by the United States are more likely to be resisted.

*The Degree of International Consensus about the Regime*
Some regimes operate with some consensus about their norms, or their norms are stated explicitly, as is the case with the Missile Technology Control Regime (MTCR). Other regimes are in the process of formation (global climate change) and/or are divided over the norms that should

guide them. China finds it easier to enter regimes that lack a consensus. In such cases, it can choose the norms to which it will adhere. But the lack of consensus renders China's participation less meaningful. Its range of choice, along with that of other members of the regime, has not been narrowed. Obviously, China's latitude is limited when a regime enjoys a consensus about its norms. While China does join such regimes, it is more likely to complain thereafter that rules were formed without it. Its degree of actual compliance, then, depends on the cost-benefit calculus. Ambiguities in the human rights and intellectual property rights regimes, for example, give China the opportunity to maneuver and manipulate, while the financial regime imposes strict standards.

*The Evolution of the Regime*
International regimes themselves evolve. As a member of a changing system, China confronts both opportunity and challenge. It then can shape the nature of the change, but it must accept the responsibility to participate in the setting of the rules. In several instances, by the time China has equipped itself to enter a regime and support its purposes, the regime itself is in the process of change. China then has difficulty adjusting to the changes. The domestic bureaucracies that gained from the prior purposes and practices and hence were proponents of a constructive Chinese involvement then seek to keep the international regime committed to its original purposes and structures. They fear that the changes in the international regime could alter the benefits they receive and divert resources to competing domestic agencies. Domestic bureaucratic rigidities, in short, tend to produce Chinese conservatism on the world scene.

It is worthy of note that China has had a minimal impact on the regimes in which it has participated. On the whole, it has been passive in most regimes it has joined. Only in the environmental and human rights sphere has China actively sought to shape the norms of the international regime; even in those important areas, China has made its case within the regime rather than outside it. Neither the worst fears of a disruptive China in the U.N. system nor the best hopes of a constructively and extensively involved China have been realized.

## ADVANCING DOMESTIC POLITICAL INTERESTS

Chinese participation in international affairs is an extension of its domestic politics. When the leaders derive more benefits than participation costs them, they will involve themselves in a regime. These benefits include enhanced domestic status, financial resources, or useful ideas and information. But when the costs exceed the benefits, they will not cooperate. This may seem like a trivial observation, but it is worth noting that Chinese leaders are rational actors within their own political environment.

In addition, the degree of consensus in the uppermost echelons of government also affects China's entry. If there is a strong consensus among the top leaders that integration serves China's interests, or if a single leader attaches importance to an otherwise lower-priority issue and energizes the effort, entry might go forward. The opposite is also true: no support at the top means a greatly reduced chance of participation.

Moreover, participation in an international regime ultimately is in the hands of Chinese bureaucracies. But usually their domestic missions are more important than their external responsibilities, and their domestic missions shape their response to the international involvement. To understand China's policies, one must understand the bureaucratic politics and interests at work. As in the United States, most foreign policies involve several agencies and require coordination among often competing ones. When the bureaucratic interests of China's participating agencies diverge, the likelihood increases that participation will lack coherence, consistency, and continuity. This emerges clearly in the case studies on trade, energy, arms control, and telecommunications. At the same time, when a single agency is responsible for formulating policy, creating its implementing agencies, and enforcing the policy, the likelihood of coherence and consistency is greater. Chinese behavior also reflects the responsible agencies' capacity to implement policy, especially their financial resources, the quality of personnel, the regulatory context, and the priority attached to the issue at lower levels. The weaker the institutional capacity, the weaker the compliance with international commitments.

Finally, ethnic Chinese who reside outside the PRC also have had an enormous effect on how China has behaved in international regimes. But this has varied greatly from regime to regime. Hong Kong tycoons, Taiwanese investors, and American academic economists of Chinese ancestry have had a discernible impact on Chinese behavior in the international trade and financial areas, but the influence of overseas Chinese has been less noticeable in the security realm, where their contacts appear weak. In the realm of human rights, the message they deliver is ambiguous, with some championing the human rights agenda and many others encouraging Beijing to reject foreign pressure.

## TACTICS

The case studies also reveal that Chinese behavior is guided by certain deeply ingrained strategies and tactics. The list includes the following:

- Retaining flexibility in foreign policy conduct and avoiding enduring commitments and entangling alignments. Exclusion from an international regime is painful, but so too is the constraint arising from inclusion in the regime.

- Free riding and seeking influence without shouldering responsibility, acquiescing to policies of international regimes that manifestly serve China's interest while expressing reservations about the policies. Then extracting side payments for acquiescing while whispering to opponents of the policies that the major powers forced China to yield.

- Voicing China's objectives clearly, succinctly, and repeatedly, and making compliance with these objectives the litmus test of whether the interlocutor wants "good" or "friendly" relations with China, and placing the burden of maintaining "good" relations on the other side.

- Mobilizing support for China's position among developing countries.

- Taking advantage of the ambiguities in the norms of international regimes.

- Adopting an aggrieved posture, capturing the moral high ground, and placing the interlocutor—whether a country, a regional organization, or an international regime—on the defensive, claiming it owes China special consideration because of past injustices.

- Maintaining secrecy and opacity.

- Entering into agreements knowing China lacks the institutions to implement them not out of insincerity but as part of an effort to entice the international regime to assist the nation in acquiring the necessary institutional capacity.

## CHANGES IN CHINESE REGIME BEHAVIOR

Although the broad objectives and tactics have remained the same, the eight case studies reveal that Chinese behavior in international regimes has changed somewhat since the 1970s. China's changing capabilities, the rise of new leaders, and a different strategic setting have had their effect.

The early days were characterized by a certain idealism—a desire for China to contribute positively to the regime involved—although the contribution the Chinese desired to make was on behalf of the developing world against the established order. Increasingly, engagement appears calculated more in terms of the short-term costs and benefits for China. Two examples capture the evolution. On joining the United Nations as a permanent member of the Security Council, China volunteered to increase its dues, from 4 percent to 5.5 percent of the total U.N. budget. The request was unprecedented; no nation had ever sought to increase its payments to the United Nations. But in 1979 China asked for and was granted lower dues, 0.79 percent of the budget, in line with other developing countries. In the economic sphere, China in the early 1970s was an ardent supporter of the developing world and advocated major transformations of the international economy; it loomed as a potential threat to established telecommunications or financial regimes. Today it derives revenue from its participation in those regimes, and often seeks more.

In the early 1970s China adopted a low profile in the regimes that it joined. While its rhetoric was often ideological and strident, its behavior was disciplined and restrained; certainly this characterized China's early behavior in the United Nations. Eager to join the regime, the Chinese were not overly concerned with the details of entry. But by the late 1980s and early 1990s the Chinese had become more assertive and tougher in their negotiating positions. For example, the Chinese delegation demanded major changes in the Montreal accords on protecting the earth's ozone layer before China would accede to the agreement. In such trade matters as intellectual property rights and entry into the WTO, Chinese negotiators also have proceeded from well-crafted positions that are intended to defend their country's economic interests. Retreat from initial bargaining positions in area after area has occurred only after considerable external pressure has been brought to bear.

Five factors help explain the evolution from idealism to practicality, from ideology to economic rationality, and from reticence to nationalistic assertiveness: generational change, a learning curve, evolution in the domestic policy process, an altered international environment, and Chinese economic success.

*Generational Change*
China's kaleidoscopic modern history has produced sharp differences among generations. Each generation endured distinctive traumas and socializing experiences in its formative years, such as the Japanese invasion (1931–1945), the Great Leap Forward and the resulting famine (1957–1962), and the disruptions of the Cultural Revolution (1966–1976).

These experiences did not weld each generation into a cohesive whole; instead, every generation splintered over its members' diverse reactions to the defining trauma, and each group for its lifetime grappled with the distinctive issues the trauma posed. Those who matured in the 1920s and 1930s, deeply affected by nationalistic sentiment, wondered how best to cure China of its weakness and leave behind its inferior status, through ideologically militant defiance of the outside world or an idealistic effort to join and contribute to it. Those maturing in the Soviet era wrestled with their response to the Russian system: whether to conform to it or seek to change it. Those who survived the Cultural Revolution and prospered had learned to seize opportunities in an often bewildering environment.

The evolution in Chinese motivations for participating in international affairs partially reflects generational succession. In the 1970s the formulation and implementation of policy lay with communist recruits of the 1920s to mid-1940s. They included ideologues and idealists, rustics from peasant backgrounds and urbane, well-educated Chinese who had been exposed to the West in their youth. That generation harbored ambivalent attitudes toward the West but clearly relished the opportunity to play pivotal roles in the initial stages of China's reintegration into the world. By the mid-1980s that generation was fading. Party recruits of the late 1940s and the 1950s who had risen in the post-1949 bureaucracy, many of them trained in the Soviet Union and Eastern Europe, were coming to the fore.

In the 1990s the Cultural Revolutionaries, who are entrepreneurial and assertive, and often lack extensive formal education, have begun to make themselves felt. This generation clearly relishes the opportunity to calculate how China's rise can benefit them and their country. Many of its members appear eager to accelerate China's involvement in world affairs, but in an assertive and nationalistic way. Soon after them will come a very different cohort that matured in the Deng era, many among them with substantial experience in the West. On balance, this evolution in human talent is gradually equipping China for extensive involvement in world affairs, although at present there is a deficiency of qualified people that is partially remedied by ethnic Chinese from Taiwan, Hong Kong, and Southeast Asia.

## CHANGES IN THE POLICY PROCESS

Early on in China's entry into the international community, the Chinese political system was highly centralized. Foreign policy was in the hands of a few people who brought discipline and coherence to the process. The subsequent expansion of China's involvement in world affairs, coupled with the administrative decentralization, makes it impossible for a few people at the top to control foreign relations. While a handful of individuals can enforce their will on matters of highest priority to them, they cannot monitor every transaction that crosses the Chinese border, as was the case in the early 1970s. The ideological tone of China's early engagement reflected Mao's dominance of the system. The apparent pragmatism of the mid-1990s is a product of bureaucratic bargaining and a consultative, consensual policy process.

Moreover, the domestic budgetary system has changed. Every government unit and enterprise in China is under increasing budgetary pressure and has incentives to earn foreign currency and establish sources of domestic and foreign revenue. Local environmental agencies, for example, depend on the fines they collect from polluters to finance construction of their office buildings. Research centers use a substantial part of the per-diem consulting charges that are billed to international funders to support their administrative staff. Arms manufacturers sell their wares abroad to help finance purchases of technology. Avarice has replaced ideological principle in China's engagement with the world.

## A LEARNING CURVE

The nature of China's participation also has changed because of lessons learned. Foreigners have engaged in a huge educational effort to enhance China's understanding of and capacity in various international regimes. Chinese agencies and individuals have sought instruction, and the outside world has been glad to teach.[2] The messages that foreigners convey, however, are often discordant. International corporations and lawyers seek to convince the Chinese of the benefits of protecting intellectual property at the same time that Taiwanese, Korean, and Hong Kong businesspeople teach about the profits to be earned from intellectual property rights (IPR) infringement. While the U.S. government lectures China on human rights, Lee Kwan Yew encourages China to ignore American advice. Norwegian, Indonesian, Kuwaiti, and American petroleum experts offer different advice on structuring joint venture agreements to explore and develop oil reserves.

Listening to this discordant advice, the Chinese have learned a great deal about international standards of conduct and how to evade them. In every realm there are now policy communities in Beijing—although not in every provincial capital—that understand the international regimes China is joining. The intellectual gap between Beijing and the international community has narrowed, albeit more in some realms than in others. The Chinese have learned how to extract the benefits that international regimes offer and minimize the costs they impose. Overall, then, China has become less distinctive. Its foreign policy calculus increasingly resembles that of other major powers.

## A CHANGED INTERNATIONAL ENVIRONMENT

Since the late 1980s a series of events has increased Beijing's sense of vulnerability: the tragedy of June 4, 1989, the Soviet Union's collapse, the Persian Gulf war, Taiwan's transition to democracy and the resulting enhanced international stature of the island, the growth of regional and multilateral forums in Asia, and the Asian economic debacle of 1997. China's leaders believe they have lost the diplomatic maneuverability and strategic value that the cold war provided them. Asian regionalism deprives Beijing of opportunities to play one power against another. The collapse of Marxism-Leninism has increased China's susceptibility to potentially disruptive foreign ideas. Thus despite the many gains China has secured in relations with the world and its greater involvement in international regimes, its leaders do not feel that their environment is clearly more hospitable and less threatening than in the mid-1980s.

# Implications for U.S. Policy

Secretary of State Madeleine Albright has stated that the United States has multifaceted interests with regard to China and that none of these prevails over all others. Our findings lend weight to her observation. At the same time, U.S. policy must exhibit a sense of priorities. American policy therefore must go beyond the slogan of "constructive engagement" and recognition that U.S. interests are multifaceted. Even though no single interest is overriding, U.S. policy must display a sense of priorities and an understanding of the interrelationship among its many interests. A realistic China policy must provide satisfactory answers to three fundamental questions: What are the priorities? What strategies should be pursued to encourage China to participate constructively in world affairs? What precautionary measures should be taken in case that effort should fail? The agenda is a long and challenging one.

## ESTABLISHING A SENSE OF PRIORITIES

To aid the conduct of diplomacy and to provide the Chinese with sufficient guidance on the objectives of American policy, the United States must convey a sense of priorities. Our study suggests that these should be in the areas of security, economic relations, and encouragement of the rule of law. In the jargon of our section on mapping the policy debate, we place greater emphasis on mutual accommodation than on confrontation, and while drawing on insights from all three perspectives on world affairs, we are drawn to the realist, neoliberal, and ideationalist agenda in that order of preference.

In the security realm, China has yet to acknowledge the interdependent nature of security. Its leaders pursue Chinese security while engendering a sense of insecurity among potentially hostile neighbors. Eliciting Chinese cooperation to deter nuclear proliferation and an arms race in the Asia-Pacific region clearly is a priority objective. In the economic domain, China has taken only the first step on some major domestic economic reforms, particularly of state-owned enterprises, that are vital to its continued progress in abiding by norms in trade and finance. It seeks unfettered access to American markets but remains protective of its own; it seems unconcerned about its growing trade surplus with the United States. Finally, Chinese officials claim to seek the rule of law while resisting establishment of the basic conditions for it. Without the rule of law, China's commerce will continue to rest on poorly regulated and insecure ground. Corruption will flourish. Moreover, unconstrained by law at home, rulers are more able to behave arbitrarily abroad. And the rule of law cannot be attained if Chinese citizens or foreigners remain vulnerable to opaque laws, arbitrary arrest, lengthy detention, lack of legal counsel, harsh imprisonment, and punishment by police answerable only to themselves or individual rulers.

These issues help identify the priority objectives for U.S. participation with China in international regimes: encouraging its adherence to the International Atomic Energy Agency and the Missile Technology Control Regime standards in preventing spread of nuclear technology, nuclear weapons, and advanced missiles and missile technology; eliciting its contribution through multilateral and bilateral dialogue to maintaining peace and stability in Korea, the East and South China seas, the Taiwan Straits, and the Indochina peninsula; securing its membership in the WTO on terms that protect a liberal trading regime; and facilitating its development of the rule of law.

## MULTILATERALISM

The record demonstrates that American bilateral efforts are most effective when reinforced through multilateral efforts and supported by the bilateral efforts of others. The United States will not be successful if it unilaterally seeks to impose the conditions of China's involvement in world affairs. Integration proceeds best when there is an international consensus on the norms to which the outside world expects China to adhere. China's behavior in international financial markets, its eventual agreement to cease nuclear testing, the tempering of its assertiveness in the South China Sea, its assistance in bringing peace to Cambodia, and its endorsement of APEC goals to remove trade barriers are examples of the process at work.

Nevertheless, multilateralism cannot be a substitute for bilateral approaches. Often the institutions undergirding international regimes are weak and unable to elicit compliance with their norms. In many regimes there is no agreement on what norms should be respected. And America's interests toward China do not entirely converge with those of its partners.

The United States should consult widely with its Asian and European partners to secure as much support as possible for its priority objectives toward China. If the United States finds itself isolated on an issue, it should think twice about pressing the matter. It also should recognize that mutual adjustment is necessary to secure China's commitment. China should help to shape the rules that affect its interests.

## ENGAGING IN STRATEGIC DIALOGUE

To repeat one of our most important findings, many top Chinese leaders reject the notion of interdependence and are relatively uninterested in fostering a shared perspective on world affairs. They see the world through very different eyes. But the record shows that when intensive, high-level, strategic dialogue with China's leaders was conducted in the 1970s and 1980s, and again in 1996–1998, progress was made in shaping Chinese thinking. Over time Chinese perceptions can be influenced through dialogue, provided the Americans in their turn are willing to listen carefully to Chinese views. The dialogue cannot be a lecture.

From June 4, 1989, until 1996, such consultations were drastically curtailed. The two summits between President Clinton and President Jiang in October 1997 and June 1998 renewed the process. The agenda is extensive.

- The destabilizing consequences of the collapse of the Soviet empire challenge both countries. Both have an enormous interest in ensuring that Russia neither disintegrates nor becomes virulently nationalistic. Dialogue is required on how the two countries can best encourage Russia's transformation into a stable, effectively governed country that does not seek to dominate its neighbors.

- America's efforts to adjust its security treaty with Japan in northeast Asia and to expand the North Atlantic Treaty Organization (NATO) eastward in Europe must be explained to China's leaders; the message should be that those changes are an important means of enhancing the stability of both regions by continuing to anchor Germany and Japan in an alliance system in Europe and Asia, respectively. Both efforts are intended to prevent the reappearance of age-old regional rivalries. Chinese leaders currently fear that the adjustments in the U.S.-Japan security alliance is intended to assist Taiwan and constrain them, as some Russians fear NATO expansion is directed against them. Unless these adjustments are well understood and accepted in Beijing and Moscow, their inadvertent result could be to provide a rationale for enhanced Russian-Chinese strategic cooperation.

- As to dialogue on strategic weapons, progress on START III would compel China (as well as Russia and the United States) to assess the role of nuclear weapons in the post–cold war era. START III–level talks will almost certainly require the adoption of a minimum deterrence strategy by the United States, which would meet the conditions China has set for placing its nuclear forces on the negotiating table. At the same time, the United States should advance strategic nuclear arms talks among the Perm Five members of the Security Council to discourage China's nuclear force modernization. India's nuclear proliferation in the South Asian subcontinent will complicate this process immeasurably.

- Continued, close consulations to reduce tensions in South Asia and cope with nuclear proliferation in the subcontinent are particularly important. Through coordinated policies—as occurred when the People's Republic chaired the June 1998 meeting of the Perm Five members of the U.N. Security Council soon after the Indian and Pakistani nuclear detonations and again through the joint statement issued during the June 1998 Clinton-Jiang summit—the United States and China can maintain pressure on India and Pakistan to join the Nuclear Nonproliferation Treaty and the Comprehensive Test Ban Treaty without any condition. They can help to prevent India and Pakistan from acquiring legal status as nuclear weapons states and discourage them from deploying deliverable nuclear weapons.

- Military-to-military contact has been resumed and should be expanded to foster understanding and cooperation among air, naval, and ground forces. Technological exchanges should occur in such areas as military medicine, surveillance of drug trafficking, disaster relief, conversion of military production to civilian use, and force demobilization. Ship visits should occur regularly, including continuation of past patterns to Hong Kong. Discussions should be held on how to prevent accidental encounters in waters patrolled by both the Chinese and the American navies. Joint military exercises should be encouraged. Moreover, the United States should encourage Japanese self-defense forces and the South Korean military to engage in regular contact with the Chinese military. The objective is to help make China comfortable with the security environment created by U.S. treaties with Japan and South Korea.

- Dialogue is also required at the highest levels in the economic area. The implications of the 1997–1998 Asian economic debacle pose challenges to both economies and require coordinated responses. America's top economic officials should seek to elicit from their Chinese counterparts a better sense of their timetable for further economic reform. How do China's leaders foresee addressing their fundamental problems? And China's top economic officials deserve to hear American officials explain why China's early adherence to WTO standards actually would serve Chinese interests. As in the security realm, it is important for Chinese and American leaders, as well as leaders from industrial democracies other than the United States, to have a shared perspective concerning the trends in the world economy and how those trends can be shaped to serve the common interest. With this goal in mind, it seems appropriate to invite China to attend meetings of the Group of Eight.

- The U.S. government should continue a separate dialogue with China on human rights, one that is frank, vigorous, and rooted in mutual respect. The focus should not be on the release of specific dissidents, although those languishing in prison should not be forgotten; instead, the discussion should concentrate on how the two nations can cooperate such that each makes progress toward realizing the broad goals of the U.N. Declaration. The United States should encourage other industrial democracies to undertake their own, separate human rights discussions, recognizing that some of them, perhaps Canada, Australia, or Sweden, might elicit a more positive response.

## PROMOTING INSTITUTIONAL DEVELOPMENT

Institutional weakness impedes China's effective participation in many international regimes. The People's Republic lacks an adequate central revenue system, regular sources of local finance, a strong central banking system, a professional civil service, the effective rule of law, an independent judiciary, effective civilian control over the military, a robust system of representative assemblies, and a well-defined system of property rights.

Many Chinese officials desire not only to remedy these deficiencies but also to encourage investigative journalism and formation of government-licensed nongovernmental organizations. International, regional, and national organizations, both governmental and nongovernmental, enjoy considerable opportunity to cooperate with China in all these realms. To cite some examples from our chapters:

- The United States Arms Control and Disarmament Agency could be assigned an important role in arms control discussions. This would prompt the Chinese government to use and strengthen its own recently elevated agency within its Ministry of Foreign Affairs. The Chinese have offered some arms control proposals. No harm would come from very tentatively exploring the details of their proposals.

- Cooperating with the new State Intellectual Property Rights Administration (previously the State Patent Administration) would foster that agency's ability to enforce China's IPR regime.

- Chinese experts in the telecommunications and computer industries wish to learn about America's experience in restructuring its industries to benefit from the telecommunications revolution. Assistance in this realm would accelerate the dissemination of advanced communications technologies in China and the concomitant widening of access to information and to the outside world.

- The World Bank and the International Monetary Fund are providing advice on how to strengthen the banking and revenue system. The United Nations Development Programme is assisting the Chinese effort to create a national system of electing village leaders. Such efforts should be encouraged.

- Chinese officials have indicated their receptivity to dialogue on the fundamental issues of governance in the modern era: for example, the appropriate allocation of power between a central government and lower levels, the role of the state in the resolution of civilian disputes, the organization and role of representative assemblies, the provision of welfare for the unemployed and the elderly, and the regulation of property rights. Many Chinese recognize that their political system, like those of other countries, faces unprecedented challenges brought on by rapid technological change and economic growth. No country has a monopoly on wisdom concerning effective governance, and many Chinese officials are prepared to talk about their problems and their search for solutions.

The international community and the United States should seize upon these and many other, similar opportunities. The quiet ferment in Chinese universities, in research institutes, and at the intermediate and lower levels of the Chinese bureaucracy suggests China could be on the eve of considerable institutional change, and the United States could and should be part of that process to the extent opportunities arise for cooperation. Our study suggests that cooperation is strongest when the outside world reinforces and assists indigenously generated change.

## ENVIRONMENT AND ENERGY

The environmental and energy realms are so important that they deserve special mention. The United States must energetically assist international agencies such as the World Bank, the Asian Development Bank, and the U.N. Development Programme in extending aid to China in these areas. The United States itself should lift its ban on U.S. assistance through the auspices of the U.S.-Asia Environmental Partnership. This low-cost program could promote environmental protection in China and advance American business interests in selling environmental technologies.

Of primary concern to the United States and other countries, as well as to many Chinese, is China's rapidly increasing impact on global climate change. The United States should encourage China in the research and development of new energy-efficiency and renewable energy technologies. It should facilitate the transfer of such technologies, removing the constraints on government assistance to American vendors for trade development and private insurance in this realm. This is good for the global environment, good for business, and good for the health of the Chinese people.

In addition, training Chinese personnel in key bureaucracies, such as the State Planning Commission and the State Environmental Protection Agency, in such areas as environmental economics is an inexpensive but highly effective means of assistance. Finally, as with trade issues, the United States should assist China's environmental system to become more transparent by aiding its efforts to develop environmental databases and insisting on reporting requirements in global environmental accords.

## INCENTIVES, SANCTIONS, AND LINKAGES

Since China's officials respond more favorably to incentives—payoffs and benefits—than to sanctions and exacting of costs, rewards can be distributed to build consensus. It is better to concentrate on leading the Chinese to win-win situations while resisting their proclivity to insist on side payments to agree to such solutions.

On the other hand, sanctions and linkages—when limited and credible—do work. Chinese leaders engage in linkages and sanctions against other countries, and they respond to the threat or use of them by others. The threat of a well-targeted and limited sanction, especially in the trade realm, is more effective, however, than efforts to link two broad and diverse areas of Chinese behavior (i.e., human rights performance and trade). Negotiation deadlines tied to the threat of sanctions are often the only way to force the Chinese coordinating agency to establish discipline among the several bureaucracies that make up a Chinese negotiating team. However, once an agreement has been reached and the sanctions averted, the recalcitrant bureaucracies may feel under little obligation to adhere to the agreement unless they have received a payoff.

Establishing linkages between widely separate spheres of Chinese behavior is much more difficult. For example, responding to a foreign threat to impose economic sanctions because of its human rights record requires intervention at the highest levels, since only top leaders have the authority to make the trade-offs such linkages require. Only they can issue binding and connected orders to such diverse bureaucratic domains as the public security apparatus and the manufacturing sector. And China's top leaders are unlikely to yield often to such pressures; their colleagues and subordinates would perceive them as weak. Moreover, by forcing such issues to the highest levels, the agenda becomes overloaded. Top leaders should not have to negotiate issues that are better handled quietly through bureaucratic channels; their energies are best suited to the priority issues.

## BEHAVING CREDIBLY AND AVOIDING HYPOCRISY

Our study stresses the essential rationality of China's leaders. Within the context of their domestic political situation and their perceptions of the international context, they seek to maximize their benefits and minimize costs. The United States therefore should provide China's leaders with clear and consistent signals, indicating in credible fashion U.S. objectives, capabilities, and strategies. Do not promise what cannot be delivered; do not issue empty threats; match words with deeds; and do not criticize China for behavior that the United States exhibits. The United States should not behave toward China in a hypocritical fashion, claiming its objective is to participate with China in international regimes on a mutually acceptable basis while acting unilaterally in global and regional affairs or not meeting its own international commitments. There are many examples of such discrepancies, and none escapes Chinese attention. Specifically:

- The United States decries Chinese violations of multilateral and bilateral sales agreements, but its 1992 sale of F-16 jet fighters to Taiwan tested the limits of the 1982 arms sales agreement it reached with China. The United States wants China to temper its weapons sales and dual-use technology transfers in Asia—particularly in South Asia and the Middle East—lest the sales stimulate conflict, but it refuses to detail how its own arms sales in Asia, particularly to Taiwan, contribute to regional stability. The United States chastises Chinese arms salesmen for chasing profits, while its own sales have skyrocketed in recent years. The United States, let us remember, is the largest arms merchant in the world by far.

- The United States is handicapped in criticizing China's U.N. record when it is in arrears in meeting its own financial obligations to the United Nations. Moreover, China has signed the covenant on social and economic rights as well as the covenant on civil and political rights.

- The U.S. embrace of protectionist impulses encourages China to emulate it, while American support for a liberal trade regime, as with APEC and the WTO, places China under pressure to do the same.

In these instances, China's response to American inconsistencies is similar to that of most countries. It seizes upon them as a rationale to justify its own departure from the norms. The United States places itself at a disadvantage in holding China's leaders accountable for their failure to adhere to their commitments and international norms. Greater consistency between rhetoric and action would enhance U.S. credibility and effectiveness, not just with regard to China but elsewhere as well.

THE ROLE OF NONGOVERNMENTAL ORGANIZATIONS
AND THE PRIVATE SECTOR

The private sector greatly facilitates China's integration into the international system and its adherence to international norms. Universities, foundations, nongovernmental agencies, professional associations, and corporations are playing important roles in this area. Our study reveals, for instance, that the private sector has helped to nurture the various policy communities in Beijing that now play pivotal roles in China's participation in each international regime: disarmament, environmental regulation, international banking, civil aviation, telecommunications, and even introduction of the rule of law.

Much more can be done. For example, business can play several vital roles in the environmental sphere.

Most important, companies can set an example by upholding high environmental standards. It is in their self-interest to do so, to avoid liability, for better public and investor relations, and because of competitive pressures. In addition, the International Standards Organization 14000 certification procedure will encourage Chinese businesses to become certified in order to qualify as vendors of goods and services to other companies. Foreign companies can share information on an informal basis and work with their Chinese counterparts through business associations to address common problems.

With regard to human rights, it is important to recognize the vital role played by Amnesty International and others in creating an international climate that has placed human rights on the agenda and made it a worldwide concern. The nongovernmental organizations and business communities can employ quiet diplomacy, technical assistance, training, institution building, and grants to work with the Chinese government to improve the human rights situation in areas of mutual interest that include child labor, prison labor, women's rights, the independence of the judiciary, and the rule of law.

## The Precautionary Measures

A forthcoming posture toward China may fail. The arguments of the confrontationalists cannot be totally dismissed. China could emerge as an assertive and disruptive force on the world scene. Or it could disintegrate, the chaos spilling over its borders and bringing turmoil to the region. The strategy of mutual accommodation is intended to minimize the chances of these outcomes. What precautionary measures are necessary? Our study prompts six recommendations:

First, the strategies and tactics that China has used with such success in the early stages of its entry into international regimes, as well as its statecentric, zero-sum approach to many issues (especially in the security realm), dictate a hardheaded approach toward it. Its leaders must be treated with dignity; to demean the leaders of such a great nation is inexcusable. But U.S. negotiators must remain aware of Chinese tendencies to free ride, to adopt an aggrieved posture to extract extra benefit, and to trade on unwarranted expectations of their nation's future strength. Such tactics should be vigorously resisted.

Doing so requires approaching China with a keen sense of U.S. interests. All the policies recommended in our study flow from a sense of those interests; they are intended to advance enlightened U.S. purposes. Each American initiative must stand on its own merits. China will seize generous and well-intentioned offers of cooperation that serve its interests alone, but it will give little in return.

Third, the United States must retain a robust military presence in Asia and cultivate strong relations with Japan, South Korea, the ASEAN states, Australia, and New Zealand. It also must encourage the development of regional and subregional organizations. These measures are aimed not against China but rather at promoting regional stability. This web of regional, subregional, and bilateral ties exists to discourage disruptive behavior from any quarter.

Fourth, the United States must retain a full range of unofficial relations with Taiwan—political, economic, cultural, and military. While the United States has no obligation to support provocative Taiwan policies that predictably raise the mainland's ire, it has a moral and domestic legal obligation to ensure Taiwan has the capacity to sustain its self-defense. Shirking this responsibility would damage American credibility in Asia. The long-run U.S. objective is clear: a peaceful reconciliation arranged by the two sides without duress.

Fifth, China's entry into international regimes must occur on terms that protect the core purpose of each regime. This is particularly true for its negotiations to join the WTO.

Finally, the United States must retain an independent capacity to understand Chinese domestic and foreign affairs. It must nurture a national capability to deal with China intelligently. This requires not allowing national analytical capabilities—especially in think tanks and universities—to become dependent on funding from China or Taiwan. The U.S. government must cultivate and reward its foreign service officers, commercial counselors, military officers, and intelligence analysts who have expertise on China. At present, the government makes inadequate use of those within its ranks who have devoted their careers to mastery of China.

## Rebutting the Skeptics

Many skeptics doubt that the course we recommend is workable. They note the historical love-hate relationship that has long existed between China and the United States: periods of mutual attraction, heightened expectations, and extensive cooperation followed by dashed hopes, mutual recriminations, and enmity. The skeptics assert that the two nations remain captive to the cycle.

Analysts differ over why the United States and China have been unable to sustain a constructive relationship. Some believe that the profound differences between the two civilizations preclude protracted cooperation. Political and ideological differences intervene. As the two approach each other, their differences repel them.

Others claim that the differences in wealth, power, and global responsibilities inevitably engender divergent interests and perspectives. As a global power and a leader of the industrial democracies, the United States defends an international system it helped to create and that advances its interests, while China, as a rising power, seeks to challenge the established order. Tension and conflict are the predictable result.

Finally, some skeptics doubt the stability and continuity of the Chinese system. They note that China is in a transition period whose outcome is uncertain. They urge the United States not to invest time, energy, and money in a Chinese elite and system that may not survive and recommend cultivation of the next generation of leaders. But these skeptics overlook the fact that uncertainty about the leadership is a permanent feature of the Chinese political landscape, successors cannot be identified, and the transition is likely to persist for several more decades.

All these cautionary notes have validity. They provide sober reminders of the enormous challenges ahead and warn those dealing with China neither to harbor illusions nor to allow expectations to soar. But what is the appropriate response to these concerns? To look upon China as a potential enemy and work to isolate, weaken, or divide it, thus helping to create what the United States should seek to avoid? Surely not. The United States and its partners traveled that road from 1949 to 1971, to no avail.

There is no real alternative to the course we recommend and that every president since Richard Nixon has adopted. As President Clinton declared during the June 1998 summit:

> "[I]t is important that whatever our disagreements over past action, China and the United States must go forward on the right side of history

for the future sake of the world. The forces of history have brought us to a new age of human possibility. But our dreams can only be recognized by nations whose citizens are both responsible and free. Mr. President, that is the future America seeks to build with China, in partnership and honest friendship.

Tomorrow, Hillary and I will visit the Great Wall. The wall's builders knew they were building a permanent monument, even if they were unable to see it completed in their lifetimes. Likewise, we know we are building a friendship that will serve our descendants well, even if we ourselves will not see its full development across the next century and into the new millenium.

Our friendship may never be perfect. No friendship is. But I hope it will last forever."[3]

The record suggests that enlightened self-interest on both sides will prevail, as has largely been the case since 1972, when China and the United States embarked on their epic journey to participate together in world affairs.

## Notes

1. China's membership in international governmental organizations has grown from 21 in 1977 to 49 in 1995; its participation in international non-governmental organizations has grown from 71 in 1977 to 1,013 in 1995.

2. David Zweig and Chen Changgui, *China's Brain Drain to the United States: Views of Overseas Chinese Students and Scholars in the 1990s* (Berkeley: Regents of the University of California, 1995); and David M. Lampton, *A Relationship Restored: Trends in U.S.-China Educational Exchanges, 1978–84* (Washington, D.C.: National Academy Press, 1986).

3. "The Leaders' Remarks: Hopes for a Lasting Friendship, Even if Imperfect," *New York Times*, June 28, 1998.

# 2

# China and the United Nations

## SAMUEL S. KIM

THE UNITED Nations celebrated its 50th anniversary in October 1995 but also seemed to be experiencing a crisis of overextension. The major features that have characterized the U.N. system were found not only in the largest ever gathering of world leaders in modern times but also in the earlier failure to convene a second Security Council summit in January 1995, as originally planned to kick off the United Nations' great leap into its second half century.

In virtually all of its multitasking, from peacekeeping, to human rights, to sustainable economic development, the prospects of the world body for building a global consensus based on a broader conception of security within a more fluid transitional world political framework seemed at one and the same time daunting, promising, and open-ended. On one hand, the dangerous pattern of superpower conflict suddenly has withered away, opening up new pathways for U.N. rejuvenation. On the other hand, despite or perhaps even because of the initial euphoria and hyperactivism in the early post–cold war years, the United Nations soon began to experience what former Secretary-General Boutros Boutros-Ghali called "a crisis of overcredibility." Local and regional armed conflicts, previously overshadowed and repressed by global superpower cold war contention, have been breaking out in many parts of the world. Of the 89 armed conflicts between 1989 and 1992, for example, all but three were "internal conflicts" and "state-making" conflicts. In responding to such post–cold war security and humanitarian challenges, U.N. "peacekeepers" soon found themselves involved in a wide range of more demanding but less clearly mandated state-building activities, such as supervising cease-fires, demobilizing forces, destroying weapons, overseeing the return of refugees, providing humanitarian assistance, supervising administrative structures, training new police forces, and supervising and organizing elections. All the same, the member states, especially those of the Security Council, are asking the world organization to do more and more with less and less—without opening their wallets or delegating more power, or revamping the half-century-old Big Five anachronism of the Security Council.[1]

With the end of the consensus-forming clarity of superpower conflict, the foreign policies of most states, including the United States and China, have increasingly become mired in and symptomatic of hypernationalistic domestic politics. The end of the bipolar world also means that the political leaders everywhere are more subject than ever before to the dictates of global market forces with little countervailing socialist challenge. The statecentric nature of the United Nations and the reality of new post–cold war nationalistic behavior of member states have been conflated, but this conjuncture has exposed some serious promise/performance gaps for mobilizing and sustaining effective multilateral responses to global problems that threaten common security. The so-called U.N. crisis today can be better understood mainly as a crisis of *national* policy in the *global* organization. Indeed, the most fundamental challenge for the United Nations in the coming years will be how to stay relevant and viable as a global yet statecentric organization in a multi-centric and multipolarizing world where state sovereignty has been subject to the relentless twin pressures of global integration from above and substate fragmentation from below. The institution and principle most affected by the eruption of ethnonational wars is the state system and the principle of state sovereignty.

Still, there is little doubt about the fundamental legitimacy and author-ity of the United Nations as the first truly global organization in all of human history. With the membership explosion of the 1960s, and espe-cially since the entry of the People's Republic of China and the two Ger-manies in the early 1970s, the United Nations has become the most legitimate institutional expression of the idea of global community, help-ing to facilitate, however imperfectly, global consciousness-raising, con-sensus-building, standard-setting, and law-making processes to deal with problems that threaten international peace, human security, social, economic, and ecological well-being. The General Assembly has shifted its primary attention to the development of a more synergistic conception of human security by sponsoring a series of global conferences on human development. These include the United Nations Conference on the Envi-ronment and Development, Rio de Janiero, 1992; the World Conference on Human Rights, Vienna, 1993; the International Conference on Popu-lation and Development, Cairo, 1994; the World Summit on Social Development, Copenhagen, 1995; the Fourth World Conference on Women, Beijing, 1995; and the Second United Nations Conference on Human Settlements (Habitat II), Istanbul, 1996.

How does China fit into the post–cold war U.N. challenge of establishing a more peaceful, equitable, democratic, and ecological world order? By dint of what it is and what it does, China inescapably becomes part of both the world order problem and the world order solution. As one of the so-called Perm Five (P5) China is ipso facto involved in the conflict-management process of the Security Council. No major international conflict of a military, social, demographic, and environmental nature in the world at large and especially in the Asia-Pacific region can be resolved or abated without China's constructive engagement. Because China is one of the five acknowledged nuclear weapons states, its cooperation remains indispensable in any meaningful global and regional arms control and disarmament processes. Inescapably, the Beijing government's treatment of nearly one-fourth of humanity within its porous borders already has become a continuing global human rights issue and one of the most vexing problems taxing China's precious global time and diplomatic resources. A U.N. human rights regime either without China's participation or treating the Chinese case to be an exception renders that regime a virtual paper tiger. There can be little chance of stabilizing world population growth at a tolerable level unless the Chinese improve their family planning programs and services. China already has become an environmental polluting giant of sorts, contributing to global warming faster than any other major country. By the year 2020 China's rising generation of carbon dioxide and other greenhouse gases would make it the world's largest emitter, possibly accounting for as much as 25 percent of global emissions.

Remarkably, in the post-Tiananmen years of the first half of the 1990s, the issue of Sino-U.N. interaction has acquired new urgency by the so-called rise of China phenomenon. That development is marked by China's emergence as the world's fastest-growing economy, a rising revisionist non–status quo military power with a real increase of about 40 percent in military expenditures during the first half of the 1990s, long-standing claims to extensive territories along its periphery throughout the Asia-Pacific region, and an assertive China that can say no to foreigners and increasingly relies on hypernationalism as a unifying ideology. The politics of mutual adjustment—how the world organization might adjust to the ambitions and prerogatives of a rising China and how a rising China might adjust to the principles, norms, and objectives of the world organization—poses one of the major challenges of the post–cold war world order.

# The Evolving Pattern of China's
# U.N. Participation

It is essential to step back a little to better appreciate the changes and continuities in China's attitudes and policy toward the United Nations and to better assess the various possibilities and limitations of China's constructive engagement in the establishment of a peaceful post–cold war world order.

In contrast to China's very negative attitude toward the League of Nations during the interwar period and especially after 1931, both the Republic of China (ROC) and the People's Republic of China (PRC) after 1949 assumed a generally positive posture toward the United Nations. Nonetheless, the PRC posture rotated through the stages of naive optimism, frustration, disenchantment, rebellion, disinterest, revived hope, and a sophisticated diplomatic campaign to gain its seat. In the 1950s China adopted a wishful attitude in its elusive quest for international recognition and legitimation through U.N. membership. As the goal continued to prove elusive and hope faded in the 1960s, China became increasingly critical of the United Nations. This negative attitude culminated in a radical *system-transforming approach*, especially in 1965, with China's call for an alternative "revolutionary United Nations" in the wake of Indonesia's withdrawal from the world organization. Greatly buoyed up by increased support in the 1970 General Assembly vote on the perennial Chinese representation issue, the PRC leadership quickly incorporated the objective of winning a U.N. seat into its new foreign policy grand strategy by accelerating its banquet diplomacy, people-to-people diplomacy, state-to-state relations, and aid diplomacy. On October 25, 1971, the General Assembly crossed the Rubicon on the China question by adopting General Assembly Resolution 2758 (XXVI) to replace the ROC representative with one from the PRC; the recorded vote was 76 to 35 with 17 abstentions.

After the much-heralded entry into the United Nations in late 1971, however, China's participation remained highly selective and symbolic throughout the 1970s. General Assembly Resolution 2758 was a milestone in the quest for absolute international legitimation, opening the door wide to the PRC's entry into the specialized agencies of the U.N. system. And yet China opted to enter into only eight of the specialized agencies. China adopted a *system-reforming approach*, especially at the Sixth Special Session of the General Assembly in April 1974, which adopted two historic resolutions on a new international economic order. Beijing treated the United Nations as a legitimizing dispenser of normative claims for the Third World rather than as a vehicle for promoting

Chinese national interests and as an arena for antihegemonic (anti-Soviet) and to a lesser extent anti-U.S. struggle rather than as a functional actor in the service of Chinese development.

A comprehensive network of linkages between China and the rest of the world of international intergovernmental organizations (IGOs) was not established until the 1980s, when Beijing joined practically all important IGOs in the U.N. system, including the World Bank and International Monetary Fund. As shown in Table 2–1, China's IGO membership increased from 21 in 1977 to 51 in 1996. Even more revealing was the astonishing 14-fold growth in international nongovernmental organization (NGO) membership in 1977 to 1996 (from 71 in 1977 to 1,079 in 1996). An equally significant rise in a great variety of multilateral treaties and agreements China signed and acceded to is another indicator of this expanding nexus with the U.N. system. Thus, for the first time in modern history, China has finally joined the U.N.-centered global system with an accompanying engagement in the myriad activities of multiple international organizations. In the United Nations proper, China decided to participate in the Conference on Disarmament (CD) in 1980 and the Human Rights Commission in 1982. In late 1984 China captured its seat in the International Court of Justice with the election of PRC jurist Ni Zhengyu as a judge on the court.

With the steady expansion of membership in the world of international organizations in the 1980s, China's orientation also became distinctively *system-maintaining*. Accordingly, Beijing became more interested in what the U.N. system could do for China's modernization and less interested in what China could do to reform the United Nations. In late 1985, on the occasion of the 40th anniversary of the founding of the United Nations, when the effectiveness of the world organization had reached its nadir, Zhao Ziyang, the first PRC prime minister ever to address the General Assembly, praised it in unprecedented and almost surrealist terms: "In world history it is rare for a political international organization to have such enduring vitality like that of the United Nations, whose universality and importance grow with the passage of time."[2]

In the post–cold war and post-Tiananmen years, China's generally positive view of the United Nations has been sustained, if not greatly enhanced. This posture is clearly evident in Prime Minister Li Peng's participation in the first-ever Security Council summit in January 1992, the first-ever Earth summit at Rio in 1994, and the first-ever World Summit on Social Development at Copenhagen in 1995, as well as President Jiang Zemin's attendance at the 50th anniversary of the founding of the United Nations in New York in October 1995. The United Nations has continued to receive good press coverage in China. As the *People's Daily*

Table 2–1.  Participation of Selected Countries in International Organizations, 1960–1996[a]

| Country | 1960 | 1966 | 1977 | 1984 | 1986 | 1987 | 1989 | 1992 | 1994 | 1995 | 1996 |
|---|---|---|---|---|---|---|---|---|---|---|---|
| **China** | **2** | **1** | **21** | **29** | **32** | **35** | **37** | **44** | **50** | **49** | **51** |
|  | 30 | 58 | 71 | 355 | 403 | 504 | 677 | 856 | 955 | 1,013 | 1,079 |
| **Taiwan** | **22** | **39** | **10** | **6** | **6** | **6** | **6** | **7** | **7** | **8** | **10** |
|  | 108 | 182 | 239 | 429 | 419 | 464 | 554 | 695 | 775 | 809 | 865 |
| **Japan** | **42** | **53** | **71** | **60** | **58** | **60** | **58** | **61** | **62** | **61** | **63** |
|  | 412 | 636 | 878 | 1,296 | 1,222 | 1,420 | 1,583 | 1,749 | 1,863 | 1,889 | 1,970 |
| **France** | **90** | **100** | **104** | **93** | **67** | **81** | **83** | **88** | **85** | **88** | **87** |
|  | 886 | 1,168 | 1,457 | 2,227 | 1,704 | 2,264 | 2,598 | 2,879 | 3,038 | 3,127 | 3,255 |
| **United Kingdom** | **76** | **90** | **91** | **79** | **63** | **72** | **71** | **70** | **71** | **74** | **71** |
|  | 742 | 1,039 | 1,380 | 2,021 | 1,607 | 2,091 | 2,416 | 2,681 | 2,846 | 2,918 | 3,031 |
| **United States** | **59** | **68** | **78** | **65** | **33** | **59** | **64** | **66** | **62** | **64** | **64** |
|  | 612 | 847 | 1,106 | 1,593 | 804 | 1,579 | 1,933 | 2,127 | 2,273 | 2,327 | 2,418 |
| **USSR/Russia** | **29** | **37** | **43** | **73** | **69** | **69** | **61** | **48** | **48** | **58** | **62** |
|  | 179 | 295 | 433 | 668 | 646 | 714 | 806 | 1,074 | 822 | 1,093 | 1,300 |
| **Global** | **154** |  | **252** | **365** | **369** | **311** | **300** | **286** | **263** | **266** | **260** |
|  | 1,255 |  | 2,502 | 4,615 | 4,649 | 4,235 | 4,621 | 4,696 | 4,928 | 5,121 | 5,472 |

[a]Figures for intergovernmental organizations are bold throughout the table; figures for international nongovernmental organizations are in roman type.
*Sources:* Adapted from Union of International Associations, *Yearbook of International Organizations 1985/86*, 3rd ed., Vol. 2 (Munich: K. G. Saur, 1985), pp. 1479, 1481–83; *Yearbook of International Organizations 1986/87*, 4th ed., Vol. 2 (Munich: K. G. Saur, 1986), tables 2 and 3; *Yearbook of International Organizations 1988/89*, 6th ed., Vol. 2 (Munich: K. G. Saur, 1988), tables 2 and 3; *Yearbook of International Organizations 1989/90*, 7th ed., Vol. 2 (Munich: K. G. Saur, 1989), tables 2 and 3; *Yearbook of International Organizations 1992/1993*, 10th ed., Vol. 2 (Munich: K. G. Saur, 1992), pp. 1613–15; *Yearbook of International Organizations 1994/1995*, 12th ed., Vol. 2 (Munich: K. G. Saur, 1995), pp. 1681, 1683–85; *Yearbook of International Organizations 1995/1996*, Vol. 2 (Munich: K. G. Saur, 1996), pp. 1682–87; and *Yearbook of International Organizations 1996/1997*, Vol. 2 Munich: K. G. Saur, 1997), pp. 1637, 1639–41.

put it, the United Nations "has truly become the largest and most authoritative intergovernmental organization in the world. Its unique influence on international affairs cannot be replaced by any other international organizations."[3] The United Nations also is depicted as the prime global arena where China projects its national identity as a Group of One: "China will not enter into alliances with any countries, but can coordinate with different sides, and can say and dare to say what others cannot easily or dare not say. China enjoys high fame and plentiful friends in the U.N."[4]

Despite the turns and twists in China's U.N. policy over the years, however, the predominant image of the United Nations is still one of a statecentric system anchored in such principles as state sovereignty, state equality, state responsibility, and state rights maintained by and for states. Contrary to realist and neorealist theory, the United Nations is important for China's accelerated march to superpowerdom. What makes the United Nations all the more important in the Chinese case is Beijing's unification problem. In fits and starts Taiwan is breaking away, Hong Kong is hard to control, Tibet wants an exit with voice, the Muslims in the Northwest are unhappy, and the Mongols would like to be independent. Lacking co-optive soft power and ideological appeal, Beijing instinctively invokes the sacrosanct principle of sovereignty in its efforts to maintain its control over Hong Kong, Tibet, Inner Mongolia, Xinjiang, and Taiwan. Faced with the recent, growing challenge of Taiwan's quest for dual recognition via "flexible diplomacy," for instance, Beijing responds: "A country can have only one legal government which acts as its representative in the international arena and which exercises sovereignty in its relationships with other countries. This is an indisputable and most important principle of international law which the United Nations, the most important international organization in the world, has abided by for decades."[5] China's unusually swift recognition of 12 newly independent states in the wake of the collapse of the Soviet Union in December 1991 was prompted by fear that Taiwan would jump the gun. The greatest leverage Beijing had in this connection was its veto power in the Security Council and the threat to use it in blocking the entry of any of these newly minted states into the world organization—*no acceptance of the Beijing Formula, no U.N. entry.*[6] There is also a sense in which such a pro forma establishment of diplomatic networking is to make a virtue of necessity, bespeaking a deep anxiety about the viability of one sovereign, unified, multinational Chinese state amid turbulent global politics and growing ethnonational conflicts in many trouble spots of the world.

China's voting behavior in the General Assembly suggests the extent of Sino-American differences on a range of global issues. As shown in

Table 2–2, the coincidence figures on all the recorded votes in the General Assembly in 1994 to 1996 place China—and Cuba, North Korea, Iran, Iraq, Laos, Syria, and Vietnam—in the lowest-scoring-countries category even though China's coincidence voting percentage vis-à-vis the United States roughly doubled, from 10.95 percent in 1989 to around 22 percent in 1994 to 1996. China cast 13 identical votes, 44 opposite votes, 14 abstentions, and 6 absences in the 1994 plenary session; 14 identical votes, 51 opposite votes, 13 abstentions, and 5 absences in the 1995 plenary session; and 19 identical votes, 45 opposite votes, 10 abstentions, and 4 absences in the 1996 plenary session. Measured in terms of the coincidence figure on recorded votes considered important to U.S. interests, China's voting coincidence rate dropped down to 12.5 percent in 1994 (1 identical vote, 7 opposite votes, 6 abstentions, and 1 absence) and to 9.1 percent in 1995 (1 identical vote, 10 opposite votes, 4 abstentions, and 1 absence) and rose to 22.2 percent (2 identical votes, 7 opposite votes, and 3 abstentions) in 1996. Since there is no veto in the General Assembly, the impact of Sino-American differences in the domain of global normative politics seems minimal. However, China's voting coincidence rate of 22.2 percent in the 1996 General Assembly plenary session stands out in sharp contrast to a combined average of 74.5 percent with France (81.8 percent), Russia (60.0 percent), and the United Kingdom (81.8 percent) in the Security Council, suggesting the extent of Sino-American differences prevailing in the primary domain of global high politics.

Indeed, the General Assembly—and global conferences initiated and sponsored by it—seemed made to order for the politics of collective legitimation and delegitimation. During its participation in the General Assembly, Beijing has experimented with various blends of confrontation with both superpowers, first with the Soviet Union in the 1970s and now with the United States in the 1990s. At the general level of policy pronouncement, China is still engaged in a habit-driven search for any affirmation in the world body of its national identity as a moral regime and of its role as a champion of international justice for the global underdogs. Indeed, China's symbolic identification with the Third World bespeaks a deep sense of historical grievances and an intense craving for great-power status dramatizes its nationalist sentiment that it has been unjustly denied its rightful place in the international system by those more powerful.

## CHINA'S RESPONSE TO U.N. REFORMS

Beijing's participation in the Security Council offers a more concrete real-world case for assessing China's security thinking and behavior as made manifest on a host of reform proposals now on the U.N. agenda.

Table 2-2. Voting Coincidence of China, France, USSR/Russia, and the United Kingdom with the United States in the General Assembly, 1989–1995

| Country | 44th GA 1989 (%) | 45th GA 1990 (%) | 46th GA 1991 (%) | 47th GA 1992 (%) | 48th GA 1993 (%) | 49th GA 1994 (%) | 50th GA 1995 (%) | 51st GA 1996 (%) |
|---|---|---|---|---|---|---|---|---|
| *China* | 10.9 | 16.3 | 16.4 | 16.4 | 10.6 | 22.8 | 21.5 | 22.2 |
| France | 69.0 | 76.7 | 70.5 | 63.8 | 71.0 | 75.8 | 76.9 | 81.8 |
| USSR/Russia | 9.5 | 16.7 | 41.9 | 59.5 | 68.6 | 66.6 | 73.1 | 60.0 |
| United Kingdom | 77.8 | 81.8 | 79.6 | 73.5 | 80.0 | 84.3 | 85.1 | 81.8 |
| Average[a] | 16.9 | 21.3 | 27.8 | 31.0 | 36.8 | 48.6 | 50.6 | 63.9 |

[a]This is an overall average of all the member states of the United Nations, not an average of the Perm Five in the Security Council.
*Sources:* Adapted from United States Department of State, *Voting Practices in the United Nations 1994* (Washington, D.C.: Department of State Publication 10245, March 1995), pp. 33–37; *Voting Practices in the United Nations 1995* (Washington, D.C.: Department of State Publication 10327, March 1996), pp. 31–35; *Voting Practices in the United Nations 1996* (Washington, D.C.: Department of State Publication 10438, March 1997), pp. 54–58.

The question of an appropriate perspective on U.N. reform is closely keyed to attitudes about sovereignty and its corollary, the state system. The U.N. Charter model of world order is a hybrid of statist principles and globalist aspirations. The Charter system can be said to have embodied an indeterminate mandate appealing to both statist system-maintaining instincts and globalist system-transforming possibilities. In short, the Charter system endowed the United Nations with the potential to move in either direction, setting the new world organization afloat in the sea of postwar global politics. Given the indeterminate mandate and the presence of mutually competing principles, the Charter system has become all things to all states.[7]

The starting point for understanding China's response to the challenges of U.N. reform is to recognize that in the post-Tiananmen and post–cold war era the old Westphalian conception of state sovereignty has returned with renewed vigor to the rhetoric of Chinese foreign policy. If China's foreign policy pronouncements in the United Nations are taken at face value, sovereignty remains both the sine qua non and the lingua franca of its international comportment and the chrysalis of international order. Indeed, the most basic characteristic of post-Tiananmen Chinese foreign relations is the supremacy of state sovereignty: *no state sovereignty, no world order or regional order.*[8] More broadly, however, the sovereignty-centered image of world order reflects a deeply rooted realpolitik outlook that world politics remains a neo-Darwinian jungle where state interests are best promoted through self-help and unilateral security.

## REVITALIZING THE COLLECTIVE SECURITY SYSTEM

During the long cold war years, the Security Council had proven unable to implement the Charter-based collective security system. In light of the widely held belief that the United Nations had to exercise some minimal authority for the maintenance of international peace and security in order not to repeat the fate of the League of Nations, a politically more feasible and militarily more modest alternative has evolved over the years. Known as "peacekeeping," it was conceived as a mechanism to bridge the growing gap between what should be done and what could be done; it fell in the gray zone between the pacific settlement provisions of Chapter VI and the enforcement provisions of Chapter VII of the U.N. Charter. Not surprisingly, the track record of U.N. peacekeeping during the cold war years was mixed, with the success curve dropping to disappointingly low levels in the 1970s and followed by a still sharper drop in the mid-1980s.

However, events in 1987 to 1993 served as a reminder that it was premature to write off the United Nations in the maintenance of international peace and security. To a significant extent, the post–cold war challenge of preventing, controlling, restraining, weakening, or encapsulating regional armed conflicts has devolved on the Security Council. Having extricated itself from the paralysis of East-West confrontation, the Security Council has decided not to let state sovereignty get in the way of intervening in certain situations perceived to be threatening to international peace or the collective moral consciousness of the world community.

Against this backdrop and at the request of the first-ever Security Council Summit, held in late January 1992, then Secretary-General Boutros Boutros-Ghali issued a landmark report, entitled "An Agenda for Peace," calling on the member states, and in particular the Perm Five, to redefine state sovereignty to strengthen the world organization's capacity for preventive diplomacy, peacemaking, peacekeeping, and postconflict peace building. While paying the mandatory lip service to the principle of state sovereignty, the secretary-general made clear what would be required for the world organization to meet the rising demands of global security: "The time of absolute and exclusive sovereignty . . . has passed; its theory was never matched by reality."[9] Of the Perm Five, China has jumped the gun by projecting the most skeptical posture toward Boutros-Ghali's agenda.[10] Apparently his report contained too many sovereignty-diluting features, thus provoking Beijing's public opposition: "UN reform should contribute to maintaining the sovereignty of its member states. Sovereign states are the subjects of international law and the foundation for the formation of the United Nations. The maintenance of state sovereignty serves as the basis for the establishment of a new international order."[11] More specifically, China argued that all U.N. activities, whether in preventive diplomacy or peacemaking, whether in peacekeeping or postconflict peace building, should strictly observe the principles of state sovereignty and of noninterference in the internal affairs of member states.[12]

Lacking anything but lukewarm support and even indifference from the major powers and faced with the twin crises in Bosnia and Somalia, the secretary-general issued on January 3, 1995, an addendum to "An Agenda for Peace" entitled "Supplement to an Agenda for Peace." Boutros-Ghali suggested various alternatives to the currently overextended and micromanaged peacekeeping operations, such as (1) U.N. authorization for member states themselves to take the initiative, as happened in U.S.-led Desert Storm operations under Security Council Resolution 678 and in the early phases of the U.N. Mission in Haiti; (2) establishment of a rapid reaction force; (3) greater role and burden sharing by regional organizations; and (4) transfer of decision-making responsibility from the Security Council to the General Assembly or other intergovernmental bodies.[13]

China responded to this supplement with an I-told-you-so attitude reiterating its minimalist approach: (1) the twin principles of state sovereignty and noninterference in a state's internal affairs always must be observed in any peacekeeping operation; (2) all disputes must be settled by such pacific means as good offices, mediation, and negotiation; (3) the General Assembly should play a more active and effective role in the maintenance of international peace and security; (4) as an expression of democratization of international relations, the Security Council should hear the views of all member states, and its decisions must reflect their common will and interests; (5) any future peacekeeping operation must proceed from the prior consent of the parties concerned, impartiality, and the nonuse of force, except in self-defense and within the limits of its financial means; and (6) full play should be given to the role of neighboring countries and relevant regional organizations.[14]

In practice, China's position on U.N. peacekeeping has evolved over the years in a dialectical situation-specific way, balancing its realpolitik interests with concerns for its international reputation as the champion of Third World causes. During China's preentry period as a whole (1949–1971), both ideology (in the form of the Maoist theory of just war) and experience (the trauma of the U.N. intervention in the Korean War) conditioned its negative attitude toward U.N. peacekeeping activities. And yet China argued forcefully in support of the U.N. interventions and sanctions in the Suez Crisis of 1956 and in colonial and apartheid questions involving Portugal, Southern Rhodesia, and South Africa while at the same time condemning the United Nations Emergency Force, enacted via the Uniting for Peace Resolution as ultra vires on the grounds that the Security Council alone was empowered to take such action. All U.N. peacekeeping operations up to 1971 were characterized as docile special detachments of the international gendarmerie of U.S. imperialism. Once China had secured a seat in the Security Council, its position shifted through three stages: (1) principled opposition/nonparticipation (1971–1981), (2) support/participation (1982–1989), and (3) contingent support/minimal participation (1990–present). During the opposition/nonparticipation period, China showed a negative attitude toward such operations, even if opposition was expressed in the form of nonlethal "nonparticipation in the vote" and disassociation from any financial obligations. Then came a policy change as part of Beijing's opening to and more active involvement in the world of international organizations ushering in the support/participation period. On December 14, 1981,

China for the first time voted for the extension of the U.N. peacekeeping force in Cyprus (UNFICYP). In the 1980s China "safely" projected itself as a champion of U.N. peacekeeping and no longer abstained from voting except for a single occasion (Security Council Resolution 502 of April 3, 1982, on the Falklands). With Soviet prodding and support, China formally made a request in September 1988 to become a member of the U.N. Special Committee on Peacekeeping Operations and was unanimously accepted two months later. In the first official statement issued as a new member in April 1989, Ambassador Yu Mengjia urged the international community to give "powerful political support" to U.N. peacekeeping, because the facts had proven convincingly that it had become an "effective mechanism" in realizing the purposes of the charter and an integral part of its efforts in finding a political settlement for regional conflicts.[15] In November 1989 the Chinese government decided for the first time to dispatch 5 Chinese military observers to serve in the U.N. Truce Supervision Organization (UNTSO) in the Middle East and 20 Chinese civilians to serve as members of the U.N. Transitional Assistance Group (UNTAG) to help monitor the independence process in Namibia.

The 1990–1991 Gulf crisis was the most serious and propitious test of the Chinese commitment to the Charter-based world order. Initially, Beijing's response was a nonresponse. It waited to see how others would react, perhaps hoping that the United Nations would downplay this naked aggression, as it did with Saddam Hussein's 1980 invasion of Iran, without putting Beijing on the spot. This wait-and-see posture was tempered by a sense that multiple dangers lurked in the situation. Despite its initial vacillation and ambiguous posturing, Beijing soon awakened to the dialectical possibility of seizing on the crisis for simultaneously diverting the world's attention from its high post-Tiananmen profile and applying its weight again in global high politics. By abstaining rather than voting for or against Security Council Resolution 678 (which authorized the use of "all necessary means to uphold and implement" all relevant Council resolutions) on November 29, 1990, China allowed itself ample room for multiple interpretations of its "principled stand"—indeed, another demonstration of its multiprincipled diplomacy of projecting itself as all things to all nations. Despite repeated pronouncements during the Security Council proceedings that "China does not have nor does it wish to seek any self-serving interests in the Middle East, and its only concern is to maintain peace and stability of that region," Beijing managed to extract maximum payoffs from Washington in exchange for the most minimal support.[16] All the same, China's abstention on Resolution 678 was justified as its own way of "adhering to principles and upholding international justice." China cannot support the use of force in the name of the United Nations, on the grounds that the "United Nations, as an international organization for the maintenance of peace and security, is responsible both to international security and to history."[17]

In the face of both America's military Persian Gulf victory under the banner of that resolution and the growing number of U.N. peacemaking and state-making activities, China began to retreat by redefining its stand in a contingent manner—to wit, peacekeeping operations could be established and conducted only in compliance with the principle of noninterference in internal affairs, since the U.N. Charter does not authorize involvement in the internal disputes of its member states.[18] Having extracted maximal geopolitical mileage from the Cambodian conflict, Beijing seemed poised to drop its Pol Pot card, giving support to the establishment of the U.N. Transitional Authority in Cambodia (UNTAC), one of the most costly but arguably successful peacemaking and state-making operations in U.N. history, involving some 22,000 military and civilian personnel at an estimated cost of $2 billion. In April 1992 China dispatched 47 military observers and 400 military engineers to join the UNTAC, only to retreat once again via the abstention escape route when the Council decided in Security Council Resolution 792 on November 30, 1992, to impose economic sanctions on the recalcitrant Khmer Rouge faction.

Even in such a multilateral setting, China makes its preference for bilateralism over multilateralism loud and clear. While giving moral support to the idea of a nuclear-free Korean peninsula (who doesn't?), Beijing repeatedly has denied any role or responsibility in the Korean nuclear issue and continues to claim that this dispute is directly and exclusively between the Democratic People's Republic of Korea (DPRK), on the one hand, and the United States, the Republic of Korea (ROK), and the International Atomic Energy Agency (IAEA), on the other. In other words, it is none of China's business. At the same time, Foreign Minister Qian Qichen made it clear on many occasions that his government is not only opposed to economic sanctions but also against bringing up the issue at all in the IAEA and the Security Council. When push comes to shove in the council, Beijing would issue a thinly veiled threat to vote against any proposed resolution. Because China alone among the Perm Five had taken such a hard line, the Security Council had first to delay and then to dilute any draft resolution so as to make it more palatable to Chinese sovereignty-bound minimalism. On May 11, 1993, the Security Council adopted a resolution (825) by a vote of 13 to 0 with only China and Pakistan abstaining, merely calling on the DPRK to reconsider its announced withdrawal from the Nuclear Nonproliferation Treaty. It was against this backdrop that the issue was taken out of the Security Council and became a subject of U.S.-DPRK bilateral negotiations in New York between June 2 and 11, 1993. On March 28, 1994, China brushed aside demands for a rather mild Security Council draft resolution, insisting successfully on a still milder "presidential statement." On May 29, 1994, the Security Council, in diluted diplomatic language once again aimed at appeasing Beijing, tried to send another statement that "further Security Council consideration will take place" to achieve Pyongyang's full compliance.[19]

For China, afflicted since 1989 with the twin legitimation crises at home (the Tiananmen carnage) and abroad (the collapse of transnational communism at its epicenter), international sanctions, especially U.S.-sponsored sanctions against a socialist regime, triggers the sound and fury response of state sovereignty. There is another logic driving Chinese behavior on the North Korean issue in the Security Council. As one Security Council representative put it, "And they used the North Korean debate as a case to illustrate a deeper point—if you can't force the North Koreans to do what you want, how do you imagine you could ever force the Chinese to do anything? Nothing can be done against the Chinese. . . . We lobbied them as part of the non-aligned movement (NAM) countries on the Bosnia and the Haiti missions. Again, they believe in *bilateral dealing*, they come, they smile, they leave."[20]

Whether the cold war ended or not, the United Nations, for China as for so many other member states, is still a statecentric intergovernmental organization. The dogged determination to define national identity in terms of state sovereignty, state status, and state security stands in the way of responding positively to any proposal for a regional or global collective security system. China's post–cold war security strategy was revealed in an internal document on January 28, 1995. According to the document, the Chinese Communist Party (CCP) and military have agreed to oppose any idea of establishing an Asian collective security scheme, as proposed by Japan and other countries. Such a regional collective security system would increase the possibility that Southeast Asian nations may rehash their arguments over the "Chinese threat theory" (*Zhongguo weixian lun*), especially over the Spratly Islands dispute, and thus impinge too closely on Beijing's expansive regional security zone for comfort.[21]

## INSTITUTIONAL REFORM

The General Assembly first considered the Charter review question in 1955 in compliance with Article 109(3) of the Charter, and adopted a resolution deciding in principle that a conference to review it should be held "at an appropriate time." The Assembly disposed of the issue by establishing committee of the whole to keep the matter under review. Following heated debates in the General Committee and the Sixth (Legal) Committee, the 29th Plenary Session of the General Assembly in 1974 finally established the 42-member Ad Hoc Committee on the Charter of the United Nations, with a mandate to discuss and consider suggestions and observations from member states on the need and desirability of Charter review. Predictably, debates on the review question, whose core issue centered on the who, how, and what aspects of the veto, generated more heat than light, and not much headway was made on the issue.

The end of the cold war gave rise to the growing recognition that a new world order requires a new framework of global governance. All existing international institutions—particularly the Security Council, the U.N. development system, and the Bretton Woods economic institutions—need considerable restructuring if they are to meet the new challenges of common security in the post–cold war era. A U.N. working group, set up in early 1994, has been debating the question of Security Council reform with no consensus on any particular formula in sight other than the general need to reform. The most recent prevailing opinion of the working group in the General Assembly is that any enlargement in permanent membership should move beyond adding Japan and Germany and that there should be no enlargement in permanent membership, although some degree of enlargement in nonpermanent membership should take place. Another proposal—the so-called third proposal—calls for the establishment of five new permanent seats, to be filled by rotation among the members of each of the United Nations' five regional groups. Yet the debate in the General Assembly has remained academic, as there could be no reform or enlargement proposal against the wishes of any of the Perm Five members in the Security Council.

The nature of Chinese support on the question of U.N. institutional reform, and especially on the expansion of Security Council membership, is more rhetorical than real, more generalized than specific. The restructuring of the General Assembly and the Security Council, we are told, should be accomplished through consensus of the member states after serious and careful study and discussion in line with the principles of balance and rationalization. "All proposals for the restructuring of the General Assembly and the Security Council should be made with a view to strengthening rather than affecting the current mechanisms that have been proved effective through practice."[22] This was another way of saying that any institutional reform or restructuring has to be done through formal constitutional amendment—a rigorous and well-nigh impossible process, given the two-thirds plus the Perm Five requirement (Article 108).

Without initiating any specific proposals, China seems more willing to go along with whatever the Third World wants to do to make the General Assembly more democratic and its procedures more rational. Reforming the historical anachronisms that still mark the permanent membership of the Security Council is an entirely different matter.[23] Here more than on any other institutional reform issues, China prefers to vacillate and equivocate and let the remaining Perm Five do all the stonewalling, even as it habitually argues that "the important thing is to change the tendency of a few big nations and rich nations to control and manipulate the UN and to ensure that all nations, big or small, rich or poor, can take part in discussing and solving major world issues on an equal footing."[24]

Throughout discussions about Security Council reform, Beijing has remained cautious, noncommittal, and reactive. China has neither advanced its own specific proposal nor reacted specifically to various reform proposals on the U.N. agenda. Instead, its pronouncements, always couched in vague language, are subject to multiple interpretations, reflecting China's larger concern for maximizing its status and leverage in global high politics. Any reform should be done under the strict guidance of the U.N. Charter and in a manner that provides due consideration to the principle of fair and equitable distribution, so that the Security Council will become more representative, more efficient, and more capable of dealing with major international problems. China gives moral support to the Third World demand for greater representation in the Security Council, but in a manner that would make its own "fair balance and full consent formula" virtually impossible to implement—membership expansion should seek a fair balance between developed and developing member states as well as among various regions of the world, and membership expansion should be acceptable to all through negotiation and consensus building, giving special consideration to the fact that the developing countries make up a majority of the U.N. membership.

China sees no imminent danger that its veto power will be diluted through expansion of membership, because there is tacit agreement among the Perm Five that "reform should only consist of an increase in members and they oppose discussing the veto question or taking any action in this regard. . . . Considering the global influence that the United States, Britain, France, and Russia still exert and the legal complications involved in amending the U.N. Charter, the standing of the permanent members will not be fundamentally challenged by any reform in the near future. . . . The five powers have insisted that any reform of the 15-member council must not dilute their power of veto."[25]

The logic of Beijing's defensive mechanisms is obvious. Beijing has a vested symbolic and strategic interest in keeping the Security Council exactly as it is. Not only would an increase in the number of permanent members dilute its own high-profile role as a Group of One and the champion of the Third World, but any changes in the use of the veto power also would reduce its fungible leverage. As will be noted later, China gets what it wants by threatening to use its veto power, as was made amply evident in the Haiti case in the Council in 1996. Any successful expansion of permanent membership would inevitably emasculate its status and leverage as the only non-Western, Third World country in the cockpit of U.N. politics. One Chinese international relations scholar goes so far as to echo the Soviet party line in the 1970s—since the veto is the keystone of the existence of the United Nations, it should not be tampered with or even restricted in its usage.[26] The rise of pop nationalism found its way clear to Beijing's U.N. diplomacy as a group of 15 hypernationalistic activists, headed by Tong Zeng, issued a statement/letter on November 19, 1996, addressed to and hours ahead of a three-day visit by Secretary of State Warren Christopher, strongly protesting against "the U.S. government supporting Japan's bid to become a permanent member of the U.N. Security Council to draw Japan over to its side." Japan is not qualified for permanent membership, according to the letter, because "many Japanese politicians had been reluctant to apologize for its war atrocities and tried to whitewash history."[27] Although this unusual protest letter was formally addressed to the U.S. government, its target audience was the Chinese government, which, eager for more low-interest loans from Tokyo, has been reluctant to antagonize Japan and has not taken a strong public stand on the issue.

During the postentry Maoist period (1971–1976), China was uncharacteristically active on the Charter review question, which it viewed as part of the larger struggle for "the establishment of a new international relations based on equality." China managed to project itself as the only permanent member of the Security Council willing to give moral and political support to the underdogs' demands for a more egalitarian world order, even at the possible risk of diluting its own privileged U.N. status. In contrast, China's posture in recent years has been noticeably system-maintaining. Chinese references to and commentaries on the Charter review question have virtually vanished. Instead, China has enjoyed its self-styled role as the only developing country among the Perm Five fighting for the causes of the Third World, especially through its support for a Third World candidate for the post of secretary-general. Of the 21 vetoes China cast from 1971 to 1996, 19, or 90 percent, had to do with recommendations regarding the appointment of the secretary-general. In late October and early November 1981 there was a Sino-U.S. "veto war" in the behind-the-scenes proceedings in the Security Council—with the United States casting 16 vetoes against China's favorite Third World candidate, Salim Salim of Tanzania, and China casting 16 vetoes against the candidacy of Kurt Waldheim of Austria—which paved the way for the election of a dark-horse compromise Third World candidate—Javier Pérez de Cuéllar of Peru.[28] In 1991 Boutros Boutros-Ghali as a leading candidate for secretary-general received positive Chinese press coverage for his expressed opposition to opening the Pandora's box of enlarging the permanent membership.[29] President Clinton's misguided and electorally inspired campaign against Boutros-Ghali for a second term, culminating in the U.S. solo veto in the Security Council on November 19, 1996, enabled Beijing to exercise its maxi/mini Third World championship diplomacy, defending the secretary-general and attacking the United States in both procedural and substantive terms.[30] Once Boutros-Ghali suspended his candidacy to pave the way for other African candidates to compete, China stayed largely on the sidelines, although it effectively ended the candidacy of Senegalese Foreign Minister Moustapha Niasse because Senegal has ties with Taiwan.

Thus the fight for a Third World candidate for the post of secretary-general is well suited to China's maxi/mini code of conduct. On one hand, such posturing is believed to enhance the credibility of Beijing's claim of assuming championship without leadership, although there is no evidence supporting such a claim, as made evident in the perceptions of other representatives in the Council. On the other hand, it papers over, or at least compensates for, China's refusal to support the long-standing demand of Third World countries such as India, Brazil, and Nigeria for more equitable representation among the Council's permanent members.

## Assessing the Reciprocal Impacts

### CHINA'S IMPACT ON THE UNITED NATIONS

In a general sense the greatest impact of Chinese participation on the development of the United Nations as a world organization has been largely symbolic. The 25-year relationship between the two can be characterized as one of mutual adjustment, mutual legitimization, and mutual enhancement of symbolic capability. With China's participation in all the remaining U.N.-related agencies and programs in the 1980s, the world organization has been made more legitimate, more representative, and more relevant in responding to global problems and issues. At the same time, the disruptive impact of Chinese participation that was so widely and wrongly predicted and feared during the exclusion period has not come to pass. The irony is that China is still not a satisfied status quo power, since it retains extensive territorial disputes with virtually all of its Asian neighbors. But within the world organization it is a satisfied conservative system maintainer, not a liberal system reformer nor a revolutionary system transformer. With China's growing participation in U.N. organs and U.N.-sponsored conferences, the global consensus-building, standard-setting, and norm-clarifying processes have become more legitimate but also more difficult and protracted. Apart from its positive and legitimizing symbolic impact, China's U.N. participation has had varying and differentiated consequences in a variety of issue areas.

In the Security Council, China has exerted considerable leverage, if not normative influence, not by hyperactive positive engagement but by following an indeterminate strategy vacillating between tacit cooperation and aloofness. China's voting behavior in the Council is closely keyed to and conditioned by its maxi/mini diplomacy. Despite its "principled opposition" to a wide range of issues in the Security Council, China generally has expressed its principled opposition in the form of "nonparticipation in the vote" in its early postentry years and abstention in recent years. In 25 years, from late 1971 to the end of 1996, China cast 21 vetoes—19 on recommendations regarding the appointment of the secretary-general (December 1971, December 1976, and October 1981), one on Bangladesh's membership issue (August 25, 1972), and one on a Middle East question (September 10, 1972). As already noted, China and the United States got drawn into a tit-for-tat exchange of vetoes on the appointment of the next U.N. secretary-general; the United States cast 16 vetoes against Salim Salim of Tanzania, and China cast 16 vetoes against Kurt Waldheim of Austria.

Since late 1981 the veto has vanished from Chinese voting behavior.[31] Given its long-standing assault on the veto as an expression of hegemonic behavior, China tried hard—and successfully—not to allow itself to be cornered into having no choice but to cast its solo veto. Instead, abstention has become a kind of normative veto, an expression of "principled opposition" without standing in the way of the majority will. As shown in Table 2–3, in the past seven years (1990–1996) the veto in general has become a rarity, with a total of 6 (4 by the United States and 2 by Russia). During this period China cast 29 abstention votes, 64 percent of all 45 abstentions among the Perm Five. Thus China sometimes is forced to affirm a resolution (as in the case of resolution 827, on the international war crimes tribunal in Bosnia) that violates its most cherished principle of the nonviolability of state sovereignty with nothing more than the habit-driven ritualistic pronouncement of "principled position." The most obvious explanation for such behavior is the desire to retain maximum leverage as part of its indeterminate strategy of becoming all things to all nations on many issues intruding on the Security Council agenda. To abstain is to apply the Chinese code of conduct of being firm in principle but flexible in application or to find a face-saving exit with a voice in those cases pitting China's conflicting realpolitik geopolitical interests against idealpolitik normative concerns for its international reputation. In short, the pattern that emerges with respect to China's voting behavior in the Council, particularly abstentions on Chapter VII enforcement resolutions, is neither positive engagement nor destructive obstruction but one of pursuing the maxi/mini strategy in a situation-specific and self-serving way.

China's impact, whether constructive or otherwise, is also a function of how other member states perceive the manner in which Beijing plays its role as one of the Perm Five in the Security Council. During the postentry Maoist period (1971–1976), the PRC's representatives already had established a reputation in the U.N. community as a first-rate professional team, winning friends and influencing delegations to a degree many observers found rather astonishing.[32] In contrast, China's behavior in the Council in recent years as perceived and conveyed by the representatives of other member states is one of aloofness (i.e., a low level of engagement) on most issues and cases. As one European representative put it, "Informal consultations continue on a P3 or P4 basis, but the Chinese are not interested anymore. The Chinese are feeling less and less in common with the P5. They don't feel they should have to sacrifice their independence because they are a P5 member, and they feel they stand to lose more by identifying with the P5 than by allying themselves with the NAM." He goes on to say: "Stepping back to appraise their level of engagement, I would say that they see the game is being played in town and they want to be in on it. But beyond that they don't feel a need to contribute constructively. That is why I would say my catch-word . . . is disappointment after three years."

Another representative, from a Latin American country, concurs, saying how aloof the Chinese have become from the general agenda of the Security Council and quoting "Dean Acheson, 'Let Me Sleep Unless . . .' in this case, the 'unless' for the Chinese are the topics of human rights, Taiwan or sanctions. . . . They never take part in the give-and-take of preparing resolutions, e.g., never part of the debate on Somalia, they were totally removed, had no opinion. If they can, they let others weave

together a resolution, then say they can live with it; they don't waste any time on things that are not fundamental to their interests."

And yet aloofness may be a close function of the extent to which Beijing micromanages China's behavior in the Council. As one Latin American representative put it, "The Chinese are *totally dependent on Beijing, to the last comma*. . . . they will only venture a strong opinion verbally, but then abstain, not veto." This overdependence on Beijing also may be a function of the extent to which the quality of China's U.N. representatives has declined over the years. The heady days when China was represented by the who's who in the Chinese foreign policy establishment (e.g., Huang Hua, Chen Chu) have long since gone. U.N. press corps' nickname for China's chief representative Li Daoyu (now China's ambassador in Washington) was "Ambassador Looking Out the Window."

Aloofness does not mean that China wants to be excluded from the only game in town. It also may be a function of an increasingly reactive foreign policy. "They generally wait to see what everyone else's position is, where the NAM stands, where the country [Beijing] itself stands," according to one representative. "They do wait and see, determine what the majority feel." Another representative put it this way: "On procedure behind the scenes . . . they very much resent being left out of the process. But they don't want to be part of the drafting process, so they will always insist on seeing the finished 'work of art' before the official submission, making everyone wait for a week or two while they send it to Beijing, then they always make a correction, sometime a very ridiculous one [revision], before the draft is submitted openly."

The Rwanda case underscores another logic—the Tibet factor—of China's delaying tactic. "We tried for weeks to get the Council to use the word 'genocide,' and the U.S. and China were the two most difficult parties. . . . The Chinese couldn't bring themselves ever to accept criticism of the murders taking place in those places, even though the nonaligned were desperate to get it. The Chinese found themselves in a weird alliance with this Hutu guy sitting around the U.N. The word 'genocide' was needed to characterize the events; with the U.S. the word 'genocide' was a trigger that called for certain responsibilities, while with the Chinese it was a more generic issue."

Despite the habitual claim that support for and solidity with the Third World is a basic principle in Chinese foreign policy, China has emerged as perhaps the most independent actor in global group politics, a veritable Group of One. As a member of the Japanese permanent mission to the United Nations put, "When I first arrived at the U.N., I expected the Chinese to have a very high profile, particularly among developing countries. I was startled to find that the general opinion of the Chinese was very low among these countries, including the Asian countries, who privately voiced their disappointment at the lack of Chinese support for their development needs. They see the Chinese as spending all their energy on developing their nuclear power when they could be putting those same funds into assistance of poor neighbors." That said, however, China still enjoys a better access and credibility among Third World member states, especially in the U.N. Human Rights Commission, than any other member of the Perm Five.

In short, China's impact on the work of the Security Council is neither positive nor negative; rather China pursues a reactive minimalist approach, as made evident by the fact that the Chinese veto has become as rare as China-initiated Security Council resolutions. Beijing is always eyeing the Security Council with Taiwan or Tibet in mind and is quick to protest what might seem to be a pattern of interference in any nation's internal affairs.

Still, permanent Security Council membership with the veto power serves as a great-power status symbol as well as a highly useful and fungible instrument of renewable leverage in the service of China-specific interests. Like nuclear weapons, the real power of the veto lies not so much in its actual use as in the threat to use it or not to use it. With the demise of the strategic triangle, China's permanent membership in the Security Council remains the only way it can portray itself as a global power. After the recent and unexpected revival of Taiwan's U.N. bid, Beijing's veto power has been touted publicly as the powerful sword and impregnable shield that defend the integrity of People's China as the only legitimate Chinese government in the United Nations.

More than in any other issue areas, China's impact is measurably palpable in its contribution to U.N. financing. Teetering on the brink of bankruptcy, the world organization closed out 1996 with a budget shortfall of $2.3 billion ($600 million in the regular budget and $1.7 billion in the peacekeeping budget), with the United States as the largest fiscal deadbeat, owing a debilitating $1.3 billion in back dues. Viewed in this light China, without any outstanding debt, seems like part of the solution. And yet a reality check suggests otherwise. In the past 25 years, China made two surprising and dramatic policy changes with instant impact on U.N. financing. As if to add more credibility to China's touted national identity as the only Third World country that gave but never received any bilateral and multilateral aid during the postentry Maoist period (1971–1976), Beijing, in an unprecedented move in the history of U.N. budgetary politics, requested in 1973 to have its assessment rate raised from 4.0 percent to 5.5 percent. Faced with an incipient financial crisis triggered by the U.S. demand that its assessment be reduced from

31.52 percent to 25 percent, the General Assembly's Committee on Contributions was not in a mood to ponder the legal implications of China's unusual request and promptly accepted it. This action was a dramatic way for China to demonstrate its proper self-ascribed preeminent status in the global community during the Maoist period.

In an equally dramatic if not unprecedented move, China in late 1978 abandoned its policy of self-reliance by requesting aid from the United Nations Development Programme (UNDP), the largest multilateral technical aid organization, while advancing a request a year later that its scale of assessment be revised downward (based on its own "complete national income statistics"). Despite the considerable controversy surrounding the accuracy of the Chinese statistics, China's assessment rate was reduced from 5.5 percent to 0.79 percent and now stands at 0.72 percent. This has decisively changed the cost-benefit calculus for Chinese participation not only in the United Nations proper but also in the U.N. system as a whole (with all the specialized agencies that follow the scales of assessment determined by the General Assembly). (See Figure 2–1.)

Then in 1980 came China's entry into the World Bank and International Monetary Fund. In three short years, China had renounced its unique status as the only developing country to decline multilateral aid and instead had acquired the largest number (200) of multilateral technical aid projects. By 1989 China overtook India to become the world's biggest recipient of multilateral aid. In effect, economic and functional intergovernmental organizations in the U.N. system (e.g., UNDP, United Nations Children's Fund, U.N. Fund for Population Activities, World Food Program, and World Bank) were redefined as capital filling stations on the way to the promised land of development and prosperity, providing technical expertise and information as well as cost-effective financial fuel for China's accelerated modernization drive. That China's switch on U.N. peacekeeping *followed* a drastically reduced assessment also speaks directly to the logic of post-Mao maxi/mini U.N. diplomacy. In the course of another Security Council debate on alternative arrangements of financing UNFICYP, Chinese U.N. Ambassador Li Daoyu flatly declared in 1990 that China's position on those financial arrangements remained unchanged and that China was not committed to any change in the force's financing.[33]

Thus post-Mao China has adopted and followed a maxi/mini realpolitik of reaping maximum benefits with minimal financial responsibility—taking as many free rides as possible as a major recipient of aid from U.N. agencies while it contributes very little through its extremely low rate of assessment and negligible voluntary contributions. Currently

**Figure 2–1.   China's Contributions to the Budgets of the U.N. System, 1971–1985**

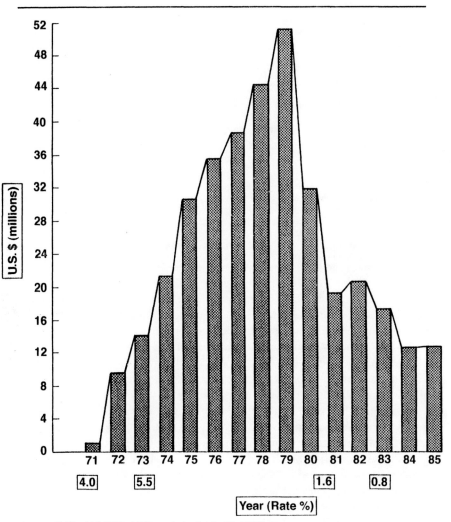

*Source: Shijie zhishi* [World Knowledge], No. 21 (1985): 9.

China is the largest recipient of both Japanese bilateral aid and the World Bank's multilateral aid (about $3 billion per year), despite the fact that, according to the World Bank's new measures of purchasing power parity (PPP), China in 1991 became the world's second-largest economy. From 1980 to 1996 the World Bank's multilateral aid commitments to China

Table 2–4.    The Shifting Assessment Rates of the Perm Five for the
U.N. Budget, 1946–1997

| | Proposed 1946 (%) | Adopted 1946 (%) | 1953 (%) | 1964 (%) | 1974 (%) | 1984 (%) | 1995 (%) | 1997 (%) |
|---|---|---|---|---|---|---|---|---|
| China | 2.75 | 6.30 | 5.62 | 4.57 | 5.50 | 0.88 | 0.72 | 0.74 |
| France | 5.50 | 6.30 | 5.75 | 5.94 | 5.86 | 6.51 | 6.32 | 6.42 |
| USSR/Russia | 6.00 | 6.62 | 12.28 | 14.97 | 12.97 | 10.54 | 5.68[a] | 4.27 |
| United Kingdom | 10.50 | 11.98 | 10.38 | 7.58 | 5.31 | 4.67 | 5.27 | 5.32 |
| United States | 49.89 | 39.89 | 35.12 | 32.02 | 25.00 | 25.00 | 25.00 | 25.00 |
| Perm Five Total | 74.64 | 71.09 | 69.15 | 65.08 | 54.64 | 47.60 | 42.99 | 41.75 |

[a] Figure for 1995 is for the Russian Federation only. To compare with figures for the USSR, add 1.33 percent (the total of the other 12 former Soviet republics admitted to U.N. membership in 1991–1992). The Russian contribution rate is scheduled to drop to 4.45 percent in 1996 and 4.27 percent in 1997.

Sources: Adapted from Jeffrey Laurenti, National Taxpayers, International Organizations: Sharing the Burden of Financing the United Nations (New York: UNA-USA, 1995), p. 29; and General Assembly Resolution 49/19 (December 23, 1994).

exceeded \$25 billion for 173 projects.[34] According to World Bank figures released in 1994, China has about 2.5 percent of gross world product. Using PPP, China's share increases to 8 percent of gross world product.

As one of the Perm Five in the Security Council, China should be contributing a significant percentage of the peacekeeping budget, certainly higher than 0.978 percent. The United Kingdom, with the second-lowest assessment rate among the Perm Five of 6.372 percent, contributes nearly seven times as much as China. At the regular budget assessment rate of 0.74 percent, China's contributions to the U.N. regular budget—and all the specialized agencies of the U.N. system follow the assessment rates determined by the General Assembly in their own regular budgets—are surpassed by such other Third World member states as Brazil (1.62 percent), South Korea (0.82 percent), and Mexico (0.79 percent). In short, as shown in Table 2–5, China today is a U.N. financial regime taker, not shaper, because what it gains from the United Nations in the form of multilateral financial and technical assistance far exceeds what it contributes to U.N. regular and peacekeeping budgets.

Thus, as issues of U.N. financial and Security Council reform arise in such a linked fashion, China is hard put to defend its meager contributions to the various components of the U.N. budget. Beijing still argues that the existing formula for U.N. assessments is appropriate and that

**Table 2–5. The Shifting Peacekeeping Burden of the Perm Five**

|  | Regular Budget Assessment Rate (%) 1974 | Peace-keeping Assessment Rate (%) 1974 | Regular Budget Assessment Rate (%) 1994 | Peace-keeping Assessment Rate (%) 1994 |
|---|---|---|---|---|
| *China* | 5.50 | 6.357 | 0.77 | 0.978 |
| France | 5.86 | 6.773 | 6.00 | 7.616 |
| USSR/Russia | 12.97 | 14.990 | 6.71 | 8.518 |
| United Kingdom | 5.31 | 6.137 | 5.02 | 6.372 |
| United States | 25.00 | 28.894 | 25.00 | 31.735 |
| Total Apportioned Among Perm Five | 54.64 | 63.151 | 43.50 | 55.219 |

*Source:* Jeffrey Laurenti, *National Taxpayers, International Organizations: Sharing the Burden of Financing the United Nations* (New York: UNA-USA, 1995), p. 30.

China's assessment should not be raised. China has taken the position that recent assessments of its economic strength are "exaggerated by Western standards" and argues that many "unconventional" calculations of its economic output and growth rate do not take into account the nation's economic base or the structure of its economy. In addition, because of China's 1.2 billion population, its per-capita gross national product (GNP) is still extremely low. China's statements regarding U.N. financial reform have been vague but have emphasized the importance of responsible payment of contributions by member states: "We believe that the fundamental way to deal with the inadequacy of the fund for UN peace-keeping operations is to have a situation in which all Member States would faithfully meet their obligation under the Charter to make their assessed contributions unconditionally, in full and on time. In this regard, China has conscientiously fulfilled its obligations. We call upon other countries, particularly those with huge arrears, to pay off their arrears as soon as possible."[35] For the home audience, however, the United Nations' financial crisis is said to be no more or less than a symptom of the decline of American hegemony in the world organization:

> The real cause is that the gap between the increasingly inflating hegemonic attitude and strategic schemes on the one hand and the increasingly more evident tendency of multipolarization within the U.N. on the other has become bigger and bigger. However, with the rise of the Third World, the multipolarization tendency in the U.N. has become more and more apparent. The United States finds it more and more difficult to do as it pleases in the U.N. Without being able to do anything about it, the United

States can only resort to financial threat and has attempted to use economic means to compel the U.N. to submit to control.[36]

Despite its active participation in all the U.N. regimes, China's substantive contribution to or impact on arms control and disarmament (ACD), economic, and environmental issues has been modest. As a professed Marxist-Leninist state (as encoded in the preamble of its present—1982—constitution), China would have been expected to make an ideological assault on "bourgeois" international law. Yet in a curiously self-serving manner, China has embraced the sovereignty-centered system of the old Westphalian legal order. Not surprisingly, few of the U.N. conventions and agreements on a wide range of global issues and problems—and few of the many U.N. reform proposals currently afloat—bear Chinese initiative or sponsorship.[37]

One area where China has had more negative than positive impact is in the U.N. human rights regime anchored in the United Nations Human Rights Commission. Beijing put forward proposals for "reforming" the commission: (1) the commission needs a complete and thorough reform and "rationalization" (meaning further underresourcing of its already underresourced budget); (2) the commission has "an imbalanced seat distribution favoring certain regions over others" despite the fact that the 53-member commission is as representative as any U.N. subsidiary organ can be, certainly far less unrepresentative than the U.N. Security Council, which Beijing wants to keep exactly as it is; and (3) some "working groups or individuals of the Commission have based their reports on biased views in disrespect of the specific legal system of a certain country" (the commission does not respect China's cultural relativist line).[38] While Beijing is calling for "rationalization" (downsizing and underresourcing) of the Human Rights Commission, the overwhelming majority of the member states are "expressing concern that the underresourcing of the Centre for Human Rights of the Secretariat is one impediment to the human rights treaty bodies in their ability to carry out their mandates effectively."[39]

Beijing's divide-and-conquer human rights diplomacy was successful, if measured only by the failures of the Human Rights Commission even to consider a resolution on China. In the 1997 session, the vote on China's "no-action motion" on a draft resolution alleging violations of human rights "in China by local, provincial and national authorities and severe restrictions on the rights of citizens to the freedoms of assembly, association, expression, and religion, as well as to due legal process and to a fair trial" was 27–17–9—the widest margin of failure of the seven annual attempts to debate and eventually put a resolution on China to a vote.[40] No other state under U.N. human rights scrutiny—including Cuba, Iran, Iraq, Russia, or Sudan—ever advanced a no-action motion, preferring to debate draft resolutions on their merits. Despite repeated pronouncements about its willingness to engage in international dialogue on human rights issues, Beijing successfully has preempted the introduction of even a mild draft resolution, thus denying the raison d'être of the Human Rights Commission. Paradoxically, the key to the success of Beijing's divide-and-conquer strategy lies in linkage power politics, a politics that runs contrary to what China has been saying publicly, especially to the United States; that is, that there should be *no* linkage between human rights and trade or aid. Beijing, in fact, has been practicing linkage sanctions diplomacy through promises of aid projects to developing countries and threats of withholding commercial contracts to industrialized countries. Beijing's battle cry to Third World countries—"You could be next"—often finds receptive listeners and ready responses in the Human Rights Commission.[41]

## THE UNITED NATIONS' IMPACT ON CHINA

As the most universal international organization, the United Nations has multiple principles, objectives, and functions, and as such it exerts diverse and varying degrees of influence on the behavior of its member states. As the most authoritative dispenser of international legitimation, the United Nations has remained indispensable in the legitimation of newly independent or minted states and in the Chinese quest for absolute legitimation. From 1949 to 1971 the quest of the two Chinas—PRC and ROC—for international legitimation has been closely keyed to the jagged development of the U.N. politics of collective legitimation and delegitimation. With Taiwan launching its U.N. bid in 1993 and post-Tiananmen China determined to maximize its international legitimation to make up for the growing legitimation deficits at home, once again the United Nations is primed for mobilizing and affirming China's national identity as the sole legitimate government—and as a great global power whose political influence is pronounced repeatedly to the domestic audience as growing by the day.

The General Assembly is the surest and shortest way to China's global forum shopping and to the global politics of collective legitimation and delegitimation. "The assembly was created," Woodrow Wilson once remarked about the League of Nations, "in order that anybody that purposed anything wrong should be subjected to the awkward circumstance that everybody could talk about it."[42] In an age of the global transparency revolution, the United Nations in general and the General

Assembly in particular, operating in global prime time and the global limelight, generate normative pressure by structuring expectations and restraining behaviors of its member states. Like it or not, China's international reputation is inescapably keyed to and conditioned by its deeds, not its words. Do as I say, not as I do, does not work in U.N. politics. Image costs become an important factor in the conduct of Chinese multilateral diplomacy. The calculus of image costs and benefits seemed to have increased significantly in the 1980s, as China became more engaged in a wider range of U.N. disarmament, economic, human rights, and environmental regimes as well as in a great variety of U.N.-sponsored global conferences. The image factor also may explain the rarity of Chinese obstructive behavior in such security-sensitive institutions as the CD and Security Council, where China would rather abstain or compromise than to cast a costly lethal veto. All in all, the image factor that accompanied greater participation has engendered substantial flexibility—adaptive/instrumental learning—in the pursuit of national interests in the world organization. China has not shifted from realpolitik to idealpolitik; it merely has learned how to adapt its realpolitik strategy to the changing rules, norms, and governing procedures of the ACD, human rights, and economic and environmental regimes in the U.N. system. Inevitably, such an adaptable strategy introduces many ambiguities and contradictions into China's balancing act between its realpolitik interests and idealpolitik concerns for international reputation.

Increasingly, the General Assembly has interpreted its ambiguous mandate expansively and thereby has become the principal catalyst of the international law-making process—the most recent example being efforts in the International Law Commission and the General Assembly's Sixth (Legal) Committee to hammer out a statute for a new International Criminal Court. China's U.N. participatory behavior and treaty behavior provide ample evidence of the United Nations' impact in bringing about the changes and shifts in Chinese global policy. Even in the most sensitive ACD domain, Beijing's public position has shifted progressively from initial dismissive nonparticipation (the 1970s), to reluctant selective participation (the 1980s), to comprehensive entrapped participation (the 1990s). As if to demonstrate that there is more than meets the suspicious eye in such changes, China in the period from 1982 to 1992 acceded to 9 of the 12 multilateral ACD conventions that it had previously evaded, denounced, or ignored.[43] China finally acceded to the Non Proliferation Treaty (NPT) in March 1992, signaled its willingness to participate in negotiations in the CD for a Comprehensive Test Ban Treaty (CTBT) in September 1993, agreed to accept the norms and parameters of the Missile Technology Control Regime (MTCR) via a bilateral agreement with the United States in October 1994, and finally put in abeyance several preconditions, after conducting what it called the last (underground) nuclear testing and after obtaining several concessions from the United States on the CTBT's verification regime, to join the remaining four nuclear weapons states on the first-ever accord among the Perm Five on nuclear disarmament.

In the field of human rights too, from 1980 to 1989 China successively signed and acceded to 8 of the 25 major U.N. human rights conventions on racial discrimination, apartheid, women, genocide, torture, refugees, and the child (but not the two most important human rights conventions and one optional protocol—the International Covenant on Economic, Social and Cultural Rights [ICESCR]; the International Covenant on Civil and Political Rights [ICCPR]; and the Optional Protocol to the ICCPR that, together with the Universal Declaration of Human Rights, constitute the International Bill of Rights). (See Chapter 4.) Since the early 1980s China has begun to sign on to all the major international environmental treaties. (See Chapter 9.)[44] China became one of the early ratifiers of the Biodiversity Treaty, which emerged from the Rio Earth Summit in 1992. On May 15, 1996, the National People's Congress ratified the United Nations Convention on the Law of the Sea (UNCLOS), which had finally entered into force in November 1994 after 12 years of the politics of ratification process.[45]

The United Nations has served, as well, as the chief catalyst for setting in motion within China the bureaucratic politics of continuing institutional adaptation and agency creation to better prepare the country's positions on a great variety of global issues and problems. In spite of its generally reactive and "damage-limitation" approach at the U.N. Conference on the Human Environment, held in Stockholm, Sweden, in June 1972 (Stockholm '72), China's debut at this epochal conference can be said to have served as a reality check on the ecological reality principle. In 1974 China joined the post-Stockholm global trend in establishing its Office of Environmental Protection. A decade later that office became the National Environmental Protection Agency (NEPA), which in 1988 became an independent agency responsible for all aspects of environmental policy and management. China's participation in the World Bank and the International Monetary Fund (IMF) since 1980 also has prompted changes in policies, policy processes, and institutions within the country.[46] The major multilateral economic institutions— such as the UNDP, World Bank, IMF, the General Agreement on Trade and Tariffs (GATT), and the World Trade Organization (WTO)—have greatly expanded the range and influence of external actors accepted as legitimate participants in China's modernization drive.

The United Nations and all of its satellite international regimes have served as the major training ground for Chinese diplomats and negotiators abroad as well as the chief catalyst for spawning various global policy communities—epistemic communities—within China. Participation in the CD has generated a steady annual increase in the number of Geneva-trained ACD experts on the Chinese delegation as well as a broader ACD policy community within China. The size and breadth of this policy community grew vertically and horizontally in the 1980s and 1990s, with at least 280 specialists having already written articles and essays on ACD issues for leading journals.[47] Thanks to China's participation in the U.N. Human Rights Commission, a human rights policy community and human rights scholarship were born and developed in the 1980s.[48] There is a burgeoning environmental policy community in China. As of 1992 there were 200 institutes employing 17,000 to 20,000 scientists and technicians engaged in environmental research, 71 environmental studies departments and programs in Chinese universities, and some 2,000 organizations and units involved in environmental work, employing 650,000 people.[49]

The United Nations and U.N.-sponsored global negotiations and conferences also have elicited a Chinese response in the form of white papers. In the 1990s China released a series of the white papers on human rights and human rights–related subjects—most notably "Human Rights in China" (1991), "Progress of Human Rights in China" (1995), and "Progress in China's Human Rights Cause in 1996" (1997), all prompted by a felt need for alternative theories and formulations to cope with the clear and continuing challenge at home and abroad. That China was willing to make such a response rather than walk out of the human rights regime is an acknowledgment—however reluctant—that human rights are a valid subject of international dialogue and a sign of willingness to respond to international concerns. Faced with the global complaint about the lack of transparency in military/security policy, China even produced its first-ever ACD white paper, "China's Arms Control and Disarmament," in November 1995, which only makes more transparent China's already stated "principled stand." Most tellingly, China's "Agenda 21" was produced and presented as Beijing's specific response to the global clarion call issued by the 1992 Rio Earth Summit: "Our government has drawn up 'China Agenda 21—A White Paper on China's Population, Environment, and Development in the 21st Century,' in accordance with the requirements outlined in the document of the 1992 U.N. Conference on Environment and Development, and in light of China's reality. This document will play an important guiding role in our country's formulation of long-term and mid-term national economic and social development plans."[50]

The process of participation in the U.N. lawmaking process is inevitably linked to China's international legal behavior and its legislative politics at home. As post-Mao China joined more and more international institutions, conventions, and regimes in the U.N. system, the logic of a great legal leap outward became increasingly self-evident and self-fulfilling. In the course of its participation in the making of the UNCLOS, for instance, China gradually has accepted the principles of *jus cogens* and of the common heritage of mankind, broadening its conception of the sources of international law and relaxing its conception of absolute sovereignty. The 1980s and 1990s witnessed a flurry of environmental legislative activities enacting a series of specific laws and regulations on water pollution and marine resources; the preservation of land, grasslands, and fisheries; mineral, water, and soil conservation; and wildlife protection. As Lester Ross and Mitchell Silk suggest, "environmental protection has been among the most heavily legislated sectors of public policy in the post-Mao period."[51] Even in the area of human rights, the National People's Congress enacted in 1994–1995 a new Prison Law, the Labour Law, the PRC Law on Judges, the PRC Law on Procurators, People's Police Law, the State Compensation Law, and the Administrative Punishment Law.

On the thorny issue of the relationship between domestic and international law, the Chinese government responds either with a "who, me?" denial or in broad and sweeping terms amenable to multiple interpretations. In a statement made before the U.N. Committee against Torture on April 27, 1990, for example, Chinese Ambassador Fan Guoxiang made a remarkable concession of sovereignty, claiming the primacy of international law over domestic law. In the Chinese legal system, he asserted, "the provisions of the international treaty prevail over domestic law, except where China has entered reservations to the treaty at the time of ratification or accession."[52] Yet this claim was situation-specific, as it was advanced to argue that there was no need for supplementary domestic legislation to implement China's ratification of the U.N. Convention against Torture. "All the relevant provisions of the Convention were reflected in Chinese legal instruments, including the Constitution, the Criminal Law, the Criminal Procedure Law, the Administrative Procedure Law and the Regulations on Arrest and Detention. . . . There was therefore no special legislative procedure for incorporating an international convention into domestic law."[53]

China seemed determined enough to slow down the process of establishing an international criminal court in the General Assembly's Sixth Committee by advocating a "step-by-step evolutionary approach." On the principle of complementarity between domestic and international criminal law, Chinese Ambassador Chen Shiqiu argued, "the International Criminal Court should not supplant national courts or become a supranational court or act as appeal court to the national courts." "Any proposal, out of whatever motivation, to make the Court a supranational judicial body in violation of the complementarity principle is unrealistic and harmful and will have a hard time finding universal acceptance in the international community."[54]

In finally ratifying the UNCLOS on May 15, 1996, after 14 years of careful watching and waiting, the Chinese government said nothing about the primacy of international law over domestic law. The Law of the People's Republic of China on Its Territorial Waters and Their Contiguous Areas, adopted by the People's Congress on February 25, 1992, stipulates sweeping claims via a unilateral legislative sleight-of-hand of China's territorial sovereignty over "the mainland and its offshore islands, Taiwan and the various affiliated islands including Diaoyu Islands, Penghu Islands, Dongsha Islands, Xisha [Paracel] Islands, Nansha [Spratly] Islands, and other islands belonging to the People's Republic of China" (Article 2) and as such clashes head-on with the many provisions of the UNCLOS.

The United Nations' impact on China's compliance behavior is modest but not trivial. China's growing participation does not ipso facto translate into its greater commitment to multilateral cooperative security, just as a growing commitment to U.N.-sponsored treaties does not ipso facto translate into greater compliance. The general ranking and sequencing of preferences of Chinese adaptive realpolitik behavior is first to seek unilateral free rides. If free rides become difficult or impossible, China will seek to delay or divert negotiations with several preconditions and then drop these preconditions and sign on in exchange for concessions from its main negotiating adversary (usually the United States).[55]

Realpolitik China seems to have used its participation in the United Nations and U.N.-related regimes as cost-effective ways and means of learning how to remain noncommittal or feign compliance more efficiently within rather than outside these institutions. Such adaptive realpolitik translates into a maxi/mini code of conduct guiding China's consecutive and simultaneous participation in multiple security games on multiple chessboards—the maximization of security benefits through free rides and/or noncommittal strategies and the minimization of normative (image) costs. In this way China projects its role as a constructive and positive player in the U.N. disarmament game without constraining its own nuclear development.

In light of such strategies, Beijing's declaration of its willingness to participate in CTBT negotiations in the fall of 1993 constitutes, potentially, a significant shift from a unilateral "who, me?" denial (i.e., the espousal of differentiated rights and responsibilities in the global ACD processes) to security interdependence and an important constraint on the further development and testing of its nuclear weapons program. Yet once inside the CTBT negotiation processes, China has been behaving in a realist fashion, trying hard to slow, divert, and delay the completion of the CTBT, which would constrain its nuclear testing program.[56] In the home stretch of the negotiating process, China has injected several preconditions for a successful completion of the treaty that are not acceptable to other participants. These included (1) the right of declared nuclear weapons states to conduct peaceful nuclear explosions; (2) no-first-use pledge and negative security commitments by the nuclear weapons states, and (3) the use of international monitoring system over national technical means of individual states for treaty compliance verification.

In 1996 as the treaty negotiations moved toward a finale, China's "principled stand" shifted and mutated. In late March as the CTBT negotiations reached a cul-de-sac largely because of China's demand regarding the conduct of peaceful nuclear explosion, Chinese Disarmament Ambassador Sha Zukang publicly declared that "no country can impose its will on China under any circumstances."[57] Faced with President Boris Yeltsin's jawboning to sign the CTBT, China came up with a new escape clause—"mankind needs to keep developing 'peaceful' nuclear weapons in case a giant asteroid is discovered careening through space on a collision course with the earth."[58] Faced with the deteriorating image as it stood alone in advocating the peaceful use of nuclear blasts, China in June dropped its peaceful nuclear explosion precondition, but it and the United States were still deadlocked over the treaty's provisions for on-site inspections in the event of suspected blasts' occurring in signatory states. Two months later both countries agreed to a deal whereby Beijing promised to use its influence on Pakistan to join and also to help Washington take the CTBT to the U.N. General Assembly in the event that India vetoed the treaty in the Conference on Disarmament—in return for U.S. concessions to meet China's demand to make it more difficult to launch international on-site inspections under the pact. To launch an inspection, the number of votes needed at the treaty's 51-member executive council is being raised to 30 from a simple majority of 26, as in the latest draft text. Yet in the wake of the General Assembly's approval of the CTBT by a 158-to-3 vote on September 11, 1996, Ambassador Sha captured the high moral ground by issuing a clear call to India to join rather than fight while at the same time criticizing the treaty as not having reflected proper and reasonable demands from many developing countries (including the PRC) and by attacking the current practice of "bypassing the Conference on Disarmament and directly submitting the treaty text to the U.N. General Assembly."

That the most critical concession China obtained from the United States in forming the united front of the Perm Five had to do with the CTBT's verification regime does not augur well for China's full compliance with the treaty, even if some legal way can be found to overcome India's unit veto legally required for the treaty to come into force. Even in the non–zero-sum game of global ecopolitics, there is ample evidence of China's lax or feigned compliance. Concerning its Agenda 21 ozone depletion substance commitments, for example, China now argues that it cannot meet those commitments in aerosols by 1997 and foam by 2000, unless the multilateral fund provides $1 billion in near-term funding for China's chlorofluorocarbon substitution.[59]

As Abram Chayes and Antonia Chayes sharply argue, however, the free ride or noncompliance problem has been greatly exaggerated on the basis of the misconceived "enforcement model" of compliance—sanctions with teeth. Compliance at the international level is not a simple on/off, or "either/or," phenomenon. Instead, what is required to maintain compliance with treaty obligations and regime norms at an acceptable level is an iterative process of discourse—what they call the "managerial model" of compliance—among the parties involved, in which not only national positions but also conceptions of national interest evolve. Such an iterative process of discourse and learning combined with diffuse international reputation—membership in good standing in the international organizations and regimes—generates the major pressure for compliance with treaty obligations and regime norms.[60] Assessed in terms of the managerial model, relying primarily on a cooperative discourse approach instead of a coercive sanctions one, China's compliance behavior seems more malleable than subversive.

## An Overall Evaluation

In seeking a retrospect/prospect appraisal of changing Sino-U.N. interactions over the years, it seems useful to recall Karl Marx's famous observation about history-making: that we do not—and cannot—make our own history just as we please but only "under circumstances directly encountered, given, and transmitted from the past."[61] Since the collapse of the traditional Sinocentric world order in the late nineteenth century, the proud and frustrated "sick man of Asia" has had enormous difficulty overcoming the tyrannies and grievances of the past and the persistent tension between the temptations and fears of external dependency and the abiding quest for national identity via civilizational autonomy and political and normative self-sufficiency. This frustration, combined with the belief that China, by dint of its demographic weight and the greatness of its civilization, has a natural and inalienable right to great-power status, explains the wild swings of national identity projection over the years, mutating through a series of varying and alternating global roles.

For Mao in 1932, the League of Nations as the first universal international organization in modern times was still nothing less than "a League of Robbers by which the various imperialisms are dismembering China."[62] In contrast, the United Nations from its inception became indispensable in China's quest for international legitimation and great-power status drive. Paradoxically, America's policy of containment and isolation became progressively self-defeating and self-contradictory, as it demonstrated its lack of legitimacy and the United Nations' lack of legitimacy on the Chinese representation issue while at the same time adding significantly to the prestige of the PRC, excluded from the so-called world organization.[63] As Mao put it in 1957, "the longer you [the United States] stall, the more you will be in the wrong and the more isolated you will become in your own country and before world opinion."[64] Thus the single greatest contribution the United Nations made to China—and the single greatest diplomatic victory China accomplished—was the adoption of General Assembly Resolution 2758, which at one and the same time recognized and accepted the PRC as a great power in the world organization. As the most authoritative dispenser of international legitimation and the most universal intergovernmental organization, the United Nations' importance for China's quest for absolute legitimation remains undiminished even in the post-Tiananmen and post–cold war years. The United Nations is the source of China's standing as a great power; the veto power in the Security Council is China's ultimate sword and shield to safeguard its own state sovereignty.

The post-Mao era witnessed the acceleration and intensification of Sino-U.N. linkages and interactions; Chinese membership and participation in all the remaining U.N.-related regimes and Chinese accession to U.N.-sponsored multilateral treaties increased steadily. This growing and widening engagement with the United Nations and U.N.-sponsored global conferences has produced the feedback and spillover effects of facilitating certain adjustments and shifts in Chinese multilateral diplomacy as well as in the policymaking and policy-reviewing processes and institutions within China. Judging by the phenomenal growth of Chinese IGO and NGO membership, positive participatory experience, the emergence of epistemic communities, and a number of policy adjustments and shifts over such global issues as arms control and disarmament, U.N. peacekeeping, North-South relations, human rights, science and technology, and environmental protection and sustainable development, some Chinese global learning indeed has occurred. Once in the world organization, China for the most part has been acting as a satisfied system maintainer, not a system reformer or system-transforming revolutionary, playing multiple games on multiple global chessboards by the established rules, rather than by attempting to replace or repudiate them.

Still, all the policy shifts and changes in the post-Mao era can be seen better as adaptive/instrumental learning rather than cognitive/normative learning at the basic level of worldview and national identity. Despite China's participation in the Security Council and global ACD fora for more than two decades, there is no hard evidence of any paradigm shift from unilateral self-help to cooperative common security. Instead, China via its adaptive realpolitik has exploited and probably will continue to exploit its participation in international ACD regimes as a more cost-effective way of learning how to free ride within rather than without these regimes. In attempting to reconcile the seemingly irreconcilable—unilateral realpolitik security interests versus idealpolitik concerns for its international reputation—Beijing trumpets its declarations of antihegemonism and no-first-use pledge as both necessary and sufficient conditions for peace and stability in the Asia-Pacific region, indeed as the surest and shortest pathway to global peace. In this way China projects its "principled stand" on a range of global issues, asking others to follow what it says, not what it actually does.

Since the early 1980s, while China has forged wider cooperative relations with the world community, this trend has continued only as long as China's leaders, for their own domestic political purposes, have continued to believe their interests coincided with full global engagement.[65] And yet the very process of this Sino-U.N. interaction, whether intended or unintended, greatly widened and deepened the ambit of China's involvement in the U.N. system, eroding and blurring the boundary between externally conditioned and internally determined policies. While sovereignty has remained central in Chinese rhetoric, its unbridled premises have been progressively chipped away in practice. Practically all the multilateral economic, science, and technology regimes in the U.N. system have been reconceptualized as cost-effective sources of bridging China's information, knowledge, capital, and technology gaps in the service of the modernization drive. They have been allowed to enter, some by design and others inadvertently, the castle of Chinese sovereignty as conceptual Trojan horses influencing the process by which Chinese national interests are redefined and Chinese national priorities are restructured for a better fit with the logic of the global situation. Viewed in this light, Chinese globalism is not more important than Chinese nationalism, but the former is important in the service of the latter.

The apparent absence of cognitive/normative learning at this time does not necessarily mean that China's realpolitik views are immutably predetermined or that changes conducive to cooperative common security are totally lacking or cannot occur in the future. The adaptive-cognitive learning distinction, therefore, may be better seen as a continuum rather than a dichotomy. Once entrapped in the political processes of the U.N. regimes, there is no easy exit—to wit, Chinese adaptive realpolitik, once constrained and more deeply enmeshed, inevitably calls for the readjustment or restructuring of certain policies, principles, and institutions of Chinese foreign policy. Despite some rigorous encounters in the U.N. arms control and disarmament, human rights, and security regimes in recent years, China has not withdrawn from them. Unlike the United States, China has yet to withdraw from any international regime or IGO it has joined since 1971. With the exception of the Haiti and Guatemala cases in 1996 and early 1997, China's obstructive behavior has become as rare as its veto in the Security Council. Thanks to the entrapment effects and potential image costs, China by fits and starts has accepted basic international norms and governing procedures (including the universality of human rights despite its cultural relativism) in multilateral fora. Despite a somewhat problematic compliance record on the NPT and MTCR norms, China in recent years has made a significant move away from the unilateral security "who, me?" denial toward finally accepting and signing onto the CTBT.

In China's protracted encounter with the outside world, foreign technical, commercial, religious, educational, and military advisors have come and gone without making much of a dent in Chinese world order thinking.[66] Viewed against this historical backdrop, China's growing participation in the United Nations in the 1980s and 1990s, accompanied by a growing adaptive learning process, is all the more remarkable. Although China cannot be said to be fully cooperative in every issue area of international relations, it has pursued a more accommodative, although occasionally erratic posture over the last 150 years. Indeed, the general pattern and direction of China's international behavior, albeit more in the global political economy than in global high politics, has been a slow but steady movement from conflict to cooperation. And China is more cooperative in a high-profile multilateral institutional or negotiating settings than in low-profile bilateral negotiations. In the course of its born-again modernization drive, post-Mao China increasingly has become so dependent on foreign trade, investment, borrowing, and technology transfers that no easy socialist exit from the capitalist world system exists that would not entail a major economic crash landing or the loss of its "global citizenship."

Are we better or worse off if China becomes more or less actively engaged in the United Nations? The answer is obvious and somewhat paradoxical. Yes, we are all far better off if China becomes more fully engaged and integrated *and* if we adopt and pursue strategies of multi-layered enmeshment followed by multilateral containment. Despite the priority of domestic over external pressures as the ultimate shaper of Chinese international conduct, the United Nations still matters. The most significant impact that it can bring to bear on China lies not in its supervision of the implementation of China's international treaty obligations or imposing U.N. sanctions. Rather, it lies in the standard-setting, norm-clarifying, and lawmaking processes of the United Nations, engendered by the continuing iterative process of China's multilateral integration into each of the U.N. organs and conferences. Because of high normative pressures and high image costs, China can be forced more easily to shift toward more cooperative directions if it is more fully integrated into global regimes (thus raising the costs of withdrawal) and if negotiations are conducted in authoritative global institutions such as the Conference on Disarmament and the Security Council.

But this vertical engagement approach is not enough. The growth of epistemic (policy) communities within China coupled with a dramatic increase in China's NGO membership in the 1980s and 1990s—granted that most Chinese nongovernmental organizations remain extended arms of the state[67]—provide some grounds for cautious optimism about gradually cracking the absolute and exclusive hard shell of state sovereignty that still constrains the United Nations' effectiveness by expanding and strengthening horizontal Chinese and transnational NGO linkages and interactions. After all, initiating and sustaining effective global responses to the challenge of establishing a new post–cold war world order require nothing less than the integrated and synergistic engagement of all social actors and institutions at and across all levels, from local communities to global intergovernmental organizations.

# Notes

The author wishes to acknowledge that this chapter benefited from exchanges and discussions with and valuable suggestions from the members of the Council on Foreign Relations Task Force—especially Elizabeth Economy, Michel Oksenberg, Dinah Lee, Harry Harding, Andrew Nathan, Art Rosen, Linda

Perkins, Allan Y. Song, and Alastair Johnston. Edward Luck, William Feeney, and Peter Van Ness also provided useful comments and suggestions on an earlier version. In addition, the author's involvement as a member of the U.S. side in the work of a Sino-American commission on the Study of U.N. Reform in 1995–1996 was of immeasurable help. The Chinese members represented by the Shanghai Institute for International Studies were Liang Yufan, Zhu Majie, Chen Luzhi, Wang Baoliu, Qian Wenrong, Ding Xinghao, Yu Guanmin, Guo Longlong, Zhang Zuqian, Luo Weiguo, Zhang Xingyan, Li Mintao, and Zhao Nianyu; the American members represented by the United Nations Association of the United States (UNA-USA) were Ronald I. Spiers, John Bolton, Janet Welsh Brown, Edward C. Luck, Jonathan Moore, Allan Y. Song, and Samuel S. Kim. None of the above-mentioned persons should be held accountable for the views and interpretations—and the errors that may persist—in the chapter.

1. In 1995 the United Nations oversaw 17 peacekeeping operations, more than half of the total of 33 launched since 1948. The number of U.N. peacekeeping personnel registered more than sevenfold increase—from under 10,000 troops and military observers in the 1980s to over 70,000 in 1994. Such hyperactivism began to recede beginning in 1994, as is evidenced in the declining number of resolutions and peacekeeping personnel. The Security Council passed 93 resolutions in 1993 (an all-time record), compared with only 13 in 1987; 78 in 1994; 67 in 1995; and 57 in 1996. The commitment to U.N. peacekeeping declined as well, from 67,269 troops in July 1995 to 25,296 troops in July 1996. For more detailed analysis and reports, see Secretary-General Report, "Supplement to an Agenda for Peace: Position Paper of the Secretary-General on the Occasion of the Fiftieth Anniversary of the United Nations," U.N. Docs. A/50/60 and S/1995/1 (3 January 1995), and Report of the Secretary-General on the Work of the Organization, GAOR, 51st Sess., Suppl. No. 1 (A/51/1).

2. Zhao Ziyang, "Work Together for a Better World," *Beijing Review* 28 (November 4, 1985): 15.

3. *Renmin ribao* [People's Daily], September 19, 1995, p. 6. For similar pronouncements before the U.N. audience, see U.N. Docs. A/49/PV.8, p. 12, and A/50/PV.8, p. 9.

4. A statement made by Li Zhaoxing, vice minister of Foreign Affairs, who became China's new permanent representative at the United Nations in May 1995. *Renmin ribao*, October 23, 1995, p. 7.

5. Wu Daying, "On Taiwan Authorities' Programme," *Beijing Review* 34 (July 8–14, 1991): 35. Even before Tiananmen, Beijing was so alarmed by Taiwan's "elastic diplomacy" that it submitted an official "warning" document to the Security Council. See U.N. Doc. S/20355 (December 28, 1988).

6. The Latvian foreign minister, Janis Jurkans, specifically mentioned this point during his visit to Taipei in December 1991. See James L. Tyson, "Taiwan, Besting China, Sets Up Ties to Baltics," *Christian Science*

*Monitor*, December 27, 1991, p. 8; *Free China Journal*, January 31, 1992, p. 1.

7.  For instance, the principle of nonuse of force (Article 2[4]) is qualified by the principle of the inherent right of individual or collective self-defense (Article 51), just as the principle of unanimity (Article 27 [3]) is qualified by the principle of the sovereignty of all member states (Article 2 [1]).

8.  For extended analysis see Samuel S. Kim, *China In and Out of the Changing World Order* (Princeton, N.J.: Center of International Studies, Princeton University, 1991).

9.  "An Agenda for Peace: Preventive Diplomacy, Peacemaking and Peace-Keeping," U.N. Doc. A/47/277 and S/24111 (June 17, 1992), p. 5. Apparently, sovereignty too makes strange bedfellows in and out of the United Nations. Senator Jesse Helms, chairman of the U.S. Senate Committee on Foreign Relations and arguably the most passionately anti-PRC American politician, cites this passage of "An Agenda for Peace" as evidence of the United Nations' creeping supranational attack on state sovereignty (read: American sovereignty). See Jesse Helms, "Saving the U.N.: A Challenge to the Next Secretary-General," *Foreign Affairs*, Vol. 75, No. 5 (September/October 1996): 3.

10. Paul Lewis, "U.N. Set to Debate Peacemaking Role," *New York Times*, September 6, 1992, p. 7.

11. This point is made in Foreign Minister Qian Qichen's major speech at the 46th Session of the General Assembly, which comes close to being China's annual state of the world report. For an English text of the speech, see FBIS-China, October 1, 1992, pp. 4–8.

12. U.N. Doc. A/47/PV.37 (October 28, 1992).

13. U.N. Doc. A/50/60 and S/1995/1 (January 3, 1995).

14. U.N. Doc. S/PV.3492 (January 18, 1995), pp. 12–15.

15. Xinhua, in FBIS-China, April 13, 1989, p. 4. For a glowing scholarly account, see Liu Enzhao, "Lianheguo weichi heping xingdong" [U.N. peacekeeping forces], *Guoji wenti yanjiu* [Journal of international studies], No. 2 (1989): pp. 53–61.

16. China, through its fence-straddling strategy, managed to force Washington into becoming an excessively anxious supplicant. To secure a "voluntary" abstention in place of a possible Chinese veto, the Bush administration ignored the continuing repression in China and agreed to resume high-level diplomatic intercourse (by granting a long-sought White House visit by Foreign Minister Qian) and to lift the World Bank's sanctions by supporting its first "nonbasic human needs" loan since Tiananmen.

17. Being "responsible to history," Foreign Minister Qian Qichen later explained in an interview for the home audience, means that "the Chinese

people still clearly remember that the Korean War was launched in the name of the United Nations." See U.N. Doc. S/PV.2963 (November 29, 1990), p. 62, and *Renmin ribao*, December 17, 1990, p. 7.

18. Hu Yumin, "UN's Role in a New World Order," *Beijing Review* Vol. 34, No. 23 (June 10–16, 1991): pp. 12–14.

19. In this case, however, China did make a major contribution by default by transferring the issue from the Security Council to direct U.S.-DPRK bilateral negotiations, culminating in the landmark Geneva accord (the U.S.-DPRK Agreed Framework of October 21, 1994).

20. This statement and all other statements of peer representatives in the Security Council draw from Dinah Lee's extensive field interviews with a cross-national sample of Security Council representatives conducted in December 1995–January 1996.

21. See FBIS-China, January 30, 1995, pp. 1–2.

22. *Beijing Review* (November 1–7, 1993), p. 8. For a more detailed discussion, see Guo Longlong et al., *Lienheguo xinlun* [New discourse on the United Nations] (Shanghai: Shanghai Jiaoyu chubanshe, 1995), pp. 278–282, 304–309.

23. The historical anachronisms and rigidities are suggested by the fact that the Perm Five are constitutionally entitled to perpetuate their status. According to Article 108, no provision in the Charter can be amended without the consent of all the permanent members of the Security Council. The result is that, since its inception in 1945, the Charter provisions on the permanent membership have remained untouched despite the fact that U.N. membership itself has more than tripled and despite the profound changes in the sources, nature, and ranking of "great power" in the world. The number of the council's nonpermanent members was last adjusted in 1963, when it was increased from five to ten. Since 1963 the member states have increased by 50 percent.

24. *Renmin ribao*, September 19, 1995, p. 6.

25. FBIS-China, October 27, 1994, p. 4; *Beijing Review*, No. 43 (October 23–29, 1995): pp. 15–16.

26. Yu Huizhe, "Zouxiang 21 shiji de Liangheguo—Liangheguo jizhi he gaige wenti yantaohui—ceji," [Sidelights on the United Nations toward the 21st century—forum on the problems of U.N. machinery and reform], *Shijie jingji yu zhengzhi* [World economics and politics], No. 2 (1994); pp. 55–59, esp. p. 59.

27. Reuters on-line, November 19, 1996. Apparently there occurred in 1995–1996 a new wave of pop nationalism in China, as made manifest in the best-selling book, *The China That Can Say No*, and a popular television series, *A Beijing Man in New York* [*Beijingren zai Niuyue*]. For a discussion and analy-

sis of how this latest tide of pop nationalism represents "the coming of age of Chinese narcissism" and functions as "a form of consensus beyond the bounds of official culture," see Geremie R. Barme, "To Screw Foreigners Is Patriotic: China's Avant-Garde Nationalists," *The China Journal*, No. 34 (July 1995); pp. 209–234. See also Song Qiang et al., *Zhongguo keyi shuo bu* [The China that can say no] (Beijing: Zhonghua gongshang lianhe chubanshe, 1996), and Cai Jianwei, ed., *Zhongguo da zhanlue* [China's grand strategy] (Haikou: Hainan chubanshe, 1996).

28.  Thirty-two vetoes were cast in the 16 rounds of balloting in the Security Council, October 27–28, 1981, and November 4–7, 1981. Ling Qing, a former Chinese U.N. ambassador, publicly revealed that China had cast 16 consecutive positive votes—and another permanent member (the United States) 16 consecutive vetoes—on Salim Salim of Tanzania as a Third World candidate for the post of U.N. secretary-general in behind-the-scenes closed meetings of the Security Council in late 1981. See Ling Qing's interview, as published in *Ban Yue Tan* 6 (March 25, 1986): 28–31, in FBIS-China, April 18, 1986, pp. A4–A6. For the veto record of the Perm Five from February 12, 1946, to the end of 1990, see Sydney D. Bailey, *The Procedure of the U.N. Security Council*, 2nd ed. (Oxford: Clarendon Press, 1988), pp. 200–211; and Anjali V. Patil, *The U.N. Veto in World Affairs, 1946–1990: A Complete Record and Case Histories of the Security Council's Veto* (London: Mansell, 1992), pp. 426, 483, 486.

29.  Xinhua (New China News Agency), in FBIS-China, August 13, 1991, pp. 1–2.

30.  See *Renmin ribao*, November 22, 1996, p. 6.

31.  On January 10, 1997, China cast its solo veto, killing a resolution authorizing a small U.N. peacekeeping mission for Guatemala because of that country's diplomatic ties with Taiwan. The other 14 Security Council members voted in favor of sending 155 military observers to verify Guatemala's new U.N.-brokered peace accord. This is a sui generis Taiwan-connected case.

32.  For a detailed analysis of China's behavior in the Council based on extensive field interviews, see Samuel S. Kim, *China, the United Nations, and World Order* (Princeton, N.J.: Princeton University Press, 1979), pp. 178–241.

33.  For Ambassador Li's remarks, see FBIS-China, December 19, 1990, p. 3.

34.  *China Daily (Business Weekly)*, July 14–20, 1996, p. 1.

35.  U.N. Doc. A/47/PV.37 (October 28, 1992).

36.  FBIS-China, pp. 96-171, August 29, 1996 on-line via WNC. See also Liu Enzhao, "Lianheguo de caizheng weiji genyuan" [The roots of the U.N.'s financial crisis], *Guoji wenti yanjiu* [Journal of international studies], No. 4 (1996), pp. 45–48.

37.  For diverse perspectives and interpretations of the place of international law in China's international relations, see Ronald St. John Macdonald, ed., *Essays in Honour of Wang Tieya* (Dordrecht, The Netherlands: Martinus Nijhoff Publishers, 1994).

38. For excerpts from Tian's speech, see FBIS, China, 95-040 (February 28, 1995) on line via WNC.

39. General Assembly Resolution 51/87 (December 12, 1996). For a more serious scholarly analysis of the marginalization and fragmentation of the human rights program and activities, see B. G. Ramcharan, "Reforming the United Nations to Secure Human Rights," in Saul H. Mendlovitz and Burns H. Weston, eds., *Preferred Futures for the United Nations* (Irvington-on-Hudson, N.Y.: Transnational Publishers, 1995), pp. 193–219.

40. U.N. Doc. E/CN.4/1997/L91.

41. Barbara Crossette, "China Outflanks U.S. to Avoid Scrutiny of Its Human Rights," *New York Times*, April 24, 1996, p. A12.

42. Quoted in Sydney B. Bailey, *The General Assembly of the United Nations: A Study of Procedure and Practice*, rev. ed. (New York: Praeger, 1964), p. 8.

43. See *SIPRI Yearbook 1993: World Armaments and Disarmament* (New York: Oxford University Press, 1993), p. 728.

44. See Alastair I. Johnston, "Defective Cooperation: China and International Environmental Institutions, 1990–1994" (Harvard University, August 1995), pp. 22–23, unpublished paper.

45. *Renmin ribao*, May 17, 1996, p. 6.

46. For detailed analysis and explanation, see Harold K. Jacobson and Michel Oksenberg, *China's Participation in the IMF, the World Bank, and GATT: Toward a Global Economic Order* (Ann Arbor, Mich.: University of Michigan Press, 1990).

47. For the development of China's arms control policy community in the 1980s, see Alastair Iain Johnston, "Learning versus Adaptation: Explaining Change in Chinese Arms Control Policy in the 1980s and 1990s," *The China Journal*, No. 35 (January 1996), pp. 36–43. For a list of some prominent experts in China's ACD policy community, see Chapter 3.

48. For a most comprehensive and thoroughgoing analysis, see Ann Kent, *China, the United Nations and Human Rights: Compliance, Learning and Effectiveness* (Philadelphia: University of Pennsylvania Press, forthcoming).

49. Hao Yufan, "Environmental Protection and Chinese Foreign Policy," in Thomas W. Robinson, ed., *The Foreign Relations of China's Environmental Policy* (Washington, D.C.: American Enterprise Institute, 1992), p. 166; FBIS-China, May 19, 1993.

50. Foreign Minister Qian Qichen's speech at the 49th plenary session of the General Assembly delivered on September 28, 1994. For full text, see FBIS-China, 94-189 (September 29, 1994), pp. 1–5; quote at p. 4. See also U.N. Doc. A/49/PV.8 (September 28, 1994), p. 11.

51. Lester Ross and Mitchell A. Silk, *Environmental Law and Policy in the People's Republic of China* (New York: Quorum Books, 1987), p. 3; part 6 contains English texts of all of these environmental laws and regulations.

52. Committee against Torture, *Initial Reports of States Parties Due in 1989,* Addendum, "China," supplementary report, October 8, 1992, U.N. Doc. CAT/C/7/Add.14 (1993), part 2, para. 61, at 16.

53. Committee against Torture, *Summary Record of the 50th Meeting,* U.N. Doc. CAT/C/SR.50 (Geneva, 1990), para. 3, at 2.

54. Xinhua, October 31, 1995 in FBIS-China, 95-210, October 31, 1995, pp. 2–3. See also U.N. Doc. A/AC.244/1 (March 20, 1995), pp. 8–12.

55. For a cogent analysis along this line, see Johnston, "Learning versus Adaptation."

56. See Ching Kuan, "Bleak Prospects for Comprehensive Test Ban Treaty," *Wen Wei Po* (Hong Kong), August 22, 1996, p. A4, in FBIS-China, 96-166, August 22, 1996 on-line.

57. Reuters on-line, March 28, 1996.

58. Patrick E. Tyler, "Chinese Seek Atom Options to Fend Off Asteroids," *New York Times,* April 27, 1996, p. 4.

59. Elizabeth Economy and Michel Oksenberg, "International Law and Global Environmental Change: The China Case," in Harold Jacobson and Edith Brown Weiss, eds., *Improving Compliance with International Environmental Accords* (forthcoming); and Johnston, "Defective Cooperation."

60. Abram Chayes and Antonia Handler Chayes, *The New Sovereignty: Compliance with International Regulatory Agreements* (Cambridge, Mass.: Harvard University Press, 1995).

61. Karl Marx, *The 18th Brumaire of Louis Napoleon,* in Lewis Feuer, ed., *Basic Writings on Politics and Philosophy: Karl Marx and Friedrich Engels* (New York: Doubleday & Co., 1959), p. 320.

62. This characterization was contained in a telegram of the Chinese–Soviet Government (dated October 6, 1932) signed by Mao. Cited in Stuart R. Schram, *The Political Thought of Mao Tse-tung* (New York: Praeger, 1963), pp. 266–267. For additional references, see Jerome Alan Cohen and Hungdah Chiu, *People's China and International Law: A Documentary Study,* 2 vols. (Princeton, N.J.: Princeton University Press, 1974).

63. See Rosemary Foot, *The Practice of Power: US Relations with China since 1949* (Oxford: Clarendon Press, 1995).

64. Mao Zedong, "Talks at a Conference of Secretaries of Provincial, Municipal and Autonomous Region Party Committees," January 1957, in *Selected Works,* vol. 5 (Beijing: Foreign Languages Press, 1977), p. 363.

65. Jacobson and Oksenberg, *China's Participation in the IMF,* p. 163.

66. This thesis is eloquently argued and developed in Jonathan Spence, *To Change China: Western Advisers in China 1620–1960* (New York: Penguin Books, 1980).

67.  As Gerald Chan writes, "In China, the top office-bearers of member organizations of INGOs are usually government officials or they have strong ties with the state." Gerald Chan, *China and International Organizations: Participation in Non-Governmental Organizations since 1971* (New York: Oxford University Press, 1989), p. 152. This observation applies to the Chinese side of the Sino-American Commission on the Study of U.N. Reform.

# 3

# China and Arms
# Control Institutions

## MICHAEL D. SWAINE AND ALASTAIR IAIN JOHNSTON

T HE UNITED States and most of the international community, including China, have articulated a basic interest in the maintenance of
global peace and security, the encouragement of a prosperous and
economically expanding Asia-Pacific region free from destabilizing
arms races or threatening military powers, and the advancement of
global and regional nonproliferation regimes and practices. Differences
among states are largely over how to weight these goals, how best to
meet them, and how to distribute the costs of meeting them.

China is a major player in the advancement of these interests. It is one
of the Perm Five members of the U.N. Security Council, thus giving it
influence in dealing with major global issues such as weapons proliferation, humanitarian intervention, and peacekeeping. It is one of the five
declared nuclear weapons states, a growing military power, and, like the
United States, a producer of nuclear, chemical, and missile-related
equipment, materials, and technology. It is also a major participant in
the international arms control world, and its compliance with multilateral proliferation regimes is necessary to help stop the spread of
weapons of mass destruction (WMD), missiles, and other means of
WMD delivery. Moreover, it plays an important role in regional security
issues, such as the North Korean nuclear issue.[1]

One of the sources of debate among major states regarding how to
pursue these general regional and global interests is China's program of
military modernization, both conventional and nuclear.[2]

- Although China has embarked on a sustained effort to modernize its conventional and nuclear armed forces, its military budget and strategic plans remain largely opaque to the rest of the world. Particular uncertainty exists about China's nuclear weapons capabilities, its strategic intentions (both globally and within the Asia-Pacific region), and the long-term goals of its nuclear modernization program.

- China has claims to territory along its periphery throughout the Asia-Pacific region. Although these claims are pursued peacefully, the ability to use force is considered an important, if implicit, bargaining tool in most of these cases. China's military exercises in 1995–1996, including missile firings in the vicinity of Taiwan, raised concerns among states in the region about the compatibility between China's claims and behavior on one hand and the pursuit of the region's sense of peace and stability on the other. Many states worry that Chinese acquisition of credible power projection capabilities in the absence of mechanisms for peacefully resolving these disputes could contribute to regional arms races and insecurity spirals in the region.

- Until the Comprehensive Test Ban Treaty (CTBT) takes force, China is not constrained by any extant international arms control regime from modernizing and expanding its nuclear forces, unlike the United States and Russia. However, China can obstruct or advance many important arms control processes. Indeed, although it has shown signs of positive support for nonproliferation measures in recent years, until signing the CTBT in 1996, it continued nuclear testing at a time when the other nuclear powers—with the exception of France—were observing an informal test moratorium. China was also a source of some of the roadblocks to the speedy conclusion of the treaty. It is not particularly enthusiastic about a fissile material production cutoff, even less so if this cutoff were to reduce existing stockpiles. Moreover, China's support is essential in future efforts to reach agreement among the five declared nuclear powers to reduce their strategic nuclear weapons stockpiles drastically. But it is not clear whether the conditions China might demand would facilitate or hinder agreement.[3]

- China has sold technologies with potential application for the development of weapons of mass destruction, as well as missile delivery system technology, to countries in sensitive regions. Specifically, it has supplied technologies to nuclear programs in Pakistan, Iran, India, Argentina, Brazil, Iraq, Syria, South Africa, Saudi Arabia, and Algeria.[4] China variously argues that some of these transfers have not in fact occurred, or that they fall under activities allowed under rules of the International Atomic Energy Agency (IAEA), or that these activities are no worse than U.S. transfers of military-related technologies that also could be used for WMD delivery.

These factors point to the need to understand better China's emerging post–cold war security views and military doctrine, its associated program of conventional and nuclear weapons development and arms sales, its views on conventional and nuclear arms control and nonproliferation processes (including the major institutions involved in the arms control policy arena), and its record of participation in and compliance with various nonproliferation and arms control regimes. A clearer understanding of these critical areas is necessary in order to develop more effective bilateral and multilateral policies to adjust successfully to growing Chinese military power and to strengthen international standards regarding the proliferation of WMD and related technologies.

This chapter therefore outlines the major features of the Chinese government's strategic outlook, military doctrine, and major conventional and nuclear arms programs, identifying areas of greatest impact on regional stability and arms control. It also provides an overview of China's leaders' changing outlook toward and participation in the major conventional and unconventional (i.e., nuclear, chemical, and biological weaponry) international arms control regimes. We examine the impact of Chinese involvement on international arms control regimes and processes and on Chinese participation, summarize Chinese views and behavior toward arms control, and provide recommendations for U.S. and international policies to improve constructive engagement with China in the arms control arena.

Our analysis indicates that overall Chinese views and behavior toward both conventional and unconventional weapons development are motivated primarily by a relatively hard realpolitik, state-centered, balance-of-power calculus centered on maintaining and increasing China's relative economic, technological, and military power. This calculus assumes that China is a weak state in most areas relevant to the development of a modern military force, especially when compared with major potential competitors in the Asia-Pacific region, such as the United States and Japan. Given this perceived weakness, Chinese leaders believe their country therefore must modernize its conventional and strategic force structure; they also believe that improving China's relative power will not only enhance its security vis-à-vis other major powers in the region, but also will contribute to greater regional and international status. China's strategic weapons development program suggests that its military might be diversifying its approach to the use of nuclear weapons in ways that could complicate various current and future arms control efforts. Our analysis also shows that China's greatly expanded participation in various forms of arms control has consisted primarily of efforts to adapt its weak-state, realpolitik approach to a changing international arms control agenda while at the same time trying to minimize constraints on its own military capabilities. Evidence that China's leaders accept security concepts based, for instance, on a recognition of the security dilemma or on the concept of common security is still hard to come by, although these concepts do seem to be influencing how some Chinese arms control specialists in the policy process think about security.

In pursuing its realpolitik interests in military modernization and arms control, China at the same time remains acutely sensitive to its international image as a peaceful leader of less-developed countries and a strong advocate of complete WMD disarmament. Its involvement in various international arms control regimes continues to expand, and the cost of retreat or withdrawal increases proportionately, especially given growing international sentiment for arms control. Moreover, China's increasing involvement in arms control has produced a growing Chinese arms control community with expanding links to foreign arms control circles. Together these factors highlight a tension in Chinese diplomacy between a realpolitik desire to minimize commitments and preserve relative power capabilities and an identity-based desire to maximize status as a participant in the legitimate international institutions that regulate state behavior. These and other features of Chinese arms control behavior suggest a variety of measures that might help constrain the former and encourage the latter, designed to integrate China even further into international arms control processes.[5]

## Chinese Nuclear and Conventional Arms Development Programs and Their Implications for Arms Control

The end of the bipolar U.S-Soviet strategic rivalry, the subsequent emergence of an increasingly interactive political and economic environment in the Asia-Pacific region, a concentration by most regional states on economic growth over military expansion, and the emergence of a host of Chinese domestic problems (e.g., growing crime and corruption, an array of social and economic inequities, and sporadic ethnic unrest) have produced a less-threatening yet arguably more complex and uncertain security environment for China. Specifically, this post–cold war environment presents six basic requirements for Chinese security policy:[6]

1.  To increase China's overall global and regional stature as a major power, particularly through the display of high-technology weaponry and efforts to "show the flag" beyond its borders.

2.  To deal with the uncertain future conventional and nuclear military postures of the United States, Japan, the Association of South East Asian Nations (ASEAN) states, India, and Russia.

3.  To maintain a credible threat of force toward an increasingly separatist-minded and economically potent Taiwan.

4.  To improve Chinese military and diplomatic leverage over and access to nearby strategic territories claimed by Beijing, such as in the South China Sea.

5.  To defend access to vital oceanic routes in the event of conflict.

6.  To strengthen China's ability to deal with domestic social unrest and ethnically based border instabilities.

These requirements have led to a transformation in China's strategic outlook, military doctrine, and resulting force requirements, from that of a continental power requiring a minimal nuclear deterrent capability and large land forces for "in-depth" defense against threats to its northern and western borders, to that of a combined continental/maritime power requiring a more sophisticated conventional and nuclear force structure and a military doctrine centered on the concepts of local war, active peripheral defense, and rapid response, including the projection of power into enemy-controlled space.

These core elements of China's post–cold war conventional military doctrine, first enunciated by the Chinese leadership in the early and mid-1980s, assume that limited or regional conflicts or wars of relatively low intensity and short duration could break out virtually anywhere on China's periphery, demanding a rapid and decisive application of force, in some instances outside of China's continental borders.[7] Many such conflicts would be linked to disputes over territory and perhaps involve regional arms races and weapons proliferation issues. Such possibilities are suggested by points 3 to 5 above. Other elements of the doctrine, associated with points 1 and 2, assume that Chinese forces eventually will need to attain broader power projection and other capabilities either to support China's longer-term desire for great-power status or to deter the U.S. use of forward-deployed forces in the region, or both.

Taken together, from the Chinese perspective, these contingencies and aspirations demand a conventional force structure centered on a diverse range of advanced weapons with medium- and long-range force projection, mobility, rapid reaction, and offshore maneuverability capabilities. These requirements, in turn, imply the creation of a smaller, highly trained and motivated, technologically advanced, versatile, and well-coordinated military force operating under a modern combined arms tactical operations doctrine utilizing sophisticated command, control, communications, and intelligence (C³I) systems. These conclusions were reinforced by the lessons China learned about advanced forms of warfare from observing U.S. military performance during the Gulf war.[8]

China's resulting conventional weapons modernization program emphasizes (1) improved tactical, mobile, solid-fueled missiles (both ballistic and cruise, possibly with both conventional and nuclear warheads); (2) longer-range strike aircraft; (3) improved submarine warfare and antisubmarine warfare capabilities; (4) improved surface ships, especially in long-range missile attack, air defense, and fire control; (5) C³I and early-warning/battle management capabilities; (6) long-range transport and lift capability; (7) airborne early-warning (AEW) aircraft; and (8) midair refueling capability.[9]

Some analysts believe that, as a result of the tensions over Taiwan in 1995–1996, China's weapons programs likely will place an increasing emphasis on acquiring capabilities designed to strengthen the credibility of Beijing's military options against the island and to deter the United States from deploying aircraft carriers in an effort to counter such options. Specific conventional military systems relevant to such capabilities include (1) large amphibious landing craft, especially those capable of traversing wide, shallow mud flats as are found on the west coast of Taiwan; (2) medium-range fighter/interceptors and attack helicopters; (3) short- and medium-range ballistic missiles; (4) conventional attack submarines; (5) improved C³I and carrier detection systems; and (6) long-range, standoff, antiship weapons, including cruises missiles and anticarrier torpedoes.[10]

Programs in these areas indicate that a potential danger to regional stability would result from the interactive dynamics of Chinese naval modernization (including naval air support) coming up against forward-deployed U.S. naval forces. The relative peace and stability in the western Pacific at present arguably can be linked to the absence of competing power projection capabilities among the major powers in the region. Once the previously land war–oriented regional powers begin to acquire the capability to apply military force across large expanses of ocean and engage in sea or air denial operations, however, the security situation in Asia will change. A number of weaker states in the region worry that Chinese military modernization may be more intrinsically destabilizing than the U.S. forward presence. This fear suggests that some means eventually must be developed to coordinate the growth of Chinese maritime capabilities (including both naval and long-range air assets) with the requirements of U.S. military power in the region in ways that accommodate the legitimate interests of both states and also constrain any destabilizing behavior.

These military requirements, along with the potential threats to China's nuclear deterrent presented by proposed theater missile defense (TMD), national missile defense (NMD), and WMD deployments, also are apparently encouraging China to enhance its nonconventional capabilities, particularly nuclear weapons. Officially, China states that it does not possess chemical or biological weapons, that its nuclear weapons are entirely for self-defense, and that its efforts to improve its nuclear weapons are focused entirely on improvements in warhead safety, reliability, and survivability. Beijing's traditional stance has centered on the notion that Chinese nuclear weapons are to be used only to deter a nuclear attack, and never against a nonnuclear power. Hence China often stresses that it has long adhered to a policy of no-first-use (NFU); it has a bilateral NFU agreement with Russia and has demanded a complete ban on nuclear weapons, while the other four declared nuclear powers (the United States, Russia, Britain, and France) have continued a first-use policy and developed a widened nuclear deterrence strategy.[11]

However, as Appendix A indicates, China recently has sought to "improve the survivability of its missile forces by reducing the prelaunchtime period, to find less vulnerable basing modes, and to make general improvements in accuracy, range, guidance, and control."[12] In general, China's nuclear weapons modernization program emphasizes (1) the development of land-and sea-based intercontinental ballistic missiles (ICBMs) with improved range, accuracy, survivability, and penetration against limited missile defense; (2) the development of a new generation of solid-fuel, short- and intermediate-range ballistic missiles; (3) the apparent development of smaller warheads, which theoretically would allow a multiple, independently targetable reentry vehicle (MIRV) warhead capability[13]; and (4) an improvement in China's nuclear weapons $C^3I$ through the advancement of space capabilities and the continued importation of advanced communication technologies, such as fiber optics, and microwave equipment.[14]

These initiatives *may* reflect changing assumptions about the utility of nuclear weapons and hence Chinese nuclear strategy. In the past, China's nuclear doctrine and deterrence theory comprised what often has been referred to as minimum deterrence (*zui di weishe*). This concept hinges on the belief that China's limited number of high-yield nuclear warheads constitute a credible deterrent because they can inflict what is perceived to be unacceptable damage on a handful of enemy cities with a simple, undifferentiated countervalue second strike (a so-called city-busting capability). Under minimum deterrence, there is no need for nuclear force levels beyond what can inflict unacceptable damage.[15]

These developments suggest that there are strategists in China who advocate the development of a new nuclear strategy, specifically a version of what is usually called limited deterrence (*youxian weishe*). Similarities exist between this concept and the American doctrine of flexible response, which posits a range of strategic and substrategic capabilities to deter or defeat highly damaging or overwhelming conventional attacks, deter any level of nuclear conflict, and in a nuclear war contain escalatory pressures.[16]

Specifically, a limited deterrence doctrine might emerge from Chinese concerns about the need to (1) counter a future limited use of theater nuclear forces in a conventional attack; (2) deter an attack by highly accurate and powerful conventional standoff weapons such as long-range cruise missiles or precision-guided munitions; (3) permit warning strikes to shake or undermine an enemy's determination to launch nuclear strikes, destroy its strategic intentions, and thus contain nuclear escalation; or (4) negate the potential neutralization of China's deterrent capability by strategic-capable TMD or ballistic missile defenses (BMD).[17]

All this suggests that China's decision makers may be increasingly uncertain about the credibility and reliability of their past minimum deterrence and believe a more well-rounded and reliable nuclear warfighting capability has military value for deterring and fighting wars in the post–cold war era, especially given China's presumed conventional weaknesses.[18] Beijing also might believe that a more sophisticated nuclear capability will augment China's ongoing search for great-power status, noted earlier. If true, China therefore has few incentives to give up nuclear weapons or constrain its own programs unilaterally, at least over the short to medium term. If the concept of limited deterrence is indeed a factor in the future configuration of Chinese nuclear forces, China will try to resist any restrictions on acquiring flexible options for its nuclear force. Indeed, limited deterrence seems to encourage a limited nuclear buildup, since China's current strategic arsenal is obviously inadequate for the task.

## Conventional and Nonconventional International Arms Control Regimes and Chinese Participation

As a general concept, arms control processes are designed primarily to reduce the risk of war, particularly nuclear war, to reduce the damage resulting from war, to reduce the costs of preparing for war, and sometimes to strengthen global and regional stability and security. However, individual states, multilateral institutions, and nongovernmental organizations support arms control efforts for a variety of reasons, sometimes reflecting common security notions and sometimes reflecting unilateral security interests based on realpolitik assumptions about the nature of international politics. The premise or justification for arms control based on common security often rests on the recognition of the security dilemma. This realization posits that any unilateral effort to increase military power ultimately will weaken a state's security by forcing other states to engage in dangerous arms buildups, counteralliances, or, worst of all, preemptive warfare. Hence one's own security can be assured only when other states also feel secure, and arms control efforts can provide such common security. This situation can lead to arms control policies, including unilateral disarmament measures, that are designed to reassure other states of one's own cooperative and/or defensive intentions. The core notions of (the short-lived) Soviet "new thinking" on arms control reflected these cooperative security assumptions.[19] Common security is also the predominant approach to security *within* the community of Western liberal democracies, although not necessarily between this community and nondemocracies.[20]

This notion of common security stands in contrast to most realpolitik approaches to security. The realpolitik approach regards the international environment as largely anarchic, populated by power-seeking nation-states that generally hope to dominate or balance against potentially threatening states in order to maximize their security at the expense of others. Thus realpolitik strategies generally stress the acquisition of superior coercive capabilities and the offensive doctrines suited to their use. Such strategies usually place a premium on unilateral approaches to security and are highly sensitive to relative material capabilities among states. Yet they do not exclude temporary alliances among states faced with a common, superior threat. This strategic approach usually rejects the basic "security interdependence" argument of common security and generally argues that a state is more secure if other states are weaker in relative terms, and thus less secure.[21] However, a realpolitik approach to international politics does not preclude support for arms control initiatives. Such initiatives could serve to prevent more advanced states from increasing their military capabilities further, prevent technologically inferior states from acquiring greater capabilities, limit proliferation of new capabilities to other states, deceive other states into believing one's own state is essentially a cooperative one, or improve one's own "reputational capital" for expenditure in some other issue area. These aims are all compatible with a realpolitik approach to security. It is important for analytical rigor to distinguish realpolitik from common security approaches so as to be able to understand and observe differences among states that pursue unilateral, bilateral, and multilateral security strategies. Otherwise all behavior becomes realpolitik, and the concept becomes unfalsifiable, hence analytically useless.

Why some states adopt cooperative security strategies and other states realpolitik ones is, of course, a complex and controversial question that cannot be dealt with here. Suffice it to say, evidence for the existence of both kinds of security strategies suggests that although realpolitik approaches may be more common, they are not deterministically imposed on states by the international system, and they do not exclusively characterize major-power behavior. There is some choice, or at least there are factors that are changeable. It is important to note that states that endorse common security strategies are not acting altruistically; nor are they not self-interested. They simply recognize that their own security rests on reassurance strategies based on institutionalized commitments to avoid destabilizing unilateral behavior. To use game theory metaphors, unilateral realpolitik security strategies are premised on a view of the world as, at its most benign, a prisoner's dilemma and, at its most malign, a zero-sum, deadlock environment, where defection (arming to exploit other's weaknesses) is considered the most efficacious security strategy regardless of what other actors do. Common security approaches, however, are based on a view of the world as an "assurance game" where all players recognize mutual cooperation as the most preferred outcome, and where cooperation—namely, credible reassurance signaling—is the most efficacious security strategy. Thus, for example, German-Russian security relations in the post–cold war era are characterized more accurately as an assurance game than as a prisoner's dilemma: reassurance through the promotion of nonthreatening security institutions is the preferred strategy, even though both are major powers with a long history of animosity and conflict in eastern Europe.[22] Similarly, current Japanese security strategies rest, in part, on sending reassurance signals to neighbors through constitutional and operational restraints on the use of military power. These kinds of strategies, premised on a sensitivity to the factors that trigger security dilemmas, are all self-interested, but they are qualitatively different from unilateral security strategies premised on efforts to enhance relative power to deter or coerce potential adversaries. Depending on an actor's assessment of the type of security relationship—which can easily vary depending on the "interlocutor"—it is quite possible for states to pursue realpolitik strategies in one relationship and common security strategies in another.

That said, China's longtime approach to security appears to be primarily a persistently realpolitik one, keyed to the cardinal principal of strategic independence (*zhanlue dulixing*) and reinforced by China's predominant self-image as a relatively weak yet rising great power deserving greater status and respect from other major powers. Many of these powers bullied and coerced China during its "century of humiliation" from the mid-nineteenth to the mid-twentieth century. That experience pervades much of current Chinese strategic thinking. Many Chinese appear to believe that China must reclaim its long-standing and proper historical status as a preeminent power in Asia and should be accorded equal consideration and respect by those powers that oppressed it in the past. This mind-set is reinforced by an apparently deeply socialized view that China's rise will be uniquely nonthreatening and that to believe otherwise is to contribute to the perpetuation of the "China threat theory." (There are parallels here to myths about American exceptionalism and the benignancy of American imperialism historically.) Such beliefs leave less room for common security concepts, and more space for competitive, statecentric nationalism in conceptualizations of the international system.[23] As we shall see, however, they do not preclude support for *some* forms of arms control.

The core of the international arms control effort consists of several major WMD and conventional arms control agreements. These include existing treaties, such as the Comprehensive Test Ban Treaty, the Nuclear Nonproliferation Treaty (NPT), the Biological Weapons Convention (BWC), the Chemical Weapons Convention (CWC), the Missile Technology Control Regime (MTCR), the United Nations Conventional Arms Register, the United Nations Convention on Certain Conventional Weapons (CCW), the Ottawa Treaty banning antipersonnel land mines, and various agreements currently under negotiation, such as the fissile material production cutoff. Activities in support of many of these and other regimes are primarily, although not exclusively, centered in the U.N. Conference on Disarmament in Geneva (CD).

China's views toward and involvement in these and other, lesser arms control processes have changed substantially since the late 1970s. During the Maoist period, the Chinese approach to arms control was highly negative and dismissive. China criticized arms control regimes as discriminatory, serving to "limit the activities of the have-nots while placing no requirements on the haves to disarm."[24] Beijing thus refused to participate in multilateral arms control processes and denounced these processes, as well as the U.S.-Soviet bilateral arms control agreements, as sham disarmament or as efforts by the superpowers to institutionalize their hegemony.

The reform period has witnessed a shift in Chinese perspectives from viewing arms control as largely an adjunct of the East-West struggle and without any benefits to China, to a recognition that China could gain from arms control efforts and would have to become involved in international arms control regimes.[25] As a result of this shift, China began to develop a more comprehensive, less-dismissive, stance toward arms control. In the past 10 to 15 years Beijing has signed onto agreements or made arms control commitments that it had previously opposed vigorously. Indeed, China's participation rates have increased dramatically: In 1970 it had signed about 10 to 20 percent of all arms control agreements it was eligible to sign. By 1996 this figure had jumped to 85 to 90 percent. Chinese participation can be divided into the following eleven arms control or arms control–related areas.[26]

## NUCLEAR TEST BANS

China entered the Conference on Disarmament in 1980. In 1981 Beijing signaled that it would not oppose setting up a working group on nuclear test bans in the CD and then indicated it would join such a group in 1985. In 1986 China announced it would no longer test nuclear weapons in the atmosphere (it had in fact stopped doing so in 1981), in effect committing itself to the same constraints on testing as found in the Limited Test Ban Treaty of 1963. China had denounced that treaty for years and still refuses to sign it formally. In 1993 China for the first time showed a willingness to participate in negotiations for a CTBT and to conclude the treaty by the end of 1996. It subsequently signed the CTBT and joined the global moratorium on testing in mid-1996. It should be noted that, like China, the United States opposed a comprehensive test ban treaty well into the 1990s.

## NUCLEAR NONPROLIFERATION

China officially acceded to the NPT in March 1992 and in 1995 supported its indefinite extension. This marked a reversal in Chinese policy. China's traditional position has been that the NPT was discriminatory, perpetuated the U.S.-USSR nuclear hegemony, denied the right of states to acquire legitimate means of defense, and had no direct effect on improving China's own security. Beijing had insisted that the United States and the Soviet Union first needed to stop vertical proliferation before the world could stop horizontal proliferation. Apparently these arguments no longer hold much currency in Chinese strategic thinking.

## FISSILE MATERIALS PRODUCTION

In the fall of 1994 China agreed to participate in U.N.-sponsored talks on establishing an international convention to end the production of fissile materials (separated plutonium and highly enriched uranium) for nuclear weapons purposes, known as the fissile material production cutoff (FMPC). The primary goal of the FMPC convention will be to attain the signatures of the five declared nuclear powers and three undeclared powers (India, Israel, and Pakistan).[27]

## CHEMICAL AND BIOLOGICAL WEAPONS

China has signed and ratified the Chemical Weapons Convention and the Biological Weapons Convention. It participated in the CWC talks from their inception and remained active until their conclusion in fall 1992. This was the first time China has played an important role in formulating the terms of a major multilateral arms control agreement. The CWC has provisions for on-site challenge inspections (OSI) of facilities in any member state. (The CTBT also has OSI provisions, but it has not entered into force.[28]) Since the CWC entered into force in May 1997, OSI have been conducted in several countries, including some in China.

## MISSILES AND MISSILE TECHNOLOGY EXPORTS

China is not a member of the Missile Technology Control Regime, but in the early 1990s Beijing began to adjust its past claim of being exempt from the voluntary guidelines of the MTCR by issuing statements supporting the principle of missile nonproliferation. China then began to accommodate multilateral controls aimed at halting the spread of missiles and missile technology. It has accepted increasingly strict limits on the sale of missiles, culminating in October 1994 in a bilateral agreement with the United States to refrain from selling MTCR-class missiles. China has agreed that it will ban the export of ground-to-ground, MTCR-class missiles.[29] Questions remain, however, as to whether China actually has honored its commitments in this area, as will be discussed. In October 1997 China also indicated to the United States that it would no longer export cruise missiles to Iran.

## SELF-INITIATED ARMS CONTROL PROPOSALS

Beijing has introduced its own proposals on nuclear arms control in the United Nations in recent years. It has proposed a convention on the complete elimination of nuclear weapons, similar in form to the Chemical Weapons Convention. It has also "called for a 'no-first-use' of nuclear weapons treaty among the five declared nuclear powers and negative security assurances [NSA] by the nuclear weapons states that they will not use nuclear weapons against non-nuclear states." Both are long-standing Chinese positions.[30] At various points from the mid-1980s on, China also has proposed agreements imposing limits on naval forces, conventional arms, and weapons in outer space. China also claims that its reduction of the People's Liberation Army (PLA) by 1 million personnel from 1985 to 1987 and proposals for a further reduction of 500,000 made in September 1997 make it an exemplar in unilateral disarmament (although the decisions to reduce were motivated by cost reductions and operational flexibility, not arms control).

## U.S.-SOVIET STRATEGIC ARMS LIMITATION TALKS (START)

China has expressed its support for U.S.-Soviet strategic arms limitation and arms reduction processes, which previously it had regarded as "sham" disarmament. It also basically endorsed the 1987 Intermediate-range Nuclear Force (INF) treaty.

## CONVENTIONAL ARMS TRANSPARENCY

China has formally acceded to the U.N. Conventional Arms Register, negotiated after the Gulf war and approved by the U.N. General Assembly in 1991. The purpose of the registry is to promote transparency in arms transfers. It calls on members to provide, voluntarily, annual data on imports and exports of several categories of conventional weapons. China has supplied data each year since then and has participated in negotiations on how the registry should be expanded.[31] However, it opposes any tighter reporting requirements and does not currently favor a separate registry for Asia-Pacific states, as has been suggested by some in the track-two (unofficial) security dialogues taking place among those countries.

## THE USE AND EXPORT OF LAND MINES

In 1982 China formally acceded to the 1980 U.N. Convention on the Prohibitions or Restrictions on the Use of Certain Conventional Weapons Which May Be Deemed to Be Excessively Injurious or to Have Indiscriminate Effects. Of greatest interest is Protocol II of this convention, which restricts the use of land mines, booby traps, and other devices under certain conditions. In 1996 China agreed to sign onto the revised version of Protocol II, which prohibits the transfer of land mines that are undetectable and do not contain self-destructive and self-deactivating devices. China also pledged to abide by a moratorium on the export of antipersonnel mines, called for by a consensus vote of the U.N. General Assembly in December 1995. China has made these agreements even though it is a producer and exporter of land mines. Like the United States, however, China opposes the recently concluded Ottawa Treaty banning antipersonnel land mines. The Chinese military contends that with China's extensive borders, land mines are legitimate and necessary defensive weapons.

## CONFIDENCE- AND SECURITY-BUILDING MEASURES (CSBMs)

In recent years China has participated in a variety of bilateral and multilateral confidence- and security-building measures. These include the ASEAN Regional Forum; border confidence-building measures (CBMs) with Russia and India; a five-power treaty with Russia and three Central Asian states that provides for exchanges of military observers, limits on military exercises near the border, the setting up of hot lines and other CBMs; and a program of CBMs with the United States that includes military-to-military visits and exchanges, exchanges on defense conversion, dialogues on strategy and transparency, ship visits, and a recently concluded agreement covering incidents at sea.[32]

## A GROWING ARMS CONTROL COMMUNITY

Finally, a growing although still small and decentralized arms control community has emerged within the national security policy bureaucracy, as part of China's rapidly expanding role in the preceding regimes and processes. This community is a direct result of China's increasing involvement in technical arms control processes that impinge on extant or potential military programs. As the international arms control agenda has become more technical, China has brought technical specialists into the policy process. This in turn has helped create opportunities for interaction with technical arms control specialists inside and outside governments in other countries. Through this interaction Chinese arms controllers have received assistance for training, conferences, and research. This cadre of arms control experts is located primarily in three clusters of institutions: the Ministry of Foreign Affairs (primarily in the new Arms Control and Disarmament Department, formerly a division under the International Organization Department, and in a new division, in the Asia Department, set up to handle multilateral security dialogues in the Asia-Pacific); the PLA General Staff Department (including the chemical defense subdepartment, the intelligence subdepartment, and the equipment subdepartment), and the nuclear weapons and missile technical communities (i.e., the China Academy of Engineering Physics, the China Aerospace Corporation, the General Equipment Department, and the Commission on Science, Technology and Industry for National Defense's [COSTIND] Arms Control and Disarmament Program). Estimates vary concerning the total size of China's arms control community. One senior Chinese arms control expert estimates that there are at least 100 people involved, although many are part-time participants in arms control research. Some of the most important agencies responsible for WMD arms control policy are listed in Appendix B.[33]

## A Shift Away from Realpolitik toward Common Security?

China's greatly expanded pattern of participation in global and regional arms control regimes during the 1980s and 1990s clearly suggests that a measurable shift has taken place in its approach to arms control. This shift could be motivated primarily by an emerging acceptance of the value of common security approaches or, alternatively, by realpolitik approaches to arms control, especially those dictated by the interests of a relatively weak yet growing power. The former would suggest a basic change in how China understands its security and the role of arms control in this calculus, a consequence of its exposure to a wide range of non–zero-sum relationships with new trading partners and international economic institutions, which present new possibilities for negotiation, joint economic gains, and logrolling. Such a shift could consist of movement toward accommodationalist, common strategies of mutual restraint, in the absence of exogenous (dis)incentives (e.g., institutional rules and/or sanctions).

This summary of China's defense doctrine and conventional and unconventional weapons programs indicates, however, that such a fundamental conceptual shift is at this point a less likely explanation for change in most of Chinese arms control policies. With a couple of possible exceptions, it is more likely that China's expanding involvement in arms control regimes stems from realpolitik motives, whereby policy reflects realpolitik-based responses to changing relative capabilities and a changing international environment favoring greater arms control.

A closer examination of China's specific behavior toward several of the major arms control regimes confirms the likely dominance of realpolitik approaches over common security views in its approach to most arms control issues.[34] However, such an examination also provides clues as to how China might be encouraged (or induced) to participate even more actively in arms control regimes.

## The Interactive Effect of Chinese Involvement in Arms Control Regimes

International arms control treaties and conventions in which China has participated over the past 15 years "differ significantly in their scope, permitted activities, required activities, and compliance mechanisms."[35] China's activities in these fora have become significant only since the early to mid-1990s. Moreover, the specific record of China's expanding involvement in arms control regimes reveals a wide variety of motivations and calculations. Nonetheless, there are some common themes in and characteristics of Chinese participation worth noting.

NUCLEAR TEST BANS

China's signing of the CTBT in the near term would suggest Beijing's willingness to place some restraints on its nuclear modernization effort, given the presumed importance of continued nuclear testing to that endeavor. How much of a restraint, of course, depends on how ambitious China's nuclear modernization goals are and how successful China's testing program prior to the CTBT has been. Until late summer 1996, outside observers did not sense much strong support in China for the CTBT. Indeed, Beijing's position in the CTBT talks seemed to have been largely designed to slow down the process, in the view of many CD delegates and nongovernmental observers. Specifically, China had posed several preconditions for successful completion of the treaty that were generally unacceptable to other participants in the talks and that would seriously delay its signing and implementation. These included the right of declared nuclear states to conduct peaceful nuclear explosions; no-first-use and negative security assurances commitments by the nuclear states; and the exclusive use of an international monitoring system (IMS) that would then exclude the use of national technical means (NTM) by individual states for treaty verification.[36] China also had proposed a lengthy procedure leading to the treaty's entry into force following its signing. Indeed, many CD members suspected that Beijing wanted to delay talks past 1996, possibly in order to permit it to complete the modernization of its nuclear warheads.[37]

China claimed it had legitimate reasons for pushing these proposals, however. For example, some Chinese officials and scientists support peaceful nuclear explosions as potentially cost-effective and technically feasible methods for mining and oil and gas exploration. Chinese views reportedly have been influenced by Russian scientists, as Russia has used nuclear explosions for these purposes; few foreign experts outside

Russia agree with this rationale, however. In addition, China fears that the United States or Russia could use national technical means primarily to call for investigations of China or to suppress evidence to hide their own activities in violation of a CTBT; NTM also could be used for intelligence-gathering purposes. In addition, many Chinese seem to genuinely believe that pledges regarding the first use and negative security assurances would enhance international security and are not simply political statements. In fact, China apparently believes a NFU pledge by all nuclear powers would provide a greater deterrent to war than the CTBT or nuclear arms reduction agreements.[38]

In addition to all these concerns, and perhaps most important, China had long been cautious about signing the CTBT (or, for that matter, a five-power nuclear arms reductions agreement or any other regime that might restrict its nuclear programs) because it feared that the viability of its nuclear deterrent would be undermined in the future by the deployment of ballistic missile defense systems in the United States or Russia.[39]

On the other hand, China also realized that any obvious move to delay or dilute a CTBT could tarnish its image among a large group of developing states who saw the treaty as a core pillar in the extension of the Nonproliferation Treaty. (Many such states had demanded that the nuclear states sign a comprehensive nuclear test ban as a prerequisite for NPT extension.) There had been a wave of international protests of Beijing's nuclear tests in 1995 and 1996. Beijing finally ceased nuclear testing in late July 1996, but indicated that it wants the issue of peaceful nuclear explosions to be reexamined in a decade.

In May 1996 China dropped its potentially treaty-killing positions on no-first use and peaceful nuclear explosions when a "clean" draft treaty eliminating this language was accepted as the basis of endgame negotiations. After intense negotiations, primarily with the United States, over a compromise on the intrusiveness of the CTBT verification regime, China signed the treaty.[40] There has been some speculation that China dropped the obstructionist bargaining positions once it was clear that India would not sign the treaty. Since the parties to the negotiation agreed that India's signature (along with the P-5 and Pakistan and Israel) were required for the treaty's entry into force, India's opposition would block the treaty from becoming international law.[41] China would thus not be constrained by a legal instrument, while India would bear the pressure for undermining the CTBT.

However, on balance the evidence suggests that India's strong opposition to the treaty (which did not come until after May 1996, when China had already dropped its obstructionist positions) was not a central factor in China's accession. Independent of India's blocking entry into force,

China is still bound by international practice to abide by a treaty it has signed even if the treaty has not entered into force. China is politically bound, as well, to abide by its voluntary moratorium on testing. Moreover the treaty has provisions for revision that in principle could be used to eliminate India's signature as a condition for entry into force. Thus relying on India to keep China essentially free to test would have been high risk politically. Finally, there is evidence that China probably decided finally in late 1995, or possibly by April 1996, to sign the treaty. This was before India developed a negotiating posture that essentially vetoed the near-term possibility of entry into force.[42]

In the absence of evidence of technological or financial side-payments to join (e.g., transfers of computer simulation technology), and given the constraints the regime places on China's ability to modernize its nuclear warheads, a powerful reason, then, for China's participating in and acceding to the treaty seems to be a concern about image and status. In interviews the authors have conducted with Chinese nuclear weapons scientists and military officials a common response to questions about why China signed is that China had little choice once it was clear that the CTBT was supported by an enormous majority of states who saw it as a pillar of the nuclear nonproliferation regime. The language used to justify the decision is the language of status and image. China could not buck this "great international trend." There was "psychological pressure" to join once the other P-5 had joined the negotiations and there was clear support from developing counties. China's signature was consistent with its being a responsible major power, and joining the treaty was part of a "global atmosphere," such that China would have been isolated had it opposed or sabotaged the treaty.

## NUCLEAR NONPROLIFERATION

China's support for the Nonproliferation Treaty likely reflects a complex mixture of predominantly realpolitik motives. First, China's NPT adherence does not place any significant restrictions on its WMD capabilities. It was a relatively painless step that "enabled China to gain further legitimacy and status as a great power while pursuing various diplomatic, economic, and strategic interests. Beijing's leaders have stated since 1984 that China does not encourage nuclear proliferation."[43] As a nuclear power, China is not subject to inspections by the International Atomic Energy Agency unless it decides to submit to them. Moreover, China was already an IAEA member (since 1984) when it acceded to the NPT. No military-related facilities, and only a handful of civilian sites, are under IAEA safeguards.[44]

Second, although China joined the NPT and the Zangger Committee (in 1997), it has not joined the Nuclear Suppliers Group (NSG), which has sought to establish tighter controls over nuclear transfers than those specified in the NPT. In 1993 NSG members agreed to a policy requiring full-scope safeguards for countries that received transfers of nuclear technology. China has been the only state transferring nuclear technology that did not require these safeguards. It has signed nuclear cooperation agreements with over a dozen states. In each instance Chinese officials have insisted that any transfers be conducted under safeguards consistent with IAEA obligations and that the transfers be only of materials intended for peaceful purposes. Little is known about formal Chinese procedures for export controls on nuclear materials and equipment. By joining the NPT but not the NSG, China thus retains its option to provide nuclear technology to countries that would be barred from receiving such exports from NSG members.[45] Some Chinese arms control specialists, however, have advocated unofficially that their government accept full-scope safeguards, and there are discussions under way in the Zangger Committee to require its members to apply such safeguards. Informed observers speculate that, in the end, China will accede to these to preserve its status in the committee.[46]

Third, evidence indicates that China signed onto the NPT in large part because of image concerns. International support for nonproliferation has grown considerably since the end of the cold war. Support for the treaty also was growing inside China's arms control technical community in the late 1980s. But the timing of China's signature suggests that scoring diplomatic points was a critical factor in determining when it would sign. In the early 1990s, after France declared it would accede to the treaty, China was the only declared nuclear state that was not a party to the NPT; hence it was in a class with undeclared nuclear powers India, Pakistan, and Israel. China probably hoped to deflect criticism of its nuclear export policy, especially in the aftermath of the broader criticism it received from the international community for its violent suppression of the Tiananmen demonstrations of June 1989. In addition, China's position on NPT extension during the review conference of April–May 1995 suggested that it was motivated by image concerns rather than by a support for global nonproliferation. China hedged its position on extension until determining whether a large majority of states favored indefinite or limited extension, and then supported the predominant viewpoint.[47]

Fourth, from a purely security perspective, some in China view the NPT as an essential tool in efforts to halt the spread of nuclear weapons in Asia. The possibility of this spread has become far more real in recent years, given the rapid economic growth rates and advanced technologi-cal capabilities of many (especially northeastern) Asian states.[48] Until India's and Pakistan's recent nuclear tests, it was in China's interest as the only Asian power with nuclear weapons to restrict their proliferation in the region. After these tests, the Chinese may now have a stronger interest in using the NPT and other arms control measures to contain ver-tical and horizontal proliferation in this region. Nonetheless, it is not clear how pervasive this view of the NPT is inside the Chinese policy process. Until the Indian tests, some Chinese arms control experts had questioned just how serious the nonproliferation problem was for Chinese and global security, arguing that this was primarily an American interest.

The preceding motives suggest that China had many realpolitik rea-sons for signing onto the NPT. However, these reasons do not necessarily prevent China from defecting from certain treaty requirements. For exam-ple, China's adherence to the treaty prohibition against members' trans-ferring nuclear weapons capabilities to nonnuclear states has been questioned by the U.S. government in the past. There is no public evi-dence that China has violated this prohibition, and within East Asia, the Chinese apparently have remained highly cautious about the transfer of WMD-related technologies or delivery systems.[49] However, there are some indications that China assisted Pakistan in its nuclear weapons pro-gram in the past, although it is not clear which aspects of this assistance occurred before and which after its signing of the NPT.[50] In 1998 the U.S. government indicated that the Chinese government is meeting U.S. expectations to stop the flow of nuclear technology to Pakistan and Iran.[51]

FISSILE MATERIALS PRODUCTION

China reportedly has ceased production of fissile materials and officially stated its support for a fissile materials production cutoff convention, although it is known to be less enthusiastic about such a convention than other states. Beijing's position on this issue, like that of the rest of the Per-manent Five, does not necessarily indicate a willingness to restrict China's nuclear weapons program. Many experts believe that China already has ample stockpiles of fissile materials on hand, enough to produce at least 200 additional warheads. Hence adherence to the convention likely would present few costs to Beijing, at least over the short to medium term. Nevertheless, some experts also believe that China's final decision on whether and when to sign onto a convention has yet to be taken. The con-vention would prohibit production indefinitely; signing requires consid-erable confidence that production will not be desired, even over the long term. Hence China might decide to delay or avoid signing a convention altogether, especially if, as was suggested earlier, it is indeed changing its nuclear doctrine in ways that demand more warheads on a wider variety of delivery vehicles. On the other hand, many experts believe that China likely will not want to be seen as the only declared nuclear power not to cease the production of fissile materials permanently.[52]

## CHEMICAL AND BIOLOGICAL WEAPONS

China has maintained a consistent position that all nations capable of manufacturing and producing chemical weapons should stop testing, producing, transferring, and deploying them and pledge against their use. Certain aspects of China's behavior suggest that it will try to conform to the requirements of the Chemical Weapons Convention.[53] However, although China declared itself to be a non–chemical weapons state when it signed the CWC, there is some suspicion in the U.S. intelligence community that this is not an accurate description and that China might have transferred components or technology for chemical (or biological) weapons to other states.[54]

Moreover, China's negotiating position on the CWC primarily reflected its fear of manipulation by foreigners and its desire to preserve its independence. The CWC was the first arms control treaty China signed that had provisions for on-site challenge inspections of facilities in any member state. But early on Beijing expressed some concern over this provision, fearing that parties to the CWC would use the pretext of a challenge inspection to gain access to sensitive facilities for commercial or military espionage. Hence China insisted that requests for challenge inspections should be "reasonable, specific, and precise." China also supported insertion of a procedure for stopping inspections, although it had to compromise on the details: a three-quarters vote by the CWC's executive council is required to stop a challenge inspection if it is considered frivolous, abusive, or outside the scope of the convention. China also has sought to formalize an understanding that any challenge inspection would be preceded by discussion and consultation. Partly for these reasons the PRC was slow to ratify the CWC.[55]

As in the case of the CTBT, some of China's concerns about the CWC are justifiable. For example, China has stressed its difficulties in complying with various disclosures required within 30 days of the treaty's entering into force (e.g., to disclose all chemical production and, in some cases use, of chemicals that fall into three schedules). Gathering these data is hampered by the sheer number of labs and other chemical facilities that the Chinese must guarantee will act in compliance with the treaty, and by China's lack of experience in preparing for on-site inspections and the types of technologies that can be used to minimize intrusion. China can delay work on treaty implementation procedures because of these concerns, but not without image costs.

## MISSILES AND MISSILE TECHNOLOGY EXPORTS

An enormous amount of confusion and a lack of accurate public information surround China's behavior in the Missile Technology Control Regime. The regime is a "voluntary arrangement among countries that share a common interest in arresting missile proliferation." It is not a treaty. The MTCR consists of "common export policy guidelines applied to a common list of controlled items that each MTCR member implements in accordance with its national legislation."[56] Its terms are imprecise (e.g., the agreement allows for certain transfers on a case-by-case basis), and its requirements for compliance vary depending on the status of the adherent. Also, it has no multilateral enforcement or verification mechanism. Thus violation of the MTCR is not a violation of codified international law. Only U.S. domestic law provides for punishment for violation. MTCR-related sanctions are required by U.S. law and only when there is "overwhelming" proof of violations. But U.S. charges of Chinese violations of MTCR commitments have been supported only by satellite imagery and other classified information. Moreover, the United States first raised formal complaints about Chinese missile transfers in 1991, before China made any commitment to adhere to the MTCR. Even though China was not a member, Washington then decided to impose sanctions that denied China various dual-use and high-technology items.[57]

Nevertheless, China made several unpublished "promises," "pledges," and "commitments" to adhere to the terms of the MTCR in 1992 and again in 1994. This put China in a similar category to several other designated "adherent countries" that have agreed unilaterally to abide by the terms of the agreement or stated their intention to abide by them but do not participate in the meetings of the member countries. Although China has pledged to adhere to the MTCR, it is not formally considered a member country under U.S. law: such countries are required to conclude a formal memorandum of understanding (MOU) with the United States regarding adherence to the MTCR and to have in place a system of export controls for missiles and missile technologies, neither of which is evident in the Chinese case. Nonetheless, as an informal adherent, China is expected to live by the decisions of the MTCR members without being able to influence them. China has repeatedly criticized such an arrangement, with some justification. The United States has been unwilling to press hard for China's formal entry into the MTCR because of concerns about, among other things, having to share sensitive intelligence, and because formal membership probably would exempt Beijing from U.S. sanctions.[58]

China's 1992 commitment was articulated in a series of written diplomatic exchanges with the United States. However, while American expectations were clear, the terms of China's 1992 MTCR commitments were limited and ambiguous. China's renewed commitment to the MTCR, expressed in a signed bilateral agreement and joint statement with the United States in October 1994, was more explicit and phrased in a more jointly agreed manner than its 1992 commitment. The 1994 agreement included a pledge not to export particular MTCR-class missiles, as defined by the United States, to other countries. However, Beijing still does not accept the revised MTCR guidelines and annex of 1993 and 1994. It has agreed to adhere only to the MTCR guidelines and annex of 1987, in force at the time of its MTCR pledge. The Chinese government has claimed, with some justification, that the United States has shifted the goalposts without consulting Beijing. For instance, in 1993 the MTCR partners adjusted the guidelines to include missiles capable of delivering any type of weapon of mass destruction. This change required all member states to restrict more items.[59]

It is difficult to determine accurately whether China has complied with its MTCR pledges. Reports in December 1992 alleged that China had shipped M-11 missiles or equipment to Pakistan; U.S. sanctions were again imposed. China denied it had violated the MTCR.[60] However, some denials were ambiguous, not specifying whether China was denying the existence of the transfer or that the sale violated MTCR guidelines.[61] In general, accusations of Chinese MTCR violations often are raised solely by the United States, on the basis of its use of national technical means, and not by other parties to the regime. The unwillingness of other states or international organs to pressure China over potential MTCR violations thus has made the issue hostage to unrelated U.S.-China problems.

It does seem clear, however, that China's compliance with the MTCR (insofar as it has occurred) does not stem from any strong support for the measure as a major nonproliferation regime. China has long insisted that such a control regime also should apply to sales of aircraft capable of carrying WMDs, many of which are sold worldwide by the United States and Russia. In addition, China apparently agreed to become an adherent country to the MTCR only if the United States lifted sanctions imposed in June 1991 on two Chinese defense industrial companies for transfers of missile technology to Pakistan.[62] Such a quid pro quo arrangement suggests that Chinese compliance with the MTCR was motivated by factors other than simply a concern over missile proliferation.

## FIVE-POWER NUCLEAR ARMS REDUCTIONS

China's agreement to engage in nuclear arms reduction talks would signify an important step toward its acceptance of mutual security restraints that serve to place real limits on Chinese nuclear force levels. However, although China has stated officially that it will participate eventually in such talks, it has vacillated since 1981 regarding the terms for such participation. China insists the two superpowers must take the lead, since their stockpiles are so much larger than that of the other nuclear powers. From 1982 until around 1988 Chinese officials said China would not seriously discuss reductions until the two superpowers agreed to reduce their arms by one-half. After the United States and Soviet Union had pledged to reduce their stockpiles by 50 percent, however, and thus made dramatic reductions possible, China restated its early 1980s position and stipulated that the superpowers would need to make unspecified "drastic reductions" before it would participate in discussions.[63]

This position suggests that Beijing has tried to avoid putting its own strategic nuclear capabilities on the table. Such a strategy is quite consistent with realpolitik adaptation by a relatively weak nuclear power, based on an aversion to constraints on relative capabilities.

## CONVENTIONAL ARMS TRANSPARENCY

Despite participation in various activities intended to promote defense transparency, China has avoided providing much detailed information on its military doctrine and modernization plans, and provides little information that has not been made public previously. The argument exhibits a realpolitik pathology: as a weaker state vis-à-vis the United States, Russia, and Japan, China gains an advantage by keeping stronger states guessing about its capabilities. The hope is that these states exaggerate these capabilities to some extent, thus adding to China's deterrent and status. Chinese strategists call this "asymmetric transparency" (*bu dui zheng touming du*). This calculus suggests an insensitivity, however, to China's status as a stronger state vis-à-vis weaker states along its periphery. The logic of asymmetric transparency suggests that China should be more transparent than some of its Southeast Asian neighbors. It generally is not. Ironically, the "China threat theory," which China denounces, is perhaps an unintended consequence of this strategy of playing off "worst-case" analyses in other states.

## THE USE AND EXPORT OF LAND MINES

China's support for limits on the use and export of land mines is motivated by realpolitik and image concerns. Its ascension to the 1980 U.N. Convention on Certain Conventional Weapons (CCW) did not present many obstacles to China's use of land mines, given the many loopholes in that document.[64] China's more recent support for a revised version of Protocol II constituted a reversal of its past position. China had argued previously that since land mines were an essential defensive weapon for poorer countries, their restriction thus would provide advantages to countries with high-tech weapons capabilities, China's long border made land mines an essential and legitimate means of defense, and the costs of converting its large stockpiles and its production lines to meet the three criteria in the revised Protocol II (detectability, self-defusion, and self-destruction) would be enormous. The Chinese military was a particularly strong advocate of these arguments. According to knowledgeable observers, China eventually ended its opposition primarily because the Chinese Foreign Ministry was able to make the successful argument that the potential costs to China's image from not signing outweighed the economic costs of converting production, because support in the international community for both the revised Protocol II and the moratorium had grown considerably. In particular, China would have been subjected to heavy international criticism if it had chosen to obstruct adoption of the agreement. In addition, the moratorium on the export of land mines is not a legally binding agreement. Nonetheless, the Chinese shift in position, although certainly not monumental, indicates a willingness to override military concerns. China has balked, however, along with the United States, at joining the Ottawa Treaty, banning all antipersonnel land mines.

## A GROWING ARMS CONTROL COMMUNITY

As international arms control issues have become more complex and technical, and impinge more directly on China's image and security, the nation's growing arms control community apparently has exerted more influence on its arms control policymaking process. China also exhibits denser and more institutionalized internal and external linkages. Initially through the early 1980s the specifics of China's arms control and disarmament policy were relatively simple, and primarily the responsibility of the Ministry of Foreign Affairs International Organization Department. The job was a relatively easy one—criticize the United States and Soviet Union and stick to vague and impractical proposals.

By the mid-1980s, however, as test bans, chemical weapons issues, Star Wars, and nuclear winter moved onto the international arms control agenda, Foreign Ministry generalists required input from technical specialists in COSTIND, the China Academy of Engineering Physics and its affiliate, the Institute of Applied Physics and Computational Mathematics, and from seismologists, chemists, and the uniformed PLA. In effect an interagency process was born. Initially, much of this interaction took place in irregular cross-unit conferences and meetings or on the Chinese delegation to the Conference on Disarmament in Geneva. By the mid-1990s, however, on CD-related issues in particular, there is a relatively well-developed routine process for devising bargaining positions. While the Ministry of Foreign Affairs—in particular the ambassador for disarmament and the Arms Control and Disarmament Department (prior to 1997, a division)—takes the lead in organizing the interagency meetings and in developing the agenda and basic talking points in China's bargaining position, it must seek and balance the interests of the technical community (mostly represented by specialists from the China Academy of Engineering Physics, the Institute of Applied Physics and Computational Mathematics, and COSTIND's Arms Control Program) and the PLA (coordinated by a "leading small group" on arms control that reports to the Central Military Commission). Arms control issues and policies also are often floated informally in regular seminars that invite specialists from across these units. Senior political leaders now interfere in the process only to resolve disputes among these three groups of actors and to establish broad parameters for policy (e.g., should China sign the CTBT or not).

As the interagency process has developed in response to the global arms control agenda, certain tensions have arisen in Chinese arms control policy. On one hand, China's cooperation is more central than ever before. A CTBT or fissile material production cutoff would lack credibility if not agreed to by a major nuclear power. This means that more international attention is being paid to Chinese behavior and its performance in international arms control arenas. Thus image costs and benefits are even more salient in the policy process and provide the Ministry of Foreign Affairs a certain weight in the process that might not exist otherwise, given the highly technical nature of some of these issues. Thus this ministry apparently prevailed over PLA views on whether to sign the CWC, the land mine protocols, and perhaps even the NPT. On the other hand, precisely because of the technical nature of these issues and the fact that they cut closer than ever before to Chinese military programs and capabilities, the Foreign Ministry is less able to argue about the technical merits of an agreement or process. Thus some of the more obstructionist positions in

China's bargaining in the CTBT were apparently in the Chinese negotiating brief because of strong support from the testing community.

The changing international arms control agenda has not been the only factor contributing to the development of an interagency process. Tentative contacts with Western governmental and nongovernmental arms control experts, beginning in the early 1980s and continuing in the 1990s, have opened China's arms control community to a wide range of alternative views on arms control. These contacts have been a conduit for funding, research ideas, conference opportunities, and other assistance for institutional development. In general, experts among foreign nongovernmental arms control groups tend to stress cooperative security and hence the futility, or even the danger, of attempting to attain security through the unilateral pursuit of superior capabilities. They tend to believe that in the short run, global arms control processes should aim to strengthen assured destruction deterrence by limiting strategic defenses, warhead modernization, ballistic missile proliferation, and improved accuracy. Evidence for the transmission of these types of ideas to China remains murky, but the ideas that have been transferred have not been inconsequential for Chinese arms control policy. (More on this point below.) There is some evidence that these contacts have helped buttress arguments in favor of signing the NPT and the CTBT, and joining the Fissile Material Production Cutoff talks. They also have exposed some members of the community to ideas about minimum deterrence, ideas that run contrary to arguments made by some strategists in the uniformed PLA about limited deterrence. There is also intriguing evidence that some of those in the policy process handling China's diplomacy in the ASEAN Regional Forum (ARF) have been influenced by the interactions they have had with multilateralists from other states and are pushing for greater involvement in the ARF from a genuinely internalized belief that mutilateral security dialogues are good for Chinese security. In the last year or so the official Chinese discourse on the ARF also has adopted the language of common security (even using the game-theoretic language of assurance games). This fact would suggest the potential for at least some softening in the realpolitik understandings of security that have dominated China's security policies. The evolution of China's ARF policy may provide some lessons for designing other arms control institutions that encourage cooperative security thinking.[65]

However, realpolitik assumptions about the international system continue to pervade Chinese discussions of arms control. For example, many Chinese arms controllers reject the argument, made by Soviet new thinkers and by smaller activist multilateralist states, that global interests have replaced, or are largely coterminus with, national interests. In fact, many Chinese analysts argue that interdependence can accentuate interstate conflict by trampling on sovereignty of nation-states, by preventing them from controlling their economic, military, and political resources, and by providing opportunities for states to interfere in the internal affairs of others. They also argue that the effectiveness of arms control has been severely limited by several general features of the international regime; for example, states with a technical advantage in one area will prevent arms control from touching that area; states with technological disadvantages will advocate arms control to restrict the state with the advantage; arms control agreements come to fruition only when the states involved are evenly balanced in military technology; and arms control tends to be successful for technologies that are out of date.

This argument implies that China should support arms control only that places asymmetrical restrictions on the capabilities of more technologically advanced states and should agree to substantive arms control commitments only once it achieves technological parity with its primary rivals. Cooperative security thus should begin with improvements in the bilateral relations between states and include reciprocated unilateral actions. It should not always or predominantly involve multilateral conventions, or transparency on the part of weaker states. Such views tend to describe China's predominant arms control behavior.

## Assessment[66]

The following conclusions are suggested by our analysis.

First, China's greatly increased involvement in arms control regimes consists primarily of realpolitik adaptation to a changing security environment by a regime that views itself as a relatively weak state militarily, when compared with the major industrial powers. In other words, in the face of an increasingly intrusive international arms control agenda, Chinese arms control behavior in most instances reflects efforts to devise the most effective means to avoid placing China's capabilities on arms control tables, and is designed to preserve and improve its relative capabilities. There is also an element of free-riding in Chinese actions, visible in the fact that China:

- is more supportive of measures that result in reductions of other states' capabilities (e.g., U.S. and Russian strategic force reductions) and less supportive of measures that restrain its own capabilities;

- has sought to avoid or delay full implementation of arms control regimes that might limit or reduce Chinese capabilities (CTBT, participation in strategic arms reductions);

- has not initiated new arms control talks or regimes in areas that might limit or reduce Chinese capabilities, especially in the conventional area (CSBMs), but it is participating in a growing number of CSBM dialogues and processes (five-power CBM treaty; ARF);

- supports measures that bear little or no cost to China and offer substantial image benefits (NFU, NSA)[67];

- is reluctant to reveal its capabilities through transparency measures;

- supports measures that help create a stable, peaceful international environment for reform-based economic construction (NPT, FMPC);

- *might* have violated specific nonproliferation regimes, such as the NPT and the MTCR in the case of Pakistan, presumably to maintain political leverage and strengthen, in its view, the strategic balance in South Asia.[68]

Second, Chinese arms control behavior also is motivated by China's desire to maintain its international image as a peace-loving, nonthreatening underdeveloped leader of the non-Western world. Hence Beijing wishes to avoid appearing as an outlier or violator of arms control norms when these are supported by a large group of politically significant nations.[69]

Third, Chinese arms control behavior behavior suggests a general order of preferences:

- China most enthusiastically supports pure free-riding opportunities. If pure free-riding becomes difficult, then China may try to slow down, divert, or delay negotiations. If this proves difficult, then China may try to build coalitions of like-minded states to build bargaining power and to lower the image costs of obstructionist behavior.

- China next favors low-cost unilateralism (e.g., NFU, NSA); symmetrical bilateralism (Sino-Russian CBMs); and symbolic multilateralism (e.g., nuclear weapons–free zones in Latin America, Africa, and the South Pacific, none of which provides direct security benefit terms or clear security costs, although they do have some clear image benefits), and low-cost multilateralism (e.g., regional security dialogues).

- China least supports what it perceives to be asymmetrical bilateralism and multilateralism (e.g., strategic nuclear arms control involving China; CTBT; the MTCR).

Fourth, China's cautious approach to some arms control measures is motivated at least in part by very pragmatic factors: a concern over intrusive inspections, fears of freezing China into a permanent position of inferiority regarding certain weapons and technologies, and purely logistical and procedural problems, such as a shortage of trained people or a lack of expertise in negotiating and implementing arms control agreements.

Fifth, China's existing record of arms control behavior does not show a clear pattern of noncompliance, partly because China has not been involved in or has yet to enter into regimes with strict verification or compliance procedures that would enable easy measurement against an established compliance standard. At the low-cost end, China has little difficulty providing reports to the U.N. arms registry or complying with its commitments under the South Pacific, Latin American, African Nuclear Weapons Free Zones, and Outerspace and Seabed treaties. The compliance questions raised by the United States focus mostly on the NPT and the MTCR, the latter an agreement in which China is not formally a member and which is enforced unilaterally by domestic American law rather than internationally agreed-upon sanctions. These examples alone would suggest that Chinese compliance is, on average, likely to be higher on high-cost or high-stakes issues when these are addressed in formal multilateral agreements.

Sixth, China's development of an arms control community presents opportunities for encouraging a less-opportunistic or less–zero-sum approach to arms control. Although by no means a predominant voice, contacts with the foreign arms control community have encouraged the development of views supportive of common security, minimum deterrence, and the normative value of compliance with extant commitments.

## Recommendations

The following general recommendations on how to improve constructive engagement with China on arms control follow from the preceding analysis.

The challenge for the United States and the world community is to find more effective ways of addressing Chinese security concerns while involving China as a more committed stakeholder in the future security environment, at both conventional and WMD levels. This will require:

- Better communication by the United States of its preferred future strategic role for China and by China of its short- and long-range strategic concerns, through a permament, regular (preferably annual) bilateral security dialogue leading to a set of security and arms control understandings between the two powers. This dialogue should aim to bring together on both sides as many actors from different agencies as possible. It should focus on encouraging and expanding interagency coordination on the Chinese side while enhancing the authoritativeness of the Ministry of Foreign Affairs in this process. It should move progressively toward a technical level so that both sides focus bureaucratic resources on developing an understanding of technical and doctrinal issues at the heart of the future global arms control agenda. On the U.S. side, the lead on arms control policy might be taken by the Arms Control and Disarmament Agency so as to encourage the organizational and political development of China's emerging counterpart organization (the Arms Control and Disarmament Department), thus tipping the interagency balance in favor of arms controllers drawn from the Ministry of Foreign Affairs and the technical community.

- More determined efforts by the United States and Russia to reduce the strategic weapons inventories amassed during the cold war. A determined effort to move to a START III will compel both the United States and China finally to come to terms with the role of nuclear weapons in the post–cold war era. START III levels almost certainly will require the adoption of some form of minimum deterrence strategy by the United States. This will meet the conditions China has set for putting its nuclear forces on the negotiating table. START III negotiations thus should be a prelude to, or develop in parallel with, a Perm Five strategic nuclear arms negotiation, thus putting pressure on China to restrain its nuclear force modernization. A Perm Five nuclear arms negotiation also will allow for a more credible discussion of no-first-use with the Chinese. Any such negotiations will have to focus on the verification of NFU through, for instance, detailed discussion of deterrence stability, crisis stability, and nuclear use doctrine. Greater transparency on these sorts of issues not only would improve the bilateral and multilateral political atmosphere but also would ensure that first use was a relatively low probability. Thus the condition for placing a Chinese issue, NFU, on the Perm Five agenda will be Chinese transparency on doctrinal and operational issues, Chinese adherence to a multilateral strategic arms agreement, and the explicit adoption of a minimum deterrence strategy.[70] This suggests that the United States and China probably will have to think about how to ensure that both sides' nuclear forces are purely for second-strike purposes. The U.S. push for the development of national missile defense capabilities and any Chinese missile defense programs as well are incompatible with this goal.

- An increased sensitivity by the United States and its allies in Asia toward the unintended effects of U.S. security policies (e.g., deployment of strategic-capable theater missile defense systems) that could pressure the Chinese to accelerate their nuclear program. In general, any serious, ongoing U.S.-China security dialogue should include both arms control and ballistic and theater missile defense issues. The development of a credible dialogue with China in the latter area requires a thorough reappraisal of the security costs and benefits of missile defenses. It also must include an evaluation of alternative means of addressing potential missile proliferation. The security costs of planned U.S. missile defense systems are likely to be higher and the security benefits lower than is assumed by proponents of missile defense. It is hard to believe that China will accept U.S. development and deployment of BMD/TMD without a response. Under present conditions, the likely Chinese response will be to increase warheads and delivery vehicles and to develop countermeasures (e.g., chaff, decoys, reduction of the radar and infrared signatures of reentry vehicles). The credibility of the American effort to compel China to abide by arms control commitments is not likely to be enhanced if the United States is perceived as violating or circumventing the antiballistic missile treaty by developing and deploying THAAD systems or a national missile defense system. In general, the United States needs to be more self-reflective about the consistency of its approaches to many arms control agreements, commitments, and norms. For example, F-16 aircraft are, under some circumstances, more efficient platforms for delivering weapons of mass destruction than Chinese ballistic missiles.[71]

- Increased CBMs, such as a wide range of bilateral and multilateral exchanges, including military-to-military interactions and exchanges. While symbolic exchanges between senior military officers, heads of military academies, ship visits, and the like are important indicators of the state of play in the political relationship, ritualistic contacts between top military or political officials alone will not do much to reduce pressures to escalate if or when the United States and China are next in a militarized crisis.[72] A more stable, cooperative military-to-military relationship must be established through the creation of a durable set of organizational and personal incentives extending throughout both military establishments. Functional exchanges should appeal to the core interests of important military departments on each side, in order to ensure an ongoing commitment of their financial, personal, and organizational resources to the Sino-U.S. military relationship. In addition, specific topics and fora should serve to facilitate the emergence of extensive networks between the two sides, especially at middle and lower levels.

Interactions and exchanges should occur in several general areas. Visits by senior officers (e.g., commander-in-chief, Pacific forces) should include the development of an agenda for discussion of issues of mutual interest to air, ground, and naval components under their command. At lower levels, dialogues and visits in functional areas of mutual interest such as military medicine, drug trafficking, military justice, naval- and ground-based search and rescue, piracy, disaster relief, storage and restoration of military equipment, logistics and long-range planning, and force demobilization should be considered.[73] In addition, on the Chinese side, exchanges should focus on further developing expertise in the Chinese military academy system and in the General Staff Department on CBMs, joint crisis management techniques, international law and armed conflict, and U.N. and regional peacekeeping operations. These exchanges also should, to the extent possible, bring in Foreign Ministry experts from the Arms Control and Disarmament and Asia departments (which now handle global arms control and regional CBM issues, respectively) so as to encourage the development of a technical expertise on these issues in the civilian bureaucracy. On the U.S. side, exchanges should focus on developing among U.S. military planners an expertise in Chinese military doctrine and capabilities, modern Chinese nationalism, and post-Mao reforms. The "expertise gap" is formidable, with the number of genuine experts on U.S. military affairs in China outnumbering those with both a deep area knowledge and functional expertise in the United States. These exchanges also should include the gaming of hypothetical crises or historical cases of interstate crises. Both sides need to be clear about how each responds to an intense challenge to core values within a short time frame. The United States should persist in efforts to set up joint crisis management exchanges with Beijing. Formal crisis management and preventive diplomacy agreements also should be put on the bilateral agenda.[74] These proposals should be framed in a language that does not imply an automatic symmetry between U.S.-China relations today and U.S.-Soviet relations during the cold war, however.

In order to use targeted sanctions more effectively or to issue linkages to encourage Chinese participation in or compliance with arms control endeavors, the United States needs to greatly sharpen and prioritize its policy objectives toward China. The use of negative sanctions also will be more effective and justifiable if done according to international or multilateral agreement rather than on the basis of American domestic law. More fundamentally, such sanctions will require much more sophisticated study of the degree to which they have worked in the past. As yet there has been no effort to trace through the relationship between unilateral American threats of punishment or offers of side payments on one hand and Chinese compliance on the other.[75]

China's concern with image suggests that critical global arms control processes should be conducted in high-profile, authoritative multilateral institutions such as the Conference on Disarmament, rather than in low-profile or secretive bilateral negotiations such as the MTCR. This will not be easy, since China is leery of engaging in many multilateral arms control processes precisely because it knows that such processes are likely to be the most effective in limiting its military capabilities. But once these issues are on the international agenda, China is loath to back out even when the process is not necessarily in its military interests. The CTBT and CWC are good cases in point. The United States is a critical actor in defining the international arms control agenda. Thus it needs to focus more resources and attention on multilateral arms control that takes into account the impact on Chinese capabilities. The United States should actively support China's formal membership in a nondisciminatory, internationally enforced MTCR and in the Nuclear Suppliers Group, and China should be invited to all multilateral discussions of nuclear safety among the major industrialized powers. The same principle applies for regional arms control. To the extent that the ARF gradually adopts stricter templates for "defense white papers" or begins discussion of some of the contractual CBMs that China agreed to in the five-power treaty with Russia and three central Asian states, China will be compelled to accept the new agenda; the image costs of turning its back on the forum are too high to ignore at the moment.

The growth of China's arms control community and its expanding links with its foreign governmental and nongovernmental counterparts might help produce greater Chinese support for common security approaches. Hence the United States, other states supportive of arms control processes, and nongovernmental organizations should encourage and facilitate both official and unofficial contacts and exchanges in this area. Funding is an important issue here. For example, the development of arms control training programs in China's Foreign Affairs College would help develop an arms control expertise in the Ministry of Foreign Affairs, as the college is one of the primary sources of ministry recruits. Bringing arms control experts from the uniformed military to Western universities, and providing research materials and templates for arms control research projects ongoing inside China, also would be a valuable investment. The relevant military units include the General Staff Department (GSD) and subdepartments, the Academy of Military Science Strategic Research Department, the National Defense University Strategic Studies Institute (the last two of which have relatively new arms control research programs), and, ideally, the Strategic Missile Forces Command College. Finally, funding is needed for research and recruitment in the technical arms control community in COSTIND (e.g., the Arms Control and Disarmament Program under the China Defense Science and Technology Information Center), in the new arms control office in the Institute of Applied Physics and Computational Mathematics, and in the aerospace community. Arms control is not an especially attractive career move for smart scientists just out of college, given the opportunities to sell their skills in the market economy. But it can be more attractive if travel, conference, and training opportunities are available.

Chinese sensitivity regarding fissile materials production suggests that the United States and Russia should consider placing a significant amount of their existing fissile material stocks, including material from dismantled warheads, under international safeguards. Doing so would reduce the amounts available to both powers and thus address China's concerns that an FMPC convention does not affect its capabilities, given its huge stockpiles. It also would establish a bilateral precedent for a multilateral FMPC II that managed existing stockpiles, thus placing even greater constraints on China's option to increase the size of its nuclear forces.

The preceding recommendations indicate that a future multilateral arms control agenda that includes fissile material production controls, plus deep reductions in strategic nuclear weapons, strict ballistic missile controls, and tight restrictions on ballistic missile defense systems will place the maximum restraint on China's nuclear modernization. The existence and restrictiveness of these regimes depends on American initiative to put these onto the Conference on Disarmament agenda or into some separate Perm Five forum. Ultimately deep reductions in nuclear weapons and the promotion of nuclear stability as Chinese power grows rests to a large degree on fundamental decisions by the United States about the structure and purpose of its own weapons of mass destruction. Moreover, avoiding future political and military confrontations with China resulting from its acquisition of significant conventional naval and air power projection capabilities rests on a sustained U.S. commitment to the attainment of a strategic understanding with Beijing that could place limits on certain conventional capabilities on both sides. Unless it moves in the directions listed earlier, the United States hardly can expect China to accede to this agenda or to any other agenda that places restrictions on its military capabilities. China's response will be, as it has been in the past, that it is simply following the example of other great powers.

## Notes

The authors would like to express their deep thanks to Wendy Frieman, Paul Godwin, Bates Gill, and members of the study group on arms control for their comments, criticisms, and ideas. They would also like to thank those in the U.S. and Chinese policy communities who have provided invaluable insights and information but who prefer to remain nameless.

1. These points are largely taken from testimony by Kent Wiedemann, deputy assistant secretary of state for East Asian and Pacific affairs, before the Senate Foreign Relations Committee Subcommittee on East Asian and Pacific Affairs, July 25, 1995, and from a statement by Assistant Secretary of State Winston Lord before the House International Relations Committee, Asia and Pacific Affairs Subcommittee, February 9, 1995.

2. For an official U.S. government interpretation of the implications of China's military modernization programs, from which several of the following points are drawn, see the statement of Ambassador Winston Lord, Assistant Secretary of State, Bureau of East Asian and Pacific Affairs, before the Senate Foreign Relations Committee, Asia and Pacific Affairs Subcommittee, October 11, 1995.

3. Banning Garrett and Bonnie Glaser, "Chinese Perspectives on Nuclear Arms Control," *International Security* 20, No. 3 (Winter 1995–96): 43, 48. In anticipation of post-START III strategic arms control, the Chinese technical and military arms control community has been tasked with researching everything from verification of deep cuts to the effects of such cuts on China's nuclear strategy. Some of the conditions for Chinese participation in a deep-cuts regime, proposed unofficially, are likely to run into opposition from the United States (e.g., five-power no-first-use declarations, controls on ballistic missile defenses).

4. Shirley Kan and Zachary Davis, "China," in Mitchell Reiss and Robert Litwak, eds., *Nuclear Proliferation after the Cold War* (Washington, D.C.: Woodrow Wilson Center Press, 1994), pp. 146–47.

5. The interesting question is whether China's image concerns will diminish as its relative power grows. At times in the past U.S. diplomacy has appeared unconcerned about international opposition or praise. If China follows the American route, then the window of opportunity to manage Chinese behavior by playing on its image concerns may by limited.

6. Much of the following discussion of China's defense policy is drawn from Michael D. Swaine, *China: Domestic Change and Foreign Policy* (Santa Monica, Calif.: RAND, 1995), pp. 88–89; and Michael D. Swaine, "Strategic

Appraisal: China," in Zalmay Khalilzad, ed., *Strategic Appraisal 1996* (Santa Monica, Calif.: RAND, 1996), pp. 202–4.

7.  In 1985 Deng Xiaoping announced a "strategic decision" to shift the guiding doctrine of Chna's military modernization from preparation for an early, large-scale, and nuclear war to preparation for a somewhat more peaceful environment, where conflict would be limited to local, small-scale wars.

8.  Operation Desert Storm confirmed the obsolescence of the Maoist notion of People's War, centered largely on a protracted war of attrition against a massive conventional invasion, conducted by large numbers of slow-moving infantry and armor-led forces, backed by reserve and militia units engaged in guerrilla warfare. This doctrine relied essentially on the use of World War II–era ground warfare tactics involving huge numbers of foot soldiers (i.e., "the human factor"), largely armed with light weapons and deployed in mobile combat along a fluid front. In place of these features, weapons, technology, and systems for the rapid, coordinated deployment of smaller air, land, and naval forces are now viewed by most Chinese strategists as the decisive elements in modern warfare. See the articles on doctrine in the symposium on the People's Liberation Army, *China Quarterly* (June 1996).

9.  This is a wish list of desired capabilites. See Appendix A for further details on extant capabilities.

10. This paragraph is taken from Michael D. Swaine, "Chinese Military Modernization: Motives, Objectives, and Requirements," paper prepared for the Joint Economic Committee, United States Congress, Washington, D.C., July 1996.

11. For details, see "China: Arms Control and Disarmament," *Beijing Review* 38, No. 48 (November 27–December 3, 1995): 10–25; and Liu Huaqiu, "Evaluation and Analysis of China's Nuclear Arms Control Policy," *Xiandai Junshi* [CONMILIT], November 11, 1995, No. 226, pp. 15–18.

12. Robert Norris, Andrew Burrows, and Richard Fieldhouse, *Nuclear Weapons Databook. Volume Five: British, French, and Chinese Nuclear Weapons* (Boulder, Colo.: Westview Press, 1994), p. 372.

13. Beijing might perceive a need for a rapid increase in the number of deployed warheads to overwhelm a Asia-based TMD or a U.S.-based NMD system.

14. Alastair Iain Johnston, "Prospects for China's Nuclear Force Modernization: Limited Deterrence versus Multilateral Arms" *China Quarterly* (June 1996): 548–577. Also see Mark A. Stokes, "China's Strategic Modernization: Implications for U.S. National Security," USAF Institute for National Security Studies, October 1997.

15. Alastair Iain Johnston, "China's New 'Old Thinking': The Concept of Limited Deterrence," *International Security* 20, No. 3 (Winter 1995–96): 5–42.

16. Ibid.

17. A related concern is whether a U.S. TMD system deployed in Japan will reduce China's ability to deter any Japanese involvement in a conflict between the United States and China over Taiwan. If the penetrability of conventionally armed missiles, for instance, is degraded by TMD, some Chinese strategists believe that China will have no tools with which to coerce Japan into inactivity.

18. We have used tentative language to describe the apparent relationship between China's nuclear modernization program and the transition from a minimal to a limited deterrence strategic doctrine for several reasons. First, the Chinese government denies that it has adopted a doctrine of limited deterrence, even though such a doctrine is discussed frequently in Chinese written sources. Second, only recently have Chinese leaders and nuclear strategists begun to discuss explicitly the formulation of a nuclear weapons strategy. For decades China possessed no articulated nuclear doctrine. Minimum deterrence is a term used primarily by outside observers to describe China's historical approach to the use of nuclear weapons. Third, in the past nuclear weapons development in China apparently has been target- and technology-, not doctrinally, driven. Fourth, we have no understanding of the relationship between those who think about doctrine (e.g., in the Academy of Military Sciences, the National Defense University, or the Strategic Missile Forces Command College), those who draw up operational doctrine, those who make research and development and acquisition decisions, and political leaders who decide on use. It is possible that pro–limited warfighting arguments at the first and second levels do not get translated into policy choices at the third and fourth levels, largely because of the existence of major technological, financial, and political obstacles. Such disconnects occur in the U.S. case, so it is entirely possible that they also exist in the Chinese case. In any event, this question ought to be put on the top of the agenda in discussions on transparency between the United States and China. Finally, with its accession to the CTBT, China faces some new constraints on developing a limited deterrent—for example, limits on certain types of new warhead designs— although its last series of tests may have given it sufficient information to develop smaller warheads suitable for MIRVing. MIRVing would be consistent with a limited deterrence doctrine.

19. See Bobby Herman, "Norms and National Security: The Soviet Case," paper presented to SSRC Workshop on Norms and National Security, University of Minnesota, January 1994; Sarah E. Mendelson, "Internal Battles and External Wars: Politics, Learning, and the Soviet Withdrawal from Afghanistan," *World Politics* 45, No. 3 (April 1993): 327–351; Emanuel Adler, "The Emergence of Cooperation: National Epistemic Communities and the International Evolution of the Idea of Nuclear Arms Control," *International Organization* 46, No. 1 (Winter 1992); Andrei Kortunov, "Realism and Morality in Politics," in A. Gromyko and M. Hellman, eds., *Breakthrough: Emerging New Thinking* (New York: Walker, 1988), pp. 101–145;

Andrei Melville, "Nuclear Revolution and the New Way of Thinking," in ibid.; Janice Gross Stein, "Political Learning by Doing: Gorbachev as Uncommitted Thinker and Motivated Learner," *International Organization* 48, No. 2 (Spring 1994): 155–83.

20. On the concept of common security—originally explicated by the Palme Commission—see David DeWitt, "Common, Comprehensive, and Cooperative Security in Asia-Pacific," *CANCAPS Papers*, No. 3 (March 1994). On the norms of interaction among democracies, see Thomas Risse-Kappen, "Collective Identity in a Democratic Community: The Case of NATO," in Peter J. Katzenstein, ed., *The Culture of National Security: Norms and Identities in World Politics* (N.Y.: Columbia University Press 1996). For a discussion of rational reassurance strategies for status quo states, see also Lisa Martin, "The Rational Choice State," in John Gerard Ruggie, ed., *Multilateralism Matters: The Theory and Praxis of an Institutional Form* (N.Y.: Columbia University Press, 1993); and Charles Glaser, "Realists as Optimists: Cooperation as Self-Help," *International Security* 19, No. 3 (Winter 1994–95).

21. Garrett and Glaser, "Chinese Perspectives," esp. pp. 49–50.

22. See Celeste Wallander, *Balancing Acts: Security, Institutions, and German-Russian Relations after the Cold War* (Ithaca, N.Y.: Cornell University Press, 1999).

23. This is not unique to China: realpolitik is the predominant American approach to security outside of certain interactions with the Western democratic community. Indeed, there are obvious parallels between the predominant understandings of the international system that hold sway in China and those among American national security elites. The U.S. determination to maintain and enhance its military primacy in the post–cold war world is premised on a belief that the world is a dangerous place of uncertain threats, where a unilateral capacity to apply offensive forces is the basis of strategic security.

24. Wendy Frieman, "Introduction to Chronology of Chinese Arms Control Behavior" manuscript, p.1. Up to the mid-1980s, China argued that test bans that involved China were discriminatory and would serve only to consolidate the nuclear superiority of the superpowers.

25. Garrett and Glaser, "Chinese Perspectives," p. 46.

26. This list includes Chinese involvement in confidence- and security-building measures that are designed to reduce security anxieties but are not, strictly speaking, part of an arms control regime. The information on Chinese participation contained in this list is drawn from: Alastair Iain Johnston, "Learning versus Adaptation: Explaining Change in Chinese Arms Control Policy in the 1980s and 1990s," *China Journal* (January 1996): esp. 49–57; Garrett and Glaser, "Chinese Perspectives on Nuclear Arms Control," esp. pp. 47–48, 53; Lisbeth Gronlund, David Wright, and Yong Liu, "China and a Fis-

sile Material Production Cut-off," *Survival* 37, No. 4 (Winter 1995–96): 147–50; Kan and Davis, "China," pp. 147–52; Frieman, "Introduction to Chronology of Chinese Arms Control Behavior"; U.S. Government Accounting Office, "Export Controls: Some Controls over Missile-related Technology Exports to China Are Weak" (Washington, D.C.: GAO/NSIAD-95-82, April 1995).

27. Under the NPT, the five declared nuclear states can produce an unlimited amount of fissile material for weapons. India, Israel, and Pakistan are not NPT members, and their nuclear programs are not capped at present. A fissile material cutoff probably offers the best chance for drawing the undeclared nuclear weapons states into a nonproliferation regime, and for this China's participation is essential. India will not sign an FMPC convention unless China does, and Pakistan will not sign unless India does. China has halted production of fissile materials for weapons and taken some steps that would make it difficult to resume such production. Gronlund, Wright, Yong, "China and a Fissile Material Production Cut-off," pp. 147–48, 162.

28. Frieman, "Introduction to Chronology of Chinese Arms Control Behavior," p. 2.

29. Kan and Davis, "China," pp. 151–52; U.S. GAO, "Export Controls."

30. Garrett and Glaser, "Chinese Perspectives," esp. p. 47.

31. Frieman, "Introduction to Chronology of Chinese Arms Control Behavior," p. 9.

32. The United States announced in August 1996 that it would disband the U.S.-China Joint Commission on Defense Conversion, largely because of a lack of accomplishments. The Republican-controlled Congress also voted against providing the commission any funds.

33. For a detailed discussion of the expansion of China's arms control community, see Johnston, "Learning versus Adaptation" pp. 36–43; Garrett and Glaser, "Chinese Perspectives," esp. p. 45.

34. Again, it is important to stress that China is by no means an exception in this regard. Major powers usually follow realpolitik strategies in the national security and arms control arenas.

35. Frieman, "Introduction to Chronology of Chinese Arms Control Behavior," p. 1.

36. As indicated earlier, China has long asserted that it will never use nuclear weapons first and that it will never use nuclear weapons against a nonnuclear power.

37. Garrettt and Glaser, "Chinese Perspectives," pp. 53–60; Frieman, "Introduction to Chronology of Chinese Arms Control Behavior," pp. 5–7.

38. Garrettt and Glaser, "Chinese Perspectives," pp. 60–69. China is unlikely to be in a position in which first use of nuclear weapons would present an

advantage (although proponents of limited deterrence can think of situations in which an NFU pledge would be a disadvantage). China has no extended deterrence commitments to allies, as does the United States.

39. Deployment of national missile defense systems could drive China to offset this threat by increasing the size of its existing strategic forces and improving the quality of its nuclear warheads (MIRVs, etc.). Such efforts would, of course, then require China to reconsider its commitment to participate in further global arms control efforts with Russia and the United States. China thus opposes revision of the ABM Treaty to allow for expanded U.S. or Russian BMD systems or TMD in Asia, which China contends would violate the treaty. China is especially concerned that the THAAD (theater high-altitude air defense) system under development by the United States could be upgradable to defend against strategic ballistic missiles and thus threaten the viability of the Chinese nuclear deterrent. Ibid., pp. 73–74.

40. China also announced, after the completion of its last nuclear test in late July 1996, that it would observe the informal international moratorium on testing. China had indicated for many months prior to this announcement that it intended to stop testing by the end of 1996, although its official bargaining position left open the right to continue testing after signature and up until the treaty's entry into force.

41. India has argued for many years that the treaty would permit the five declared nuclear powers to maintain their nuclear superiority and at the same time prevent nonnuclear and undeclared nuclear powers from ever acquiring nuclear weapons to defend themselves. But it was not until after May 1996 that India insisted that it would not sign the CTBT unless it includes a timetable for strategic disarmament by the declared nuclear powers. See "India to Block Completion of Pact to Ban Nuclear Tests," *New York Times*, July 31, 1996, p. 4.

42. Some observers believe that the Chinese successfully completed, in July 1996, a series of tests of the sort of low-yield warheads that could be used for both MIRVed ICBMs and shorter-range tactical missiles. If true, China would have risked relatively little while improving its image considerably by dropping or shelving its major objections to the treaty. On the other hand, many Chinese nuclear weapons scientists and U.S. nuclear weapons specialists have noted that the treaty is a sacrifice, that it constrains China's options for warhead modernization in ways that U.S. options, with advanced in-lab and computer technologies, are not.

43. Kan and Davis, "China," p. 150.

44. Frieman, "Introduction to Chronology of Chinese Arms Control Behavior," p. 8; Kan and Davis, "China," pp. 150–51; and personal correspondence with Bates Gill.

45. Frieman, "Introduction to Chronology of Chinese Arms Control Behavior," p. 8; Kan and Davis, "China," pp. 153–54, 163. In July 1996 China reportedly

pledged to stop cooperating with nuclear facilities not under international safeguards.

46. Our thanks to Bates Gill for this point.

47. Johnston, "Learning versus Adaptation," pp. 49–51; Kan and Davis, "China," pp. 150–51.

48. Jonathan Pollack, "Chinese Policies towards Weapons of Mass Destruction in East Asia," pp. 12–14.

49. Ibid., p. 12.

50. China reportedly has provided a design for a 25-kiloton implosion device to Pakistan and has been helping Islamabad operate a uranium enrichment plant. It also reportedly supplied Pakistan with enough weapons-grade uranium to fuel two nuclear weapons. In 1986 China reportedly sold tritium to Pakistan. (Tritium is used to achieve fusion in hydrogen bombs and to increase the yield of tritium-boosted nuclear bombs.) Kan and Davis, "China," p. 148. For a more detailed and updated overview of Chinese nuclear cooperation with Pakistan as well as with Iran, Algeria, Iraq, and Syria, see Shirley A. Kan, "Chinese Proliferation of Weapons of Mass Destruction: Background and Analysis," *Congressional Research Service Report* 96-767 F, September 13, 1996, Library of Congress, Washington, D.C., pp. 27–36; and Shirley A. Kan, "Chinese Proliferation of Weapons of Mass Destruction: Current Policy Issues," *Congressional Research Service Report* 96-767 F, updated October 17, 1996, Library of Congress, Washington, D.C., pp. 4–5. These reports and other, similar studies suggest that China's nuclear cooperation with Pakistan presents the greatest potential case for Chinese noncompliance with the NPT.

51. See the testimony of Robert J. Einhorn, deputy assistant secretary of state for nonproliferation to the House of Representatives Committee on International Relations, February 4, 1998, in Northeast Asia Peace and Security, "Special Report," February 6, 1998.

52. Gronlund, Wright and Yong, "China and a Fissile Material Production Cutoff," pp. 151, 162.

53. For example: (1) China has produced domestic legislation to spell out the legal obligations of chemical firms and laboratories for compliance with treaty provisions; (2) it agreed to and accepted three CWC-related inspections at the end of 1997; and (3) it participated in the international lab tests to prepare for treaty verification. Frieman, "Introduction to Chronology of Chinese Arms Control Behavior," p. 3; personal correspondence with Bates Gill.

54. See Kan, "Chinese Proliferation of Weapons of Mass Destruction: Background and Analysis," pp. 37, 40.

55. Frieman, "Introduction to Chronology of Chinese Arms Control Behavior," pp. 2–4.

56. Both quotes are taken from U.S. Government Accounting Office, "Export Controls," p. 1. At present, 25 states are formal partners to the MTCR, while

an additional 7 states, including China, have adhered or declared an intention to adhere to the MTCR guidelines.

57.  U.S. Government Accounting Office, "Export Controls"; Frieman, "Introduction to Chronology of Chinese Arms Control Behavior," pp. 4–5.

58.  Frieman, "Introduction to Chronology of Chinese Arms Control Behavior," p. 4; Kan, "Chinese Proliferation of Weapons of Mass Destruction: Background and Analysis," p. 19.

59.  This paragraph and the one following it are drawn from U.S. Government Accounting Office, "Export Controls," pp. 1–4, 16–17; and Frieman, "Introduction to Chronology of Chinese Arms Control Behavior," pp. 4–5. The former source also states (p. 17): "Under the terms of its October 1994 commitment, China and the United Stated will conduct in-depth discussions concering a Chinese commitment to the current MTCR guidelines and annex and prepare the way for eventual Chinese MTCR membership."

60.  For a detailed summary of Chinese policy and behavior regarding the MTCR in the specific context of the alleged missile shipments to Pakistan, see Kan, "Chinese Proliferation of Weapons of Mass Destruction: Background and Analysis," pp. 17–25.

61.  Shirley Kan's detailed treatment of the record leads her to conclude that "there has been no determination that China transferred complete missiles which exceed MTCR guidelines, since the 1987 sale of CSS-2 IRBMs to Saudi Arabia or since China first promised to abide by the MTCR in 1992." See ibid., p. 42.

62.  Kan and Davis, "China," p. 152.

63.  Johnston, "Learning versus Adaptation"; and Liu Huaqiu, "Evaluation and Analysis of China's Nuclear Arms Control Policy," pp. 15–18.

64.  For example, the convention does not prohibit the use of nondetectable mines, the provisions for remotely delivered mines are not strong enough, the provisions on the use of hand-enplaced mines are too weak, and it has no effective implementation or monitoring mechanism. See International Committee of the Red Cross, "Anti-Personnel Mines: Not an Indispensable Weapon of High Military Value," communication to the press, Geneva, March 28, 1966. This document states that, given the above flaws, "the 1980 Convention has had little or no effect on the use of anti-personnel mines in recent conflicts."

65.  On the role of transnational activities by nongovernmental organizations in the transmission of "new knowledge," see Peter Haas, "Introduction: Epistemic Communities and International Policy Coordination," *International Organization* 46, No. 1 (Winter 1992): 1–35; Adler, "The Emergence of Cooperation," pp. 101–145; and Matthew Evangelista, "The Paradox of State Strength: Transnational Relations, Domestic Structures, and Security Policy in Russia and the Soviet Union," *International Organization* 49, No. 1 (Winter 1995). For the clearest enunciation of common security with Chinese characteristics and the notion of mutual security, see "Chinese Paper

at the ARF-ISG-CBMs in Brunei," November 3–5, 1997, p. 3. This is not to suggest that there are no participants in the Chinese policy process who view the ARF as a useful realpolitik tool for balancing U.S. influence in the region. Clearly there are, but as a general observation, the strongest proponents of "mutual security" are not those who are the strongest advocates of reducing the U.S. military presence in East Asia.

66.   Our thanks to Paul Godwin, who also provided some valuable suggestions regarding the recommendations section.

67.   Some Chinese strategists claim that China's NFU pledge is a real operational constraint on its nuclear forces: it makes China more vulnerable to a first strike than it would be absent NFU. This is impossible to verify, as we have no information about China's operational nuclear plans.

68.   This at least suggests that possible Chinese proliferation behavior regarding Pakistan might be sui generis in nature, reflecting China's unique political relationship with a long-standing strategic ally in a critical region on its southern flank.

69.   China's concern with its international image is also arguably part of its overall realpolitik perspective; that is, it could reflect the desire of a weak state facing highly industrialized powers such as the United States and Japan to avoid alienating potential political supporters in the international community. This concern is listed separately, however, because historical and cultural factors (e.g., the traditional role of the Confucian state as moral exemplar to other states, China's humiliation at the hands of imperialist powers, and the aspirations to Third World leadership of the Chinese Communist Party) greatly accentuate Chinese sensitivity in this area. Moreover, many internal arguments for participation are put in terms of sui generis status enhancement, not in terms of instrumental reputation.

70.   NFU is a controversial subject in the U.S. strategy community. There is strong opposition to abandoning the right to first use. Moreover, the constraints on first use have been loosening in the post–cold war period. The United States threatened nuclear use against Iraq if Iraq used chemical weapons. Previously the United States stated it would not use nuclear weapons against a nonnuclear state unallied with another nuclear state. This would have excluded Iraq as a target of nuclear use in the post-Soviet world. This expansion of the U.S. conditions under which it might use nuclear weapons, however, only undermines the already shaky taboo against nuclear use at a time when real nuclear disarmament is a reality. It is also likely to be read by Chinese strategists as a justification of nuclear utility concepts in China. On the other hand, if American and European reports of Iraqi use or deployment of WMD are accurate, then the U.S. threat was probably not credible. As for the extended deterrence arguments against NFU, as past U.S. presidents have admitted, first use under the auspices of extended deterrence was not entirely credible during the cold war because it was unlikely the United States would sacrifice Chicago

for Bonn. It is hard to see how first use is any more credible or militarily necessary in the absence of a superpower threat such as the Soviet Union posed during the cold war.

71. For a detailed discussion of these issues, see Lisbeth Gronlund, George Lewis, Theodore Postol, and David Wright, "Highly Capable Theater Missile Defense and the ABM Treaty," *Arms Control Today* (April 1994): 3–8; and Gronlund, Wright and Yong, "China and a Fissile Material Production Cut-off." A major obstacle to a serious U.S. arms control dialogue with China in both WMD and conventional weapons areas is the perceived American interest in maintaining (or, in some istances, expanding) the U.S. margin of military superiority over all potential challengers (e.g., through NATO expansion, narrowly defined concepts of counterproliferation, national missile defense plans). This suggests that issues of concern to China, such as ballistic missile defense or U.S. military intentions in East Asia (including the relationship with Japan and Taiwan), are off the table. This is unlikely to change, but Washington should at least be sensitive to the effects of U.S. military power on Chinese security calculations.

72. Indeed, military interactions could erode confidence and goodwill if the expectations of one or both parties are persistently frustrated by the process. This is what appears to be happening at present: while the U.S. side often shows visiting Chinese officers the most advanced weapons and facilities in the U.S. military, Beijing is unwilling to provide reciprocal access to its armed forces to visiting U.S. officers. In addition, the Chinese are extremely reluctant to engage in a genuine working-level strategic dialogue with the United States or to permit more functional-oriented dialogues among officers at lower levels. While it is unrealistic, and unnecessary, for the United States to demand symmetrical reciprocity from the Chinese side, Beijing should nonetheless understand that the value of military-to-military ties lies primarily in the political arena and hence that a perceived lack of reciprocity will likely strengthen domestic U.S. opposition to a more expansive level of engagement with China.

73. Sino-U.S. functional exchanges in the areas of disaster relief, piracy, and drug trafficking are likely activities for integration into the multilateral arena, in coordination with other regional states. In addition, visits by Chinese military personnel to U.S. peacekeeping training centers could lead to discussions of the establishment of a joint peacekeeping training center for the region.

74. A recent U.S.-PRC agreement for handling incidents at sea could evolve into a permanent structure for dispute resolution. It also could serve as a basis for the development of regular contacts between senior and midlevel naval officers on both sides, which should be a major goal of the relationship, given China's growing maritime capabilities.

75. For some suggested policy sanctions and trade-offs, see Kan and Davis, "China," pp. 159–60.

# 4

# China and the International Human Rights Regime

## ANDREW J. NATHAN

THE CHINESE government is an active participant in the international human rights regime. It has acceded to nine human rights conventions, participates in the U.N. Human Rights Commission, and has stated its respect for international human rights law, including the Universal Declaration of Human Rights (UDHR). In late 1997 China signed the International Covenant on Economic, Social and Cultural Rights, and in 1998 it signed the International Covenant on Civil and Political Rights. As China responds to the human rights diplomacy of other states and tries to influence the future evolution of the international human rights regime, questions relating to the application and implementation of the regime form a major focus of its diplomatic activity.

## The International Human Rights Regime and Chinese Participation

The concept of human rights is associated with the rise of capitalism and liberal democracy. But when socialist states and Third World authoritarian regimes participated in drafting the documents that defined the postwar international human rights regime, the documents delinked the human rights idea from these historical associations. Although the international regime is incompatible with institutions that are totally unfree, it does not require particular kinds of political or economic systems. Human rights is today an international idea, not a code word for Westernization.

The benchmark of international human rights law is the Universal Declaration of Human Rights, adopted by the United Nations General Assembly on December 10, 1948. This is a declaration of principles, which does not require the accession of states to come into effect. In recent years the Chinese government has asserted its respect for the declaration and referred to it as a standard for favorably evaluating its own human rights performance.

In 1966 the General Assembly adopted the International Covenant on Economic, Social and Cultural Rights and the International Covenant on Civil and Political Rights, which converted the UDHR into legally binding treaties. Both entered into force in 1976, after ratification by a sufficient number of countries. China gave favorable commentary on the covenants in the mid-1980s, and the 1984 Sino-British Joint Declaration committed China to allow them to continue in force in Hong Kong for 50 years after China's takeover of the former British colony in 1997. China now has signed the economic covenant and the political one. It has the right to enter reservations against either and then needs to ratify both in order to give its accession legal effect.

The Chinese government has its own interpretations of the meaning, scope, and limits of human rights. But regarding the international human rights regime itself, its declaratory policy since 1991 has been increasingly affirmative. In its first human rights white paper, issued that year, the government acknowledged the "international aspect" of human rights. At the United Nations on January 31, 1992, Premier Li Peng stated, "China values human rights and stands ready to engage in discussion and cooperation with other countries on an equal footing on the question of human rights."[1] In his Government Work Report in March 1992, Li stated, "We believe that the human rights and fundamental freedoms of all mankind should be respected everywhere. . . . China agrees that questions concerning human rights should be the subject of normal international discussion."[2]

In April 1994 Foreign Minister Qian Qichen declared, "China respects the Universal Declaration of Human Rights, the Proclamation of Teheran, the Declaration on the Right to Development, and other international documents related to human rights."[3] In a second human rights white paper, issued in December 1995, the government stated, "China respects the purposes and principles of the Charter of the United Nations related to the promotion of human rights and fundamental freedoms. In recent years China has, as always, actively supported and participated in international activities in the human rights field and has made new efforts to promote the healthy development of international human rights since the cold war."[4] And in his press conference with President Clinton in

October 1997, Chinese President Jiang Zemin stated, "[It] goes without saying that, as for general rules universally abided by in the world, China also abides by these rules."[5]

The international human rights regime has become increasingly detailed, underscoring its applicability to states with different kinds of political, economic, and legal systems. Nations have negotiated at least 25 major human rights covenants, conventions, and protocols, as well as a host of more specialized instruments. China has acceded to 9: the Convention on Prevention and Punishment of the Crime of Genocide; the Convention Relating to the Status of Refugees; the Protocol Relating to the Status of Refugees; the International Convention on the Elimination of All Forms of Racial Discrimination; the International Convention on the Suppression and Punishment of the Crime of Apartheid; the Convention on the Elimination of All Forms of Discrimination against Women; the Convention against Torture and Other Cruel, Inhuman, or Degrading Treatment or Punishment; the International Convention on the Rights of the Child; and the Convention Concerning Equal Remuneration for Men and Women Workers for Work of Equal Value. China also has ratified a number of key International Labour Organization (ILO) conventions relating to workers' rights.

Many human rights conventions establish special bodies for enforcement. In addition, the U.N. Human Rights Commission works through specialized rapporteurs and working groups ("thematic mechanisms"). These mechanisms function by reporting and asking governments for reports, and have no other enforcement powers. China has submitted reports to U.N. bodies in keeping with the requirements of conventions it has signed, although human rights groups have evaluated the reports as deficient. On the recommendation of the 1993 Vienna World Conference on Human Rights, the U.N. General Assembly established the office of a human rights commissioner. The recently appointed second commissioner, Mary Robinson, made her first official visit to China in late 1998.

The international human rights regime is conducted partly through dialogue among governments. The right of governments to express concern about each other's rights performance is well established. China frequently responds to human rights–related comments and inquiries from other states and has entered into formal human rights dialogues with a number of governments, including those of the United States, Australia, Canada, several European countries, and the European Union. The use of trade or other sanctions to punish violations is more controversial. U.S. practice in this area has been more assertive than that of other countries. The United States promoted the application of sanctions to South Africa and the imposition of sanctions against China for the 1989 Tiananmen massacre. China argues against linking human rights and economic issues. But it has not argued that sanctions for human rights violations are illegal under international law, and it voted for U.N.-mandated sanctions on South Africa.

In the official Chinese view, normally it is up to each sovereign state to oversee its own fulfillment of international human rights standards. But in academic discussions scholars in law departments and institutes have acknowledged that in certain cases the concerns of the international community override the domestic jurisdiction of states. Some say that a human right becomes of international concern when a sovereign state enters into treaties or otherwise undertakes to subject itself to international law with regard to the particular right. Others variously cite, as valid objects of international intervention, violations that are heinous, "large-scale, gross," and that constitute international crimes, such as genocide, apartheid, or violations occurring in consequence of invasion or military occupation; violations that threaten the peace and security of neighboring countries or the world, such as aggression, racial discrimination, and international terrorism; violations that create flows of refugees; violations of the rights to self-determination or development (which Chinese theorists consider human rights); violations constituting colonialism and neocolonialism, hegemonism, racial segregation, or slavery; and violations committed by Nazi, fascist, or militarist states or forces.

Such discussions leave room in theory for China to back international intervention in some possible future human rights calamity. But they have little application to Chinese diplomacy today. Their common theme is that the international human rights regime should be used to oppose fascism, hegemonism, and imperialism but not to interfere in the internal affairs of socialist and Third World countries, such as China. The literature is not explicit about what forms international intervention may legitimately take.

The international human rights regime also includes nongovernmental organizations (NGOs) that monitor the performance of governments (and sometimes of political movements out of power). The most important groups are Western-based, but human rights NGOs recently have emerged in the developing world as well. By publicizing abuses (a strategy known as stigmatization), human rights NGOs seek to mobilize psychological and political pressure against violators. Most of the organizations deal with many countries and many kinds of rights issues. Among those that have given attention to China are the Fédération Internationale des Droits de l'Homme, Freedom House, Amnesty International, Human Rights Watch, the International League for Human

Rights, the Lawyers Committee for Human Rights, and the Committee to Protect Journalists.

Organizations focusing specifically on China include Human Rights in China (New York–based, and consisting chiefly of Chinese citizens) and several organizations concerned with human rights in Tibet. In 1993 China established its own nominally nongovernmental human rights organization, the China Society for the Study of Human Rights. Headed by former New China News Agency chief Zhu Muzhi, the association has entered the international propaganda fray with counterattacks on Western criticisms of Chinese policies and denunciations of U.S. human rights abuses.

Chinese policymaking on international human rights issues follows the same pattern as policymaking on other foreign policy issues. The most complex and politically sensitive problems are decided by the top leader; for example, so far as we know Deng Xiaoping personally super-vised the management of the Wei Jingsheng case until he became too ill to do so. Other important policies are decided at the level of the Polit-buro Standing Committee and the State Council. The Information Office of the State Council issued China's white papers on human rights. The Ministry of Foreign Affairs manages representation on human rights at the United Nations and other diplomatic venues.

A circle of study groups and university-based human rights research projects surrounds the central policymaking and implementing institu-tions. The most influential is located at the Institute of Law of the Chinese Academy of Social Sciences. Some of these institutions have received Ford Foundation support and sent personnel for short- and long-term study in the West. Some studies are provided in "internal" (*neibu*) form, while others are published in specialized periodicals and books. In informing the central authorities about foreign thinking on human rights law, academics often have argued that the Chinese gov-ernment should adopt a more proactive, affirmative position in its human rights diplomacy. These views have had visible effect on the evolving official stance. But the scholars operate under central leader-ship and never publicly dissent from government policy.

Human rights is different from most other foreign policy issues (but similar to foreign economic policy) in that it has numerous links with domestic policy. The prison authorities under the Ministry of Justice are involved with prisoner mistreatment and export of prison labor prod-ucts, both issues that have figured in China's human rights diplomacy. The Ministry of Civil Affairs runs the system of state orphanages, which was the object of human rights criticism. Similarly, many other govern-ment agencies are involved in issues that have arisen or might arise in human rights diplomacy. Human rights is an international regime whose implementation or violation takes place almost entirely at home.

## International Concerns and Chinese Performance

Few foreign concerns about Chinese human rights involve social, economic, and cultural rights. This is partly because the Chinese government has performed creditably in this area, especially since the initiation of Deng Xiaoping's reforms. Living standards have increased, compulsory education has been extended to nine years, housing stock has improved, and in major cities many residents lead comfortable lives. Adult literacy stands at 79 percent according to official figures, and at 69, life expectancy exceeds that in many middle-income countries. For such reasons, the United Nations Development Programme (UNDP) has assigned China a middle-range ranking on its "human development index" that places it far above its ranking in terms of per-capita gross national product.

Yet recent evidence suggests that the Chinese performance in social, economic, and cultural rights is not as good as has widely been thought. A new World Bank study finds that more than 250 million Chinese live in conditions of grinding poverty.[6] Violation of many social and economic rights was essential to the Maoist project of industrializing through expropriation of surplus from the peasantry. Deng's reforms reversed some of these policies but also have dismantled some of Mao's socialist-style welfare provisions. Poorer Chinese face declining availability of medical care and education. Rural residents can enter the cities as migrant workers but are not allowed to transfer their legal residences and are subject to a variety of discriminatory practices. As accelerated reform of state-owned enterprises leads to more layoffs of Chinese workers, we may hear more about denial of urban welfare rights and suppression of independent trade unions. In short, more research needs to be done before we can evaluate the Chinese government's social and economic rights performance accurately.

For now, foreign and most Chinese criticisms center on political and civil rights. In this realm there are pervasive and systematic violations, many of them carried out as matters of government policy. The facts are seldom in dispute. There is a range of violations that are conducted by government agents, transgress China's international obligations, and are indefensible under even the most culturally relativist standards.

Although such violations sometimes are carried out under the color of Chinese law, often they transgress the clear face language of the

Chinese constitution, the law of criminal procedure, and other enactments. Egregious examples include the treatment of Wei Jingsheng, who after his release from a 15-year political conviction was arbitrarily detained for over a year, then given a second 14-year sentence for such innocent acts as purchasing stock in an art gallery, publishing articles in the Hong Kong and U.S. press, and meeting with U.S. Assistant Secretary of State John Shattuck, and finally was forced into exile; and the case of Wang Dan, who was kidnapped by government agents for over a year, then given a trial without adequate defense and sentenced to 11 years for such acts as publishing articles critical of the government and participating in a self-help group for dissidents; he also was forced into exile.

The major issues of recent international concern are as follows:

- The imprisonment or arbitrary detention for their political beliefs of people who have not used or advocated violence and/or such persons' forced exile. The victims include democracy movement activists arrested for such acts as writing articles and petitioning the National People's Congress (NPC), Tibetans detained for verbally supporting independence, Mongols detained for a cultural revival movement, people detained for protesting about personal grievances, and people accused of divulging state secrets for circulating publicly available information. Although many Chinese citizens have gained new liberties of personal movement and of private political expression under Deng's reforms, those who publicly criticize basic government policies continue to be denied their rights.

- Religious repression: arrests and beatings of adherents of the autonomous Catholic and Protestant movements; interference in freedom of religion through intrusive pratices of state registration and supervision of churches; detention of Tibetans for religious practices; and the house arrest of a six-year-old child who was designated by the Dalai Lama as the incarnation of the Panchen Lama. Such persons often are charged as counterrevolutionaries, yet in many instances they have carried out no counterrevolutionary acts.

- Problems related to criminal procedure: lack of procedural safeguards against police abuse, especially during the process of "shelter and investigation" (*shourong shencha*), when police hold suspects without indictment or notice to relatives; insufficient safeguards against unlimited detention without trial; failure to provide fair trials (no publicity, insufficient provision for notice to family and preparation of a defense, lack of a presumption of innocence); lack of independence of the judiciary; and the widespread use of "reeducation through labor" as a form of imprisonment at police initiative without benefit of trial. The 1995 Judges Law and 1996 amendments to the 1979 Criminal Procedure Law addressed some of these issues but did not resolve them.

- Torture and abuse of inmates of prisons and labor camps, and imposition of forced labor on inmates. The Chinese government has signed the convention against torture, has intermittently campaigned against the use of torture by police and jailers, and has reiterated the outlawing of torture in its 1994 Prison Law. But the practice remains prevalent. In the case of many political prisoners, apparently it is condoned by the central authorities. Prominent political prisoners mistreated in prison included Wei Jingsheng, Liu Gang, and Xu Wenli; those denied adequate medical care included Chen Ziming and Bao Tong.

- Forced resettlement, suppression of dissent, and violation of labor rights in connection with work on the Three Gorges dam project and—although less is known about them—in connection with other large infrastructure projects.

- Forced abortion and sterilization as part of population planning practices. These acts violate declared central government policy yet are carried out by local officials on what appears to be a widespread basis.

Other civil and political rights violations less noticed in the outside world include denial of the right to strike, denial of the freedom of the Chinese and foreign press, mistreatment of gays, eugenic practices, and state interference in the practice of Islam and Buddhism.

China's foreign policy also contends with a second category of issues, consisting of problems that have drawn foreign attention but whose status as rights violations is debatable in one way or another—because there is some question whether the practices are occurring, or whether the government can be held responsible for failing to end them, or in what way they violate international or domestic law. Such issues include the following:

- Capital punishment. Its use is not against international or Chinese law. Yet China uses the penalty exceptionally widely and with grossly inadequate safeguards. Moreover, international law considers public execution, still widely practiced in China, to be a violation of human dignity.

- Harvesting of organs from condemned prisoners for transplantation. Organ transplant does not violate international law, but in China the need for organs apparently leads to frequent violations of due process, and authorities seldom obtain donor consent. Commoditization of organs violates both Chinese government policies and the laws of some foreign countries.

- Kidnapping, trafficking, and abuse of women and girls. The government has campaigned against these practices. Nonetheless, they continue on a widespread basis, and some plausibly argue this is possible only with the cooperation of local officials.

- "Cultural genocide" in Tibet. Some argue that government intrusion into Tibetan religious institutions and the movement of non-Tibetan migrants into Tibet takes place on a scale that constitutes cultural genocide.

- Export of prison labor products to the United States. This violates American law but not international law. When the prison labor is compulsory, as appears to be the case in Chinese prisons and labor camps, it is prohibited by ILO conventions.

The international concern with human rights in China is selective in ways that reflect the political dynamics of the issue in the West. Politicians and human rights organizations respond to constituencies that are interested in some issues and not others. Yet the core issues involve rights that are unambiguously protected under the international regime and widely violated by the Chinese government. Although some of the items are questionable in one way or another, as a whole it is wrong to describe the core issues as constituting a "Western agenda" of doubtful validity under international law or doubtful relevance to Chinese values. Nor does the foreign agenda constitute a hidden program to overthrow the Chinese government. Human rights are a limited set of goals, independent of regime type and for the most part compatible with China's constitution, laws, and declared policies. The sometimes expressed notion that outsiders have no standing to criticize China until their own rights records are perfect makes little moral or political sense. Certainly it lacks a basis in international law, which, like any other kind of law, does not make a perfect record a precondition for a concerned government or NGO to accuse another government of lawbreaking.

It is often pointed out that the Chinese government is not the worst rights violator in the world. This is true, and the rights picture in China is better now than under Mao. But China is a major violator. Because of the secrecy of the Chinese political system and the limited manpower devoted to human rights research in the outside world, the error in outside estimates usually has turned out to be underestimation rather than overestimation of the extent of Chinese human rights abuses.

Rights violations are not all carried out or defended as a matter of state policy. In some cases the Chinese government does one thing and says another—not only internationally but also at home, where the constitution and laws contain relevant rights provisions. In some instances the government serves its propaganda needs by claiming to grant rights that, out of fear of political turmoil or economic cost, it actually denies (e.g., freedom of political speech). In other situations the government seems to lack the capacity or political will to correct violations of its stated policies by its own officials (e.g., abuse of prisoners, neglect of orphans, forced abortion and sterilization). Sometimes foreign policy authorities are unable to control domestic policy domains in which human rights violations occur, such as public security, civil affairs, and social welfare. As with intellectual property rights, market access, or weapons proliferation, the implementing bureaucracies are often located in other bureaucratic systems, or at lower levels of government, where they are able to take advantage of the decentralization of power to escape supervision. And yet—again just as with these other issues of regime compliance—it would be illogical not to hold the Chinese government as responsible as any other government for the acts of its agents.

## China's Management of the Human Rights Issue

From its earliest days the People's Republic of China (PRC) addressed human rights proactively as part of its foreign policy. In 1955 China acceded to the Bandung Conference Final Communiqué, which stated, "The Asian-African Conference declared its full support of the fundamental principles of human rights as set forth in the Charter of the United Nations and took note of the Universal Declaration of Human Rights as a common standard of achievement for all peoples and all nations."[7] In the 1950s and 1960s the PRC argued that sovereignty and self-determination were human rights and criticized as violators the United States, France, South Africa, and Israel, among others. In the 1960s and 1970s human rights featured prominently in Chinese polemics against the Soviet Union. The *People's Daily* ridiculed the Soviet constitution—on which in this regard the Chinese constitution was closely modeled—for granting rights and freedoms and then denying them to those who would use them to infringe on the interests of the regime.

After its admission to the United Nations in 1971, China played an increasingly active role in human rights diplomacy. In 1979 the PRC began to attend meetings of the U.N. Human Rights Commission as an observer, and in 1982 it was elected to the commission. China participated in the Subcommission on Prevention of Discrimination and Protection of Minorities and in working groups concerned with the rights of indigenous populations, freedom of communications, the rights of children, the rights of migrant workers, and the issue of torture. With other Third World countries, it promoted the idea of a "right to development," which the U.N. General Assembly enacted by resolution in 1986. China's representatives voted in favor of U.N. investigations into human rights violations in Afghanistan and Chile and denounced Israel, South Africa, Vietnam, Afghanistan, and other governments on human rights grounds.

It was not until the Beijing massacre of June 4, 1989, that China became a major target of other countries' human rights diplomacy. Many imposed sanctions, including diplomatic cold shoulders of one kind or another, cancellation of cultural exchanges, freezes on bilateral aid and loans, voting for temporary suspension of World Bank and Asian Development Bank loans, and interruption of military sales and links. The main sanctions were lifted starting in 1990, although several minor American sanctions remain in place at this writing. As sanctions were eased, Western governments and politicians felt it necessary to maintain verbal pressure. From 1991 onward an endless procession of important visitors made public and private representations on human rights, including the French prime minister, the Japanese prime minister, two Australian parliamentary delegations, many U.S. congressional delegations, a European Community (EC) delegation, the Polish foreign minister, a Canadian parliamentary delegation, a delegation of EC ambassadors visiting Tibet, and German Chancellor Helmut Kohl.

Industrialized nations gave sanctuary to refugee dissidents, and some gave permanent residency to Chinese visiting scholars and students. After 1989 China experienced a two-year decline in its credit rating, foreign investment, export orders, and tourism. The renewal of normal trading rights with the United States (most-favored-nation [MFN] privileges) was threatened annually from 1990 through 1994 by public and congressional desires to push China toward human rights improvements. In 1993 Beijing's bid to host the 2000 Olympics encountered international opposition on human rights grounds and was defeated.

China came under criticism in U.N. bodies concerned with human rights. In August 1989 the U.N. Subcommission on Prevention of Discrimination and Protection of Minorities adopted by secret ballot a resolution mildly critical of China, marking the first time that a permanent member of the Security Council had been censured in a U.N. forum for its human rights performance. The 1990 session of the Commission on Human Rights considered a resolution to condemn China, although the resolution was not adopted. No such resolution was offered in 1991, when the United States needed China's support in the Security Council for the Persian Gulf war. But similar resolutions came before the commission every year through 1997, in each case to be sidelined after Chinese lobbying. The efforts to defeat these resolutions became major foci of Chinese diplomacy, engendering intense negotiations with the United States and the European Union.

Chinese problems also were discussed at one time or another in reports or meetings of the United Nations' Special Rapporteur on Religious Intolerance, Working Group on Arbitrary Detentions, Special Rapporteur on Summary and Arbitrary Executions, Committee against Torture, Special Rapporteur on Torture, and Working Group on Enforced or Involuntary Disappearances. In 1996 the U.N. Committee on Torture, after hearing NGO reports, asked China to stop public executions, ensure the independence of the judiciary, and establish a system to investigate complaints of police brutality. The same year the U.N. Committee on the Rights of the Child urged China to combat infanticide of girls and expressed alarm over high mortality rates in state orphanages. The rapporteur on religious intolerance visited China in 1994 and the Working Group on Arbitrary Detention did so in 1997, each issuing reports critical of some major Chinese government policies.

Human rights arguably took an indirect toll on Beijing's bargaining position on other issues. In Sino-U.S. relations, Tiananmen, combined with the trade deficit and arms exports, created a synergy of anti-Beijing sentiments that thrust China's preferred priority issue, Taiwan, so far down the agenda of bilateral issues that it was hardly discussed, at least in public, until 1995. The anti-China atmosphere also weakened Beijing's negotiating position in talks over intellectual property rights and market access; in both negotiations, faced with the threat of trade sanctions, China made concessions to American demands. The fact that China was on the defensive on human rights weakened its ability to block American and French arms transfers to Taiwan and probably helped explain the replacement of a conciliatory Hong Kong governor with one who confronted Beijing on the issue of Hong Kong democratization. According to Michael Swaine, China's accession to the Nonproliferation Treaty (NPT) probably was accelerated by its desire to "deflect criticism of its nuclear export policy, especially in the aftermath of the broader criticism it received from the international community for its violent suppression of the Tiananmen demonstrations of June 1989." (See Chapter 3.) The international response to the Beijing massacre amplified the incident's impact in Hong Kong and Taiwan, helping spur the democracy movement in the former and independence sentiment in the latter.

Beijing's response to international human rights pressures demonstrated realism, central coordination, strategic consistency, and tactical flexibility. As in other areas of foreign policy, we lack "smoking-gun" central committee documents to demonstrate cause and effect; but as in analyses of other foreign policy areas, we can inspect the policy record to reach an informed interpretation of Beijing's goals and methods, and consequently of the impact of foreign pressure on Chinese policy. China's policy combined resistance and selective concessions, in a mixture designed simultaneously to rally Third World support, especially in multilateral settings, to appeal to advocates of realpolitik in the West, and to construct policy dilemmas for human rights advocates.

China mounted a variety of ideological counterattacks on its critics. First, official spokespersons pointed to a series of double standards: that China drew condemnation while other countries in which violations were in some sense worse (e.g., Israel, India) were ignored; that Westerners who said nothing about Mao's violations complained about less-severe violations under Deng; that prosperous Westerners insisted on immediate implementation of modern standards in a developing China; that the West itself had committed human rights violations at least as deplorable as those it was criticizing; and that the West continues to be rife with human rights problems from which it distracts attention by criticizing others. They alleged that the West's real motives were political, to weaken China internationally and domestically.

Second, Chinese spokespersons argued that cultural standards differ. No culture's concept of human rights has greater claim to be accepted than any other's. Thus the foreigner has no moral right to judge. Third, Chinese spokesmen raised the issue of sovereignty, arguing that problems foreigners consider human rights violations are matters of domestic Chinese law and, if they need fixing, are within the purview of the Chinese government to fix. Finally, the government argued that China's rights record was excellent, at least as good as its critics'. The rights to survival and development are better assured in China than in the West. Only by continuing to build socialism could such rights be further assured.

Such arguments garnered support from regional leaders such as Prime Minister Mohamad Mahathir of Malaysia and former Prime Minister Lee Kuan Yew of Singapore. At the same time, the cultural relativism, double standard, and national sovereignty arguments proved congenial to Americans of the realist school, who believed that a moralistic foreign policy was neither justified nor useful.

Propaganda arguments dovetailed with diplomatic activity carried out in conjunction with like-minded governments. For example, the 1990 U.N. Human Rights Commission meeting decided to shelve action on a motion dealing with human rights in China, after China gained either support or abstentions from the Soviet Union, Ukraine, Yugoslavia, Cuba, and most participating African and Latin American countries. In 1990 China helped block a Western initiative to establish an emergency mechanism to enable the Human Rights Commission to be called into session following a major event such as the Tiananmen massacre.

China cooperated with other governments to resist strengthening the international machinery. In 1992, for example, it joined the Philippines, Syria, and others to limit the mandate of the U.N. Special Rapporteur on Torture. In preparation for the 1993 Vienna World Conference on Human Rights, China worked with other Asian governments to promote the principles of noninterference in the internal affairs of states; nonselectivity (i.e., U.N. bodies should not single out specific countries for criticism); the priority of collective, economic, and social rights encompassed in the notion of a right to development; national sovereignty; and cultural particularism (the nonuniversality of human rights values across regions).

The Chinese government response to international human rights pressure also included hard-line actions on particular cases. Wei Jingsheng, the political prisoner given perhaps highest priority abroad, and certain other well-known prisoners were subjected to harsh treatment for years as if to make the point that international pressure was counterproductive. After his release in 1993 as part of Beijing's campaign to host the Olympics in 2000, Wei was redetained in 1994 along with his assistant, Tong Yi, a few weeks before President Clinton had to decide whether to extend most-favored-nation status; subsequently Wei was given another long jail term and subjected again to harsh prison treatment before his release into exile in 1997. Long sentences were handed out for political crimes to victims to whom the outside world paid relatively little attention and to exemplary cases such as Wang Juntao and Chen Ziming. In November 1992 China interrupted its dialogue with the United States on human rights issues, as a protest against F-16 fighter sales to Taiwan and a warning to incoming President Clinton. Selective use of hard-line measures helped sustain a Western policy debate on whether human rights pressure on China was productive.

While rhetorically and diplomatically rejecting human rights interference, the government at the same time offered a series of measured concessions. In 1990–1991, at times when such releases would affect the politics of MFN status in the U.S. Congress, Beijing announced the release of three batches of Tiananmen prisoners, totaling some 881 persons; lifted martial law in Beijing; permitted dissident Fang Lizhi to leave his refuge in the U.S. embassy to go abroad in 1990; agreed to initiate a human rights dialogue with U.S. officials; gave assurances to U.S. Secretary of State James Baker that Chinese citizens would not be prevented from going abroad for political reasons; and freed labor activist Han Dongfang in 1991 when he was in danger of dying in prison. The government supplied information on, and improved the treatment of, high-profile prisoners such as Wei Jingsheng, Wang Juntao, and Chen Ziming, subsequently released each of them, and allowed Wang and later Wei to leave the country for medical treatment.

In 1992 and again in 1994 China signed a memorandum of understanding with the United States to restrict export of prison labor products to this country. In 1993 and 1994, in the lead-up to the annual U.S. MFN decision, Beijing provided information to American diplomats on political prisoners and held inconclusive talks on prison visits with the International Committee of the Red Cross (ICRC). The regime gave passports to dissidents whose right to go abroad had been the subject of U.S. concern and to the family members of political exiles.

Beijing also moved further toward accepting human rights as a valid subject of international dialogue. China dispatched two human rights delegations to the West in 1991–1992 to engage in dialogue and gather information. In 1991 the State Council issued its first white paper on human rights, followed by white papers on the criminal law (1992), the situation in Tibet (1992), family planning (1995), and children's rights (1996), as well as second and subsequent editions on some topics. Although generally unyielding in tone, such documents were significant as a sign of willingness to respond to international concerns. As noted earlier, government statements on the binding nature of the international human rights regime became increasingly affirmative.

The most important effects of international pressure probably were to be measured in actions the regime did not take. In contrast to earlier practice, many dissidents taken into custody after 1989 were released without punishment. In connection with the 1989 demonstrations, death sentences and prison terms of 15 years or more were given exclusively to prisoners who for one reason or another had been virtually ignored by the outside world, mostly workers and intellectuals living in remote locations. The most likely explanation was the anticipated foreign as well as domestic reaction.

The government structured its concessions in such a way as to divide its critics. Productive results were tied to friendly and quiet intercessions, such as those by Japanese Prime Minister Toshiki Kaifu and pro-MFN U.S. businessman/activist John Kamm. Concessions were timed to provide cover for the resumption of World Bank lending in 1990, to reward Japan's renewal of lending under the Third Yen Loan Package, to help George Bush beat back congressional critics who tried to revoke or add conditions to MFN status, and to reward Bill Clinton's resumption of summit diplomacy with China in 1997–1998. Although China appeared to reward quiet diplomacy instead of public pressure, such diplomacy achieved its results only against the background of political and economic pressure.

While concessions to foreign pressure mostly involved individual cases or changes in rhetoric, they coincided with a more fundamental internal evolution in the direction of rule of law. The movement toward rule of law seemed motivated chiefly by the need for modern, predictable administration. The post-Mao construction of a legal system began in 1979 with the promulgation of a criminal code and other laws. It continued after 1989 with such benchmarks as the 1994 adoption of a prison law and 1996 revision of the Criminal Procedure Law. Other reform measures included strengthening the courts, cultivating a legal profession, gradually increasing the activity and authority of the National People's Congress, and initiating village-level competitive elections. Even though progress made on paper often remained to be implemented in practice, these developments were potentially important steps toward improving the human rights situation.

Foreign pressure would not have been as effective as it was if it did not push in the same direction as internal forces. By the same token, the internal forces for change might not have moved China as fast as they did without the support of outside actors. Some foreign actors preferred quietly to assist with educational and training expenses, while others vocally invited the attention of Chinese leaders to practices that were deficient by international standards. Both internal and external forces for change strengthened the influence of policy advisors with Western legal training. Reforms advocated by both external and internal constituencies included ending capital punishment, ending counterrevolutionary crimes, establishing a presumption of innocence, providing firmer guarantees of political and civil rights, providing earlier access to defense lawyers for criminal defendants, shortening police detention of suspects, ending administrative detention, punishing police abuse of prisoners, improving judicial independence, acceding to the two international human rights covenants—indeed, virtually the whole slate of foreign human rights concerns. Often it was foreign criticism that first brought these issues to the attention of domestic specialists or that motivated policymakers to seek expert opinions on them.

Such internal debates and changes disproved the sometimes-stated view that rights concepts lack cultural support in China. They showed that a strong constituency of Chinese lawyers, scholars, journalists, and party liberals accept the universality of human rights, the legally binding status of the international law of human rights, and the political wisdom of China's bringing its domestic practices into line with international human rights norms.

After the delinkage of human rights from MFN status in 1994 by President Clinton, human rights concessions slowed at both the verbal and the substantive levels, and retrogressions occurred in the area of political rights. Among other actions, the authorities reimprisoned Wei Jingsheng, Chen Ziming, Wang Dan, Liu Xiaobo, and other democratic activists; suspended talks on prison access with the International Committee of the Red Cross; made the Sino-U.S. human rights dialogue more infrequent and devoid of substance; violated the rights of attendees at the September 1995 Beijing Women's Conference; and heightened repression in Tibet, Xinjiang, and Mongolia. But the shift of American policy to "strategic dialogue" in 1996 and the subsequent exchange of summits brought renewed Chinese concessions, including acceptance of the two U.N. covenants and release into exile of several prominent political prisoners.

## Human Rights as Realpolitik

Human rights represent Western values, and no China policy that ignores them can achieve stable public support. But in addition, promotion of human rights serves Western interests. The West will do better in building not only the human rights regime but also other regimes if it recognizes China as a realist power and acts in a realist manner itself, not flinching from a consistent stand on behalf of its interests.[8] The first requirement of a successful China human rights policy thus is to clarify the nature of the West's (and China's) interests in Chinese human rights.

Since the end of the cold war the West has devoted increasing effort to strengthening international systems of rules in such areas as arms proliferation, trade, and the environment. The international human rights regime was one of the earliest regimes the world started building after World War II. This regime provides the framework for countries to intercede peacefully against domestic abuses in other states that have the potential for having serious international consequences. It has growing utility in the post–cold war world as part of an emerging new international order.

First, the theory of the "democratic peace" that goes back to Kant remains a good guide to policy, even though it is not universally accepted by political scientists. The exercise of political rights by citizens is conducive to reducing governmental misjudgments in foreign affairs and to a more peaceful, rational, and predictable foreign policy. Countries that respect the rights of their own citizens are less likely to start wars, export drugs, harbor terrorists, or generate refugees.

In China's case more specifically, respect for human rights is a precondition for peaceful resolution of the Taiwan issue and successful management of Hong Kong under PRC sovereignty. The human rights gap is a potential source of instability in both situations. Taiwan's president, Lee Teng-hui, cites human rights violations as a reason for his government's reluctance to accept unification. Hong Kong citizens protested the Wei Jingsheng and Wang Dan trials, were horrified when China's foreign minister said that their freedom of speech after 1997 would exclude the right to criticize mainland policy on dissidents, and remain sensitive to any signs that Beijing intends to interfere in their legal system now that Hong Kong has become a special autonomous region of China. A blowup in either situation will involve American and other Western interests. Besides its economic stake in both places, the United States is committed to peaceful resolution of the Taiwan issue by the Taiwan Relations Act (1979) and to supporting Hong Kong's freedom and prosperity by the McConnell Act (1992). In promoting human rights in China, the West helps prevent these situations from exploding in its face.

Second, China's stability and prosperity have been declared interests of the West since the Kissinger era. As often noted, a stable and prosperous China will anchor a stable Asia and contribute to global prosperity through trade. A corrupt, unstable, economically stagnant China will contribute to regional disorder, pollution, and refugee flows, and in the extreme case could heavily tax outside resources for relief. China's rapid development has created such a mobilized and sophisticated population that the government can no longer legitimize itself without allowing a measure of political freedom and participation, and without legitimacy its political stability is fragile. Repression testifies to the fragility of the regime, which sees a handful of peaceful dissenters as an intolerable threat to its survival. Long-term stability will elude the Chinese government until it honors the political freedoms recognized in all four of its own constitutions since the founding of the People's Republic. This argument has been propounded within China by party reformers since the mid-1980s. It is now being promoted by officials who are experimenting with village-level elections aimed at consolidating, not undermining, the power of the Chinese Communist Party.

Third, it is sometimes argued that human rights violations are a necessary, temporary trade-off to achieve economic development. But few

Chinese rights violations (e.g., mistreatment of prisoners, violations of due process) have any plausible link to development. The few that have—such as deprivations of freedom of speech and political action, which may be considered necessary to keep political order—more often facilitate developmental mistakes than developmental achievements. Others, such as coercive population planning practices, are shortcuts to achieve targets that could be achieved equally well or better by legal methods, and probably with more secure results. Meanwhile, the violations in themselves worsen the quality of life and constitute a form of underdevelopment unmeasured in gross domestic product statistics.

The relationship between human rights and development is more often the reverse: political systems that violate political rights are prone to generate distorted communications and commit policy mistakes. Suppression of information contributed to a vast famine during the Great Leap Forward, devastation of forests, salinization of farmland, and a series of dam collapses in 1975. Repression need not be widespread to send a signal to all Chinese that they should remain silent. Rights violations throttle the channels of discussion that China desperately needs to manage its problems in the midst of rapid economic and social change. Enforced silence worsens corruption, removes checks to environmental damage, and clears the field for potential mega-disasters. Nor can China compete successfully in world markets in the age of information when it filters Internet access, tries to control financial reporting, censors the domestic and foreign press, and otherwise interferes with the flow of ideas.

Fourth, human rights diplomacy often is erroneously presented as standing in conflict with Western business interests. But even at the height of the MFN debates in Washington, U.S.-China trade boomed. In 1995, placing orders for European Airbuses, Premier Li Peng indicated that the Chinese government was penalizing the competing U.S. supplier, Boeing, for U.S. human rights pressure. But most observers believe the Airbus decision was made for business reasons, with the human rights linkage tacked on later. After Denmark sponsored a resolution critical of China at the U.N. Human Rights Commission, China suspended some business dealings with that country for a year, but then resumed normal ties. Thus counterlinkage is a reality, but it exacts short-term costs because China cannot afford permanently to distort market interests to serve diplomatic purposes.

The true relationship between rights and business reverses the conventional wisdom. Today those who make and enforce the laws (legislators, procurators, and judges) are chosen, promoted, and kept or fired at the pleasure of the political authorities and have no independence. The laws are written, adopted, and revised without substantial independent input by the legislature. Enforcement of the laws is arbitrary, and the courts have no autonomy. The lawlessness of the Chinese legal system is experienced as much by foreign businesspeople as by Chinese dissidents. What happened to Wei Jingsheng has happened in different forms to the Australian businessman James Peng, International Monetary Fund official Hong Yang, Royal Dutch Shell employee Xiu Yichun, and others. Rule of law is essential to protect American and other foreign interests (business and otherwise) in China. If law is a system of rules that are known in advance and enforceable by appeal to independent arbiters, then China's legal system will become a rule of law only when it incorporates respect for human rights.

The reasons why improved human rights in China are a matter of strategic interest to the outside world do not apply only to China. But the international interest in human rights in China is greater than in many other nations because of China's demographic and geographic size, its strategic and economic importance, its U.N. Permanent Five status, and its position of leadership in the Third World. The difference between a China and a Vietnam, a Zaire, or a Saudi Arabia—or even an Indonesia or an India—is not the international standards that apply to it but its potential impact on Western and global interests. China should be held to the same standards as other countries, but its international importance justifies giving its rights violations urgent and sustained attention even if the world does not consistently do so for every offending country.

The United States is not alone in its concern with human rights in China. There are strong human rights NGOs located in Britain, France, Australia, and to a lesser extent Japan and Germany. Paris and London have interceded intermittently on human rights issues; Bonn and Tokyo occasionally. The European Parliament has passed numerous resolutions and in 1996 awarded Wei Jingsheng the Sakharov Prize for Freedom of Thought.

The outside world's interest in Chinese human rights presents no threat to Chinese interests, properly understood. The goals of the international human rights regime are consistent with China's announced internal goals of rule of law, prosperity, stability, and more open decision making. As a weaker power, China stands to benefit from strengthening international regimes that impose limits on stronger powers and buttress the prerogatives of sovereign states as regime participants and makers. China benefits from the norms of proceduralism and multilateralism that are embedded in international regimes. Only through active participation can China take a hand in shaping regimes further to serve its needs. All these arguments apply as much to the international human rights regime as they do to the trade and arms control regimes.

## Policy Recommendations for the West

Western human rights policy toward China should center on enforcing and strengthening the international human rights regime. Internationalizing and multilateralizing the issue will help the United States work with allies and facilitate cooperation with sympathetic policymakers in the Chinese government. By disentangling human rights from democratization and "Western values," such a policy can avoid stimulating reactive nationalism. Fundamentally, multilateralism is important because a major goal of human rights policy is to strengthen multilateral institutions.

The United States should take the lead in coordinating the Group of Seven (G-7) and other approaches to China on human rights. It should hold regular high-level consultations with European allies, the European Union, and Japan and should give energetic leadership to forge common policies toward common goals. The United States should seek early ratification of the two international covenants without unreasonable reservations and should monitor China's compliance with their provisions both in the mainland and in Hong Kong, paying attention to the fulfillment of both reporting and substantive requirements. It also should urge China to extend invitations to more of the United Nations' "thematic mechanisms," such as the special rapporteurs on torture, freedom of expression, independence of the judiciary, and violence against women.[9] And although Western governments did not sponsor a resolution critical of China at the 1998 meeting of the U.N. Human Rights Commission, they should stand ready to do so if progress on Chinese human rights stalls or reverses.

The negotiating process regarding human rights should be no different from negotiating with China (or any other country) on issues related to other international regimes, such as proliferation, intellectual property rights, or market access. Both sides should realize that the regime-building process is a long one. This is not the same as "shifting the goalposts." Long-term goals should be acknowledged. Meanwhile, certain goals should be given priority, not because they are intrinsically more important but because of their human urgency; their centrality to the human rights idea; their political, ideological, and cultural bases of support inside and outside China; or their conformity with trends of development in Chinese reform. Progress on these issues will open the way to progress on related issues. Priority issues include the following:

- Release of political prisoners and international access to prisons. Although progress on individual prisoner cases may seem to make for only superficial improvement in China's human rights situation, such cases have symbolic significance and must form a focus of Western human rights diplomacy for such diplomacy to make sense to concerned publics in China and abroad. Initiatives on individual cases should be pursued in concert with efforts to open the Chinese prison system to international humanitarian organizations, such as the International Committee of the Red Cross. This would help the central government in its goal of improving conditions of detention of all prisoners, political and other.

- Legal reform and institution building. The outside world can support and accelerate Chinese legal reform and the construction of Chinese legal institutions. We should maintain a focus on key issues such as arbitrary detention, procedural safeguards in criminal trials, reform of provisions of the criminal code that violate international norms, and international access to trials. These are important because they touch on the basic nature of the Chinese legal system. Reform in these areas commands substantial support within China. Outside pressure helps focus the leaders' minds on proposals they receive from internal sources.

- Ending religious repression. This is an area of deep concern to many Western publics, and the repression is out of proportion to any realistic threat to the interests of the Chinese state.

- Guaranteeing the continuity of civil and political rights in Hong Kong.

Exposure and stigmatization of Chinese abuses is a valuable tactic and should be continued. Representations on human rights issues should be accurate and within the ambit of international law. The stress should not be on U.S.-China or West-China value differences but on Chinese compliance with international norms and Chinese cooperation with international human rights mechanisms. The human rights agenda is damaged when it is mixed with other goals, including opposition to communism, antagonism to population planning, and promotion of Tibetan independence. Western leaders should condemn publicly human rights violations and intervene personally when necessary with top Chinese officials via letter or telephone in a credible, not proforma, manner.

Substantial human rights improvements should accompany each U.S.-China summit. Summits are valuable to Chinese leaders for their symbolic affirmation of legitimacy. Such symbols of regard and support should not be awarded without adequate human rights progress.

Western policy should support constructive efforts such as educational and technical assistance, exchanges of specialists, and institution building. Both government agencies and nongovernmental foundations, universities, and exchange organizations can contribute. Promising areas of institution building include deepening Chinese involvement in the U.N. thematic mechanisms, building the court system, reforming legal codes, training the legal profession, upgrading prison administration, and improving social welfare systems. Businesses and other nongovernmental actors in the West, such as foundations and universities, should maintain and enhance educational and exchange programs that assist Chinese agencies in fulfilling the Chinese government's declared human rights policies.

Economic engagement is a complement to, not a substitute for, a human rights policy. Economic development and the opening to the West have helped raise living standards in China. But by themselves they will not solve China's human rights problems. On some fronts, economic development makes things worse (e.g., labor conditions in some foreign-invested and locally owned factories, abuse of migrant labor, eviction of farmers from land needed for development, and victimization of ordinary people by rising corruption).[10] In some areas development helps improve human rights but works too slowly (e.g., to save prisoners now being mistreated in Chinese prisons). In regard to some human rights problems, it has no effect (e.g., lack of funds was not the cause of the high death rates in some Chinese orphanages).[11]

Economic development by itself did not bring human rights improvements in South Korea or Taiwan—this required a long political struggle— and did little to improve the human rights situation in Indonesia. Deng-style economic development so far has strengthened rather than weakened political authoritarianism.[12] The linkage between development and rights is too loose, the threshold too high, the time frame too long, and the results too uncertain to make economic engagement a substitute for direct policy action on human rights. The West should participate in China's economic development while at the same time working to improve China's compliance with the international human rights regime.

The Western business community cannot respond effectively to the human rights issue by wishing it would go away. Western businesses encounter not only practical difficulties but public relations risks when they work in an environment that is abusive of fundamental human rights. The business community should help the Chinese government respond constructively to Western human rights concerns, especially in areas in which business has an interest, responsibility, and experience, such as child labor, prison labor, women's rights, social welfare, independence of the judiciary, and due process. Working through technical assistance, personnel training, institution building, and grants, businesses can encourage Chinese reform to move in directions that are good for the business climate. For its part, the human rights community should encourage consumers to take responsibility for the conditions under which the products they use are produced. Consumers should learn to look at labels and ask about labor rights, forced labor, and child labor in the factories that produce the goods they buy.

## Conclusion

In its human rights diplomacy as in other areas of foreign policy, China has behaved as a realist power, making concessions it perceived as necessary to influence states with which it was interacting and not making them when they were not seen as necessary. Since the late 1970s and especially since 1989, a Western human rights policy combining pressure and assistance has successfully supported internal evolution toward improved human rights, achieving greater results when it was firm and lesser results when it was weak.

The Chinese government used to claim that human rights could not be part of normal diplomacy because of "face," national pride in recovered sovereignty after a century of neocolonialism and exploitation, and the nationalistic "feelings of the Chinese people." Beijing persuaded many that it could not negotiate over human rights.

But the historical record shows that the main obstacle to an effective human rights policy was not Chinese intransigence but Western indecision. China has now accepted human rights as a normal part of its diplomatic agenda, and progress will continue to be made as long as the West keeps it on the agenda.

## Notes

This chapter draws from Andrew J. Nathan, "Human Rights in Chinese Foreign Policy," *China Quarterly* 139 (December 1994): 622–43, and from "China: Getting Human Rights Right," *Washington Quarterly* 20, no. 2 (Spring 1997): 135–51. Material covered in detail in those essays is abbreviated here, and I have omitted much of the documentation. For comments and criticisms, besides members of the task force, I wish to thank Joanne Bauer, Peter Geithner, Louis Henkin, Mike Jendrzejczyk, Sidney Jones, Bruce Malkin, James D. Seymour, and Xiao Qiang.

1.  PRC Mission to the U.N. press release, New York, 31 January 1992, p. 4.

2.  *Beijing Review* 15 (1992): p. XVI.

3.  Information Office of the State Council, "The Progress of Human Rights in China," December 1995, Section X.

4.  Ibid.

5.   "Clinton and Jiang in Their Own Words: Sharing a Broad Agenda," *New York Times*, October 30, 1997, p. A20.

6.   World Bank, *China 2020: Development Challenges in the New Century* (Washington, D.C.: The World Bank 1997), p. 50.

7.   New China News Agency press release, Bandung, April 24, 1955, in *Survey of the China Mainland Press*, No. 1033, April 23–25, 1955, p. 14.

8.   On China as a realist power, see Andrew J. Nathan and Robert S. Ross, *The Great Wall and the Empty Fortress: China's Search for Security* (New York: W. W. Norton, 1997).

9.   Grounding our China rights policy in the international regime will bring pressure on us to enter more fully into compliance with the regime ourselves. The United States should accede to the International Covenant on Economic, Social and Cultural Rights (it has already joined the civil and political convention) and remove the excessive reservations it has lodged against a number of U.N. conventions it signed.

10.  Sidney Jones, "The Impact of Asian Economic Growth on Human Rights," Council on Foreign Relations Asia Project Working Paper, January 1995.

11.  Human Rights Watch/Asia, *Death by Default: A Policy of Fatal Neglect in China's State Orphanages* (New York: HRW/A, January 7, 1996).

12.  Maurice Meisner, *The Deng Xiaoping Era: An Inquiry into the Fate of Chinese Socialism, 1978–1994* (New York: Hill and Wang, 1996).

# 5

# China's Integration into the International Trade and Investment Regime

## MARGARET M. PEARSON

GIVEN the great speed with which China has joined the world economy since 1978, its integration has been far from apocalyptic; rather, China's integration has been fairly smooth and has led to much less friction in the international trade and investment regime than might be anticipated by traditional realist thinkers. This conclusion is especially pertinent for the period from 1978 to 1994, during what can be called the first phase of integration. The relative ease with which China's deepening participation in the world economy occurred during this phase is reflected in large part by the fact that the short-term goals of the People's Republic of China (PRC) reformers meshed to a significant degree with the workings of the trade and investment regime. Since 1994, however, the process of China's integration into the formal regime has entered a second, plateau phase. Specifically, the rate of progress in China's integration has slowed over negotiations for its admission to the World Trade Organization (WTO), even as the volume of actual market transactions has remained impressive. The plateau results from changes in attitudes and/or political pressures, particularly within the PRC government, about the terms under which China's deeper participation in the formal trade regime should occur.

To understand these phases of integration, it is useful to map out two hypothetical models of the terms and depth of China's participation in the world economy, each of which highlights certain values and assumptions about the behavior of the Chinese leadership.[1] The first model, which is based on a philosophy of liberal trade, can be termed the *full-integration* model. It takes China's integration into the global economy—to a level and depth consistent with the most open industrial economies—as the practical and desirable outcome of China's "open policy."[2] Under such a model, it is unacceptable for China to stop halfway in its process of integration, as partial integration would be both inefficient and unfair to its trading partners. Thus, according to this model, the first phase of China's integration can be viewed as part of a steady progression toward full integration.

However, the first phase of China's integration also could be consistent with a *partial integration* model. Under the terms of this model, China views its participation in the global economy as practical and desirable yet also as a process that must be controlled carefully. China's leaders clearly acted according to this second mental model when they initiated the "open policy" in 1978, for they repeatedly expressed that they had the ability to utilize the benefits from participation in the world economy while avoiding the elements of integration that were harmful to China's economy or sovereignty.[3] Under this model, integration will slow or halt on issues that the state perceives as particularly costly to domestic, economic, or political interests.

It is clear that the *full-integration* model is considered normatively positive to most U.S. policymakers and business representatives as well as to many analysts in international organizations, such as the World Bank.[4] The model, or an approximation of it, also appears to be the model adopted by the most liberal Chinese reformers. Many outside observers also believe that, to the degree that the *partial-integration* model was ever salient, it has lost its hold over time, and many Chinese leaders have come to embrace a free trade regime. Yet, as we view the slowing of China's integration into the world economy in the mid-1990s, we should keep in mind the possibility that the second model has remained salient for many political actors. In other words, in a political environment marked by resurgent nationalism and succession politics, advocates of this second model appear to be asserting their views and gaining a sympathetic hearing. Even more important support for the second model arises as the costs of deeper integration threaten to compound stresses on the economy that result from domestic efforts to reform state-owned enterprises.

To evaluate the record of China's integration into the international trade and investment regime and analyze the recent problems in the integration process, this chapter: defines the regimes for international trade and investment; discusses the empirical record of China's involvement with the international trade and investment regime between 1978 and mid-1996; examines the impact, on both China and the regime itself, of China's integration into the international regime for trade and investment; evaluates the degree to which China is carrying out the expectations and commitments of the trade and investment regime; and assesses the degree to which China's gradual integration into the international regime has been—and can continue to be—shaped by external pressures.

## International Trade and Investment Regimes

The dominant international regime in the area of trade is consistent with the liberal precepts of free trade. Liberal norms were partially codified in the Bretton Woods agreement ratified in 1944 and in the General Agreement on Tariffs and Trade (GATT) that was created in 1947.[5] They are strengthened in the World Trade Organization, the successor organization to GATT that was created in 1995. The fundamental goal of the GATT/WTO-based regime has been to reduce tariff and nontariff trade barriers through the extension of national treatment and the broadening of most-favored-nation (MFN) trade status.[6]

In the area of foreign direct investment (FDI), no singular, broadly recognized regime equivalent to the GATT/WTO has been codified. A partial framework has been developed through various bilateral investment treaties and the guidelines written by the Organization for Economic Cooperation and Development (OECD) and the United Nations Center on Transnational Corporations (UNCTC).[7] The WTO further contributes to this partial framework by addressing a narrow range of issues related to investment, including content and foreign exchange balancing requirements, and restrictions on imports and exports of foreign investors.[8] Despite the absence of a formal structure for FDI similar to that for trade, there are de facto market-based rules for direct investment, consistent with the logic of open trade, that liberal economies tend to follow. These rules have gained increasing numbers of adherents in the current wave of global economic liberalization. Indeed, over the course of the past two decades, certain minimal rules—including the narrowing of the scope of investment prohibitions and the promulgation of guarantees against expropriation—have become commonplace. This is true even in locations such as the countries of the former Soviet Union, eastern Europe, India, Vietnam, and

China, which previously had been hostile to FDI from Western countries. The acceptance by developing countries of international investment norms has been enhanced by competition between potential host countries, pressuring governments to dismantle at least some barriers to investment and profit repatriation.[9]

Currently, no alternative regime to the market-based one exists. COMECON, the organized trade regime of the European communist countries, has been dismantled. During the 1970s, some voices (led by Willy Brandt) appeared both in the United Nations and in the developing world advocating a new international economic order (NIEO) in which the industrialized world would make an explicit commitment to aiding the development of poorer countries. In addition, some countries advocated that the U.N. Council on Trade and Development (UNCTAD) serve as an alternative forum for the negotiation of North-South trade issues. Although calls for a South-based investment regime captured global attention for a time, their influence has declined noticeably in recent years.

Although no strong alternatives to the market-based trade and investment regime exist, several factors may diminish the strength of the liberal system. First, although many nations wish to gain the benefits of membership in the WTO, they engage in mercantilist policies intended to protect their home markets. Encompassing political as well as economic interests, the GATT/WTO regime has, from its inception, been replete with distortions that reflect special interests and protectionist pressures. Many of the distortions preventing a truly free trade regime were eliminated in the Uruguay Round or, as in the case of the Multifiber Arrangement (MFA), pledges have been made to phase them out.[10] Still other forms of protectionism—notably antidumping and safeguard mechanisms on manufactures, and even stronger barriers to trade in agriculture and services—remain.[11]

Second, regional trade bodies permitted in the WTO agreement form a potential challenge to the dominant regime. There are several regional subregimes in which China does or might participate, the most prominent of which is the Asia-Pacific Economic Cooperation (APEC) forum. Formed in 1989, the APEC forum has as its vision the enhancement of trade liberalization on a regional basis in a manner consistent with (and sometimes on a timetable ahead of) global liberalization through the WTO.[12] Thus ideally APEC will complement the global WTO-based trade regime rather than compete with it. The forum at this point is too new, and its member nations too divided over the organization's charter, to be considered a viable Asian alternative to the WTO. Yet it is possible that APEC might in the future challenge or modify the dominant regime, particularly if some of the more dirigiste leanings of East Asian newly industrializing countries (NICs) (and some Southeast Asian countries) come to dominate it.[13]

Third, it is important to consider the role that is played by the vast network of overseas Chinese businesses in the Asia-Pacific and the ways they work outside the norms of the formal regime.[14] This informal network of families and firms has been an extremely important source of trade and investment for China. On one hand, to the extent that overseas Chinese traders and investors are themselves integrated into the world economy, they have been a direct and positive example to many PRC businesspeople and officials of how markets operate. On the other hand, to the extent that the overseas Chinese network provides a source of goods and capital outside of the dominant norms, it could weaken the dominant international system of norms.

## China's Involvement with the International Trade and Investment Regime

When the reformers who came to power in China in the late 1970s decided to increase China's exposure to the world economy, the absence of a genuine alternative meant that they were, in effect, choosing to interact with the liberal trade and investment regime. The motivation behind this dramatic change in policy was largely economic; it was a means to further the government's central task of rapid industrialization.[15] Consistent with the *partial-integration* model, the formula for participation in the regime was to gain the benefits of trade and investment but at the same time guard against the perceived negative impact of such interaction. The concrete benefits reformers desired included the growth of export earnings and external sources of capital and, most important, sources of advanced technology. In joining the World Bank, International Monetary Fund (IMF), and GATT, reformers stood to gain funds, advice, and (through GATT) reciprocal MFN treatment that would enhance China's exports. China stood to gain in less-tangible but nonetheless important ways as well. Integration into international regimes and organizations had international prestige value and would help legitimize the regime both at home and abroad, particularly vis-à-vis Taiwan. Integration also would help strengthen the position of domestic reformers, in their competition with conservatives, by providing political and financial support for liberalizing initiatives. At the same time as China's reformers wished to reap the benefits of integration, the reformers, with the support of conservatives in the regime, wished to guard against affronts to Chinese sovereignty and foreign exploitation. Moreover, they believed China could and should remain self-reliant by keeping trade and foreign capital subordinate to the domestic state sector.

International businesses and Western governments (particularly the United States, Japan, and the countries of the European Union) have been quite eager to have China participate in the world economy. Like China's leaders, their enthusiasm has been driven by economic considerations, including access to China's inexpensive exports and the potential for huge demand for foreign goods from Chinese consumers. Foreign investors, similarly, have seen the possibility for production of low-cost goods within China for export and for the domestic market.[16] Generally the time horizon of foreign investors has had to be very long; they wait for Chinese citizens to grow wealthier, for markets and infrastructure to develop, and for investment barriers to be dismantled. Western investors, in particular, perceiving that their domestic markets are saturated and that they must invest in China earlier than current market conditions warrant in order to avoid being preempted by their competitors, have been willing to wait for results.[17]

Similar to China's leaders, foreign governments have political motives as well. They hope that China's integration into formal trade and investment regimes will foster a common ground on which the resolution of disputes can occur more easily.[18] Foreign businesses and governments also argue that a second-order consequence will be a commitment to a more complete and transparent system of economic laws. Finally, foreign governments, and particularly the U.S. government, hope that China's integration into the world economy, and its economic marketization more generally, will spill over into the political system— that economic openness will promote democratization and a more stable strategic partnership.

The desire of the Chinese government, as well as of foreign businesses and governments, to develop commercial ties set the stage for China's gradual integration. Over the course of the 1980s, as Chinese reformers became increasingly convinced that the benefits of further involvement outweighed the dangers to sovereign control of the economy, and as the voices of economic conservatives became weaker, the government gradually liberalized many of the earlier controls. Although the process of integration was less than smooth, China's trade and investment policy became increasingly congruent with the norms of the regimes.

It is important to bear in mind that China's engagement in the world economy has occurred on two distinct levels. First, the Chinese government has entered into formal multilateral and bilateral organizations and agreements (e.g., APEC, MFA, and bilateral agreements on protection of intellectual property) and is attempting to join others (i.e., the WTO) that define and regulate the structure in which business transactions occur. This is the type of international regime on which scholars of international relations most often focus, and it has been the main locus of friction between China and the outside world. Yet these formal government-to-government agreements ultimately are designed to facilitate a second type of engagement—the vast numbers of market-based business transactions. These individual business transactions are not directed by an authoritative arbiter; although they may be informed by the rules of the formal regimes, they are carried out independently from them. The magnitude and importance of this second type of engagement is reflected in the figures for growth of trade and investment since 1978.

Before examining the record since 1978, a qualification should be made regarding the categorization of China's integration into two phases. To some degree, to draw a line at the year 1994 greatly oversimplifies a complex and multilayered process. There is a high degree of continuity between the two phases, particularly in the area of foreign direct investment, insofar as the level of transactions continued to climb. Moreover, many of the seeds for the changes of the second phase were sown prior to 1994. Nevertheless, although 1994 was not a watershed year marking a reversal of the direction of integration, major changes occurred. Most important, as it became clear that China would not be admitted to GATT, the Chinese government's attitude toward joining the major world body responsible for trade soured considerably. This change significantly slowed the momentum for China's continuing integration into the global economy.[19]

## The First Phase of China's Participation: 1978 to 1994

### TRADE REGIME INTEGRATION

In the 1980s China deepened its engagement with both the formal trade regimes and the informal regime of market transactions. In addition, it made significant changes in its trade policies and institutions. The steady growth in China's exports and imports, as shown in Table 5–1, illustrates its integration at the level of transaction. Although China has had increasing annual trade surpluses with the United States for many years, overall, its trade has been relatively balanced.[20]

It should be noted that although the speed with which China has become a major trading country is impressive, the impact of trade on its domestic economy has been more limited than might be presumed. The strongest growth in exports has been achieved by foreign-funded

Table 5–1.    China's Foreign Trade, 1986–1997 ($U.S. billions)

| Year | Exports | Imports | Total | Balance |
|------|---------|---------|-------|---------|
| 1986 | 30.9 | 42.9 | 73.8 | −12.0 |
| 1987 | 39.4 | 43.2 | 82.6 | −3.8 |
| 1988 | 47.5 | 55.2 | 102.7 | −7.7 |
| 1989 | 52.5 | 59.1 | 111.6 | −6.6 |
| 1990 | 62.1 | 53.4 | 115.5 | 8.7 |
| 1991 | 71.9 | 63.8 | 135.7 | 8.1 |
| 1992 | 85.0 | 80.6 | 165.6 | 4.4 |
| 1993 | 91.8 | 104.0 | 195.8 | −12.2 |
| 1994 | 121.0 | 115.7 | 236.7 | 5.3 |
| 1995 | 148.8 | 132.1 | 280.9 | 16.7 |
| 1996 | 151.1 | 138.8 | 289.9 | 12.2 |
| 1997 | 183.0 | 142.0 | 325.0 | 40.3 |

*Sources:* For 1986 to 1994, *China Business Review* (May–June 1995): 57 (based on China State Statistical Bureau figures); for 1995 to 1997, U.S.-China Business Council.

enterprises and PRC firms engaged in export processing (primarily collectively owned township and village enterprises [TVEs] rather than state-owned enterprises [SOEs]).[21] Moreover, even though exports from state-owned manufacturers have grown, they have held a declining share of China's annual export growth. Furthermore, the regulatory structure of China's foreign trade regime shelters the SOEs from import competition. In other words, the core of the Chinese economy has remained rather insulated from the competitive pressures of the world economy.

At the level of integration into the formal trade regime, China joined a number of multilateral organizations that were directly or indirectly related to trade during the 1980s. The story of China's integration into the World Bank and IMF has been told elsewhere and needs not be recounted in detail here. In general, the relationship between China and the World Bank and IMF during this first phase was relatively cooperative.[22] China did not seek a major leadership role but was involved productively in the policymaking of these institutions. Many of the joint projects (particularly projects involving World Bank funding) have been relatively successful. Moreover, the ongoing marketization of China's domestic economy brought it more into line with the norms of these multilateral institutions, and China adopted some of the recommended policies of both the World Bank and the IMF, such as the 1986 devaluation of the yuan. As the most definitive study of these institutions concluded for the period up until the end of the 1980s, "the rules of the two institutions have not been bent for China any more than they normally are for large new entrants."[23]

China's path toward membership in GATT was less smooth. China, which began to participate in GATT in 1982, has held only observer status except for its membership in the MFA. Its participation in the MFA was rather tense, as PRC negotiators engaged in extremely tough bargaining to keep a generous share of textile quotas.[24] In 1986 China applied for full membership in GATT. Some of the impetus for the country's application was political. PRC leaders wished to be admitted to GATT ahead of Taiwan, which also had indicated its intentions to apply for membership, and did so formally in 1991. China's leaders also hoped (seemingly mistakenly) that admission into GATT would pave the way for the elimination of the annual review of MFN trade status by the United States.[25] Some progress was made in the admission process during the first several months after the GATT working group on China began to meet in 1988. Yet GATT's requirements that members liberalize extensively their trade regimes and submit to greater international scrutiny led China's leaders to take a more cautious approach than they had with IMF and World Bank membership. Furthermore, the early momentum and optimism of China's accession was lost following the events at Tiananmen Square in June of 1989. Although the working party continued to meet periodically, its members developed a more hardened attitude, despite their declaration of support for China's accession in principle.

Complementing the domestic sources for economic reform, the government's desire to enter GATT led it to initiate numerous concrete policy changes, including the reallocation of foreign exchange toward trade, the devaluation of the yuan, and the achievement of current account convertibility.[26] Trade licenses and tariffs actually were increased in the 1980s but mainly as a transitional step away from centrally planned trade toward a market-based system. Direct subsidies for exports have been largely phased out, and export targeting is more subject to market signals. Even further progress was made in the early 1990s on the reduction of tariffs and abolition of licensing requirements. For example, major tariff reductions on 2,800 categories of goods as well as in agricultural products and services were announced in 1993. Some tariff reductions also have been made in the context of bilateral negotiations, notably the 1991 market access agreement with the United States to lower tariffs and remove other nontariff barriers. China further eliminated some of the elements of its administered foreign trade system by reducing the importance of the trade plan (particularly for exports) and, in 1991, by moving to a foreign trade contracting system in which periodic targets were set for localities for value of exports, foreign exchange earnings, and foreign exchange remissions to the central monetary authorities.[27]

Even though significant progress toward congruence with GATT norms was made during the first phase, problems remained in the liberalization of China's trading regime. Most important, while export decisions were relegated largely to the market, the protectionist trade structure for imports continued to a significant degree to be administered. To guard against competition from imports, the Chinese government continued to subsidize its state-owned industries and to erect significant nontariff barriers to trade. Indeed, as of 1994, 50 percent of imports remained subject to some form of nontariff barriers and nearly half of all imports were reprocessed into exports, thereby limiting competition for domestic producers. Moreover, even for the export sector, the vast reduction of the plan in favor of a contract system meant that local foreign trade corporations (FTC) still were subject to export targets set primarily by higher authorities. Finally, the trading system remained far from transparent, a problem exacerbated by the still-less-than-reliable accounting system and statistical reporting.[28]

## INVESTMENT REGIME INTEGRATION

There is no multilateral equivalent to the GATT for foreign direct investment. Rather, there exists a system of market-based norms, guidelines, and bilateral investment treaties. Despite this contextual difference, the story of China's integration into the international system of foreign direct investment during the first phase, from 1978 to the early 1990s, is similar to that for trade. The raw numbers of FDI grew impressively, if less steadily, than for trade. Table 5–2 shows that growth in FDI occurred slowly during the early 1980s, gathered speed in the second half of the 1980s, and then skyrocketed after 1990. Despite these impressive numbers, official figures inflate the actual amount of foreign capital flowing to China. A significant proportion of the transactions reported in later years reflects not true foreign investment but, rather, a channeling of funds of PRC origin through Hong Kong and then back into China.[29] Substantial and genuine investment, particularly in export-oriented industries and domestic manufacturing, nonetheless occurred.

China also has been making direct investments outside its own borders. By the 1990s, the level of its outward foreign direct investment was the second largest among developing countries (after Taiwan). By 1994 cumulative FDI outflows from China were estimated at $16 billion.

**Table 5–2.  Foreign Direct Investment in China, 1979–1997**

| Year | Number of Projects Pledged | Value of Projects Pledged ($U.S. billion) | Value of Projects Utilized ($U.S. billion) | Utilized Value as % of Pledged[a] |
|------|------|------|------|------|
| 1979–82 | 922 | 4.61 | 1.77 | 38% |
| 1983 | 470 | 1.73 | 0.92 | 53% |
| 1984 | 1,856 | 2.65 | 1.42 | 54% |
| 1985 | 3,073 | 5.93 | 1.96 | 33% |
| 1986 | 1,498 | 2.83 | 2.25 | 80% |
| 1987 | 2,233 | 3.71 | 2.65 | 71% |
| 1988 | 5,945 | 5.30 | 3.74 | 71% |
| 1989 | 5,779 | 5.60 | 3.77 | 67% |
| 1990 | 7,273 | 6.60 | 3.41 | 52% |
| 1991 | 12,978 | 11.98 | 4.37 | 36% |
| 1992 | 48,764 | 58.12 | 11.00 | 19% |
| 1993 | 83,000 | 111.44 | 27.52 | 25% |
| 1994 | 47,490 | 81.41 | 33.79 | 42% |
| 1995 | 37,126 | 90.30 | 37.70 | 42% |
| 1996 | 24,556 | 73.28 | 24.56 | 33.5% |
| 1997 | 21,046 | 51.57 | 42.28 | 87% |
| **Total** | **304,009** | **517.06** | **206.11** | **40%** |

[a] Invariably a proportion of pledged investment is never actually absorbed, because deals fall apart. However, because there is a lag between the time contracts are pledged (signed) and when the capital is actually contributed (utilized), some capital not absorbed in the year of signing will be absorbed in later years. (Reflecting the fact that the opportunity to actualize a contract increases over time, Chinese statistical yearbooks revise upward the figure for investment utilization in a particular year in subsequent yearbooks.)
*Sources:* MOFTEC, *Zhongguo Duiwai Jingji Maoyi Nianjian* [Yearbooks of China's foreign economic trade] (various years); "Investment Data," *China Business Review* 23, No. 3 (May–June 1996): 40.

Most of China's investment abroad involved trading (50 percent), natural resource (30 percent), and manufacturing (15 percent) ventures. However, the majority of these operations were in Hong Kong and Macao (61 percent), and thus after 1997 many of these investments will be repatriated.[30]

By the mid-1980s tensions had appeared in the government's strategy as reformers recognized that the goal of attracting foreign investment was increasingly hindered by the parallel goal of controlling it. Foreign firms, and especially those from the United States, Western Europe and Japan, perceived that controls were designed to hinder their ability to operate effectively and to gain access to China's domestic market. Disappointment in levels of investment, particularly through 1986, pressured reformers not just to clarify but also to liberalize controls. Reformers came to believe that if China was to attract sufficient capital and technology, it must go farther than originally anticipated to play by the rules of the international investment regime.

Thus, paralleling the growth in FDI transactions, and as occurred with the international trade regime, China's reformers liberalized controls on many issues related to foreign investment. For example, they increased access of foreign-invested enterprises to foreign exchange, expanded the sectors and regions into which foreign capital was allowed, made efforts to protect intellectual property, and relaxed requirements for Chinese ownership and managerial control.[31] The government also tried to make the rules for foreign direct investment more transparent and to reduce bureaucratic interference. Further tax incentives were instituted to attract foreign capital particularly to projects that would enhance China's export capacity or bring advanced technology. The scaling back of FDI controls continued despite the events at Tiananmen Square in the spring of 1989 and the conservative crackdown that followed it. Officials of the Ministry of Foreign Trade and Economic Cooperation (MOFTEC), who had become quite sympathetic to foreign business, made explicit attempts to soften the foreign reaction to the crackdown.[32] These efforts by the PRC leadership to liberalize the investment environment were accompanied by efforts by enterprises and local governments, often without the sanction of the central government, to take advantage of the Open Policy to enrich their localities.

Although the liberalization and growth in transparency was gradual and was not applied evenly across all issues, the trend toward the easing of controls was undeniable. Foreign companies expressed new optimism that they finally would gain access to the Chinese domestic market. By the early 1990s China was more open to FDI than were Japan and South Korea. Foreign investment grew to its highest levels in 1991 and, as Table 5.2 shows, continued at a record-setting pace through 1993.

## AGREEMENTS ON PROTECTION OF INTELLECTUAL PROPERTY RIGHTS

China's record on intellectual property right (IPR) protection has become a major point on contention between the United States and the PRC in recent years. What is often forgotten amid the tension is that, since first committing to provide such protection for foreign goods in the

U.S.-China Bilateral Trade Agreement of 1979, China has made far-reaching changes in its basic conception of and resources devoted to IPR protection. The official norm in China has moved away from a view of intellectual creations as social goods subject to state control and toward the limited acceptance of the Western-based view of intellectual creations as the property of the creator.[33] China has joined a number of international conventions and organizations, drafted numerous domestic laws on copyright, and established institutions responsible for these issue areas.[34] The speed with which China has moved formally to adopt a number of the norms, institutions, and procedures of the intellectual property regime suggests a significant degree of acceptance of that regime at the highest levels of government as well as from a growing policy community (often with ties to the emerging high-tech industries) in Beijing and Shanghai.

However, although the Chinese government has established many formal mechanisms of a national system to protect intellectual property, these changes have been insufficient to offer full protection of foreign IPRs. Technology to clone computer software as well as to reproduce video and audio recordings has become more widespread in China, with much of the illegal production migrating to the PRC from Taiwan. It has become clear that, despite formal acceptance at the top of the government of the idea of intellectual property and the establishment of supporting institutions, China lacks a system that can implement the existing IPR laws effectively. Moreover, the institutions designed to protect intellectual property have not yet internalized the appropriate incentives. For example, the choice to house the copyright bureaucracy within the propaganda department enhances the probability that copyrights will continue to be used as tools to serve the government's ideology and purposes, as they were beginning under the Kuomintang, rather than to protect authorship. This fact suggests that even with formal acceptance of Western norms of intellectual property, long-standing assumptions and practices related to intellectual property and innovation continue to shape the context in which seemingly appropriate institutions are implemented. At a minimum, even well-designed policies and institutions encounter resistance from provinces and localities where local officials are under tremendous pressure to show substantial results from their efforts at economic development and to whom copyright infringement may pose a strong lure.[35]

These problems led the U.S. government—through the Office of the U.S. Trade Representative (USTR)—to threaten sanctions against China under Special Section 301 of the 1988 trade bill. In 1992, at the eleventh hour of negotiations, Chinese negotiators agreed to promulgate detailed copyright regulations and join other international conventions for IPR protection. They also agreed to patent protection for two important American industries, pharmaceuticals and agricultural chemicals. U.S. bilateral pressure in this instance was highly effective in producing an agreement, although as would be seen later this agreement was insufficient to remedy all the problems in China's emerging framework for intellectual property protection.

## EXPLAINING THE INTEGRATION OF THE FIRST PHASE

The nature of integration during the first phase of integration was influenced by forces in both the international and the domestic environment. The fact that the international political and economic environment of the 1980s and early 1990s was conducive to China's integration often is overlooked. Liberalization of planned and dirigiste economies was prevalent worldwide in the late 1970s and 1980s. Economically, China was able to benefit from strong foreign demand for inexpensive Chinese exports and for access to the domestic market.[36] Thus foreign firms went to China readily, despite the barriers at its borders.[37] Moreover, foreign governments supported such moves, with the exception of the governments of Japan and Taiwan, which discouraged investment in China during much of the 1980s. Western nations were quite eager to improve bilateral relations with China for both strategic and economic reasons. The U.S. government was relatively conciliatory toward China on trade-related issues during most of the 1980s, despite periodic bilateral crises over nonproliferation and Taiwan, for example. As noted previously, however, this attitude changed considerably after the events at Tiananmen, with tensions arising over renewal of China's MFN status, the increasing U.S. trade deficit with China, and the U.S. discontent over issues of IPR and market access. The erosion of the favorable U.S.-China relationship at the end of the first phase contributed to the plateau of the second phase.

The favorable international environment during most of the first phase clearly improved the attitude of the Chinese leadership to most of the immediate aspects of international economic integration. So did the favorable economic results brought about by trade and investment, especially the rapid growth of those sectors most associated with the international economy—the TVE and foreign sectors. It was also true that the changes the Open Policy required the leadership to make during the first phase were less difficult than those that would take center stage in the post-1994 phase. Shallow integration, which reduces barriers at the border (e.g., through the reduction of tariffs and reform of the foreign exchange structure) but can coexist with state intervention in the domestic market, was less politically costly.[38] Chinese reformers could believe that on the early issues of integration there was a broad convergence between China's interests and those of the international regime.

As important as were these factors—the conducive international environment, the economic success of the early reforms, and the less divisive nature of shallow integration—most crucial for the successful integration of the first phase was the dominance within the Chinese leadership of reformers committed to the Open Policy. From the beginning, the reformers committed themselves to a strategy of rapid modernization that involved foreign trade and investment and were very effective at implementing this strategy. Their concerns, until the early 1990s, that the volume of foreign capital coming into China was less than optimal caused the continual erosion and honing of the controls described earlier. These policy changes had concrete and rapidly realized economic gains, while retaining for PRC officials some degree of control. Some changes were made under intense foreign pressure, as with the conclusion of bilateral agreements on IPR. Yet, for the most part, changes were made readily and at the initiative of Chinese policymakers, who seemed convinced of their benefits. Reformers' goals were easier to implement because of widespread public support and the fact that many issues were, politically speaking, relatively straightforward. Progressive integration did not mean an absence of frictions. But despite these difficulties, the commitment to continued integration remained.

## The Second, Plateau Phase: 1994 to Late 1997

The pattern of occasionally tense yet generally progressive integration during the first phase shifted perceptibly during 1994. Considerable momentum has continued at the level of individual business transactions, as the trade figures in Table 5–1 demonstrate. Yet despite China's ever more extensive participation in markets, its integration into the formal multilateral regime has developed serious problems. The main locus of problems has been the negotiations over accession to the WTO and China's adherence to U.S.-China agreements on IPR. These difficulties overshadow the progress that had been made in the previous decade and a half.

TRADE INTEGRATION

Both the leaders of China's reform and the major WTO member nations believe that China is too important in the global economy to be left out of the organization. Some progress has been made in the post-1994 period toward the goal of admission, and Chinese advocates of WTO admission have been persistent in pursuing negotiations. China has been forthcoming in offering tariff reductions. In addition to the earlier steps taken to reduce tariffs, Jiang Zemin at the Osaka meeting of APEC in the fall of 1995 made a surprise announcement that China would cut tariffs on 4,000 import items by 30 percent or more. Other tariff reduction offers subsequently were made. Moreover, nontariff barriers gradually have been eliminated on a large number of products since the early 1990s.[39]

Negotiations for WTO membership also have made progress, both in their bilateral form and with the WTO itself. China has agreed to eliminate many nontariff barriers. Considerable progress was made in particular in the WTO talks in early 1997, where China agreed to abide by the WTO trade-related intellectual property agreement (TRIPs) as a "developed country" upon, and to trade-related investment measures (TRIMS) two years after, accession. These negotiations also closed on many aspects of the accession protocol, including transparency.[40]

However, these areas of progress have been offset by disputes surrounding many terms of China's WTO accession.[41] The major dispute has concerned the degree to which China should be treated as a developing country on some or most issues, which means China would be permitted a longer period to comply with WTO rules. The compliance period extension varies, generally from between two and ten years, depending on the category. The Chinese government has argued that it should be offered the more generous timetable because its per-capita income figures cannot be compared with those of industrialized countries. Moreover, Chinese negotiators have argued that given that the country already has made extensive changes to integrate into the world economy, to withhold membership until China's economy has made a full market transition is unreasonable or, stated more negatively, an attempt of global hegemons to keep China from its rightful place. (It is interesting to note that the Chinese leadership's hesitation over joining the WTO with developed country status has a parallel with the attitude of U.S. government officials in the 1940s who, at GATT's founding, "were reluctant to create an international body with the potential ability to override domestic law in critical areas of economic activity.")[42]

The negotiating stance of the U.S. government has been that according to both the volume and the rate of growth of its exports, and its overall impact on the international trading system, China already is a developed country. It thus must enter the WTO on commercially sound terms.[43] Indeed, as opposed to mid-1989 when "the outline that had emerged of the prospective protocol would not force China to adopt market principles to become a contracting party of GATT,"[44] the rather full adoption of market principles on an accelerated timetable is now being pressed by WTO member governments.[45] The U.S. government also argues that if China is not required to make changes to bring it in line with WTO rules prior to admission, the WTO's leverage to force those changes in the future will decline significantly, allowing China to retain its advantaged status long after such status is warranted. Finally, negotiators from the WTO and the U.S. government alike feel that China has not liberalized on critical issues. For example, while the tariff reductions made by China are welcomed by WTO members, they now see the tariff issue is now seen as secondary to market access, and on this key issue serious responses have not been forthcoming from China.

To some degree both sides recognize that to categorize China as either developed or developing is an oversimplification. Although the countries' representatives (and their news media) often frame the debate as centered around the question of developmental status, both sides appear to recognize that an acceptable package will contain timetables for compliance on a sector-by-sector basis, with less time for compliance in some areas that are already fairly developed (e.g., textiles) and more time for compliance in relatively poorly developed industries (e.g., banking).

In addition to this broad difference in approach to China's WTO treatment, there are numerous issue-specific points of dispute. The most important of these from the U.S. perspective concern administrative (nonmarket) controls over Chinese trade, especially:

- continued PRC government subsidies (particularly through unrepaid loans) to state-owned enterprises;
- PRC market access restrictions and nontariff barriers (reflecting continuing de facto import-substitution policies), particularly on agriculture and services;
- lack of national treatment for foreign firms operating in China, particularly the inability of foreign firms to trade products unrelated to their own factories' production without going through the FTCs;
- continued lack of transparency and uniformity of rules across China;
- promulgation of industrial policies.

The main concerns of the Chinese government are:

- WTO members' insistence on using special import safeguards to prevent a flood of Chinese imports after admission[46];

- intended application by the U.S. government of the Jackson-Vanik amendment to China, thereby mandating annual review of China's MFN status even after China's admission to the WTO.[47]

The issue of industrial policies deserves special attention because of the growing importance of these policies in the thinking of Chinese reformers about industrialization, their potential effect on major foreign industries, and the lack of information about these policies outside China. Moreover, China's emerging industrial policy is relevant for the country's efforts to join the WTO because although industrial policies are not addressed explicitly in GATT or the Uruguay Round agreements, many aspects of industrial policy would conflict with WTO agreements.[48]

China's intention to rely on industrial policies for key "pillar" industries was announced in June 1994. To be considered a pillar industry, a sector must have the potential for very large output, for use of advanced technology, and for a large domestic and potentially foreign market. Such sectors include machinery and electronics, construction materials, petrochemicals, aircraft, telecommunications, and automobiles and auto parts.[49] From the Chinese viewpoint, protection for these industries—largely through special funding and preferential tax policies—is vital to the development of not only a strong economy but also a strong military. In some cases, such protection may be deemed crucial even if it hurts other sectors of the economy.

It is easy to misunderstand the goals of Chinese industrial policies. The goals differ significantly from the old-style industrial policy inherent in central planning. The architects of China's recent industrial policies—officials in the department responsible for coordinating the writing of industrial policy, the State Planning Commission's Department of Long-term Planning and Industrial Policy (DLPIP)—profess commitment to eventual market competition in the pillar industries. They express interest in building competitive industries, not in protecting uncompetitive ones through trade barriers. Indeed, there is a sentiment within the DLPIP to deny applications for an industrial policy from industries seeking only protectionism. While building competitive industries is one goal, another is controlling the process of market transformation so that it does not lead to social unrest; in other words, a central goal of industrial policy is to minimize the social costs of eventual market transition, particularly unemployment. The latter concern, while often underestimated outside of China, is held very deeply by elites in China.[50]

Although those in the DLPIP assigned to design the new industrial policies do not necessarily have protectionism as their core goal, protectionist forces nevertheless make their way into the policymaking process. Because the final promulgation of any particular sectoral policy requires the consensus of the sector's ministerial leaders as well as top leaders interested in economic policy and because officials in these sectors often are motivated to restrict foreign competition, protectionist interests gain significant influence.

## INVESTMENT REGIME INTEGRATION

International investment has not been as problematic as trade during the second phase. Although, as noted previously, certain problems arising from negotiations over the WTO are relevant to investors, the absence of an overall regime for investment implies that many problems foreign investors face in China must be handled on a business-to-business basis or through bilateral negotiations. The Chinese government has continued to make changes in its investment code, and the environment for foreign direct investment continues to improve.[51]

That interest in direct investment in China remained strong is indicated by the figures in Table 5–2. The amount of foreign capital utilized (actually absorbed) continued to rise, except in 1996. Even some of the decline in pledged investment over this period can be attributed to attempts by the Chinese government to strengthen its investment environment. In particular, the downturn in numbers of projects pledged and pledged investment in 1994 and 1995 appeared in part to be a result of regulations designed to halt the practice of setting up false joint ventures, primarily through discouraging rights to import cars duty-free.

Although the record for direct investment continued to be quite successful, both new and old problem areas remained. As a result of forces that were not China's doing, the Asian crisis caused a substantial slowing of foreign direct investment beginning in late 1997, as reflected in the decline in pledged investment in 1997. This slowdown was projected to continue for several years and reflected China's vulnerability to the heavy representation of other Asian countries in its direct investment mix as well as uncertainty of all investors regarding how China's economy would weather the crisis.

Moreover, operational difficulties in the investment environment remain. Because credit is tight throughout the Chinese economy, foreign businesses often do not get paid on time. Getting information about potential partners also is difficult. Such operational problems reflect the developing nature of China's economy and financial structure. Another type of problem arises from the Chinese government's continued regulation of the internal investment regime. Recent areas in which controls over foreign investment have been tightened (in 1994 and 1995) are in encouraged and restricted industries and regions. Restrictions have been placed on speculative real estate investment and low-value-added export processing.[52] Despite government claims of encouraging investment in certain services, investment in banking, securities, accounting, law, and insurance remains highly restricted. Incentives for investment in inland regions, which have had significant difficulty attracting foreign-funded enterprises, are being encouraged. The Chinese government also has eliminated certain benefits provided to foreign-funded projects, such as the exemption on duties on capital equipment imported by such enterprises, although this particular benefit was restored in early 1998. Some such changes would eliminate the actually better-than-national treatment that some ventures have received through preferential tax treatment, and thus represent a rationalization of the foreign investment code.

There are two major problems related to FDI at the level of the international regime itself, both of which echo issues discussed with regard to the WTO. First, the Chinese government continues to restrict market access and does not give national treatment (i.e., treatment on par with equivalent domestically produced goods) to foreign enterprises on many issues. Foreign-funded enterprises still must meet export requirements and do not have the freedom to sell goods produced in China in the domestic market. Second, China's regulations governing foreign investment continue to lack transparency and uniformity and are not standardized across provinces. Lack of uniformity is at least in part a consequence of the reformers' strategy of gaining support for the Open Policy from officials in key provinces by granting particularistic benefits.[53] Nonuniformity of investment regulations, as with that of national treatment, has in some cases benefited foreign investors, as the relative independence of the localities has meant that some projects that might not have been approved in some locations or by the central government have gained approval. Nevertheless, both transparency and uniformity are crucial for the development of a rule-based system of commercial law. Moreover, uniformity also would be in the interest of the central government, as it would enhance Beijing's control.[54]

## AGREEMENTS ON IPR PROTECTION

The most public conflict involving China's integration into the international trade regime during the post-1994 phase has concerned intellectual property protection, a dispute spearheaded by the U.S. government and U.S. entertainment and software industries. As the capacity of

Chinese enterprises to pirate software and sound and video recordings grew, it became clear that the Chinese government was failing to implement effectively the 1992 agreement on copyrights. In a manner reminiscent of the 1992 negotiations, in early 1995 the U.S. government threatened Special 301 sanctions. After vociferous threats of retaliation by China, bilateral negotiations between the USTR and MOFTEC once again led to a last-minute agreement to strengthen enforcement of IPR protection. A third round of threats of sanctions and countersanctions occurred in 1995–1996, as U.S. manufacturers of software and audiovisual recordings estimated that they were losing over $1 billion annually because of pirating by Chinese manufacturers.[55] A third agreement was reached in June 1996.

The stakes for China to solve these bilateral IPR disputes have been heightened by the fact that a record of IPR protection is requisite for China's admission to the WTO; China must demonstrate adherence to the Agreement on Trade-Related Aspects of Intellectual Property Rights.[56] With an eye toward WTO admission, and an apparent growing domestic commitment to the value of intellectual property protection, the Chinese government has made significant attempts over the past few years to implement the IPR agreement in both legislation and actual practice. Indeed, the increasingly unfavorable environment for piracy has caused at least some IPR violators to move production elsewhere in Asia.

EXPLAINING THE POST-1994 PLATEAU

Of the domestic and international factors that contributed to the positive trends of the first phase—international economic and political environment, positive economic performance, the costs to China of the issues under negotiation, and the attitude of China's leaders and populace—the international economic environment and performance factors remained steady into the late 1990s. China continued to develop good results at the level of business transactions. Moreover, the overall international economic environment for trade and investment did not worsen perceptibly until the advent of the Asian financial turmoil. But in areas of the international political environment, the costliness of issues at hand, and Chinese attitudes, changes occurred beginning in the mid-1990s. As noted previously, the enthusiasm of foreign governments toward a number of Chinese trade and investment practices that existed in the 1980s, already quite measured after the crackdown of 1989, continued to worsen in the mid-1990s. Suspicions by the U.S. government over China's WTO intentions were compounded by observations that the Chinese government was either unwilling or unable to enforce previous agreements on IPR protection. These problems elicited concerns that the Chinese government would halt the process of marketization and integration into the international trade regime at a point short of what is required for WTO membership, thereby attempting partial integration only.

Also changed during the second phase has been the fact that many of the items being placed on China's trade policy agenda require more substantial and wrenching changes on the part of the domestic economy than do, for example, tariff reductions. For example, WTO admission will subject some of China's industries to greater foreign and domestic competition, while demands by the U.S. government to participate in the enforcement of China's intellectual property laws raise the sensitive issue of national sovereignty. Thus, in some sense China disposed of the easy issues of integration first, and only then turned to face the much more difficult areas of reform.

Even more than the nature of changes required, it is first and foremost changes in the outlook of the Chinese leadership that have led to a plateau in the integration process. Chinese leaders' enthusiasm for full integration has been dampened in recent years by a more realistic appraisal of the costs and benefits to China of such integration. In terms of the benefits of WTO membership, Chinese officials recognize that they already possess most of the advantages of membership—particularly unconditional most-favored-nation status, from most countries (the United States being the main exception)—without the obligations of formal membership. But on the cost side, the ledger has grown. Although the U.S. government never promised to revoke the Jackson-Vanik amendment, thereby making less certain this key carrot of unconditional renewal of MFN status, Chinese officials apparently have come to take the U.S. stance more seriously in recent years, removing a major potential benefit to China. Increased recognition of the threat posed by deeper integration to established economic interests is an even more potent challenge. Perhaps the biggest cost that Chinese bureaucrats recognize is the potential competition to state enterprises that would result from the extensive dismantling of barriers to the Chinese domestic market. The threat from WTO admission is seen as particularly strong for five industries, most of which are (or will be) subjects of industrial policy: electronics, automobiles, petroleum refining, machine tools, and instruments.[57] As the fear of social unrest resulting from unemployment has grown throughout Chinese society, the specter of WTO membership's further exacerbating this problem has become worrisome. Protectionism, seen in part in the new industrial policies, reflects the growing influence of certain core industrial bureaucracies and their associated localities.[58]

In addition to the changes in Chinese attitudes resulting from a cost-benefit analysis, other political issues have affected the atmosphere in which the question of WTO admission is considered. Having failed to gain China's admission to GATT in 1994, China's WTO negotiators accuse the United States of having raised the bar for membership and of failing to trust that China will continue to make extensive reforms in its economy, just as it has done for the past 15 years. Even among some Chinese officials who previously were enthusiastic about China's admission there is bitterness toward the United States. Many MOFTEC negotiators reportedly have felt abused by the GATT and WTO accession process and feel the wind was taken out of their sails by China's failed bid for GATT membership. Those negotiators who remain committed to the accession process have difficulty getting key bureaucratic interests that are affected by the WTO to take the process seriously. More generally, some officials complain that China should not have to accede to rules that were created by a "hegemon." A who-needs-WTO? sentiment has grown within both the government and the population.

The resentment of Chinese officials to what they perceive as foreign, and particularly U.S., hostility is fed by growing nationalism in China. These sensitivities are particularly potent during the current political uncertainties surrounding Deng Xiaoping's succession. Yet the fact that the demands being made on China require much deeper changes than before suggest that the leadership's reactions may endure beyond the resolution of the succession problem.

This is not to say that all officials or ministries have turned against further integration. The idea continues to hold considerable sway that China, given its size and importance, should be a member of the world's trading body. As of mid-1996 support for the WTO appeared to continue among some at the topmost levels of both MOFTEC (particularly Li Lanqing) and the Chinese government (particularly Jiang Zemin). At the middle- and upper-middle levels of MOFTEC, the Ministry of Finance, and the Bank of China, among other organizations, significant support still exists for further global integration and WTO accession.[59] But these voices from the middle levels cannot be expected to carry as much influence in the current environment, and expressing pro-integration views is politically difficult. Even among the continuing supporters of WTO accession, some sentiment has developed that, while China should of course be a member of the formal trade regime, a strong push to join should be put off for several years when, presumably, the political environment in China will be clearer. A delay in joining the WTO will also simplify the environment for those formulating industrial policy. The mood in the DLPIP is to put off negotiations for

WTO accession until the industrial policy is in place (perhaps in five years), largely because WTO negotiations greatly complicate an already difficult task.[60]

Thus during the second phase Chinese officials have lost the considerable enthusiasm for joining the WTO that they showed in the first phase. Although PRC leaders have continued to take some positive steps (i.e., the tariff reductions announced at APEC), they have stated they do not expect to gain admission to the WTO any time soon.[61] Indeed, the U.S. government as of late 1998 was trying to rebuild momentum for the negotiations.

## The Impact of China's Integration

THE IMPACT OF CHINA'S INTEGRATION
ON THE INTERNATIONAL REGIME

Thus far China's integration into the world trade and investment systems has occurred without significant disruption to the regime. China has not forced a change of rules on those systems; rather the dominant trend has been for its reformers to adjust their rules to fit those of the regime. The country's relatively smooth integration into the regime is reflected most obviously in the fact that the regime has absorbed a huge volume of transactions and has emerged with neither a new set of Chinese rules for negotiation or transactions nor a new Chinese hegemony. For some individual countries China has provided export competition, but such competition is to be expected and is an integral part of the system. Moreover, the fact that China has grown to be the developing world's largest recipient of foreign direct investment has not created great disgruntlement among other countries at similar stages of development. Rather many developing countries strive to learn what they consider to be the secrets of China's success.

China's participation in the world economy has added a new element to the system of trade alliances, particularly in East Asia. Most important, perhaps, is that its trade relations with Japan, South Korea, and Taiwan have had a stabilizing influence on the region, although such relations have by no means eliminated all tensions. The most significant factor from a regime-maintenance point of view is that China's acceptance of the major multilateral organizations—the IMF, World Bank, and GATT/WTO—has blunted greatly the idea advanced by advocates of the new international economic order that these institutions are tools of U.S. imperialism. China's participation in these organizations (or, in the case of GATT/WTO, its attempt to participate) has lent them new legitimacy; in effect, the largest outsider economy has chosen to join them.

When examining China's impact on the dominant regime, it is important to consider the possibility that China will offer a challenge to it. In other words, it is conceivable that leaders might emerge in China who would attempt to devise an alternative regime, rejecting the WTO-based system as unnecessarily invasive. What might the pieces of such a regime be? The core would likely be a revised and strongly Asia-oriented APEC that adheres to many norms of free trade (such as low tariffs), and yet—like Japan, South Korea, and Taiwan—is more tolerant of industrial policy, and that is not dominated by the United States (which could continue to leverage trade policies to insert itself into areas many Asian governments feel are their sovereign rights, such as treatment of political dissidents). An Asia-oriented APEC might be even more sympathetic to a relationship-based norm of interactions that avoids binding agreements of the sort that tend to make the PRC leadership uncomfortable than to a rule of law–based norm. As it stands already, Chinese leaders appear to feel APEC is an easy forum to operate in, saying it works in the "Asian way"—not requiring signed agreements, but working according to gradual negotiations to reach a consensus. It is already true that many investments from overseas Chinese investors (who have contributed as much as 70 percent of China's FDI in the 1990s) are back-of-the-envelope deals based on personal connections rather than on the rule of law.[62] Overseas Chinese often are given preferential treatment (such as lower export requirements), sometimes a result of relationships they may have cultivated with PRC officials. A new APEC also could provide a buffer against Western criticisms over lack of protection of intellectual property or Western attempts to link trade policy to human rights. It also conceivably could be a forum in which China could resist increased attempts by organizations such as the WTO and the World Bank to use "good governance" and anticorruption as criteria for membership or lending. Support from an Asia-exclusive trade organization would be forthcoming from some other members, notably Malaysia.

The possibility of such an Asian-based regime's being realized appears remote, however, particularly in light of the financial crisis in the region. First, China's reluctance in the mid-1990s to push forward with WTO membership appears to be not a long-term rejection but, rather, a strategic retreat. Despite their anger at the United States over the WTO, most PRC elites appear to believe that China *eventually* should be a part of it, and there is no evidence that Chinese leaders plan to advocate significant changes in the regime once their country is a member. More broadly, there is no evidence of a significant constituency within China that believes the PRC should absent itself from the dominant world economic regime. China may resist integration on some issues, especially insofar as called for by the legitimate desire to protect against massive unemployment and social unrest, but such resistance is unlikely to translate into regime-threatening behavior.

Second, although the less-confrontational Asian style of negotiation has broad appeal to Asian leaders, and although relationship-based business transactions often are preferred in Asia, it remains true that a rule-of-law system that is consistent with the international regime is integral to Asian capitalism. Rule of law, good governance, and free trade norms only become more deeply entrenched as Asian countries move into increasingly sophisticated forms of manufacturing; behaviors undermining these norms, such as protectionism and piracy, if not declining, are losing official sanction within the region. To the extent that such practices remain, they are not fully consistent with the dominant international regime and certainly disadvantage those businesses that do not have access to them, but they cannot be said to shake seriously the foundations of the liberal regime. Finally, although APEC is young, the organization's direction—as a free trade–based system consistent with WTO rules and involving U.S. participation—has been set.

For all these reasons, then, China's participation in the international trade and investment regimes has strengthened rather than endangered the dominant system, and it appears that it will continue to do so.

## THE IMPACT OF INTEGRATION ON CHINA'S DOMESTIC INSTITUTIONS

China's integration into the world trade and investment regimes has had an impact on its domestic politics at several levels, including political conflict, central-local relations, trade policy, and political institutions.

At the level of political *conflict*, the initial trade and investment policy and subsequent major changes have been the subject of some domestic political wrangling between reformers and conservatives.[63] Allowing foreigners to have influence over the economy, with the specter that China would become dependent on foreigners, was difficult for many people to accept. Campaigns of the early and mid-1980s against "spiritual pollution" and "bourgeois liberalization," and protests against the Japanese economic presence, were launched by cultural and economic conservatives to combat, in part, what they perceived as negative foreign influences. Yet although these conflicts should not be ignored, they have not been extremely disruptive within China; the leadership struggle has been moderate by post-1949 Chinese standards. The question of allowing significant foreign participation in the economy was settled relatively quickly in favor of the reformers. Throughout much of the 1980s and early 1990s, reformers became more confident about reform, and conservative voices held less sway. There is considerable societal support for the Open Policy as well, and no strong domestic constituency has emerged to oppose it. (Protests against Japanese participation in the Chinese economy have occurred sporadically, but they have been short-lived.) Urban intellectuals as well as the new class of business elites in China tend to be quite unambiguous in their support for the Open Policy.[64] Moreover, there has been no antimodernization unrest emanating from the countryside, as has occurred historically when markets and capitalism have spread to rural areas.[65] This is not to conclude that objections to further integration, appearing in either nationalist or protectionist guises, cannot grow in China; after all, both forces have been evident in recent years. However, it appears unlikely that the basic direction of the Open Policy will come to be the subject of extreme conflict.

The policy has contributed to another form of conflict that may be more enduring: political conflict between the center in Beijing, on one hand, and the provincial and local governments, on the other hand. There are two dimensions to this conflict. First, in part in an effort to win over local officials to the goals of the reform, the central government has granted increased authority to local governments (although not to firms). Localities—particularly in the coastal areas—were given greater latitude, for example, to decide export subsidies and to allocate foreign exchange. These local governments gained financially from the new trade policy, particularly insofar as they were allowed to keep a share of foreign exchange earned from exports.[66] The prospect for coastal regions to gain revenues and industrial capacity as a result of exports or foreign investment created strong incentives for further integration into the world economy. It also provided them with a source of independence from the center. Independence is particularly evident in the case of Guangdong Province, where extensive contacts with Hong Kong have furthered a sense of autonomy and led provincial leaders to resist central exhortations over foreign trade and investment policy. (Such resistance has occurred recently when Guangdong officials have been less than vigilant in adhering to central directives to combat piracy of intellectual property.)

Although decentralization to the localities has been effective at producing growth in China's export sector, particularly through TVEs, power has not shifted to societal actors as much as to local governments and party organs. The local state has most benefited from the developmental strategy.[67] Moreover, as noted previously, decentralization has occurred without much attention's being paid to uniformity of laws or standards. Competition between localities for export markets or investment has led regions to undercut each other, created considerable duplication of efforts, and encouraged a geographic crazy quilt of rules that may or may not be enforced.

The second type of central-local political conflict stems from the fact that it is primarily the coastal areas that have benefited from the Open Policy rather than the inland regions. Inland provincial and local governments have felt discriminated against by past policy and wish to reap some of the benefits of China's integration into the world economy. They have demanded that they too be allowed incentives to attract foreign capital and be allowed a greater proportion of funds to develop their infrastructure. The priorities embodied in the ninth Five-Year Plan (1996–2000) reflects the success of these demands.

Although China's integration into the international trade and investment system was less conflictual politically than might have been anticipated given the massive changes it spurred, the process of integration has had a deep influence on the country's domestic policies and its political institutions. The fact that, by and large, *policies* have been made increasingly consistent with the requirements of the international regime has already been discussed. The international regime has shaped China's *institutions* in several ways. To facilitate trade and investment, China's reformers restructured the institutional framework for foreign economic affairs.[68] They did this in part by organizing the foreign trade administration under one roof (MOFTEC) during the early 1980s in order to make it more consistent with the desire to push into international markets. In 1984 MOFTEC gave up its centralized monopoly on foreign trade (previously exercised through 12 trading foreign trade corporations) by expanding the number of FTCs to several thousand and allowing them fiscal and planning independence. As discussed earlier, incentives to localities to export were increased, so that local FTCs came to handle a greater portion of exports. This incentive for local governments to press forward into export markets remains strong.

Another aspect of the restructuring of foreign trade institutions allowed the World Bank, the IMF, and GATT to gain influence in the foreign trade bureaucracies of the People's Bank of China, the Ministry of

Finance, and MOFTEC. China has tried to use these counterpart offices to shape the impact of these multilateral institutions,[69] yet the flow of influence undoubtedly has been two-way. These counterpart offices within the Chinese government often house officials who have become important allies in gaining acceptance of international norms in China.

More generally, MOFTEC as a whole has gained much greater prominence within the central bureaucracy compared to its counterpart of the pre–Open Policy years. It has been granted some expanded powers as well; for example, MOFTEC was put in charge of GATT negotiations, at least in part to isolate the issue from more protectionist ministries.[70] And, when China is admitted to the WTO, MOFTEC stands to gain even more authority as the body with primary enforcement responsibilities for compliance with the international charter. MOFTEC has helped usher issues of the international economy into national prominence. Finally, although MOFTEC bureaucrats ultimately must carry out the will of China's top leaders, it is clear that over time the institutional interests of MOFTEC have become increasingly aligned with the norms of the international regime, and it often has been an able advocate within the government for China's adoption of international practices. Many of the excellent younger and highly educated officials MOFTEC has attracted into its ranks have experience abroad, either in school, in multilateral institutions, or in foreign businesses. Those who are in the departments charged with trade relations with Western countries, and those responsible for WTO negotiations, tend to be particularly supportive of extensive integration. The careers of those in such departments hinge on having relations go smoothly in the long run; even WTO negotiators, who are responsible for protecting China's interests, historically have been some of the most committed to their nation's accession.

These examples of institutional change show that Chinese officials and elites have made a rapid move up the learning curve for trade and investment. Chinese officials have learned how to garner economic benefits from their country's participation in the international regime, which in and of itself is a strong reason to expect continued support for the regime. Increasingly, the government also has learned to garner political benefits—to use its trade position as leverage in international political disputes. Whereas during much of the first phase the Chinese government would separate its commercial and political policies, more and more the regime has been willing, for example, to make procurement decisions for political reasons (or a combination of political and commercial reasons). A prominent example was China's awarding of large contracts for purchase of aircraft to the European consortium Airbus over Boeing in the spring of 1996. Relatedly, the Chinese government is asking U.S. companies to engage in more lobbying of the U.S. government on behalf of policies that would benefit both the corporations and the Chinese government.[71]

Although China's integration into the world economy thus far has produced changes in the country's processes that are broadly supportive of that integration, it is important to recognize the limits of that impact and how those limits may affect further integration. First, MOFTEC itself comprises several institutional interests, not all of which are equally favorable toward deeper integration. Officials in the FTCs in particular, although they have benefited from China's integration into the world economy thus far and strongly favor export growth, nonetheless have a strong incentive to protect the ministry's administrative control over trade. Such administrative authority provides their bureaucratic raison d'être and gives them access to financial resources (through tariffs, fees, and even corruption). Deeper integration that sets up pressures for devolution of export authority directly to the firm—particularly pressure for direct trading rights—can be expected to face pressure from local FTCs because it has potential to deny local trade officials of some of these resources.

Second, even if those in MOFTEC who are very favorable to deeper integration were to carry the day within the ministry, the ministry does not exist in a vacuum. It is subject to antitrade interests from elsewhere in the Chinese bureaucracy. MOFTEC officials frequently recount how they must try to convince officials in other ministries—particularly ministries with protectionist agendas—of the benefits of GATT/WTO. MOFTEC has become increasingly embattled in recent years, as industrial bureaucracies work to protect their interests through industrial policies or the maintenance of import tariffs. The State Planning Commission's DLPIP, which is responsible for industrial policy, even if not anticompetition, clearly has an interest in seeing that MOFTEC's WTO negotiations are consistent with its own vision for industrial policy. Indeed, China's chief WTO negotiator, Long Yungtu, reportedly has told U.S. business groups that MOFTEC is the only party working against industrial policies.

As in the past, then, policies relevant to China's trade behavior are subject to domestic bureaucratic politics. Sometimes pro-integration forces are influential, as in the apparent difficulty actually in formulating an industrial policy for electronics that is deemed by the State Planning Commission (SPC) too protectionist and hence likely to run afoul of the WTO.[72] At other times protectionist forces appear to prevail. This was clearly the case in the formulation of the automobile industrial policy.

## Overall Evaluation

### TRENDS IN CHINESE PARTICIPATION IN THE GLOBAL TRADE AND INVESTMENT REGIME

Taking a broad overview, it is difficult not to be impressed with the speed, magnitude, and depth of China's integration into the global economy during the post-Mao era. More than could have been imagined as recently as 15 years ago, early sources of friction have been resolved. Integration into the world economy has reoriented significant portions of China's trade and foreign investment bureaucracy. From the point of view of regime maintenance, the worry that the rapid rise of a new power such as China is inevitably destabilizing has not been realized.

This positive assessment can be made particularly for the first phase, the years from 1978 to 1994. The factor most responsible for smooth integration during this period was the Chinese leadership's commitment to integration—at least at the shallow stages—which was supported by a hospitable international environment. The period from 1994 through 1998 has been more problematic, as we have seen. China's application for WTO membership has highlighted the difficulties of deeper integration. It also has raised crucial questions in the minds of both Chinese and foreign officials about how far toward a full market system China is willing to travel, and how fast; in other words, the problems reflect the ambiguity over whether China's government intends to retain significantly greater administrative controls over foreign economic interactions or is instead committed to full integration (or some approximation thereof).

The most critical barrier to deeper integration seems to be the renewal of a cautious outlook within the PRC leadership. The changed leadership outlook appears to be a result of (1) the increased power of industrial interests (aligned with key bureaucratic interests) who adhere to a partial integration model and wish to erect barriers to foreign competition, (2) a growing cognizance on the part of reformers of the costs of deeper integration, and (3) rising actual costs of integration, as any tendency of the U.S. government to admit China on comparatively lenient terms has essentially evaporated. Hence, particularly with regard to negotiations over China's WTO membership and pressures from the United States over market access and IPR, many Chinese officials appear to be behaving according to a partial-integration mindset. At the same time, those officials who might favor deeper integration have felt a need to remain cautious when succession issues dominate elite politics (although this problem has lessened as of the late 1990s) and the populace is growing more nationalistic and wary of "U.S. hegemony." The net result has been to dampen Chinese enthusiasm for continuing integration.

These barriers can be broken through in negotiations, of course. But can the impetus for foward movement come from outside China? It is precisely because the stakes of the current situation are so high that it is important to consider the possibility that actions taken outside China can significantly reverse the situation. The following section focuses on this issue.

## THE ROLE OF OUTSIDE PRESSURE IN CHINA'S INTEGRATION INTO THE WORLD ECONOMY

Two related questions should be asked about the role of external forces in shaping China's integration into the world economy: Which have been more important for shaping China's Open Policy, exogenous or endogenous pressures? In what ways is outside pressure effective, and in what ways is it counterproductive?

Evidence on the relative importance of exogenous and endogenous forces in shaping China's integration suggests that the crucial variable has been domestic; although international variables have influenced policy and leadership attitudes, they have done so at the margins.[74] It is clear that the original impetus for China's Open Policy was internal. Chinese policy communities favoring reform existed prior to the initiation of reforms; although reformers were influenced by what they saw in the outside world (particularly in Hong Kong and Taiwan), they made the decision to open to trade and investment unilaterally.[74] The reforms of China's foreign trade and investment policy and structure that were made throughout the 1980s and early 1990s, like the original decision to open the economy, were driven by the domestic desire for integration into the world economy. Outside pressure induced China to take certain specific steps toward integration, yet such pressure was unlikely to have been effective without the belief by the most influential Chinese leaders that integration (1) was consistent with ongoing domestic trends, (2) was in China's best interest, and (3) required trade-offs that would have substantial concrete benefits and rather minor costs. Moreover, the central factor behind the current plateau phase of integration is the change in leadership outlook—a rethinking of the costs of integration on the part of some reformers and the increased power of protectionist forces within China's bureaucracy—in the context of a period of succession and a new nationalism.

Even if outside pressure is influential only at the margins, the questions of when and under what circumstances it has been (and in the future can be) useful for achieving U.S. policy goals remains important. It is a difficult question to answer, however. Evidence on the effectiveness of foreign pressure is primarily anecdotal and is clouded by the fact that decision making on trade issues in Beijing and Washington usually goes on behind closed doors. It also is difficult to gauge the cause-effect relationship between foreign pressure and Chinese response because Chinese officials are loath to acknowledge that changes have been made as a result of foreign pressures, while U.S. officials may overstate the impact their negotiations have had in changing Chinese behavior. Foreign pressure on a given issue sometimes is followed by Chinese cooperation on that or a related issue, but it is not always clear that cooperation is *due* to foreign pressure, or whether pressure would have been effective with a different constellation of domestic or other international forces.

Despite these difficulties, we may gain some insights by examining the conditions under which outside influence has been most accepted within China and when it appears to have changed Chinese behavior. In general, outside influence appears to have been most effective at encouraging China's smooth integration into the world economy during the period from 1981 to 1994 (with a hiatus, driven by both foreign and Chinese reactions to Tiananmen, from 1989 to 1992). These years, of course, roughly map the first phase. Recall that favorable attitudes of both dominant Chinese officials and foreign governments, the enthusiasm by foreign businesses, a favorable international economic environment, and the ability of China to get positive and rapid economic results from policy changes (high benefits) while retaining significant control (low costs) *all* were present during these early years of integration. Under these conditions, the outside pressure to which Chinese reformers primarily responded—and from which they learned the most—was not foreign government pressure but, rather, *market* forces. Chinese policymakers responded to market inducements such as the possibility of increased exports, or to the appeal that with a liberalized environment foreign companies holding back capital would be lured into the China market. For example, in 1985–1986, the Chinese government significantly liberalized its foreign exchange controls as they applied to foreign businesses by creating swap centers and aiding joint ventures with foreign exchange shortfalls. It loosened these controls even while it was tightening authority over use of foreign exchange by domestic producers. There was no apparent sentiment among top-level reformers that, absent the reactions of foreign investors, China should relax the requirement for a foreign exchange balance at that point.[75] The Chinese government's creation in the 1980s of a program of tax incentives in order to compete with other host countries in Asia with little if any foreign governmental pressure is another example of the nation's response to outside market pressures.

While outside market forces were the most influential, under the favorable conditions of the pre-1994 years foreign *governmental* voices, both bilateral and multilateral, found an ear. Sometimes outside voices were actively encouraged. Representatives from the World Bank, the IMF, and GATT often were allowed to provide training, such as in the areas of accounting and statistics. In some cases China adopted outright certain policies suggested by multilateral institutions such as the IMF and World Bank. For example, China's reformers were responsive to foreign suggestions that more Western capital (which would bring advanced technology) or overseas Chinese capital (which would bring export capability) would result from policies to cut red tape and make laws more transparent and from promulgation of concrete investment incentives.

If the confluence of positive conditions in the first phase meant China was more open to non-coercive political and market inducements from outside, it also seemed to allow more coercive outside pressure to be relatively effective. Hence, in the relatively hospitable environment of the first phase, use of a stick seemed to result in Chinese concessions on issues that were very important and that the U.S. government chose to pursue vigorously, most notably issues of IPR and market access. But for the haranguing of U.S. negotiators, an agreement to speed up establishment of rules and institutions to protect IPR would have been unlikely, even though many central reformers apparently were sympathetic to such actions. This vision of foreign effectiveness with the stick must be qualified by the recognition that agreements between the United States and China often came only after very difficult negotiations, in which China agreed to U.S. demands at the last minute. With little clear or immediate benefit to the Chinese government, its negotiators bargained hard to preserve the status quo. Nevertheless, direct, coercive pressure from outside also induced Chinese policymakers to take steps they were unlikely to have done absent such pressure, or at a quicker pace.

The stalled negotiations over China's WTO admission, with China balking at foreign requirements that it further change its trade policies, are the most obvious result of the less-hospitable attitude on the part of Chinese policymakers. Foreign pressure over IPR in both 1995 and 1996 did, in fact, produce agreements between the U.S. and Chinese governments, suggesting that U.S. efforts to bring China into line with international norms *can* work (in the sense of gaining an agreement, though not necessarily enforcement). But even if this sort of brinkmanship can result in agreements, the spillover to other parts of the relationship that results from the acrimony produced by use of the U.S. stick may be more poisonous than if the overall U.S.-China relationship were less fragile. Moreover, agreements produced in such an environment may not create the will Chinese leaders need to enforce or implement them. Top reformers who are sympathetic to the need for greater IPR protection, or who desire WTO admission soon, find it more difficult to gain the domestic allies they need when foreigners seem to be acting as hegemons.[76] Ironically, the same forces that make strong international pressure appear more necessary than ever are less effective than such pressure was before the mid-1990s. Simultaneously, the carrot of increased access to trade and capital may not have as strong an impact on China as it did before, simply because the volume of both is already so great.[77]

Thus, in the plateau phase, both less and more coercive foreign pressure appear to have been rendered less potent because of the difficulty of U.S.-China relations, rising nationalism and protectionism within China, and, especially, a reassessment of the benefits and costs of continued integration. In what ways might outside voices enhance the probability that they will be heard in this more difficult environment? At a minimum, better overall U.S.-China relations will be more conducive to outside voices' being heard, albeit at the margins. Removing the demon factor may encourage Chinese reformers to remain more open to outside advice and may enable them to sell integration within China more easily. Thus it is important to support those Chinese officials who have in the past been advocates of a full-integration model but who now may be wavering.

An overall improvement in relations is particularly important for the issue of China's WTO admission. The United States has a long-term interest in China's participation in the WTO; although it appears China is unlikely to create an alternative regime with different rules, without China in the WTO the United States loses a key forum for seeing that China adheres to the rules of the regime. Many influential Chinese leaders also perceive their country's membership in the WTO to be important, both as leverage for further domestic economic reforms and for prestige reasons. But, while the fact that all parties have an interest in China's admission to the WTO bodes well for the long term, what occurs in the short run, particularly within China, can have a decisive impact on the terms under which admission eventually occurs. Specifically, within several years, the Chinese leadership likely will have promulgated industrial policies in key areas of interest to U.S. business, including aviation, telecommunications, construction, electronics, and petrochemicals. Even if industrial policy is not necessarily aimed at protectionism by those who help formulate it, a policy process open to strongly protectionist pressures from industry likely will generate a higher degree of protectionism than is in U.S. interests. Rather than having China return to the table after a hiatus in serious negotiations with a fait accompli of established industrial policies, it is advisable to push hard to resolve the difficulties surrounding its WTO admission, so that WTO rules will be in force during the formulation of industrial policies. Moreover, a MOFTEC that must be the watchdog for WTO enforcement within China will have a natural role to play in the formulation of industrial policy if China is a member but will have a weaker voice if others can reject its opinion as being relevant only in the future. This argument is made often by MOFTEC's WTO negotiators and surely is useful as a bargaining strategy. But its logic is supportive of U.S. interests as well.

Given the unsteady nature of U.S.-China relations, and the perception in China that the United States is acting like a hegemon, the U.S. government would be wise to rely on multilateral strategies as much as possible. Although there are differences among the United States, the European Union, and Japan with regard to China, they share a basic interest in China's deepening cooperation. The United States should be able to leverage the perceived need among its allies to stand behind it publicly and to minimize the points of difference. The U.S. government also should leverage the positive relations it has with Asian countries and in fora such as APEC, in which those with an interest in a more open Chinese market also participate. Such strategies, in tandem with a concerted effort on the part of U.S. foreign policymakers at the highest levels, may make it possible to support those forces within China that will bring a return to the more positive scenario of the first phase.

## Notes

In addition to written sources, this chapter is based on interviews with officials in the U.S. government, the World Bank, the Chinese embassy, the People's Republic of China's State Planning Commission, and several PRC scholars and government researchers. In addition to the members of the Council's task force, I wish to thank the following people for their help in providing resources and/or useful comments: Richard Brecher, Elizabeth Economy, Ann Kent, Nicholas Lardy, Robert Lee, Liu Xiaobo, Michel Oksenberg, Dan Rosen, Michael Ryan, Shi Xieqing, Michael Turner, and N.T. Wang.

1.  I thank Andrew Nathan for suggesting these two general models.

2.  As will be discussed further later, complete integration, meaning that no trade and investment barriers exist, is a standard that has yet to be reached

by any single economy or by the international trade and investment regime as a whole. Hence the realistic goal of a full integration model as applied to China is to have the PRC participate on approximately the same terms as the most open industrial economies.

3. This mental mind-set is shown to underlie China's foreign investment policy during the 1980s in Margaret M. Pearson, *Joint Ventures in the People's Republic of China: The Control of Foreign Capital under Socialism* (Princeton, N.J.: Princeton University Press, 1991).

4. On evidence of this position within the World Bank, see World Bank, *The Chinese Economy: Fighting Inflation, Deepening Reforms* (Washington, D.C.: The World Bank, 1996), pp. 6–8.

5. On the origins of the dominant liberal regime, see: Judith Goldstein, *Ideas, Interests, and American Trade Policy* (Ithaca, N.Y.: Cornell University Press 1993), pp. 153–164; and G. John Ikenberry, "Creating Yesterday's New World Order: Keynesian 'New Thinking' and the Anglo-American Postwar Settlement," in Judith Goldstein and Robert O. Keohane, eds., *Ideas and Foreign Policy: Beliefs, Institutions and Policy Change* (Ithaca: Cornell University Press, 1993), pp. 57–86.

6. Nontariff barriers include voluntary export restraints, import quotas, domestic content requirements, product standards, and subsidies. "National treatment" can be defined as "treating imports and domestic supplies equally inside a national market." Most-favored-nation treatment refers to "nondiscrimination between exporters." See Will Martin and L. Alan Winters, *The Uruguay Round: Widening and Deepening the World Trading System* (Washington, D.C.: The World Bank, 1995), p. 20.

7. China's negotiation of bilateral investment treaties is not considered in this chapter.

8. WTO rules can be applied to FDI through several agreements arising out of the Uruguay round of GATT negotiations, including the Agreement on Trade-Related Investment Measures (TRIMs), the General Agreement on Trade in Services, and the agreement on Trade Related Aspects of Intellectual Property Rights (TRIPs). See Martin and Winters, *The Uruguay Round*, p. 28; and James V. Feinerman, "A New World Order," *China Business Review*, 22, No. 2 (March–April 1995): 16–18.

9. On competitive liberalization in East Asia, see Stephan Haggard and Tun-jen Cheng, "State and Capital in the East Asian NICs," in Frederic C. Deyo, ed., *The Political Economy of the New Asian Industrialism* (Ithaca, N.Y.: Cornell University Press), pp. 84–135. TRIMs negotiated during the GATT Uruguay Round has dampened such competition as a goal. Martin and Winters, *The Uruguay Round*.

10. The MFA is to be pledged out over a ten-year period, although little action had been taken on this phase-out as of late 1996.

11. On the politics of GATT (and trade policy in general) in the United States, see Goldstein, *Ideas, Interests, and American Trade Policy*; and I. M. Destler,

*American Trade Politics*, 3d ed. (Washington, D.C.: Institute for International Economics, 1995).

12. This vision is expressed by C. Fred Bergsten, chairman of the APEC Eminent Persons Group. See Bergsten, "APEC and World Trade: A Force for Worldwide Liberalization," *Foreign Affairs* 73, No. 3 (May–June 1994): 20–26. APEC began as a consultative body in 1989 but by 1994 had grown to eighteen members and had become more of an official forum for leaders of these countries to meet concerning economic issues.

13. Malaysian Prime Minister Mahathir Mohamad has proposed an Asian consultative body, the East Asia Economic Caucus, as an alternative to APEC. With membership excluding the United States, Canada, Australia, and New Zealand, the EAEC would act as a buffer organization between APEC (which Mahathir Mohamad fears will be dominated by the United States) and the ASEAN nations. This proposal has not progressed, because of lack of support by the United States and Japan. See Jane Khanna, "Asia-Pacific Economic Cooperation and Challenges for Political Leadership," *Washington Quarterly* 17, No. 1 (Winter 1996): 259.

14. See, for example, S. Gordon Redding, *The Spirit of Chinese Capitalism* (Berlin: Walter de Gruyter, 1990); and Edward A. Gargan, "An Asian Giant Spreads Roots: Personal Ties Aid Growth in China," *New York Times*, November 14, 1995, pp. D1, D4.

15. The possibility that economic strength can be leveraged into international political or military power appears to have been a secondary part of the leadership's motivation, although in very recent years the Chinese government seems more cognizant of the ways that economic power may be leveraged into political and military power.

16. Broadly speaking, investors from Asia have set their sights primarily on production for reexport, while Western and Japanese investors have had their eye on production for the China market. Asian investors also have invested heavily in Chinese real estate.

17. On such defensive investment, as well as the appeal of the potential market, see Pearson, *Joint Ventures in the People's Republic*, pp. 31–34.

18. Resolution of trade disputes between the United States and other countries has been more successful (for the United States) when the target government of negotiation is a GATT member, as the United States can frame complaints in terms of violations of GATT rules to which a member country has committed. See Michael P. Ryan, *Playing by the Rules: American Trade Power and Diplomacy in the Pacific* (Washington, D.C.: Georgetown University Press, 1995).

19. That a significant hardening toward international norms occurred in other realms in the early 1990s has been pointed out to me by Ann Kent (regarding the international human rights regime) and Joan Lebold Cohen (regarding the arts).

20. The U.S. trade deficit with China has risen quickly since the late 1980s, from $3.5 billion in 1988 to $18.3 billion in 1992, to $34 billion in 1995. "Investment Data" *China Business Review* (May–June 1996): 41.

21. Exports of foreign-funded enterprises have grown from 1.1 percent of total exports in 1985 to 28.7 percent in 1994, and contributed about 60 percent of export growth. Nicholas R. Lardy, "The Role of Foreign Trade and Investment in China's Economic Transition," *China Quarterly*, No. 144 (December 1995): 1074.

22. This analysis of China's relations with the bank and IMF is based on discussions with World Bank officials in 1996, and on Harold K. Jacobson and Michel Oksenberg, *China's Participation in the IMF, the World Bank, and GATT: Toward a Global Economic Order* (Ann Arbor: University of Michigan Press, 1990).

23. Jacobson and Oksenberg, *China's Participation in the IMF*, pp. 127–28.

24. Ryan, *Playing by the Rules*, chap. 8. China's efforts were aided by textile importers in the United States, who lobbied hard to keep a high level of inexpensive Chinese clothing imports.

25. On these reasons, see Susan L. Shirk, *How China Opened Its Door: The Political Success of the PRC's Foreign Trade and Investment Reforms* (Washington, D.C.: Brookings Institution, 1994), pp. 71–72. On the role of another international financial organization, the IMF, in moving China to current account convertibility, see Chapter 6.

26. A domestic reason for wishing to reform the trading system was to reduce the burden of financial subsidies from the state budget to the foreign trade sector. See World Bank, *China: Foreign Trade Reform* (Washington, D.C.: The World Bank, 1994), p. 24.

27. On these changes, see Nicholas R. Lardy, *Foreign Trade and Economic Reform in China, 1978–1990* (New York: Cambridge University Press 1992), chap. 3; World Bank, *China*, p. xvi and chap. 2; and He Chang (1994), "Article Views Prospects of Admission to GATT 'This Year,'" *Zhongguo Tongxun She* (Hong Kong), in FBIS, March 17, 1994, p. 2. The scaling-back of the foreign trade plan went hand in hand with the decentralization of responsibility for the plan to local foreign trade corporations (FTCs).

28. On the slower liberalization in the import structure, see: World Bank, *China*, pp. xvi–xvii, 39–41; and World Bank, *The Chinese Economy: Fighting Inflation, Deepening Reforms* (Washington, D.C.: The World Bank, 1996), pp. 6–8. Lardy, (in "The Role of Foreign Trade and Investment,") suggests that Chinese import tariffs and nontariff barriers are quite high by international standards.

29. Such activity, which is not sanctioned by the Chinese government, reflects a surreptitious effort by domestic enterprises to gain access to the tax benefits and other privileges that are offered only to foreign investors. Moreover, local officials, hoping to look good to Beijing, may inflate statistics by

counting vague letters of intent signed with foreign firms as solid contracts. Many of these deals may never come to fruition, as is shown by the
figures in Table 5.2 on utilized investment as a percentage of pledged
investment. The decline in utilized investment as a percentage of pledged
investment in recent years suggests that inflation of statistics has
increased.

30. See World Bank, 1996, p. 8; and UNCTAD, *World Investment Report: Transnational Corporations and Development* (Geneva: UNCTAD, 1995), box II.2.

31. The liberalization of controls that resulted was played out in three broad
phases during the period from 1979 to 1988: 1979 to mid-1983, late 1983 to
mid-1986, and late 1986 through 1988. A major law that significantly clari-
fied or liberalized the environment for foreign investment marked the
beginning of each phase. See Pearson, *Joint Ventures in the People's Republic.*

32. One of these efforts included amendments to the Joint Venture Law promulgated in March 1990.

33. Neither Confucian nor Marxian traditions considers knowledge to incur
property rights. For fascinating discussions of the roots of the precommu-
nist and Marxian views of intellectual property in China, see: William
Alford, *To Steal a Book Is a Glorious Offense* (Stanford, Calif.: Stanford University Press, 1995); and Michel Oksenberg, Pitman Potter, and William B.
Abnett, "Easing the IPR Problem in China's Foreign Economic Relations,"
prepared for the National Bureau of Asian Research (Seattle: NBAR, 1996).

34. China promulgated a trademark law in 1992 (revised in 1993), a patent law
in 1984 (revised 1993), a copyright law in 1990, and computer software regulations in 1991. Other civil laws, such as the General Principles of Civil
Law (1986) and the Civil Procedure Law (1991), recognize the rights of
individuals to hold and enforce copyrights, patents, and trademarks. Institutions established to oversee these laws include the State Copyright
Administration, the National Patent Office, and the Trademark Office.
(Existing agencies, such as the Customs Service, have enforcement roles as
well.) China has joined the World Intellectual Property Organization
(1980), the Paris Convention for the Protection of Industrial Property
(1984), and the Berne Convention for the Protection of Literacy and Artis-
tic Works (1992). See Oksenberg, Potter, and Abnett, "Easing the IPR Problem," pp. 20–21.

35. This discussion is based on ibid., pp. 7, 13, 16, and 24.

36. The "miracle" economies of East Asia also benefited from a favorable
international environment for trade. In contrast, efforts to reform many
Latin American economies in earlier decades were hindered by poor international economic circumstances. See Robert Wade, "East Asia's Economic Success: Conflicting Perspectives, Partial Insights, Shaky
Evidence," *World Politics* 44, No. 2 (January 1992): 270–320.

37. China benefited by the fact that foreign investors were willing to make less-attractive deals than they might have received elsewhere in order to get a "foot in the door" to the Chinese market. Still, it is unlikely that foreign investors would have taken such steps if there were not signs that China gradually was coming into the world system.

38. On the distinction between "shallow" and "deep" integration, see Destler, *American Trade Politics*, p. 36, and Shirk, *How China Opened Its Door*, pp. xiii and 4.

39. World Bank, *The Chinese Economy*, p. 8. However, some import bans were erected under the new automobile industrial policy (discussed later). Note, too, that the tariff reductions made by China in the APEC framework would not necessarily be binding in the WTO.

40. Discussions with U.S. trade negotiator, Washington, D.C., March 1997. It should be noted that nothing is definitely agreed until everything is agreed.

41. An additional discussion of the complexities of China's admission to GATT is found in Nicholas L. Lardy, *China in the World Economy* (Washington, D.C.: Institute for International Economics, 1994), pp. 44–47.

42. Feinerman, "A New World Order," p. 16. Feinerman further notes that, by the end of the 1980s, "the United States and other countries also began to see the GATT as a means of countering the growing strength of regional trade blocs such as the European Union."

43. The U.S. government, through the USTR, has taken the lead on WTO negotiations with China. There are some differences on standards for China's admission among WTO members. Nevertheless, according to officials in the United States and from other Western nations, the U.S. position has much support from both Western allies and many nations in Asia.

44. Jacobson and Oksenberg, *China's Participation in the IMF*, p. 105.

45. The United States set additional conditions on China's accession to GATT in 1993, including convertibility of renminbi, uniform tax treatment, opening of the service market, and abolition of preferential policies for localities (such as the SEZs). Shirk, *How China Opened Its Door*, p. 73. China had achieved effective convertibility on the current account by the end of 1996 and had eliminated many preferential policies by that time as well.

46. The safeguards are allowed under the GATT/WTO as a means for existing contracting members that are subject to injuriously large increases in imports of a specific product to adopt emergency restrictions on those imports (both tariff and nontariff restrictions), if such a clause is part of the accession protocol. The United States and European Community have for a number of years insisted on this safeguard protection clause in China's accession protocol. This clause obviously qualifies the principle of nondiscrimination that is supposed to be central to GATT/WTO. (See Lardy, *China in the World Economy*, pp. 45, 135.) Similar safeguards were imposed

against Japan by European countries when Japan entered GATT in the early 1960s.

47. Article 13 of the WTO charter (formerly Article 35 of the GATT charter), the "non-application" provision, allows a country to avoid applying all or part of the charter to a new country.

48. The issue of China's industrial policies as a barrier to WTO admission recently has gained attention of WTO officials in Geneva, who at the request of the Chinese delegation prepared a paper discussing the link between industrial policy and key GATT agreements. This paper and an analysis are found in a special report in *Inside U.S. Trade*, April 5, 1996.

49. These industries were cited in interviews conducted with Chinese officials and scholars in the second half of 1996 and in World Bank, *The Chinese Economy*, p. 18. On China's industrial policy, especially in automobiles, see also "China's Accession to the WTO/GATT: Investment/Industrial Policies" (Washington D.C.: The U.S.-China Business Council), September 15, 1995.

50. One DLPIP official interviewed stated that, unlike the industrial policies of Japan and Korea, trade protectionism is not the foremost concern in China. Simple trade protectionism is not possible in China, he argued, because the post–cold war international environment will not allow it. Moreover, China's enterprises are state owned and so, unlike East Asia's private enterprises, need incentives to be competitive. Indicative of this official's liberal views, he also described with favor the current market reforms as creating a privately owned economy. The view that Chinese planners have a commitment to eventual competitiveness is also found in World Bank, *The Chinese Economy*, pp. 17–18.

51. For example, implementing regulations clarifying the status of contractual joint ventures were promulgated in September 1995. See Peter J. Halasz and Lan Lan, "New Rules of the Game," *China Business Review* 23, No. 1 (January–February 1996): 39–41.

52. The Chinese had expressed such preferences previously. For example, in 1986 the Implementing Regulations for Joint Ventures treated favorably investment projects that enhanced exports and the absorption of advanced technology. More recently China began specifying sectors in which it prefers to encourage foreign investment. The 1995 statement is the most clear-cut and firm of such sectoral guidelines.

53. Shirk, *How China Opened Its Door*.

54. China's accession to the WTO should help solve problems of both market access and transparency/uniformity in investment as well as trade. A number of problems, such as local content and foreign exchange balancing requirements (discussed previously), are addressed in the Agreement on Trade-Related Investment Measures. Michael Daniels, Richard King, and Peter Bernstein, "TRIMming Protectionism," *China Business Review* 22, No. 2 (March–April 1995): 20–21.

55. One year after signing the 1995 agreement, business representatives from software and entertainment industries were contending that China's enforcement of agreements continued to be unacceptably weak. See Kathy Chen, "China Still Ignores Copyrights, Group Says," *Wall Street Journal*, April 10, 1996, p. A9.

56. Carlos A. Primo Braga, "Protection on a Global Scale," *China Business Review* 22, No. 5 (March–April 1995): 25–27. If China is admitted as a developed country, it will have one year to apply the TRIPs provisions; on the other hand, as a developing country, China would have five years (and longer in some instances).

57. State Planning Commission Economics Research Institute Task Force, "Dui huifu guanmao zongxieding diwei hou de xiaoyi fenxi he duice" (Effective analysis and countermeasures after China resumes its place in GATT), *Guoji Maoyi* (Intertrade), No. 2 (1993): 10.

58. In contrast, according to Shirk (*How China Opened Its Door*, p. 73), the original decision to join GATT was made in a centralized fashion.

59. The major force for protection within MOFTEC is the FTCs, which, as noted earlier, have an interest in retaining bureaucratic control over trade.

60. DLPIP officials apparently find it very difficult to try to fight the domestic battles over industrial policy and at the same time keep an eye on ongoing WTO negotiations (which have an impact on industrial policy). They claim that it will be easier to make changes in industrial policy to bring it into line with WTO later, for such changes can be made by the DLPIP almost unilaterally, rather than the current process of formulating the initial policies, which require broad participation.

61. Chinese officials involved in the negotiations claimed in interviews in late 1998 that they did not expect quick admission to the WTO.

62. Much of this overseas Chinese investment flows into rural TVEs. Recall, however, that a significant proportion of investments from Hong Kong and Macao are "recycled" funds from the PRC.

63. See Shirk, *How China Opened Its Door*. Key conservatives on many issues of the Open Policy have included Chen Yun, Li Peng, and Deng Liqun.

64. See Margaret M. Pearson, *China's New Business Elite: The Political Impact of Economic Reform in China* (Berkeley: University of California Press, 1997).

65. See Karl Polanyi, *The Great Transformation* (Boston: Beacon Press, 1944).

66. This share has fluctuated. In the mid-1980s, for example, it was 42 percent, Lardy, *Foreign Trade and Economic Reform*, pp. 53, 57.

67. See David Zweig, "'Developmental Communities on China's Coast: The Impact of Trade, Investment, and Transnational Alliances," *Comparative Politics* (April 1995): 253–74.

68. The works that form the basis for the following discussion on institutional change include Lardy, *Foreign Trade and Economic Reform*; Shirk, *How China*

*Opened Its Door;* and Jacobson and Oksenberg, *China's Participation in the IMF.*

69. David Zweig, "Controlling the Opening: Enmeshment, Organizational Capacity, and the Limits of Overseas Development Assistance in China," paper presented at the annual meeting of the American Political Science Association, Washington, D.C., 1993. Unlike Jacobson and Oksenberg, Zweig emphasizes China's successful efforts to maintain control over the terms of integration with a variety of international organizations, including the World Bank.

70. Shirk, *How China Opened Its Door,* p. 73.

71. Such requests reflect a continuing Marxian perception on the part of Chinese officials that U.S. policymaking is dominated by business interests and that the most effective lobbying strategy for the Chinese government is through influence on U.S. companies.

72. Denis Fred Simon, "From Cold to Hot: Beijing Wants Electronics Industries to Play in the Big League," *China Business Review* 23, No. 6 (November–December 1996): 8–16.

73. This conclusion is consistent with that of Jacobson and Oksenberg (*China's Participation in the IMF,* pp. 140, 155) about China's cooperation with the IMF and World Bank. The question of the relative importance of exogenous and endogenous variables has been broadly debated in the field of international relations. Arguments that domestic structures shape the international system are found in Kenneth Waltz, *Man, the State, and War* (New York: Columbia University Press, 1954). A counterargument that domestic structures are shaped by the international system is found in Peter Gourevitch, "The Second Image Reversed: The International Sources of Domestic Politics," *International Organization* 32 (1978): 881–912. That the two variables exist in an iterative relationship—domestic decision makers operate within the context of international constraints but do have choices about how to respond to these constraints—is found in Peter Katzenstein, *Small States in World Markets: Industrial Policy in Europe* (Ithaca, N.Y.: Cornell University Press, 1985).

74. Even though productivity rates were declining, the Chinese economy in the late 1970s, following the Cultural Revolution, was not collapsing and so did not require reform in order to survive.

75. Had policy on foreign exchange for foreign investors closely followed the cycles of loosening and tightening of controls that were applied to domestic enterprises, this would have suggested that foreign exchange policy for joint ventures was driven wholly by internal forces. See Margaret M. Pearson, "The Erosion of Controls over Foreign Capital in China, 1979–1988: Having Their Cake and Eating It Too?" *Modern China* 17, No. 1 (January 1991): 112–50.

76. Threats of Section 301 sanctions may be losing their effectiveness more generally. These threats must appear credible in order to be effective. Whereas the specter of U.S. sanctions seemed real in the early 1990s when the tool was first used, the threat that sanctions are actually credible is, ironically, undermined by the fact that negotiations (which sometimes have levied only rather weak requirements on foreign governments) always cause sanctions to be averted.

77. China's leaders seemed to be not at all concerned about the 1994–1995 drop in pledged foreign investment, particularly because the drop came primarily at the expense only of investments it considered less valuable.

# 6

# China and the International Financial System

## NICHOLAS R. LARDY

SINCE its economic reforms began in the late 1970s China has become an increasingly important participant in the international financial system, particularly in comparison with other transition economies. It has become far and away the largest borrower from the World Bank and also is one of the largest recipients of bilateral development assistance from advanced industrial economies. More important, China in more recent years has become a significant commercial borrower and also has tapped international capital markets. It was the first transition economy to gain an investment-grade credit rating on its sovereign external debt.[1] From 1991 through the end of 1996 China issued $12.50 billion in international bonds.[2] By the end of 1996 the country had an external debt of $116.3 billion. About one-third of these borrowed funds was provided through international financial institutions and official bilateral creditors. The remaining two-thirds were provided by commercial banks and other private creditors.[3] China also tapped international equity markets, raising $13.5 billion, almost all in Hong Kong and New York, by year-end 1997. In addition, Hong Kong companies that control assets in China, known as "Red Chips," by mid-1997 had raised an additional $12 billion in share offerings and rights issues, part of which had been injected into China.[4]

China's ready and favorable access to international bond markets contrasts sharply with Russia's access. Russia did not conclude the rescheduling of its outstanding external debt to commercial banks and international agencies until late 1996, forcing it repeatedly to postpone its planned first sale of bonds to international investors.[5] When the first sovereign bond issue since the Bolshevik revolution came to market in late 1996, international investors demanded a premium of 345 basis points over U.S. Treasury bills of comparable maturity. This large premium was consistent with the noninvestment-grade status that Moody's awarded to Russian sovereign debt in 1996.

This chapter argues that in its growing participation in international financial markets, China increasingly has conformed to the implicit norms of the international financial system. Moreover, this involvement is beginning to have far-reaching consequences for China's domestic financial system. The influence of the international system on its domestic banking system to date, however, has been more modest. This slower international influence on China's banking system is the greatest obstacle to the nation's achieving its announced objective of creating an international financial center in Shanghai.

## The International Regime

Unlike most other case studies in this volume, the international regime in finance is not composed of a number of discrete formal agreements and treaties.[6] Important international financial organizations do exist, such as the World Bank, the International Monetary Fund (IMF), regional development banks such as the Asian Development Bank (ADB), and the Bank for International Settlements. And some quite specialized agreements, such as the 1992 Basle Capital Accord (discussed later), exist. These organizations and agreements collectively constitute a regime that prescribes many important norms for the international financial system. But the system as a whole is much broader than that defined by the international and regional financial organizations and specialized agreements. Thus qualitatively this regime is quite different from those in other domains.

In international finance the market itself, rather than a series of formal agreements, is the principal source of the norms of behavior. This regime differs in important ways from the regimes in other domains. First, as already suggested, it is largely implicit rather than explicit. Second, the important variables embedded in the implicit norms usually are measured on a continuum rather than in a bivariate form. For example, in the case of the international arms control regime, either countries are in compliance with agreements, such as the Comprehensive Test Ban Treaty, or they are not. As is discussed later, in international finance the key variables include transparency, timeliness, and accuracy. Compliance with the expectations of international investors with respect to these variables is almost always a matter of degree. Third, penalties for noncompliance with the norms of the international regime usually are exacted automatically by the market in the form of less-favorable financial outcomes. Governments or international organizations have only a modest role in determining the terms on which China has access to international financial markets.

## History of China's Involvement

The story of China's entry into and initial involvement with the key international financial organizations is well known.[7] The process of China's entry into the IMF and the World Bank depended critically on key individuals both in China and in the major international organizations. China's entry was part of a broader strategy fundamentally to reorient its domestic economy away from the path of economic autarky and financial self-sufficiency that had prevailed during the Maoist era. The reoriented strategy was initiated cautiously with support from Zhou Enlai in 1970–1971. In 1973, after Deng Xiaoping was rehabilitated, he joined with Zhou in playing a key leadership role promoting the reoriented economic development strategy. But the reorientation was set back by Deng's second purge in 1976 and was not vigorously implemented until after he was rehabilitated again in 1977.

The key international organizations were well prepared to respond positively to China's expressions of interest in becoming a member of the World Bank and the IMF. World Bank President Robert McNamara was strongly interested in China's participation in the bank. He responded positively to an early signal in 1973 from the Chinese, indicating that their application to join the World Bank would be welcomed. In April 1980 McNamara personally headed a bank mission to China, which paved the way for China's entry into the bank the following month, over the objections of the U.S. government.[8]

China's borrowing from the bank initially was quite modest. China's entry into the bank and the IMF in 1980 coincided with a period of domestic retrenchment designed to reduce excess demand and inflationary pressures that had built up as reform began after 1977. As a result, although the first World Bank projects were approved by its executive directors near the end of the 1981 fiscal year, there were no significant drawdowns of these loans until 1983.[9] Annual lending commitments and disbursements did not exceed the $1 billion level until 1984 and 1988, respectively.

New loan commitments by the bank were suspended for almost a year in the wake of the Tiananmen massacre of Chinese students, although disbursements from previously committed loans were sustained at almost the same level as in previous years. New lending resumed strongly in 1991, and in 1992 China emerged as the largest borrower from the World Bank, displacing India, which had occupied that position for almost two decades. China retained its position as the largest borrower from the bank in fiscal years 1993 through 1997.[10]

One of the reasons World Bank lending to China has increased so rapidly is the country's excellent record in using funds borrowed from the bank. The bank regards as exemplary the extent to which projects are started and completed on time. By contrast, projects that the bank has committed to in India often are delayed; subsequently they are completed far behind schedule. Even though the bank committed about one-fifth more funds for projects in China than in India in fiscal years 1990 to 1995, undisbursed commitments to India at the beginning of 1995 exceeded those to China. Indeed, in fiscal year 1995 repayments and interest charges that India paid to the bank exceeded the bank's disbursements of previously committed funds by about $185 million. In short, the slow pace of disbursement of more than $9 billion previously committed to projects in India meant that net financial transfers to India by the bank in 1995 actually were negative.[11]

In 1996 Chinese institutions also became members of two more specialized international financial institutions. The Bank of China became a member of the Washington, D.C.–based, Institute of International Finance, Inc. The institute is a nonprofit organization composed of major financial institutions, including commercial and investment banks, export credit agencies, and multilateral organizations. Membership in the institute will provide the Bank of China with information on global financial and regulatory issues.

In addition, China's central bank, the People's Bank of China, became a member of the Bank for International Settlements (BIS). The BIS is a financial monitoring organization owned by the world's leading central banks. China's invitation to membership was part of an expansion that will increase the number of central bank members from 32 to 41.[12] Its participation in this organization is a recognition of China's growing importance in international financial markets and the high level of foreign exchange reserves held by the People's Bank of China.

## Impact of China's Participation

It would be difficult to overstate the impact of China's interaction with the World Bank and the IMF. The bank's critical role in advising China on its economic reform, particularly in the 1980s, is well known. But that is a story that lies beyond the scope of this chapter.[13]

Much less well known is the role that the IMF has played in advising China on exchange rate policy since the very early 1980s. While the fund never makes public the advice that it offers to foreign governments on exchange rate matters, Chinese sources make clear the critical role played by the IMF at certain junctures.[14] For example, the IMF was instrumental in convincing China to abandon, beginning in January 1984, the internal settlement rate, which had been introduced on January 1, 1981, as part of an export promotion strategy. In 1986 the IMF's advice supporting a large one-time devaluation, rather than continuing a series of minidevaluations, contributed to China's decision to devalue the renminbi by 15.8 percent on July 5, 1986. That was the largest single devaluation of the currency since the introduction of the internal settlement rate in 1981.[15]

The IMF was instrumental in encouraging China to move to achieve current account convertibility by the end of 1996,[16] which was a natural outgrowth of the move to a unitary exchange rate beginning January 1, 1994.[17] On that date China replaced the dual-rate system, which consisted of the rate prevailing in the country's foreign exchange swap market and an official rate, with a single managed floating rate. Shortly after the announcement that the exchange rate would be unified, the vice-governor of the central bank and director of the State Administration of Exchange Control, Zhu Xiaohua, disclosed that China would achieve current account convertibility by the year 2000.[18] But the IMF, in its annual Article IV consultations, strongly encouraged China to move more rapidly to fulfill the obligations of Article VIII of the IMF agreement, which limits the ability of members to "impose restrictions on the making of payments and transfers for current international transactions."[19]

The most important intermediate step to achieving current account convertibility, announced on June 21, 1996, was to allow foreign-invested enterprises full access to the interbank market for foreign exchange, beginning July 1, 1996, to purchase foreign exchange for current account transactions.[20] Prior to that time foreign-invested firms generally had been restricted to the swap market.[21] In effect, this change meant the Chinese government was confident of its ability to meet the demand for foreign exchange by foreign-funded enterprises for profit remittance purposes; it no longer has to limit funds for this purpose implicitly to the amount of foreign exchange that other foreign-invested firms have been willing to sell on the swap market in exchange for Chinese domestic currency.[22]

The Chinese directly acknowledged the role of the IMF in the decision. An editorial in the newspaper of the central bank and leading state-owned banks stated that by allowing foreign firms access to the interbank market for foreign exchange, in order to convert their renminbi earnings into hard currency that could be remitted abroad, China was "meeting the demand of the International Monetary Fund ahead of schedule."[23]

The other effects on China from its interactions with the World Bank and the International Monetary Fund range from modest institutional changes, to much farther-reaching effects on the operation of the domestic economy. On the institutional side there were several important changes. First, China established a special division within the Ministry of Finance to coordinate its interaction with the World Bank.[24] China is the only large borrower to have created such a department.

Second, China established new domestic banking institutions to disburse funds provided by the World Bank and the ADB. The China Investment Bank was created in December 1981 to serve as the institution to control the allocation of project funds provided to China by the World Bank.[25] When China became a member of the ADB in 1986, the China Investment Bank assumed a similar function for ADB project loans. The China Investment Bank not only disburses foreign currency loans to finance imports of technology and capital goods, it also provides domestic currency loans to finance the local counterpart component of projects funded by international financial organizations. Thus this bank provides coordinated disbursement of all funds needed for World Bank and ADB projects.[26]

Similarly, in 1987 China established a nonbank financial institution, the China Trust and Investment Corporation for Foreign Economic Relations and Trade, to manage the concessionary bilateral government-to-government loans China receives from most industrial countries.[27] Most notable in this regard are the funds provided by the Japanese government through its Overseas Economic Cooperation Fund (OECF). The OECF committed yen loans to China totaling ¥2,190 billion for projects undertaken during fiscal years 1979 through 1998.[28]

Changes in the operation of the Chinese economy in response to conditions imposed by the World Bank emerged more gradually than the institutional changes just sketched out. One of the most important stemmed from the World Bank's requirement that awards for major bank-funded projects be subject to international competitive bidding. China originally resisted this demand, particularly for road and dam projects for which the largest share of the costs was labor rather than sophisticated engineering and design work or imported equipment.

China felt contracts for these largely domestic projects should be awarded only to domestic firms.

But the World Bank insisted that China comply with its standard international tendering procedures. Foreign firms did win many project awards. But since those firms were interested in providing the engineering and other high–value-added services in these projects rather than labor and more basic services, joint ventures between foreign and Chinese construction companies were established. Over time the Chinese firms participating in these joint ventures absorbed a great deal of engineering, technical, and managerial know-how.

Ultimately the World Bank's insistence on the use of competitive international bidding had two important consequences for China's domestic economy. First, China began to use competitive bidding on purely domestically financed roads, dams, and other infrastructure projects. This introduced competition in a sector of growing economic importance during the 1980s. For example, railroad construction companies that previously had a franchise on all Ministry of Railroad projects began to face competition from construction firms that once had been sole providers of construction services to other ministries. And they, in turn, began to bid on nonrail projects being undertaken by other government agencies. Similarly, provincial construction companies, which were once captive firms working only on government-sponsored projects in their home regions, began to bid on projects in other regions of China. Ultimately this changed the mentality of those in China who oversee public works projects and thus was an important contributor to improvements in productivity in the construction sector.

Second, Chinese construction companies began to bid successfully on large-scale construction projects outside of the country. These firms have enjoyed some success in bidding on World Bank–funded projects, particularly in Africa, and also have played a significant role in construction projects in the Middle East.[29] These have contributed to a modest strengthening of China's service account in its balance of payments.[30]

China's increasing use of international capital markets is having effects on its domestic economy that ultimately will be just as important as those flowing from its interaction with the World Bank and other international financial institutions. Most important, raising funds on international capital markets provided the regime with its first information on the real cost of capital, information not available on domestic markets because until recently, all domestic interest rates were fixed administratively. Even as late as 1998, interest rates on bank loans provided little information on the scarcity value of capital.

China's first international bond sales, in the early 1980s, were mostly private placements in Japanese banks; therefore, the function of providing information on the real cost of capital was performed only partially. Even those issues that were sold publicly were relatively small in value and thus were not actively traded on the secondary bond market. Of 40 bond issues sold between January 1982 and April 1989, there was only a single sovereign issue,[31] a 300 million deutsche mark issue of bonds sold in October 1987. Owing to the infrequency of sovereign bond issues and the thinness of trading of other issues, it was difficult to separate the cost of China risk from risks associated with other, nonsovereign borrowers, and there was no discipline of daily pricing of "China risk."

In the 1990s China's Ministry of Finance led an increasingly sophisticated approach to raising funds in the international market. China sought to raise significantly larger amounts of funds on international capital markets than it had in the 1980s. Doing so meant tapping into the deeper and more liquid Euro, Dragon, and Yankee bond markets. Moreover, these markets were well suited to the ministry's objective of selling what would become benchmark issues that would be widely traded in the secondary market. Only issues with these characteristics could provide pricing and yield information that could measure the price of China risk, by comparing the yield on Ministry of Finance sovereign offerings with the yield on U.S. Treasury bonds of comparable maturity.[32] Later this information could be compared against the market pricing of bonds issued by other, nonsovereign Chinese borrowers. And more active trading on the secondary market provided the discipline of externally imposed daily pricing.

Several bond offerings of the Ministry of Finance in the 1990s exemplified this approach: an October 1993 $300 million issue of 10-year bonds in the Dragon market; a $1 billion global offering of 10-year bonds in 1994;[33] a $400 million Yankee offering in March 1996, which was divided between $300 million of seven-year bonds and $100 million of 100-year bonds; and a $1 billion global bond offering in June 1996, which was divided into a $700 million tranche of five-year bonds and $300 million tranche of ten-year bonds. The sale of these four sovereign bond issues established benchmark issues covering a large portion of the maturity spectrum.[34]

Exploiting the public international capital market required that Chinese listing entities, including Ministry of Finance and nonsovereign borrowers such as the Bank of China, the Construction Bank of China, the China International Trust and Investment Company, and regional trust and investment companies, divulge considerably more economic and financial information than they had to for the private placements of the early 1980s. This greater degree of financial disclosure was reflected both in the prospectuses for the bond issues and in the increasing role of the rating institutions, such as Moody's Investors Service and Standard and Poor's.[35] The ratings are particularly important for the placement of bonds in public offerings, since many institutional investors are precluded from purchasing unrated bonds, and some are restricted to purchasing only the bonds of those issuers that enjoy a so-called investment-grade rating.[36]

China's entry into international equity markets posed similar challenges for more information and increased transparency. Indeed, in the early 1990s Chinese regulatory authorities spurned an initial informal suggestion that it offer their equity shares on a to-be-created second-tier Hong Kong market where the listing requirements would be less rigorous. Instead Chinese authorities chose to meet the normal listing requirements. Enormous work was required to restate the accounts of Chinese firms in standard Western format, and a much greater degree of financial disclosure than usual was required.

One final example of an area where China's increasing participation in the international financial system is having important consequences for the domestic economy is banking. Since the mid-1980s, when it formally created a central bank, the People's Bank of China, China has embarked on the modernization of its banking system. The core of this effort is twofold. One priority is to establish the legal basis for the central bank to exercise normal central bank functions. When it was created in 1984, it lacked the legal authority to do so. The Central Bank Law, which became effective in March 1995, provided the legal authority for the People's Bank of China to implement monetary policy and to exercise financial supervision over other financial institutions.[37] In most respects the law brings China's financial system into closer alignment with principles and practices of central banks in industrialized countries.

The Commercial Bank Law, passed by the Standing Committee of the National People's Congress on May 10, 1995, and effective as of July 1, similarly moved China into closer congruence with standard international commercial banking practices.[38] A few months later the People's Bank of China issued new regulations on loans that, for the first time, imposed a capital adequacy standard, a clear system for classifying loans, and a number of other constraints on bank lending that are common in Western countries.[39]

In some cases the new regulations specifically borrowed standards from international banking accords. Most notably, the regulations adopted the Basle Accord standard of capital adequacy—the own capital of each commercial bank must be equal to 8 percent of value of the bank's total assets.[40] Other limitations, specified in the regulation on loans, restrict Chinese banks to lending an amount no more than 75 percent of the value of its deposits; limit loans to any single borrower to no more than 10 percent of the value of the bank's own capital; and require liquid assets to be no less than 25 percent of liquid liabilities.[41]

This adoption of laws embodying standard international banking practices reflects three desires of China's major banks. First, they may seek to raise funds internationally through the sale of bonds. The terms on which such funds can be raised clearly depend on the evaluations of the major bond rating agencies. Concerns of these agencies about the banks' capital adequacy, system of classifying nonperforming loans, and other areas will lead to lower ratings and a higher cost of raising funds internationally.

China's four major banks also seek to expand their international operations through opening additional foreign branch banks, in part to service Chinese clients in foreign markets. The Industrial and Commercial Bank, the Agricultural Bank of China, and the Construction Bank of China, for example, all filed applications in 1993 or 1994 with the Federal Reserve Board and the Comptroller of the Currency to open branch banks in New York.[42] And the Bank of China, which already operates two branch banks and a subsidiary bank in New York and a limited federal branch in Los Angeles, applied in 1995 to open an additional limited federal branch in San Francisco. In each of these cases the central rationale for the new branches was to provide financing for the growing volume of trade between China and the United States and otherwise to serve U.S.-based affiliates of companies that have their head offices in China.

However, in the United States the regulatory approvals to open new branch banks depend primarily on these institutions' meeting two criteria. First, they must meet a capital adequacy standard. Second, U.S. law specifies that these institutions must be subject to "comprehensive supervision on a consolidated basis." The recent Chinese laws and regulations just discussed constitute the first steps in meeting these two requirements.

The third desire of China's major banks—ultimately to conform to these international banking standards—is a precondition for developing Shanghai as an international financial center, a much-discussed, if very ambitious, Chinese policy objective. Creating an international financial center depends critically on the presence of international banks that are able to conduct local currency business. The current weakness of Chinese banks effectively prevents head-to-head competition with foreign banks for renminbi business, except on a limited, experimental basis. The new laws and regulations at least establish a framework that might ultimately lead to such competition.

## The Record to Date

China's record of participation in the international financial system is mixed. The following discussion considers three separate areas: international financial institutions, international capital markets, and domestic banking.

### INTERNATIONAL FINANCIAL INSTITUTIONS

The best record is probably with the major international financial organizations. China still is regarded as an exemplary client by the World Bank and seems likely to remain one of the largest, if not the largest, borrower from the bank for the next few years.[43] And, as discussed earlier, China appears to have largely followed the advice of the IMF, moving to achieve current account convertibility on a schedule that appears somewhat accelerated compared to the country's own preferences, as reflected in earlier public statements of high-level financial officials.

### INTERNATIONAL CAPITAL MARKETS

In international capital markets, when some Chinese institutions have failed to meet the expectations of international investors, markets have imposed substantial penalties. International markets gave an exceptionally warm reception to China's initial international equity offerings in 1992 and 1993. Indeed, in retrospect some observers have argued that that market response was too enthusiastic and led to pricing that was so favorable to China that it was inevitable that it could not be sustained, even if China's behavior had been exemplary. In those years China's initial public offerings were highly oversubscribed, despite pricing that reflected very high multiples over reported earnings. For example, the initial offering in July 1993 of shares of Tsingtao Brewery, the first Chinese company to list on the Hong Kong stock exchange, was 111 times oversubscribed.[44]

However, after this initial warm reception, investors grew more skeptical, and prices of existing Chinese listings fell dramatically. Prices of Chinese H shares in the Hong Kong market in February 1996 were off about 60 percent from their peak levels of late 1993. The slide in H share prices in 1995, when the broader Hong Kong market was up 20 percent, was particularly conspicuous.

And falling prices of Chinese shares in 1995 was not limited to Hong Kong. Stock averages in New York surged to hit all-time highs in 1995, but the prices of most Chinese companies listed there dramatically underperformed the market. For example, Huaneng Power International, when it came to market in the last quarter of 1994, was touted as "a leader in the production of efficient, reliable power in China and one of the largest independent power producers in the world." In the spring of 1996 it sold for about three-quarters of its initial offering price. Since the pricing of Chinese equities in 1995 was much less favorable than that which existed only a year or two earlier, the Chinese authorities chose to bring few new issues to international markets.[45] As a result, the total value of international equities China issued in 1995, $666 million, was only one-fourth the $2.594 billion level of 1994.[46] In the latter part of 1996 a new cycle began with a trend of rising share prices that was particularly strong in the months prior to and just after the Chinese resumption of sovereignty over Hong Kong. But in the fall of 1997 share prices fell in response to the Asian financial crisis. Thus share offerings surged in 1997 but fell to a trickle in the first half of 1998.

The sharp decline in the prices of Chinese stocks reflects several factors: a decline in reported earnings in many Chinese companies, brought on partly by tighter domestic credit in China in 1994 and 1995, and a return to "normalcy" following an initially effusive market reaction to the first Chinese companies to issue shares abroad.

But the sell-off in Chinese shares also appears to reflect the slow development of the regulatory framework of China's stock markets, particularly shortcomings in protection of shareholders. Some Chinese companies listed in Hong Kong or New York, or whose B shares are listed in Shanghai and Shenzhen for sale to foreign investors, have failed to meet the expectations of international investors. In some cases Chinese firms have used the proceeds of international initial public offerings for purposes other than those promised in the sales prospectus. For example, rather than expanding beer-making capacity with the proceeds of its initial public offering on the Hong Kong market, the Shandong Province–based brewer Tsingtao on-lent the money to other firms in China. Beiren Printing put the funds it raised on the Hong Kong market into property development rather than expanding its business, as its prospectus had advised would-be share purchasers. In a few cases, especially on the B share market, firms even have failed to provide timely annual reports of economic results of their businesses, leaving international investors in the dark as to their net income and profits and other financial indicators of business performance.

The failure of some Chinese firms to meet international expectations on disclosure and transparency made the terms of China's access to international equity markets in 1994 and 1995 much less favorable than in 1992 and 1993. As a result, by mid-1996 China had completed the offerings of only about half of the firms that had been approved by the Chinese Securities Regulatory Commission for listing abroad. And the authorities accepted the fact that some of the companies they had selected would not ever be listed.[47] There also was a virtual hiatus after August 1994 in new listings of B shares, those reserved for purchase by foreign investors, on domestic stock markets in Shanghai and Shenzhen. However, beginning in 1995 more B shares came to market, but their performance continued to be mediocre. In late 1996 the average B share on the Shanghai market sold for less than half the peak level of December 1993.[48]

The terms under which China has access to international bond markets also have moved cyclically, again at least in part as a result of disappointed investor expectations. China's benchmark sovereign issue of $1 billion came to market in February 1994 at a very favorable spread of only 85 basis points over U.S. Treasury bonds of the same maturity.[49] However, in response to the news later in 1994 that Lehman Brothers Holdings and several other international investment banks were suing Chinese state-owned entities for breaches of contract, the benchmark Chinese bond sold off and the spread widened to 150 basis points toward the end of the year, even before the Mexican debt crisis. Spreads subsequently tightened to as low as just over 80 basis points in early fall of 1997. By early 1998, in response to the deepening Asian financial crisis, the spread spiked up over a period of six weeks to just over 190 points. The spread then eased but remained a relatively high 150 to 160 basis points, leading China's minister of finance in March to postpone a sovereign offering that was planned for the first half of the year. The Russians, desperate for foreign funds, did not have the luxury of postponing their international borrowing and paid a premium of 650 basis points over U.S. Treasury bonds on their $1.25 billion eurobond offering in early June 1998.[50] That was roughly twice the premium they had to pay when they first entered the international market in late 1996.

The terms under which China's nonsovereign issuers have access to international capital markets also has varied over time. In early 1995 Moody's Investors Services announced that it was reviewing its ratings on the debt of China's largest state-owned banks. This was a very important decision, since it indicated that, for the first time, the international ratings agencies were distinguishing between sovereign offerings of the Ministry of Finance, which are backed by the full faith and credit of the Chinese central government, and the offerings of other entities, such as the China International Trust and Investment Company or the four major state-owned banks. This revised approach certainly was warranted or even overdue. As early as 1993 the Chinese government had announced that its long-term objective was to require state banks to operate on commercial principles, implying that these financial institutions ultimately would be responsible for their own profits and losses. And, since at least the first quarter of 1994, the prospectuses describing the bonds and notes of these banks specifically denied that the obligations were backed by the full faith and credit of the Chinese government.[51]

Even before Moody's downgraded its ratings of the Bank of China and the three other large state-owned banks in mid-April 1995, the Bank of China was forced to put on hold a planned offering of Hong Kong (HK) $5 billion (U.S. $646.7 million) in five-year floating rate certificates of deposit. After Moody's downgraded the Bank of China's long-term debt from single-A-3 to Baa-1, the bank—unwilling to offer potential buyers a higher interest rate to compensate for the higher risk implicit in the lower rating—canceled the offering. The preliminary pricing of the debt, established prior to Moody's initial announcement, was a very favorable 35 basis points over the Hong Kong interbank offered rate.

After the Moody's downgrade, that pricing was clearly unacceptable to the market for two reasons. First, the premium over the London interbank offered rate of Bank of China three-year floating rate notes trading on the secondary market in London had gone from 40 basis points prior to Moody's announcement of a possible downgrade to 60 basis points after the downgrade decision was announced. Second, the new Moody's rating of the Bank of China was too low for its bonds to qualify for the repurchase agreement system, the so-called liquid adjustment facility, operated by the Hong Kong Monetary Authority. That made Bank of China bonds less attractive to Hong Kong financial institutions.[52]

When the Bank of China offer finally did come to market in September 1996, it was on the basis of a more favorable rating obtained from the Japan Bond Research Institute. But the bank had to cut the size of the offer to HK $2 billion, down substantially from the initially planned level of HK $5 billion. And the premium was 42 basis points over the Hong Kong interbank offered rate, higher than previously planned.[53]

Other would-be nonsovereign Chinese borrowers also appear to have withdrawn or at least postponed planned international debt offerings in part because they were not willing to pay the interest rate demanded by the international market. For example, in March 1995 the president of the China Yangtze Three Gorges Project Development Corporation announced that it would issue bonds to overseas investors to help finance the construction of the dam.[54] A year later the vice chairman of the corporation announced that the planned borrowing of $300 million was being deferred.[55]

This appears to be part of what could become a long-running story. China would like to borrow funds for the Three Gorges project from the international market without providing a government guarantee, but it has been reluctant to pay the interest rate premium that foreign investors expect to compensate them for the greater risk of lending to an unguaranteed project. The Chinese are continuing to investigate alternative mechanisms for raising international funds for the project. In the interim, the Bank of China in 1995 extended the project a loan of $120 million to meet the project's foreign exchange needs. It is possible that the State Development Bank, which was established in 1994 with a mandate to help finance long-term infrastructure projects, ultimately may be assigned the task of securing international funding.[56] In the fall of 1996 the Three Gorges Development Corporation was again testing the water, trying to gauge international investors' interest in a planned HK $930 million issue of three- and five-year bonds.[57]

International investors have confronted similar, if somewhat more complex, problems in efforts to finance electric power and telecommunications projects. China has sought to finance these projects on a nonrecourse basis, meaning that lenders to the project are repaid only from the cash flow generated by the project; no government guarantee of repayment stands behind each individual project.

Putting together viable financing packages for these projects in China, however, has proven to be far more complex and time-consuming than once thought. Potential foreign investors in such large-scale infrastructure projects face not only the usual country and currency risks associated with direct investment but also potentially large market risks associated with fluctuations in demand. In electric power projects this risk is sometimes minimized for investors by a power purchase agreement that requires the government power utility to purchase the planned output of a project at a preagreed price, regardless of whether the utility is able to resell the power to end users. An inability to agree on the pricing built into these agreements, which in turn was tied into calculations of the rate of return on capital contributed by foreign investors, became a key roadblock to completing agreements for a large number of build-operate-transfer (BOT) projects.

Formal BOT regulations issued jointly by the State Planning Commission, the Ministry of Power Industry, and the Ministry of Communications in the spring of 1996 did lead to the financial closure of the first BOT electric power project, Laibin B in Guangxi Province, and to progress toward conclusion of deals for a thermal power plant in Changsha, Hunan, and a water treatment plant in Chengdu, Sichuan.[58] But the regulations did not resolve most underlying BOT issues, so by the spring of 1998 no BOT project other than Laibin B had reached financial closure.[59]

## DOMESTIC BANKING

The impact of China's involvement in the international finance regime has been least successful, at least to date, in the area of domestic banking. Despite the new regulations, China's major banks remain woefully undercapitalized and do not appear to meet the Basle capital adequacy standards.[60] Indeed, the capital-asset ratio of each of China's four major banks has declined significantly in recent years.[61] And the banks have set aside reserves for nonperforming loans that are best described as minuscule. They are only marginally profitable in the best of times and are hugely unprofitable when inflation is high, as in 1988–1989 and again in 1994–1995.[62] Reforms announced in 1998, including an RMB 270 billion injection of capital and increased pressure on the major banks to operate on commercial terms, are designed to remedy these problems, but it is too soon to judge the degree to which these initiatives will be successful.

Most important, although China's new commercial bank law and loan regulations establish a formal structure modeled on international practices, China has only begun to address the core cause of its fragile banking system—the seemingly insatiable demand by state-owned enterprises for cheap credit. Borrowing by state-owned firms (measured by the value of loans outstanding) increased almost 40-fold between 1978, when reform began, and the end of 1997. But many of these borrowers are unable to amortize their debt, leaving China's banks with huge portfolios of nonperforming loans. Until banks are able to exercise real discretion and lend selectively on the basis of normal commercial criteria, there is little prospect that their balance sheets can be rebuilt. Ultimately this is probably the greatest constraint on China's playing a greater role in the international financial system.

## Policy Recommendations

China's engagement with the international financial system is inseparably linked to its larger opening to the outside world over the past two decades. As China sought to link its own economy to the larger international system, it was inevitably subject to the disciplines of the international financial institutions, particularly with respect to the World Bank, from which China sought to acquire both long-term funding and important forms of technical assistance and strategic advice on its economic transformation. And this was also true with respect to the IMF, which played a crucial role in guiding China to achieving current account convertibility.

But, as argued earlier, in some ways international markets have been more important than international financial institutions in providing the principal norms of behavior in the international financial system. And markets themselves have imposed penalties automatically when the behavior of Chinese firms, financial institutions, or other entities has diverged significantly from international market expectations. Yet this does not mean that there is no role for policy in this domain. The market should be allowed to continue to work, with several policy issues in mind.

The first issue is the pending application of the Bank of China to open an additional branch bank in the United States.[63] The bank appears to fall short of the capital adequacy standard set forth in U.S. law. Moreover, China's central bank does not yet exercise effective prudential supervision of state-owned banks, even within China. Thus the country fails to meet the test of subjecting its banks to comprehensive regulation on a consolidated basis, a key criterion set forth in the Foreign Bank Supervision Enhancement Act of 1991 for licensing foreign banks to operate in the United States. The Bank of China's application for an additional branch should not be approved until both of these criteria are clearly met.[64] There may be room for closer coordination with relevant bank regulatory authorities in other industrialized countries on this issue.[65]

Second, as part of the process of China's accession to the World Trade Organization, the United States is still engaged with China in bilateral talks on financial services. The United States has sought from China a commitment to provide national treatment to U.S. financial, securities, and insurance companies. In the field of banking that would mean easing very strict limitations on the opening of bank branches, allowing U.S. banks to engage in local currency business, and allowing U.S. banks to serve Chinese clients. In the securities area national treatment would require the Chinese government to allow U.S. securities firms to open local branches or subsidiaries, broker B shares without sharing commissions with Chinese brokers, and underwrite local securities issues and act as dealers or brokers in RMB-denominated securities.

National treatment in insurance would require the lifting of many limitations on the operations of U.S. insurance companies in China.[66] For example, the number of firms licensed to operate is extremely limited, and even licensed firms are restricted to doing business in only one or two cities; the types of insurance products these firms are allowed to sell also are quite restricted.

The weakness of Chinese state-owned banks will make it difficult for the Chinese to agree to full national treatment in banking services. Indeed, in the short and medium term it will be impossible for them to agree to such treatment. The fact that Chinese banks hold huge portfolios of nonperforming loans, for example, means that if interest rates were deregulated, the banks could not compete successfully against foreign banks. Foreign banks would be able simultaneously to offer higher rates on deposits and lower rates on loans than would Chinese state-owned banks.[67] Even in the absence of interest rate liberalization, foreign banks would be more profitable and would be able to offer both depositors and lenders more services than do Chinese banks. Thus allowing foreign banks unrestricted access to the domestic market would lead to a huge disintermediation problem for China. Deposits would flow from domestic to foreign banks. But since the assets of Chinese banks are tied up in nonperforming loans, these institutions would be unable to meet the demands of depositors, exposing the underlying insolvency of China's largest state-owned banks.

But the current weakness of China's state-owned banks should not deter U.S. negotiators from pressing for an agreement in principle on national treatment in financial services, with a well-defined timetable for taking various specific intermediate steps leading to full national treatment. U.S. expectations should be higher in the securities and insurance fields, since Chinese institutions should be better able to compete with international institutions than are Chinese banks. U.S. securities firms should be allowed to buy full seats on the Shanghai stock exchange, allowing them to trade directly on the exchange. At present they are required to operate through, and share commissions with, Chinese brokers.

Ultimately, however, the success of these negotiations on national treatment will depend on China's own progress in further domestic economic reform. If Premier Zhu Rongji's program for fundamental restructuring of China's state-owned industrial and commercial enterprises is implemented successfully, it will facilitate his program for commercializing the major state-owned banks. That, in turn, will remove a fundamental obstacle to moving toward capital account convertibility, national treatment of foreign banks in China, and the development of

Shanghai as an international financial center. Equally important, commercialization of the major banks will improve the efficiency with which capital is allocated in China, which will contribute importantly to sustaining positive long-term growth of the economy.

# Notes

1. Three other transition economies—Hungary, the Czech Republic, and Poland—have been awarded investment-grade ratings on their sovereign external debt. Of these only Hungary has issued a significant amount of bonds internationally.

2. David Folkerts-Landau and Takatoshi Ito, *International Capital Markets: Developments, Prospects, and Policy Issues* (Washington, D.C.: International Monetary Fund, 1995), pp. 42, 46; Takatoshi Ito and David Folkerts-Landau, *International Capital Markets: Developments, Prospects, and Policy Issues* (Washington, D.C.: International Monetary Fund, 1996), pp. 93, 101. *Zhongguo jinrong nianjian 1997* (Almanac of China's finance and banking 1997) (Beijing: Almanac of China's Finance and Banking Editorial Department, 1997), p. 52. China also had sold $4.25 billion in bonds on international markets in the 1980s, prior to Tiananmen. China reentered the market in mid-1991. Nicholas R. Lardy, *China in the World Economy* (Washington, D.C.: Institute for International Economics, 1994), pp. 59–60.

3. International Monetary Fund (IMF), *People's Republic of China—Recent Economic Developments*, Staff Country Report No. 97/71 (Washington, D.C.: IMF, 1997), p. 91. This is China's own published number on its year-end 1996 external debt, which excludes short-term trade credits and other short-term borrowing. Independent estimates place China's short-term debt at $40 billion at year-end 1996, almost three times the official figure. Moody's Investors Service, *China* (New York: Moody's Investors Service 1997), p. 10.

4. Nicholas R. Lardy, *China's Unfinished Economic Revolution* (Washington, D.C.: Brookings Institution Press, 1998), p. 153.

5. George Graham and Graham Bowley, "Russia Debt Deal Ready for Creditor Banks," *Financial Times*, May 2, 1996, p. 2; Samer Iskandar and Richard Adams, "Long Wait Whets Appetite for Debut Russian Eurobond Issue," *Financial Times*, November 18, 1996, p. 26.

6. This chapter does not consider foreign trade and foreign direct investment, probably the most important dimension of China's participation in the international economy. See Margaret Pearson, Chapter 5 of this book.

7. Harold K. Jacobson and Michel Oksenberg, *China's Participation in the IMF, the World Bank, and GATT: Toward a Global Economic Order* (Ann Arbor: University of Michigan Press, 1990).

8.  Ibid., pp. 63–64 and 74–81.

9.  Lardy, *China in the World Economy*, p. 50.

10. These statements on China's rank as a borrower are based on annual commitments of World Bank funds. On the basis of total loans outstanding at the end of 1997, India, Indonesia, and Mexico were larger borrowers than China. Each of these countries began borrowing from the bank long before China. Thus their total loans outstanding were larger than China's even though their annual borrowing in the 1990s was less than that of China. *The World Bank Annual Report 1997* (Washington, D.C.: The World Bank, 1997), pp. 190–91.

11. *The World Bank Annual Report 1995* (Washington, D.C.: The World Bank, 1995), p. 75.

12. William Hall and Gillian Tett, "BIS Seeks to Boost Market Role," *Financial Times*, September 10, 1996, p. 1.

13. For a preliminary assessment, see Jacobson and Oksenberg, *China's Participation in the IMF*, esp. pp. 109–117 and 139–46.

14. The venue for the discussions between the fund and the Chinese is the annual Article IV consultation that in recent years has occurred in the spring, usually in March or April. It is interesting to note that over the past 15 or more years many of the most important Chinese decisions on exchange rate policy have been announced within a few weeks after this annual consultation.

15. Nicholas R. Lardy, *Foreign Trade and Economic Reform in China 1978–1990* (Cambridge: Cambridge University Press, 1992), pp. 73, 114, 120, and 166.

16. Current account convertibility means that the renminbi can be readily traded for foreign currency necessary to finance trade and services transactions. Services transactions include Chinese tourism abroad, profit remittances by foreign companies operating in China, and the amortization of previously approved foreign-currency–denominated loans.

17. The unification formally was announced in a State Council document issued on December 28, 1993, "Notice on Further Reform of the Foreign Exchange Management System."

18. Xinhua, "Official Says Currency to be Convertible, 'Within Six Years,'" March 5, 1996, in FBIS, March 7, 1994, p. 38.

19. IMF, *Articles of Agreement of the International Monetary Fund* (Washington, D.C.: IMF, 1993), p. 21.

20. People's Bank of China, "Regulations on the Management of the Settlement, Sale, and Purchase of Foreign Exchange," *Jinrong shibao* (Financial news), June 22, 1996, p. 2.

21. The exception was that from March 1, 1996, the State Administration of Exchange Control allowed foreign-funded firms in Jiangsu Province,

Shanghai Municipality, Dalian City, and the Shenzhen Special Economic Zone to buy and sell foreign exchange in banks on a trial basis. The IMF commented favorably on this development, indicating that it was a positive step toward China's compliance with article VII. Xinhua, June 20, 1996, in FBIS July 9, 1996, p. 31.

22. In the past access to the swap market to buy foreign exchange was limited for joint ventures that had agreed to meet their own need for foreign exchange by exporting their product into the international market. Full current account convertibility will mean that all joint ventures will have access to the foreign exchange market, regardless of restrictions that may have been included in their initial joint venture contracts.

23. Editorial, "A Significant Reform in China's Currency Management System," *Jinrong shibao* (Financial news), June 21, 1996, p 1.

24. Jacobson and Oksenberg, *China's Participation in the IMF*, pp. 146–47.

25. The World Bank approved its first loans to China in June 1981. However, no significant disbursement of these funds occurred until after June 1982. Thus the China Investment Bank was the key financial institution disbursing these funds since the beginning of China's relationship with the World Bank.

26. Beginning in 1994, as part of the overall reform of the financial system, the People's Bank approved the conversion of the China Investment Bank into a commercial bank able to take deposits from the public and engage in a much broader range of lending activities. Although it is a separate legal entity, it remains a subsidiary of the Construction Bank.

27. The Import-Export Bank of China, which was formally established in 1994, subsequently took over responsibility for the disbursement of government-to-government loans. The China Trust and Investment Corporation for Foreign Economic Relations and Trade then became the finance arm of the China National Chemicals Import and Export Corporation, one of China's largest trading companies.

28. Lardy, *China's Unfinished Economic Revolution*, p. 74.

29. World Bank and International Development Association (IDA) payments for procurement of equipment, civil works, consultants, and the like in China, for projects in other countries, totaled $2.28 billion through the middle of 1995. China's share of total procurement financed by International Bank for Reconstruction and Development (IBRD) funds has increased significantly over the years. By fiscal year 1995 only seven and eleven other countries were more successful than China in bidding on IDA- and IBRD-funded projects, respectively. *The World Bank Annual Report 1995*, pp. 209–11.

30. China began to report earnings from labor in the service component of its balance-of-payments accounts beginning in 1983. Labor earnings averaged $80 million per year from 1983 through 1994. World Bank, *The Chinese Economy: Fighting Inflation, Deepening Reform* (Washington, D.C.: The World Bank, 1996), p. 77.

31. For a complete list of these bond issues, including their date, the market in which they were sold, the currency in which they were denominated, and the maturity of the issue, see *Zhongguo jinrong nianjian 1990* (Almanac of China's finance and banking 1990) (Beijing: Almanac of China's Finance and Banking Editorial Department, 1990), pp. 135–36.

32. Since the Ministry of Finance bonds in the 1990s were denominated in U.S. dollars, purchasers bore no exchange-rate risk. Thus the difference between the yields on Chinese and U.S. bonds of comparable maturity was the pure China risk.

33. Price and yield information on this issue, identified as China 6½ 04 because the coupon, or nominal yield, on the bonds when sold was 6½ percent and because these are ten-year bonds maturing in 2004, was reported regularly in the *Financial Times* in its FT/ISMA International Bond Service listings. As of mid-1998 the benchmark bond listed in the "Emerging Market Bonds" table is 07/06, which matures in July 2006.

34. For a more general discussion of benchmarking, see World Bank, *The Emerging Asian Bond Market* (Washington, D.C.: The World Bank, 1995), pp. 23–24.

35. Although the disclosure of information on Chinese financial institutions in Chinese publications has improved enormously in recent years, prospectuses for the debt issues of Chinese banks and nonbank financial institutions remain a valuable tool for research, since they still contain some information not disclosed elsewhere.

36. In the Standard and Poor's system, investment-grade ratings are BBB or higher; in the Moody's system, investment grade is Baa or higher.

37. "People's Republic of China People's Bank of China Law," *China Law and Practice,* June 27, 1995, pp. 23–30.

38. Ibid., pp. 32–48.

39. Provisional legislation had imposed these requirements in 1994.

40. The Basle Capital Accord was set forth by the Basle Committee on Banking Supervision in July 1988 and came into full force at the end of 1992. The committee was established by the central bank governors of the Group of Ten Countries in 1975. Its current membership consists of senior central bank officials from Belgium, Canada, France, Germany, Italy, Japan, Luxembourg, the Netherlands, Sweden, Switzerland, the United Kingdom, and the United States. However, the Basle Accord standards have been adopted by many other countries.

41. People's Bank of China, "General Rules on Loans (for Trial Implementation)," *Jinrong shibao* (Financial news), August 23, 1995, p. 2; translated in FBIS, December 12, 1995, pp. 20–30. The final version of these rules, which were to take effect August 1, 1996, was published in *Jinrong shibao* on June 29, 1996, p. 2.

42.  Until March 26, 1996, the Construction Bank of China was named the People's Construction Bank of China.

43.  However, retaining this status will depend on China's continued willingness to accept a change in the mix away from loans from the International Development Association (the bank's so-called soft loan window), which contain the largest concessionary component, and toward loans from the IBRD. IDA lending commitments to China peaked in fiscal year 1993 at $1.017 billion and have been shrinking since then, falling to only $200 million in fiscal year 1995. This is due to a World Bank decision to give greater access to IDA funds to those low-income countries that are not able to borrow commercially on international capital markets.

44.  Louise Lucas, "Higher Costs Drag Tsingtao to Surprise 96% Fall," *Financial Times*, April 17, 1996, p. 21.

45.  An alternative explanation is that Zhou Daojiong, who became chairman of the Chinese Securities Regulatory Commission in 1995, was far more conservative than his predecessor and less interested in pursuing international listings, particularly in Hong Kong and New York. Henny Sender, "Object of Desire," *Far Eastern Economic Review*, April 4, 1996, pp. 58–59.

46.  Takatoshi Ito and David Folkerts-Landau, *International Capital Markets*, p. 101.

47.  In October 1992 the Chinese Securities Regulatory Commission approved the listing of 9 Chinese companies in Hong Kong. In 1993 it approved an additional 22 companies for listing abroad. Most of the latter group were expected to come to market in Hong Kong. In 1995, 7 more firms were approved for listing abroad. By midyear 1996 there were only 20 companies listed in Hong Kong and 4 in New York. This count does not include some offshore entities that control Chinese assets that are listed in New York. Shi Liu, "Fourth Group of Companies to Be Listed Overseas," *China Economic News*, June 24, 1996, pp. 2–3.

48.  Tony Walker and Sophie Roell, "China's Markets Divide Deepens," *Financial Times*, November 12, 1996, p. 8.

49.  100 basis points = 1 percentage point.

50.  Jeremy Grant, "Fresh Jitters in Emerging Markets," *Financial Times*, June 8, 1998, p. 20.

51.  For example, the prospectus for the Bank of China's $500 million issue of five-year notes and ten-year bonds in 1994 stated that although the borrowing had been approved by "the relevant authority of China" and was "in accordance with the State plan for external borrowing," "the Bank's obligations . . . are not directly guaranteed by China." Bank of China Prospectus, March 14, 1994, p. 4.

52.  "Ratings Drop Halts BOC Issue," *South China Morning Post, Business Post International Weekly*, April 22, 1995, p. 1.

53. Louise Lucas, "FRCD Issue from Bank of China," *Financial Times*, September 17, 1996, p. 17.

54. Xinhua, "Three Gorges Planning Bond Issue," *China Daily*, March 14, 1995, p. 1.

55. Tony Walker, "Beijing Puts Off Three Gorges Issue of Bonds," *Financial Times*, March 28, 1996, p. 4.

56. In March 1996 Moody's and Standard and Poor's assigned their first ratings to the State Development Bank; Moody's rating was A-3, Standard and Poor's was BBB.

57. Tom Korski and Deborah Orr, "Dam Seeks $930m with Bond Issues," *South China Morning Post International Weekly*, October 26, 1996, p. Business 3.

58. State Planning Commission, Ministry of Power Industry, and Ministry of Communications, "Circular on Relevant Issues Concerning the Examination, Approval and Management of Experimental Foreign-invested Franchise Projects," referenced in Wu Naitao, "Rules for Experiments with the BOT Method," *Beijing Review*, May 20–26, 1996, p. 21. The first contract embodying the new principles was awarded in late 1996. Sophie Roell, "EdF Wins China's First BOT Contract," *Financial Times*, November 12, 1996, p. 6.

59. Melissa Thomas, "The Pressures of Project Finance," *China Business Review* (March–April 1998): 20–23.

60. The Basle standard calls for banks to own capital equal to at least 8 percent of their risk-weighted assets. This means banks have to own more capital to back riskier assets. For example, the risk attached to government bonds in the Basle system is zero, meaning banks do not have to own any capital to back up government bonds. China's weighting procedures appear to diverge somewhat from those set forth in the Basle agreement.

61. The capital-asset ratio for China's single largest financial institution, the Industrial and Commercial Bank of China, fell from 6.5 percent at year-end 1989 to 3.3 percent at year-end 1994. World Bank, *The Chinese Economy: Fighting Inflation, Deepening Reform* (Washington, D.C.: The World Bank, 1996), p. 35.

62. Lardy, *China's Unfinished Economic Revolution*, pp. 100–115.

63. The U.S. Federal Reserve announced on September 23, 1996, January 27, 1997, and May 14, 1997, that it had approved the applications of the China Construction Bank, the Industrial and Commercial Bank, and the Agricultural Bank to open representative offices in New York. This was pursuant to these banks' withdrawal of their applications for branches and the submission of applications to open representative offices. Since representative offices are limited to general marketing and promotional activities and not allowed to conduct banking business, the criteria for approval of representative offices are far less stringent than those for branches.

64. U.S. House of Representatives, Hearings on Recent Developments in Banking and Finance in the People's Republic of China, Hong Kong, and Taiwan, Committee on Banking and Financial Services, Nicholas R. Lardy, "Banking in China's Economic Reforms," March 20, 1996.

65. Some of these authorities appear to apply less-restrictive standards when approving foreign branch banks. For example, the Hong Kong Monetary Authority in 1995 approved the opening of branch banks by the Industrial and Commercial Bank of China, the Agricultural Bank of China, and the Construction Bank of China. The divergent evaluations by regulatory authorities in the United States and Hong Kong is somewhat surprising, since both subscribe to the principles of the Basle Committee on Banking Supervision's agreement on supervising international banks, called the Concordat. It requires all international banks to be supervised on a consolidated basis by the bank supervising authority of the bank's home country. For an explanation of the decision by the Hong Kong Monetary Authority, see David Carse, "Banking and Monetary Links between China and Hong Kong," *Hong Kong Monetary Authority Quarterly Bulletin* (February 1996): 50–55, esp. pp. 52–53.

66. Department of the Treasury, *National Treatment Study: Report to Congress on Foreign Government Treatment of U.S. Commercial Banking and Securities Organizations* (Washington, D.C.: U.S. Department of the Treasury, 1994), pp. 247–260.

67. For the same reason Chinese state-owned banks have lobbied, thus far successfully, to restrict new domestic banks, such as the Bank of Communications and the Minsheng Bank, to a limited number of branches in order to reduce the potential competitive threat they represent.

# 7

# China and the Information Revolution

## FREDERICK S. TIPSON

*Within the Party, opposition and struggle between different ideas occur constantly; they reflect the class contradictions and the contradictions between the old and the new things in society. If there were neither contradictions nor ideological conflicts through which the contradictions are resolved, the Party's life would come to an end.*
—Mao Zedong, "On Contradiction"

THE CHINESE leadership has repeatedly emphasized the central role of telecommunications and information technologies in building its modern economy. Yet the policies pursued by those same leaders contain an inherent contradiction: on the one hand, actively promoting a modern communications infrastructure of lightning speed, scope, and flexibility, while, on the other hand, repeatedly trying to control the content and uses of the information that pulses through it. During the last ten years in particular, the avenues and capabilities for communicating within China and with the world outside its borders have multiplied and intensified tremendously, even as the leadership conveys its sharp suspicions of the corrupting potential of such communications webs. Meanwhile, the global telecommunications "regime," which has provided the formal framework for international transmissions, has itself been breaking down under the twin pressures of technological revolution and economic competition in a manner that provides ever-decreasing protection for the old-fashioned prerogatives and protections of nation-state sovereignty. The leadership's posture on such issues reflects a series of political tensions whose resolution will determine much about China's future engagement with the world at large.

Of course, political tensions are nothing new to the leadership of China. Indeed, under Mao Zedong, the ruling ideology made a virtue of such "contradictions." To Mao, social progress depended on the dialectical process of resolving—and even deliberately fomenting—contradictions in order to move China forward. This chapter explores central aspects of the tensions fomented in large part by the "information revolution" that is sweeping all national societies at the end of the twentieth century. Such tensions are an inherent part of China's broader effort to manage its engagement with the rest of the world:

- To join "the club" of leading nation-states, but on China's own terms of membership;

- To participate in international "regimes" without sacrificing national "sovereignty";

- To garner the benefits of advanced technologies without accepting their "negative" consequences;

- To encourage entrepreneurial flair and market flexibility without absorbing the materialistic self-indulgence and cultural decadence that seem to come with modern capitalism (in short, to take what is deemed "good" from the outside world, and to filter out what is "bad").

This attempt to borrow selectively from outsiders is a familiar one in Chinese history. Nor is China alone among nation-states, of course, in seeking to modulate the impacts of globalization. But this particular effort likely will lead to one of three outcomes. The first possibility is that China's leaders will indeed succeed where those of other countries seem to be failing: that is, they will find the means of multiplying the number and capacity of communications channels, and applying the power of information technology to key economic and security sectors, while maintaining tight limits on the types of information that pass through this infrastructure and severely restricting public access to it. They will thereby maintain the political supervision, economic advantage, and cultural protections deemed necessary, without stifling the development of a modern economy. While China is certainly a far different country from Singapore, this effort might be considered the "Singapore approach," after the model espoused by Singapore's former leader Lee Kuan Yew.[1] (What might be called: Shake the bottle slightly but keep the cork in.)

A second possibility is that the leadership will resolve this tension either by dispensing with the pretext of comprehensive information control altogether or—as has also happened in Chinese history—by developing a rationale to accommodate a looser control regime that nonetheless appears consistent with stated government intentions, thereby allowing for a period of transition to a more open system. Whether the leadership of the Chinese Communist Party truly believes that it can manage in this process simultaneously to "build spiritual civilization" (*jingshen wenming jianshe*) in accordance with its latest pronouncements—or whether this effort is largely a rhetorical posture used to preserve a formal argument for party legitimacy—is not completely clear.[2] No doubt there are wide differences of view among the Chinese leaders themselves on such matters. It also may be that control is asserted as much for economic as for political reasons to ensure that the benefits of these new technologies accrue to Chinese enterprises (and Chinese elites) themselves. Indeed, the test of satisfactory political control may become largely an economic one. This might be referred to as the "Taiwan approach," in accordance with the gradualistic, but eventually more open, direction that Taiwan has taken in this regard.[3] (Allow new wine to ferment, and worry more about the label on the bottle than the tightness of the cork.)

The third possibility is that Chinese leaders will conclude that a modern communications infrastructure is simply not compatible with the authoritarian ideological control they must maintain to stay in power and must therefore be severely curtailed. They then would seek to limit even more drastically the people and locations given access to these networks and to scale back the ambitiousness of their plans to apply computing power to the bureaucratic and commercial entities managing the country. Such a course might complement some broader effort by the Chinese leadership to delay or reverse its current course of greater economic integration with the rest of the world. But in all likelihood, this effort would require the convulsion of a Maoist-style antimodern Cultural Revolution, which would wreak havoc with China's economy and society—and would, in any event, be a futile attempt to force the genies of communications and information technology back into their ginger jars. This might be referred to as a kind of "North Korean approach" to these issues. (Stomp the grapes as soon as they ripen.)

Indeed, this last approach could well mean the undoing of the Chinese political regime itself. Even assuming that the current leadership could find the will and the means to reverse massive changes already made, the issue would come down to one of sheer governability. The fact is that information "autarchy" is no longer sustainable for an economy like China's, with critical dependencies on trade with the outside world for the assets and technology necessary to sustain its rapid growth. And world-class economic performance, in turn, is not sustainable without the effective incorporation and exploitation of communications capabilities and information technologies. Unless the Chinese leadership does facilitate widespread access to these networks and capabilities in the interest of efficient decision making and economic modernization, the alternative may well be a society that cannot keep pace with its own economic needs and popular expectations, thereby consigning China to a 21st century of stunted growth, social depression, and political disintegration.

The resolution of this contradiction is therefore much more than just an interesting question for Sinophiles. To those who believe that a peaceful global future requires the constructive engagement of China in world politics—in order to dispel the appeal of a more militaristic, aggressive course—the working out of this tension between communications and control is central to China's future course in global affairs. The prospects for continued economic development in China, for improved human rights, for healthy international trading and investment relationships—all will be significantly affected by the management of this difficult balance. My own guess is that the Chinese will find a way to preserve the formal impression of political supervision without stifling the rapid application of information technologies—perhaps some unique variant of the Singapore and Taiwan approaches. But such an outcome is by no means a foregone conclusion, and the course will be a difficult one to manage.

In order to better understand the context of China's telecommunications challenges, this chapter begins by summarizing the technologies that make up the fundamental capabilities referenced by the term "telecommunications, computer and information technology"—which I have elsewhere referred to in shorthand as "computications" technology[4]—and suggesting the fundamental ways in which these technologies are transforming all societies. I then summarize the international telecommunications "regime" as it currently functions and gauge the impact of that regime on China's telecommunications sector, as well as the reverse question of whether China has been influential in shaping the international regime in furtherance of its own interests. Finally, I assess the implications of this analysis for U.S. policy and the prospect of constructive engagement with China in the domain of telecommunications and information policy.

## Computications Technology and Fundamental Change

Four broad categories of computications technologies are having profound effects on all human societies in the late twentieth century. Not only is China no exception in this regard, but—given the slow pace of its development earlier in this century—these technologies are changing China's culture and economy even more rapidly than those of most developed societies. The first is *video broadcast* technology, which has made the ideas and culture—the sights and sounds—of the outside world accessible to even the most remote sections of China. Perhaps almost as important, this video access also has made some of these more isolated and exotic—as well as the more important and intense—dimensions of Chinese society accessible to huge numbers of interested viewers outside of the country.

The second set of technologies includes *interactive networks* of voice, data, and images that facilitate timely two-way communications both within China and between Chinese citizens and those outside. Phone, fax, and Internet services are the principal examples of these networking capabilities. The third set of technologies result in the ever-increasing *miniaturization of processing power,* which facilitates the decentralization, flexibility, and mobility of computing and networking technologies and thereby reduces the centralized and hierarchical patterns of information access and utilization that have characterized China for centuries. The final set of technologies relates to the development of easily applied *software,* which accentuate the processing capabilities of networks of computers and result in enormous increases in individual and group productivity and innovation.[5]

Even though China has been relatively slow to invest in and disseminate these technologies on a broad scale relative to wealthier countries, the capabilities they afford have exerted a powerful collective impact on important strata of Chinese society. At great risk of oversimplifying, it is useful to consider their cumulative effects on four key dimensions of political culture: personal identity, economic value, individual and national security, and deference to authority.[6]

As for personal identity and the loyalties that result, the widespread dissemination of information, even on the limited scale achieved to date in China, tends to create irreversible shifts in the entities and symbols people identify with and commit themselves to. Individuals revise their conceptions of who they are and what is important to them, and develop new expectations as to what their values and interests are, as a result of the exposure to new possibilities and capabilities facilitated by these technologies. They also come to recognize more easily the common interests and affections they share with those far away from their immediate surroundings. Such changes need not be manifest in new political commitments, as such, in order to have profound impacts on political expectations and group demands over time.

Likewise, the impact of computications technologies on economic performance has been in part to shift the nature of economic value itself—how wealth is created, how businesses are managed, how markets behave—as the role of information has been heightened in virtually all industries.[7] Those businesses that rely most heavily on telecommunications networks and processing power—such as finance and insurance—are facilitated or degraded by the availability and quality of these capabilities. But virtually all economic activity is now dependent on achieving increasing efficiencies to remain competitive—efficiencies closely related to the ability to incorporate and exploit networking and processing technologies. Much of China's lagging state sector—with its bureaucratic, hierarchical, labor-intensive qualities—has been rendered obsolete by such changes in a staggeringly short period of time.

As networking capabilities become ever more strategic to the performance of economic activity, the availability and security of the networks themselves assume ever larger significance. Assuring sufficient capacity and reliability becomes a vital consideration in the location of major businesses. Among other consequences, these factors tend to advantage economically those parts of China that can assure such access and security—major metropolitan coastal areas, in particular—thus accentuating the disparities between regions. These technologies have significant military implications as well.

Finally, on an aggregate basis, these impacts already have transformed traditional Chinese attitudes toward authority and hierarchy. While some officials in the Chinese Communist Party may see new opportunities for information control and indoctrination through these new technologies, the more likely consequence is to reduce the need or inclination of most Chinese to defer to central authority or to accept routinely the government's characterizations of reality. To counter these effects, the leadership is engaged in a high-profile effort to establish a deeper moral basis for its authority through its campaign for the more traditional values of "spiritual civilization," but it is certainly unclear whether such an old-fashioned propaganda effort can withstand the pressures of materialism already unleashed under Deng Xiaoping.[8] In this regard (as in so many others) China shares the plight of governing authorities throughout the world who fear the political and moral consequences of rapid modernization.

Further elaboration of these broad themes is well beyond the scope of this chapter, but they are nonetheless of central importance in assessing the probable impacts of telecommunications and information technology on Chinese political culture. We turn instead to considering the interplay of China's telecom policies and the international political system.

## The International Telecommunications Regime

For the purposes of this discussion, the telecommunications regime can be said to consist of multilateral agreements and regulatory principles covering three main aspects of international communications: (1) the exchange of voice and data transmissions between states; (2) the use of the radiomagnetic spectrum, including the broadcast of radio and television programming across state boundaries; and (3) the designation of satellite locations within the geostationary orbit.[9] Traditionally, the international organization primarily responsible for all three of these dimensions was the International Telecommunication Union (ITU).[10] The ITU has been through a number of evolutionary stages since its founding in 1932, including a rebirth in 1947 as a specialized agency of the United Nations.[11] Based on a broad multilateral convention that establishes its ongoing authority, the organization functions through a series of periodic plenipotentiary, regional, and specialized conferences as well as an ongoing range of study groups and committees—all supported by a secretary-general (currently Pekka Tarjanne of Finland) and an Administrative Council and staff in Geneva. Until recently the ITU's activities were divided sharply between telephone and telegraph issues, on one hand—which were formalized in the Telephone and Telegraph Regulations—and radio spectrum–related issues, on the other—which were formalized in the Radio Regulations. More recently, however, the ITU has taken steps to reduce the separation between these two sectors in recognition of the convergence of policy and technology, as well as to create an entity focused more specifically on promoting telecommunications development in less-developed countries.

In recent years the ITU has been facing strong challenges to its consensus-building prerogatives from other international organizations, including the World Trade Organization, the European Commission, and the Asia Pacific Economic Cooperation (APEC) forum. Some commentators have argued that its slow, bureaucratic style and built-in bias toward protecting state prerogatives have resulted in the growing irrelevance of the ITU, as its efforts seem increasingly to be outpaced by rapid changes in the international market and the development of new technologies. Nevertheless, the ITU remains a forum in which broad global consensus on telecommunications matters is pursued and in which some important policy and standards issues are ultimately formalized.

## TELECOM SERVICES

Basic voice services still represent the largest source of revenues in the telecommunications industry, despite the enormous growth in computerized data transmissions in recent years. But in the telephony realm in particular, the ITU has been running to catch up with the market. In fact, with or without ITU sanction, the international regime for regulating telecommunications traffic is in a state of rapid transition—some might say *decay*—from its original framework, built firmly around the expectation of national control and state-owned monopolies, to one where the pressures for liberalization and competitive market access are rendering the notion of government and monopoly control of communications increasingly obsolete or irrelevant. Developments in technology and the expansion of infrastructure make the preservation of traditional nation-state prerogatives increasingly impractical, while the worldwide consensus for competitive provision of networks and services makes it increasingly indefensible.

Under the old model, states were to agree on a bilateral basis how all telephone traffic would be routed, what facilities were necessary for that purpose, and how they would share the revenues generated between them. Customers had virtually no options as to who would carry their international traffic and what they would pay for it. Furthermore, the range and quality of services were limited. However, as developments in digital technology and fiber-optic capacity multiplied the technical options and available routes, and as the pace of liberalization introduced new and competitive suppliers, the old model has become outdated. Resellers began this process by diverting large amounts of traffic to flat-rate leased lines (thereby avoiding the traditional, per-minute rates set bilaterally), and rerouting it according to their own lower-cost network configurations. Like the legendary American "bootleggers" with homemade liquor dodging the tax man, small entrepreneurs saw the huge opportunities in playing arbitrage with bootlegged minutes and have increasingly taken advantage of the patchwork of above-cost pricing from country to country by introducing "call-back" and third-country routing plans. New competitive carriers have followed suit to the point that even some of the largest, nationally dominant carriers have introduced versions of these reversal and redirection schemes themselves—in clear contradiction of the original ITU-based principles of jointly agreed routing and pricing.

The entire process has been further stimulated by the pressures, both political- and market-based, to allow full competition within all telecommunications services markets. The United States and the United Kingdom led the world in this regard, but Australia, New Zealand,

Canada, Sweden, Chile, and the European Union (EU) soon followed suit. Much of the developed world and many of the developing countries are now either open to competition or moving on a public timetable toward liberalization—while, in the meantime, new competitors try to jump the gun and stretch the rules in anticipation.

In this regard, the ITU was essentially undercut (or bypassed) by the General Agreement on Tariffs and Trade (GATT)/World Trade Organization (WTO), which sponsored multilateral negotiations in pursuit of a broad agreement on the terms of market access for telecommunications services—first in value-added services and then in the (bread-and-butter) basic services as well. This multilateral bypass involved a series of national "end runs" by the trade and finance ministries in key countries (including the United States), which overcame or ignored the concerns of the more conservative communications and foreign affairs agencies and pushed hard for the inclusion of basic services on the multilateral trade agenda. The United States further stimulated this development by pressing selected countries (Canada, South Korea, Mexico, the EU) for liberalization agreements on a bilateral basis.[12]

In February 1997 the Negotiating Group on Telecommunications Services (NGBT), created under the framework of the General Agreement on Trade in Services (GATS) from the Uruguay Round, reached agreement on a broad framework for the liberalization of telecommunications services under the new WTO system. That agreement came into force on February 15, 1998, following the ratification by member countries of the series of liberalization "offers" put forward by countries in the negotiations.[13] The principal commitments deal with the timing for competition in the basic network services market, the terms for interconnection with existing networks, protections against unfair or anticompetitive conduct by incumbents, and the creation of an independent regulatory authority.[14] The WTO regime is now, in effect, the minimum starting point for telecommunications market access—even in countries that may not choose to participate or accede formally in the near future.

## RADIO SPECTRUM

The ITU regime also includes norms and processes for the coordination of state allocations of the radiomagnetic spectrum. Its Radio Regulations established the International Frequency Registration Board, which maintains a frequency allocation table, designating the use of radio frequencies from 9 kilohertz (kHz) to 400 gigahertz (GHz), in an effort to achieve some compatibility of usage on a global and regional basis. All states are obligated to register their national frequency assignments for one of three reasons: (1) the potential for "harmful interference" with the communications of other countries; (2) their intended use for international communications; or (3) the state's desire for formal "international recognition" of the use of that frequency for a given purpose.

One common expectation arising from this system is that frequencies will not be used to broadcast unapproved signals from one nation-state into another. If a state has the right to determine how frequencies will be used within its territory, then presumably it has the authority to deny unauthorized transmissions over its borders. "Pirate" broadcasts can be stopped through direct police action to shut them down or by jamming their programming with broadcasting countermeasures. And one state should be able to appeal to another to take such measures itself where the activity originates in the other's territory. However, the United States in particular had a strong interest in maintaining exceptions to this principle for the broadcasts of Radio Free Europe and Radio Liberty into the Soviet bloc over the objection of the targeted states. As a result, international consensus in the 1950s and early 1960s never fully crystallized to forbid such activity.

With the growth of international communications satellites in the 1960s and 1970s, however, the issue of national sovereignty became even more heated. During the early 1970s a number of states sought to enshrine in international law the doctrine of "prior consent" for the reception of satellite signals. Despite the objections of the United States and other developed countries, resolutions enshrining a prior consent standard were passed in an ITU conference and by the United Nations General Assembly. Developing countries, including China, have argued that this is now a generally applicable principle of international law, notwithstanding U.S. resistance.

However, the prior consent issue often turns on economic rather than political considerations. Given the difficulty of preventing the receipt of unapproved satellite signals by dishes that these days can be no larger than a dinner plate, governments more often rely on the denial of customer revenues to the broadcasters and economic penalties for the unauthorized possession of receivers. Governments object to the use of receivers that are not licensed (and thereby taxed) or programming that takes viewers away from state-owned broadcast networks that find it difficult to compete.

## SATELLITE ORBITAL SLOTS

Finally, the telecommunications regime also can be said to include the principles for regulating communications satellites, which includes the management of orbital assignments as well as the designation of frequencies for their up- and down-links. Successive special World Administrative Radio Conferences, or "Space WARCs," under ITU auspices have sought to frame policies for the use of that special band of orbital locations 22,300 miles above the earth where satellites maintain an orbit in fixed relation to the earth below: the geostationary, or geosynchronous, orbit. Early efforts by developed countries were directed at reserving these limited slots for countries in a position to make immediate use of them.

Developing countries recognized, however, that these slots were a property resource for which "rent" could be charged even if the "owner," or license holder, was not in a position to launch satellites of its own. Various countries therefore have staked a claim to certain geostationary locations and have invited suitors to lease the rights to use them. At its 1994 plenipotentiary conference in Kyoto, Japan, the ITU created the Radiocommunications Advisory Group (RAG) to explore various possible approaches to the management of these issues, including an Australian proposal to require revocable deposits and a U.S. proposal to insist on "due diligence" requirements to combat orbital stockpiling.

## China's Interaction with the Telecom Regime

When the People's Republic of China assumed membership in the International Telecommunication Union from its rival regime in Taipei in 1971, the ITU was composed almost entirely of countries with state-owned monopolies for telephone service. Most of these were, in fact, government ministries with responsibility for postal, telephone, and telegraph services (PTTs)—and, in some cases, for roads and airports as well. The United States was the major exception to this pattern of government monopoly. Its telephone system was dominated by a private company, AT&T; its participation in the International Satellite Consortium, INTELSAT, was carried on through a separate private company, COMSAT; and its international telegraph/telex industry consisted of a virtual cartel of private companies, known as the international record carriers. The radio and television broadcasting industry was also private and competitive, although dominated in the early 1970s by three large, private network companies: NBC, ABC, and CBS. Elsewhere in the world, government-owned entities were generally the exclusive providers of telecommunications and broadcasting services until well into the 1980s.

The Chinese government no doubt found this pattern of government control very much to its liking. The People's Republic of China (PRC) was represented in the ITU from the outset by officials of the Ministry of Posts and Telecommunications (MPT), supported by the Ministry of Foreign Affairs, officials who must have felt quite similar to their governmental colleagues from other countries. At the first ITU Plenipotentiary Conference following its accession, the PRC sent a large delegation, and its chief representative was duly elected as one of nine conference vice chairmen. Yet, in keeping with its future role in the ITU, the delegation's participation was largely passive and ceremonial.[15]

Rather than assuming a leadership role or an aggressively reformist posture in the ITU, the Chinese government apparently saw its strongest interest as that of ensuring the best outcomes for China itself on such matters as bilateral telephone traffic, radio-frequency coordination, control of foreign broadcasting into China, and the allocation of satellite orbital slots. For example, at the 1977 World Administrative Radio Conference in Geneva, China successfully supported a plan to allocate orbital slots to countries in proportion to their geographic size rather than to any current capability or intention to use them.[16] Similarly, it became a strong advocate of the principle that no nation could broadcast into the territory of another without "prior consent."

China's subsequent participation has not departed appreciably from this pattern. It has done little to reshape the parameters of the telecom regime, finding its own interests as essentially compatible with the state-centric thrust of that regime's traditional norms. Its representatives have been less enthusiastic, of course, about the WTO- and APEC-based efforts to evoke commitments about market access and foreign investment in telecommunications operations, but, until early 1997, the slow pace of negotiations on such matters in fact provided China with a certain "cover" to legitimize its own delayed liberalization. At the same time, China evinced little overt concern about the deterioration of the old ITU regime, perhaps under the impression that it could modulate the impact of those changes on its own interests. Finally, the Chinese have not sought to take a leading role in shaping the development agenda of the ITU.

Instead, since at least the seventh Five-Year Plan, in 1985, China's preoccupation has been with the internal development of a telecommunications network sufficient to support the massive growth targets set by the Chinese Communist Party's leadership. During the current, ninth Five-Year Plan (1995–2000), the Ministry of Posts and Telecommunications intends to add 20 million new local access lines each year to its existing 70 million lines—about the equivalent of a new Bell Atlantic every 12 months—for a total of 170 million lines by the end of the century and 400 million lines by 2010.[17] The number of long-distance lines is now growing at an annual rate of over 50 percent, and 84 percent of these lines are now digital (compared with older analog technology). All provincial capitals are now linked by fiber-optic connections. This is in addition to a cellular (mobile) infrastructure that at year-end 1997 had more than 13 million subscribers—100 percent more than in 1996—and is projected to grow to more than 30 million by the year 2000.[18] Since these projections include a future teledensity in major urban areas of 30 to 40 lines per 100 people and in rural areas of more than 10 per 100—from a current nation-wide average of about 4 per 100—these targets demonstrate the magnitude of the effort to which the leadership is committed.

Paralleling this effort to develop the basic public switched network (PSN) is an ambitious program of building a "national information infrastructure" of fiber, satellite, and microwave facilities distinct from the public network to link the ministries of the central government with their provincial counterparts. This so-called Golden Bridge project is often grouped with two other programs, the Golden Customs project to create a national Electronic Data Interchange (EDI) network and the Golden Card project to build a nationwide smart card system.

Although powerfully influenced by the pressures to integrate with the global economy, there is little evidence that these ambitions were provoked or significantly influenced directly by the ITU itself. While that organization—more recently reinforced by active support from the World Bank—generally has promoted the value of telecommunications infrastructure in its members' own development plans, the ITU itself does not impose any particular commitments on internal network development. At the same time, without the ITU and its framework of operating principles and standards coordination, it is likely that China would have pursued the indigenous development of technologies to a greater degree. The ITU has provided some global discipline to the interoperability of communications technologies that has facilitated the opportunities for foreign suppliers to penetrate the China market. Even so, China's purchasing practices have been sufficiently uncoordinated that, until recently, the incompatibility of equipment was a significant barrier to the creation of an integrated national network.

Similarly, although China has participated for several years in the APEC Telecommunications Working Group, U.S. negotiators had not perceived, until quite recently, that Chinese authorities felt any immediate pressure to comply with external expectations regarding the pace of their market liberalization. Indeed, even in the least-threatening realm of value-added services, Chinese representatives had been careful to caution APEC delegates that, while they would not block consensus on market access principles, they also were not in a position to commit themselves to implementation.

The greatest multilateral influence on Chinese telecommunications policies results from the leadership's interest in seeing China become a member of the World Trade Organization. The United States has taken the public position that Chinese accession must include a willingness to commit to a reasonable timetable for the implementation of the GATS Telecom Services agreement. Nevertheless, despite informal indications from Chinese officials on occasion that such commitments were under consideration,[19] the year-end 1997 round of negotiations in Geneva produced only a very limited proposal from the Chinese delegation. China proposed no change in the prohibition on foreign participation in basic services operating entities and offered only to allow—within two years— foreign investment of up to 25 percent in two value-added ventures: one in Shanghai and one in Guangzhou.[20] Unless the United States abandons its insistence on meaningful liberalization commitments, this issue is therefore likely to remain a sticking point on WTO accession.

The WTO discussions continue a dialogue conducted with the U.S. government on telecommunications issues for several years prior to the WTO accession talks. The last formal bilateral session of this sort was held in September 1995 in Hangzhou. These discussions were similar to those conducted with many countries in the early 1990s that resembled consultations more than negotiations. Essentially, the delegations compared notes about the development of policy and regulatory issues ranging widely over the panoply of telecommunications issues. While the U.S. representatives did have an opportunity to probe particular issues in contention (i.e., foreign ownership limitations and accounting rate levels), those earlier sessions were not expected to produce resolutions or concrete agreements on such matters. The Chinese did appear sensitive to U.S. concerns but were not ready to promise policy changes or commit to timetables for liberalization on a bilateral basis. China's concern for WTO membership has clearly provided leverage of a different magnitude. Nevertheless, the economic recession begun in Asia in late 1997—prompted by currency devaluations and banking crises— seemed also to cause a lessening in China's sense of urgency on WTO membership that may reduce its sensitivity to pressures for telecom liberalization.

As for the larger trends in the international telecommunications regime, Chinese representatives to ITU meetings recently have begun to join other governments in expressing concern about the rapid transformation of the international voice and data market and the loss of state prerogatives implied by some of the newer phenomena in the marketplace. In particular, they have supported proposals to retain national control of rates and routing by preventing "call turnaround" companies and international resale. These indications of concern for the larger regime are a notable departure from the relatively passive role played previously by Chinese representatives.

With respect to China's influence on the development policies of other countries, its approach to internal telecom development, with its residue of central planning and investment, coupled with the massive scale of its economy, has not generally been seen to have clear applicability to other developing countries—except perhaps as a negative example.[21] At the same time, the sheer size of China's undertaking affects the development of the industry as a whole. Perhaps the country's greatest impact, therefore, is a result of the amount of foreign effort directed at its infrastructure development that might otherwise have been directed elsewhere, including soft financing provided by certain governments for the purchase of equipment from their national flag companies. Current restrictions on direct foreign investment in operating companies have limited demands on available foreign capital, combined with the availability of a wealthy network of "overseas Chinese" investors from Asia and North America that seems to have facilitated a certain amount of "unofficial" fudging of the investment restrictions. However, if China's current development plans remain on course and the investment rules are liberalized as indicated, the inflow of foreign investments to fund the further growth of China's communications infrastructure will increase substantially in the next decade.

## BASIC SERVICES COMPETITION

In 1994 China took the formal steps necessary to create a measure of competition in basic telecom services by authorizing a single competitor: China United Telecommunications (Lian Tong), or Unicom.[22] This new operator is actually a creation of several important ministries—Railways, Power, and Electronics—that have developed their own networks (and bridled at MPT's prerogatives) for many years.

Internal government agitation for alternative networks dates back at least to the late years of the Cultural Revolution, when the first two of these agencies, along with the People's Liberation Army (PLA), found themselves frustrated by the sporadic and lethargic performance of the MPT in providing reliable communications. In 1976 these ministries appealed to the State Council for permission to create their own "private" networks, ostensibly specialized for their own purposes, but in reality constituting limited alternatives to the public switched network constructed and managed by MPT. They received permission and, over time, built networks that are useful adjuncts to the MPT network. These networks have provided alternative sources of revenue both for the agencies themselves and for the personal benefit of some of their senior officials. The PLA followed a similar path to assure the quality of its own networks.[23]

These internal rivalries and anomalies have in fact been an important factor in the evolution of China's telecommunications policies. Decisions often have been based on considerations of internal "bureaucratic politics" between MPT and its agency rivals and critics. In this regard, MPT's lead role in China's representation to the ITU often has been a valuable positioning asset in asserting its internal authority over these competitors. On other occasions, however, as in the authorization of Unicom itself, MPT has been explicitly overruled by higher authorities in the name of reducing its control and stimulating development. Vice Premier Zou Jiahua was reported to have ordered MPT to treat Unicom as its "little brother" to see that it received fair treatment, and he intervened on several occasions to promote its progress. Likewise, the PLA has continued to intervene to protect its criminal position in certain businesses.[24]

MPT's position was also at issue in the lead-up to China's takeover of Hong Kong in July 1997. CITIC (China International Trade and Investment Corporation) Pacific, based in Hong Kong, initially was positioned as the vehicle by which the Chinese government acquired interests outside of the country. In 1991 CITIC took a 10 percent ownership position in Hong Kong Telecom (HKT), buying out the shares of Hong Kong industrialist Li Ka-shing. However, that share was subsequently reduced to less than 8 percent and later transferred entirely to Everbright Holdings Company, an investment arm of the State Council itself. Then in June 1997 China Telecom—the Hong Kong–based subsidiary of MPT—purchased 5.5 percent of the company directly from Cable & Wireless (C&W).[25] Speculation reigned that China might seek a controlling interest in HKT once the handover occurred,[26] but to date no further adjustments in ownership have been made.

Yet competition among operators—important as that may be for customers and for the development of the market generally—is probably not as decisive in the short run to the objective of information control as is the geometric multiplication of available communications channels within the country and to the outside world. The most dramatic demonstration of this phenomenon occurred during the Tiananmen crisis in 1989. Round-the-clock television coverage was certainly a decisive factor in encouraging the mass occupation of Tiananmen Square.[27] But two-way networks were also critical to these developments. It is now well recognized that the student leaders and supportive workers responsible for the sustained demonstration in Tiananmen Square had become critically dependent on fax communications both to circulate information about developments on the square and to receive expressions of solidarity and encouragement from those outside of Beijing and outside of China itself—an important factor in maintaining morale. At the time, the number and configuration of international circuits was such that it would have been relatively easy for the telecommunication authorities in the MPT and the Beijing Post and Telecom to cut off most of these circuits at the international gateway location and thereby eliminate this access. For whatever reasons, they chose not to do so—and were not forced to by higher authorities.

Since the Tiananmen crisis, however, the number of international circuits to China has multiplied almost exponentially. While the precise numbers are difficult to compile, between 1989 and 1997 circuits to the United States between MPT and AT&T alone increased more than tenfold! (See Figure 7–1.)

Fiber-optic connections between Shanghai and Japan and through Hong Kong to East and Southeast Asia have added enormous bandwidth to the connections between China's network and the rest of the world. New international gateway locations have been added, and the entire domestic network has grown in complexity, capability, and reliability. By the end of 1999 China and the United States will be linked directly by a gigantic (80 gigabits per second) submarine cable capable of carrying 4 million simultaneous phone calls. In short, the option of cutting off access to the outside world on a broad scale—at least on short notice—is now far more difficult and momentous.

Perhaps even more problematic would be a broad retrenching in China's adoption of communications and computing technologies in the modernization of its industries. The computer, the fax, and the cellular phone—in addition to the television set—are becoming staples of business life among those in the sectors experiencing the greatest growth and innovation in China's economy. Restrictions on access or use of these technologies would inhibit their essential spread—along with the even more efficient dissemination and use of information itself—to the industries that lag behind in this modernization.

## SATELLITES

China's policies on satellite communications have liberalized significantly in the last few years. In 1994 MPT authorized the licensing for pri-

Figure 7-1. AT&T Circuits in Service to China, 1989–1997

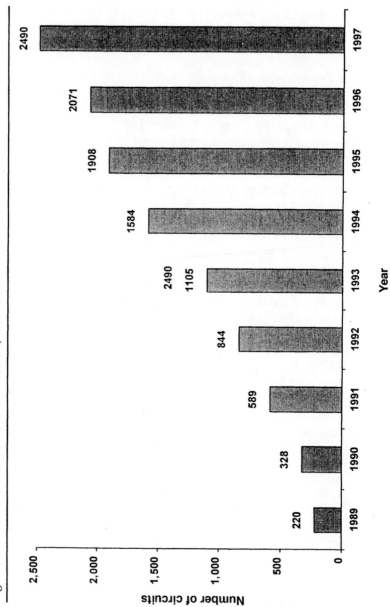

vate networks of VSAT (very small aperture terminals) systems.[28] Since then a number of large networks have been created, the largest being that of China National Petroleum, which has more than 500 terminals. Even though these networks cannot be directly linked to the public switched network, they can greatly enhance the efficiency of certain state enterprises.

On the issue of direct broadcasting satellites, China has been keeping its commercial distance from the range of commercial broadcast satellite services that seek access to its vast television audience. In April 1996, for example, the president of China Central Television (CCTV) (and vice minister of Radio, Film, and Television) dismissed as "completely groundless" reports that CCTV was about to agree with Rupert Murdoch's STAR-TV on a network arrangement.[29] Instead, he reinforced previous statements that China would develop its own cable and satellite-based television networks without foreign participation and would, in turn, expand its own programming aimed at Chinese audiences in other countries using the PanAmSat satellite system. In August 1996, another official was even more blunt in dismissing Murdoch's plans.[30] The government, of course, is indirectly an investor in the AsiaSat satellite system through a one-third interest held by CITIC. Cable & Wireless and Hutchison Whampoa of Hong Kong are the other major investors.

Nevertheless, with or without a deal involving China's active participation, STAR-TV illustrates the enormous increase in popular access to direct satellite broadcasts since the Tiananmen crackdown and the difficulties the government faces in limiting such access.[31] Most of its programming is in Mandarin Chinese (Putongua) and includes news, sports, and music video formats as well as feature films and TV serials. When STAR-TV first began broadcasting, in January 1992, Chinese authorities directed 50 Beijing-area hotels to stop offering access to their customers. But these restrictions were not seriously enforced, particularly following the easing of central government control after Deng Xiaoping's famous "trip to the South" that summer. According to a former official of the Ministry of Electronics, Chinese consumers purchased half a million satellite dishes in 1992 alone, the first year of STAR-TV's operation. In the fall of 1993 a survey of 22 Chinese provinces determined that 30.4 million homes (about 120 million people) were capable of receiving STAR-TV—which was six times the estimated number a year earlier. In July 1993 Ruport Murdoch took full control of STAR-TV.

However, on August 20, 1993, as part of a series of restrictive measures, the State Council adopted Decree No. 129, portending a crackdown on unauthorized satellite receptions. The decree created a licensing regime for satellite dishes that limited licenses to government-designated enterprises and restricted the sale of dishes to only a limited number of government suppliers. Individuals were to be prevented from acquiring satellite dishes unless they could cite "exceptional circumstances" and had to submit any existing dishes to a new approval process. This decree was not officially promulgated and publicly announced until October 5. In the meantime, Rupert Murdoch made a public statement that outraged Chinese authorities and was assumed to have been a cause of the harsher policies announced in October (although in fact they had been decided on earlier).[32]

Not long thereafter, in February 1994, a new set of implementing rules created a key distinction between those dishes installed for the receipt of domestic broadcasts and those that also were intended to receive foreign broadcasts. The approval process for the former was made much easier than for the latter. Because CCTV used the same AsiaSat satellite to broadcast in China as that used by STAR-TV, customers were able to receive both signals with only minor adjustments—so long as they were willing to risk being caught and prosecuted for unapproved receptions.

The upshot of this new effort to limit access was therefore decidedly mixed; enforcement was sporadic and geographically very uneven. Outside of the major cities, in particular, access to STAR-TV apparently was not reduced much at all. In December 1994, for example, a survey by the marketing arm of the State Statistical Bureau determined that 64 percent of the two- and three-star hotels in China were capable of receiving satellite broadcasts, and 88 percent of these hotels had STAR-TV.[33] Perhaps even more tellingly, the evidence suggests that satellite dishes, colloquially referred to as "woks," are generally available to those willing to buy them, and most dishes already owned have not been taken out of operation.[34]

## THE INTERNET

Even more pervasive impacts within China may come as a result of increasingly widespread access to the virtually boundless networks of the Internet. As other governments are quickly finding out, the Internet presents a new phenomenon in the organization and transmission of information that is not easily amenable to local rules or sensitivities. Many Chinese officials have recognized the enormous economic potential inherent in this vehicle, and there is strong support within the government for assuring broad availability for economic purposes.

However, other officials have sounded loud alarms. According to one report, Premier Li Peng was personally incensed in late 1995 by a series of electronic mail messages commemorating the 40th anniversary of the liberal Student Movement of December 9, 1935, and his outrage became a factor in the development of China's restrictive approach to Internet access early the next year.

Indeed, the State Council issued a decree on Internet access on February 4, 1996, which addressed these concerns by creating a two-tiered network structure. The first tier, the "access network," was to be the one directly accessible to users and connected to the Internet itself only through a second tier of "interconnection networks." Only four such networks were authorized, run by MPT (ChinaNet), MEI (Golden Bridge or China GBNet), the State Education Commission (CERNET), and the China Academy of Sciences (CASNET). All cross-border interconnection with the Internet was required to pass through one of MPT's international gateways. Overall authority for Internet access issues and other computer-based networks was decreed to reside in the State Council's Joint Staff Committee of National Economic Information (JSCNEI)—also known as the "leading group"—chaired by Vice Premier Zou Jiahua and formally superior to the MPT.[35] MPT and MEI were reportedly contending hotly for authority over the Internet, and the solution was to create an arbiter above them both.[36] Following this decree, the Ministry of Public Security ordered all Internet users to register with the police within 30 days or face punishment.

As of August 1996 government statistics showed that more than 50,000 subscribers had registered.[37] The marketing head of the Beijing Telegraph Office, which is licensed to distribute ChinaNet, told *China Daily* that "any individual or organization can sign up."[38] In Beijing, however, the number then stood at only 6,000 people, and analysts predicted that subscribers would be limited by capacity as well as political constraints to only 300,000 countrywide for the next few years. The government's approach, in short, was to screen and modulate Internet access at the first layer, while editing content at the second layer.[39]

One Chinese official suggested to his U.S. counterpart that it was the World Wide Web, with its graphical and video capabilities, that most concerned the government. He indicated that the authorities made a sharp distinction between the Web itself and the other electronic bulletin board/electronic mail features of the Internet, which were deemed somehow less threatening. Of course, Web sites currently are available on the Internet for everything from bomb manufacture to euthanasia—not to mention the elaborate graphical opportunities afforded to pornographers—and the four interconnection providers were given the general responsibility of filtering these out using screening software and constant vigilance. However, as the example of Li Peng's outrage at "subversive" e-mail suggests, electronic mail and bulletin boards also can convey potentially "subversive" information. The line between Web sites and other electronic interchange therefore will prove difficult to draw in practice.

By early September 1996 the government had begun to apply its Web filters and announced that it had blocked access from China to more than 100 Web sites deemed obscene or politically dangerous.[40] The Associated Press reported that the following specific sites had been blocked: U.S. news media such as the *Los Angeles Times*, the *Wall Street Journal*, the *Washington Post*, Voice of America, and Cable News Network; politically sensitive sites, including the Taiwan Government Information Office; home pages of groups that monitor human rights abuses in China, such as Amnesty International; the U.S-based *China News Digest;* and *Playboy.*

However, by early 1997 access to most of these sites had been restored—perhaps reflecting the government's concern to avoid the appearance of authoritarian heavy-handedness in the lead-up to Hong Kong's return in June 1997. Internet access, in fact, grew tremendously throughout the year, and most Web sites seemed widely available, if not always technically accessible, owing to capacity constraints. The government's Internet Information Center reported that as of the end of October 1997, the country had more than 620,000 registered Internet subscribers.[41] Since most of these subscriptions are known to be shared among as many as ten or more individual users, Internet penetration clearly is increasing rapidly among certain groups.

No doubt in recognition of this growth, and out of continued concern about the availability of information deemed problematic, the cabinet decided on December 11 to issue additional regulations governing Internet usage. The new rules, reported by the *New York Times*, included prohibitions on the use of the Internet "to split the country"—assumed to refer to the Tibetan independence movement—or for "defaming government agencies."[42] In a press conference on December 29, limited to Chinese reporters only but reported by the New China News Agency, Assistant Minister of Public Security Zhu Entao emphasized that computer information networks are indispensable to the country's economic and scientific progress. "But," he said, "the connection has also brought about some security problems, including manufacturing and publicizing harmful information, as well as leaking state secrets through the Internet."[43] The regulations also promised criminal punishments for violators as well as fines of up to $1,800 for both individual users and the companies providing access to banned material. The *Times* reported on

December 31 that, although its own Web site and those of several human rights groups did appear to be blocked, access was still available to one of the most prominent "X-rated" sites.

This "blocking-and-tackling" approach to Internet control may selectively penalize individual users and deter some others, but it is unlikely to succeed in preventing widespread access to otherwise troublesome information. The task of monitoring the Internet for potentially harmful material is a daunting undertaking. Such censorship is likely to be either sporadic and unreliable (and therefore ineffective), or so comprehensive and restrictive as to force more determined users to look for alternative means of Internet access—such as direct international phone connections outside of China.[44] As fast and clever as the censors may be, those citizens motivated to acquire "contraband" information usually can find ways to stay ahead of them.[45] More important, the politically liberalizing effects of Internet access result not merely from popular access to specific kinds of "subversive" or "corrupting" information, but from the ability to access huge databases and displays of information that, in itself, is politically neutral, but that provides a rich picture of alternative social, commercial, and cultural possibilities. The experience of the east European and former Soviet republics would suggest that it is this sort of information, not the deliberately "subversive" variety, that will have the greatest liberalizing impacts on China as a whole.

FINANCIAL REPORTING

Still another example of information control policy illustrates the clear economic basis for some of China's restrictive information policies. In mid-January 1996 the State Council announced that the government's Xinhua News Agency would assume responsibility for the distribution of all economic information from such Western services as Reuters and Dow Jones. Xinhua indicated that all financial information would have to go through its *own* review and that it would prevent the dissemination of information that was not in the "national interest." Most observers attributed the main motive for this step to an effort by Xinhua to share in the revenue generated by such services, but concern also was expressed by Chinese authorities that unfettered access to Western sources would jeopardize the reputation and viability of some Chinese enterprises.[46] The U.S. government portrayed the Chinese position not as a matter of repressive censorship but as a serious violation of intellectual property rights.[47]

Regardless of which motive was paramount, it is doubtful that censorship of economic information can be fully successful in the current state of global information dissemination. Given the decisive importance of such data and the money at stake, no serious analyst can afford to depend these days on an "edited" or official version of economic information. Filtering everything through a Xinhua censor would only render the reliability of this source so suspect as to reduce its value almost to zero. Analysts simply find other routes to obtain such information—including through the Internet itself—and Xinhua would have neither the control nor the revenue it sought. Indeed, in recognition of the need for more reliable information about the economic health of newly listed enterprises, the government at year-end 1997 also issued new accounting rules to promote more accurate financial reporting by the companies themselves.

A similar tension will no doubt continue to be played out regarding the boundaries between what are deemed acceptable and unacceptable types of journalistic reports. One year before the Hong Kong handover, the chief PRC representative there, Lu Ping, is reported to have drawn a sharp distinction regarding press reporting in Hong Kong between objective reporting—which would be acceptable to the Beijing authorities—and advocacy of a political point of view deemed by China to be subversive, including support for the independence of Tibet or Taiwan—which would be prohibited.[48] Lu suggested that such advocacy would amount to "an act" under the terms of Article 23 of Hong Kong's Basic Law and therefore could be banned or prosecuted.

Lu's distinction, of course, raised all sorts of further issues. For example, what about a critical piece of reporting that purported to be factual but had negative political implications? Even the suggestion of such difficult distinctions, accompanied by threats of prosecution, can chill the atmosphere for otherwise "objective" reporters. This point was made strongly by one of China's most noted dissidents, Liu Xiaobo, in a July 1996 letter addressed to the National People's Congress. "Monopolizing the sources of information is tantamount to throttling the spirit and survival of people's freedom," wrote Liu. "Monopoly leads to privilege, privilege leads to unfair competition, and unfair competition leads to corruption."[49]

## MINISTERIAL REFORM

As this chapter was being finalized, a major announcement was made at the National People's Congress on the restructuring of government ministries that will have a significant impact on both the policy and the operational aspects of China's information infrastructure. State Council Secretary-General Luo Gan outlined a plan that involved the abolition of 15 central ministries and commissions, including MPT, MEI, the Ministry of Radio, Film and Television Broadcasting (MRFT), and a number of related entities, including the "leading group" on information policy. In their place the Ministry of Information Industry was created, which reports directly to the State Council.[50] The new ministry has responsibility to set standards, issue regulations, allocate radio frequencies, and grant licenses. At the same time, the responsibility for operating networks and providing services was separated from the ministry—a structural separation that includes the DGT/China Telecom entities as well as those of Unicom, Great Wall, and cable television. MPT minister Wu Jichuan became the head of the new ministry. In short, China's leaders seem to be taking the first steps toward separating the policy/regulatory functions characteristic of government bodies in other countries from the operational functions of private companies—although there was no indication in the announcement of an intention to pursue early privatization of these networks.[51] Much will depend on the skill and determination of those responsible to carry out these changes as to whether they accomplish their stated purposes of integration and rationalization. But the effort to bring the government policy and regulatory functions affecting information issues together in one entity is a step that even most developed countries have not yet attempted.[52]

## Policy Implications and Recommendations

China's struggles to harness the potential of the information revolution are just one aspect of its efforts to manage the tensions unleashed by modernization and globalization. When it first joined the International Telecommunication Union a generation ago, that framework helped to facilitate its gradual, and generally undramatic, engagement with a stable, well-controlled industry. In fact, the old telecom regime provided China with a comfortable "womb" of state sovereignty within which to develop policy at its own pace. That regime "engaged" the People's Republic in those tender years on terms nicely compatible with the country's own preference for an unobtrusive, state-reinforcing framework. China participated in and conformed to the basic parameters of that traditional regime without drama or flare—but it engaged, nonetheless.

In the process, that regime also lent internal prestige and authority to those diplomatic and bureaucratic representatives from MPT and the Foreign Ministry who participated directly in ITU-sponsored or related activities. They gained access to ideas and information that provided useful advantage for their own positioning internally—and in fact may have slowed the development of competing policies and networks. In the "red vs. expert" and "nativist vs. cosmopolitan" struggles within China's vast bureaucratic apparatus, such legitimizing influences should not be underrated.

Today, however, China—and all other ITU members—are in the midst of a difficult, even painful labor to give birth to an entirely new framework for international telecommunications. And China, although a squeamish observer and not an active midwife, is now sufficiently involved in this process that it likely will be pulled along with everyone else into that brave new world of WTO trading rules, International Monetary Fund (IMF) discipline, and currency speculator/financial investor penalties. Barring some fundamental reversion to a kind of North Korean approach to the outside world, the major questions regarding China's further liberalization of telecommunications have more to do with timing and style than with whether they will occur at all. Given China's size and structure, its approach to these matters will no doubt be unique.

But whatever the process, the fact is that China already has been changed significantly and irreversibly by the technologies themselves—and most likely their impacts will only accelerate. Neither of China's most critical challenges—the transformation of its inefficient state industries and the reforms of obsolete political institutions—can be met without the aggressive application of these new technologies. Nor is the exploitation of technologies simply a matter of buying or building them. China's political and commercial culture will have to adjust to the requirements of an information-based society; doing so will involve the transformation of an authoritarian command-and-control mentality into a more open economy in which information is shared widely and rapidly, and political expediency does not protect bureaucratic inefficiencies. Whatever political gloss the Chinese leadership might contrive to justify these changes, they remain economic and social imperatives for the country.[53]

Of course, as in many other countries, in China these technologies and capabilities may develop differently in certain preferred regions and sectors and thereby could create a stratified or compartmentalized society in which some parts accelerate while others lag behind. The PLA, for example, likely will ensure that its elite ranks will have access to the finest available networks and that its principal purposes are served by them. The direction of military strategy and tactics would suggest that China's armed forces cannot afford to rely on obsolete technology and doctrine, regardless of what the party leadership may decide for other sectors. But that objective probably is facilitated, not inhibited, by the dissemination of communications technologies in the broader society as well.

Similarly, southern China may continue to lead the rest of the country in the absorption and exploitation of new technologies and techniques. Now that Hong Kong has returned to the fold, it may itself become less threatening as a model for the rest of the country—at least in the development of Shanghai and other internationally oriented port cities. Although fits and starts can be expected in the pace of their development, the basic direction is no longer in doubt.

In short, the international political implications of computications infrastructure proliferation should be clear. China has passed the point of no return in both its internal development plans and its global economic engagement. To try to slow this process appreciably, or to micromanage implementation and access, would be, in effect, to try to reverse it. It is not at all clear that the current leadership has the will, or ultimately the power, to do so, even if it should want to.[54] As its economy has become ever more linked to developments beyond its borders, China has its own stake in the effectiveness of the international regimes that facilitate this engagement. It could, of course, disregard these interests—perhaps induced by some crisis of the moment in the Taiwan Strait or along the border with Korea or the former Soviet republics. But the threads tying China to the outside world are far more binding, and far more difficult to sever, than the country's leaders probably even yet realize. Most of their efforts to control them will prove ineffective, even though they could be highly disruptive in the short term if pursued with the vindictive zeal of reactionary cadres. Indeed, to the ideological zealot—whether communist or nationalist—China's telecommunications ties to the rest of the world could come to seem like the ropes restraining a Gulliver, not the indispensable nerves and arteries between China and the global economy that Western capitalists tend to imagine.

The United States has clear economic, as well as political, stakes in the development of Chinese attitudes on these matters. China will continue to offer an enormous market opportunity for the full range of equipment manufacturers, software developers, and information providers at the high-tech tier of U.S. industry. Policies that restrict the ability of U.S. companies to participate in these markets (whether on the basis of broad most-favored-nation restrictions or selective sanctions) not only will benefit European, Japanese, and other foreign competitors at U.S. expense, but also may accelerate the development of indigenous Chinese competitors, thereby reducing the long-term opportunities for U.S.-based industries and resulting in a substantial de-positioning of U.S. competitiveness.

Beyond the profound economic implications, the changes wrought by such technologies will impact other international domains significantly. In the realm of human rights, for example, the continuing trend toward wide information access may do far more to promote openness and expose abuse—and, in turn, to change official and popular attitudes from within—than currently can be accomplished by the "selective-shaming" process relied on by external organizations. A similar effect can be hoped for on matters of environmental protection. In short, China's constructive engagement in global affairs will be deeply implicated in the future course of these changes.

No doubt most U.S. policymakers recognize the strategic significance of this sector on China's development and will look for ways to reinforce the positive aspects of these changes.[55] Successful incorporation of China into the WTO trade regime and continued progress on numerous bilateral fronts will, it is hoped, keep China's leaders in the appropriate frame of mind to manage the inevitable tensions added by computications technologies. But China's telecommunications development also will be influenced by Americans on a different level. Indeed, among those Chinese who specialize in telecommunications, computer technology, and journalism, there is an enormous demand for information and advice and a strong inclination to learn from U.S. models and experience in structuring China's industry. It is easy to underestimate, in this regard, the importance of maintaining a broad range of interactions between Chinese and American specialists to reinforce this interest and to guide development in helpful ways. While Chinese officials sometimes are accused of taking advantage of Western largesse in this regard, the value of ongoing training programs and educational exchanges for the long-run development and liberalization of China's infrastructure is vital to understand.

At the same time, the basic decisions as to how—and how fast—to adjust their information policies rest with the Chinese themselves, and no doubt will remain sources of contention among competing visions of the country's future. Depending on how its leaders choose to view international communications networks and information technologies, they are either China's worst enemy or its greatest ally. They will prove to be either part of its long-run competitive advantage or the explanation for its eventual economic slide. Without a clear commitment to exploit these technologies, and a willingness to ease up on ambitious ideological objectives, the latter "slippery slope" looms ahead. But, in all likelihood, the Chinese leadership will recognize that this course is not in the long-term interest of the country and will find its own accommodation with the technological capabilities that are transforming modern civilization. We outsiders can try to be helpful at the margins, but for the most part we must watch and hope that this particular "contradiction" will be resolved by China in its own enlightened self-interest.

The fifteenth Party Congress in September 1997 seemed to mark an important turning point in this regard. By committing himself to a fundamental reform of the state-owned enterprises, Jiang Zemin has tackled the most serious obstacle to China's economic adjustment to the outside world. By supporting Zhu Rongji as successor to Premier Li Peng—a choice ratified by the National People's Congress in March 1998—Jiang threw his support to the leader most capable of implementing this effort effectively. Recent turmoil in other Asian economies has clearly slowed the pace at which China now plans to implement such steps as full currency conversion—and even has stretched out the timetable for full WTO membership. Despite a series of concrete steps for economic reform, the leadership's ultimate vision of a "capitalist" China "with socialist characteristics" remains a fuzzy notion—particularly with respect to its political implications.

But the choice between a Taiwan-style future at one end of the spectrum and that of a North Korea at the other should leave little doubt about the right direction to take. Perhaps tiny Singapore—the city-state with the Lee Kuan Yew "attitude"—does represent an interim model (or, more likely, a useful symbol) that will allow China's leadership to resolve its competing impulses in a productive direction with only mild or intermittent efforts at political control. In this regard, we certainly can be thankful that Mao Zedong, in particular, is no longer around to "solve" this contradiction "between the old and the new things" in Chinese society in the same way he sought to resolve others. Rather, the Chinese leadership might better look for inspiration to the words of Deng Xiaoping in his famous 1992 "visit to the south":

"We should be bolder than before in conducting reform and opening to the outside and have the courage to experiment. *We must not act like women with bound feet.* Once we are sure that something should be done, we should dare to experiment and break a new path."[56]

## Notes

This chapter was completed in March 1998, while the author was still an International Public Affairs Vice President at AT&T. It contains only the personal opinions of the author in a private capacity and should not be understood as reflecting any particular point of view on the part of Hongkong Telecom, AT&T, or their respective leadership. The observations have been informed by a series of informal but confidential discussions with both government and nongovernment experts familiar with China. For a shorter summary of these thoughts (in verse), see "Getting through to China," *China Business Review,*

(November/December 1997). The author would like to thank the other members of the Telecommunications subgroup of the Council on Foreign Relations China Task Force—in particular, Daniel Lynch, now of the University of Southern California faculty, who shared important sections of his 1996 doctoral dissertation on China's information policy.

1.   This reference is not meant to suggest that Singapore has itself achieved—or can sustain—this authoritarian model, only that Lee has become a prominent exponent of the need to retain heavy political and information controls in the course of economic modernization.

2.   For understanding the current posture of Chinese leaders in this regard, I have relied heavily on a chapter from Daniel C. Lynch, *The Market Is the Message: The Political Economy of State Control over 'Thought Work' in Reformed China* (Stanford, Calif: Stanford University Press, forthcoming).

3.   For an effort to compare China's current system with those of Hong Kong and Taiwan, and to speculate on the prospects for greater convergence, see Willem van Kemenade, *China, Hong Kong, Taiwan, Inc.: The Dynamics of a New Empire* (New York: Alfred Knopf, 1997).

4.   See my remarks at the 1996 Conference of the Couchiching Institute of Public Affairs in Ontario, Canada, entitled "Future States," and available on the Internet at http://www.att.com/speeches/96/960809.oea.html. These remarks were an extension (and versification) of an earlier paper written for a Council on Foreign Relations Study Group, "Sovereignty, Non-state Actors and a New World Politics," chaired by Jessica T. Mathews. That paper, entitled "Global Communications and the Sovereignty of States," was presented in April 1995 at the Council on Foreign Relations Study Group in Washington, D.C.

5.   For overviews of the technologies and their impacts, see Arno Penzias, *Harmony: Business, Technology and Life after Paperwork* (New York: Harper Business; 1995), and Penzias, *Ideas and Information: Managing in a High-tech World* (New York: W. W. Norton & Company, 1989).

6.   Tipson, "Future States, note 4."

7.   See, in this regard, Robert B. Reich, *The Work of Nations* (New York: Alfred Knopf, 1991).

8.   The Central Committee plenary that began on October 7, 1996, adopted an extensive discourse on the meaning of "spiritual civilization," intended as the centerpiece for a central government campaign against corruption and materialism and for a rebirth of Confucian values, which will bolster the bid for long-term, post-Deng leadership by President Jiang Zemin. See "Jiang Looks to Boost His Image," *Financial Times*, October 7, 1996, p. 6. See also "Beijing Seeks Tighter Controls on Ideology," *Financial Times*, October 11, 1996.

9.   See the summary by Mark W. Zacher and Brent A. Sutton, "The International Telecommunications Regime," in *Governing Global Networks: Inter-*

*national Regimes for Transportation and Communications,* Cambridge Studies in International Relations: 44 (1996). See also Jonathan Aronson and Peter Cowhey, *When Countries Talk: International Trade in Telecommunications* (MA: Cambridge University Press, 1988) pp. 127–180.

10.  See in general George Codding and Anthony Rutkowski, *The International Telecommunication Union in a Changing World* (NY: Artech House, 1982).

11.  The ITU was in fact the direct descendant of the International Telegraph Union, created in Paris in 1865.

12.  We might contrast the statist ancien regime of the ITU ("L'etat, c'est moi"), with the more competitive "bourgeois capitalistic" regime of the nouveau WTO ("Liberté, Égalité, Fraternité"). However, this is not to suggest that reform of the ITU itself has not been a serious agenda in several quarters, including the office of the secretary-general, Pekka Tarjanne, himself.

13.  At year-end 1997, the effective date of the agreement was postponed, pending a larger number of ratifications than those conveyed by the November 30 deadline. It later became February 15, 1998.

14.  The provisions of the agreement itself on such matters are further elaborated in a "reference paper" that accompanies the text.

15.  Codding and Rutkowski, *International Telecommunication Union,* pp. 54, 65–66.

16.  Ibid., p. 50.

17.  From a statement by MPT Vice-Minister Lin Jinquan in *People's Post and Telecommunications,* October 21, 1995. The record and plans of the Chinese government for telecommunications development are documented most thoroughly in an indispensable study for the Harvard Program on Information Resources by Xing Fan, entitled "China Telecommunications: Constituencies and Challenges" (August 1996). My thoughts also benefited from the opportunity to read Stephen Chien's 1998 honors thesis at Standford, "Bureaucracies as Businesses: The Strategies of Chinese Bureaucracies and Multinational Firms in China's Telecommunications Industry."

18.  *South China Morning Post,* January 7, 1998. These figures do not include the number of subscribers linked to China Telecom's competitor, Unicom, which had an estimated 300,000 customers.

19.  For example, on December 15, 1996, one such official, Ma Jixian, outlined a three-stage (years 2000, 2010, 2020), 20-category "action plan" for the liberalization of the services sectors that will involve the reduction of tariffs, the removal of nontariff barriers, and the opening of services sectors to foreign involvement. With respect to telecommunications in particular, he indicated that China would issue by the year 2000 new "service trade rules concerning foreign-operated telecommunications networks." Walker, "Beijing Plans to Open Telecoms Sector," *Financial Times,* December 16, 1996, p. 4.

20. The proposal described the permissible scope of these two ventures as including "electronic data interchange, code and protocol conversion and on-line information and data processing," and suggested that after five years, they would be allowed to expand to an unspecified extent.

21. In India, for example, the lack of competition and foreign investment in China sometimes was contrasted with the course recommended by pro-liberalization advocates.

22. This development has been most ably and thoroughly documented to date by Xing Fan in the study cited at note 17.

23. Senior officers in the PLA have been known to operate "private" companies that lease "idle" capacity from the military network to provide services to nonaffiliated users.

24. See, for example, Asia-Pacific Telecoms Analyst, "PLA Manoeuvres towards Public Telco Network Target," *Financial Times*, November 3, 1997, p. 3.

25. C&W, which retains 54 percent of HKT, indicated at the time that it received in exchange certain assurances that it would be most favorably positioned for direct operating roles in China proper, but these prospects have not yet been realized. China Telecom also participated in an initial public offer of its shares on the Hong Kong market.

26. On January 20, 1998, Hong Kong Telecom announced that it had reached agreement with the Special Administration Region authorities to forgo the last eight years of its monopoly franchise for international services as part of a broader agreement on the terms of competition that included compensation of HK $6.7 billion.

27. The events leading to this occupation by students and workers began in April with marches in observance of the death of Hu Yaobang. The 70th anniversary of the May 4 Movement provided further impetus, followed shortly by the long-anticipated visit of Russian Premier Gorbachev. The foreign news media were present and primed for that visit, making efforts to restrict access or suppress broadcasts much more difficult.

28. VSATs are small satellite dishes that transmit and receive signals, thereby creating interactive voice and video capabilities.

29. "China Hits Murdoch TV Tie-up Ambitions," *Financial Times*, April 4, 1996. Murdoch purchased a 63.4 percent stake in STAR-TV in July 1993 from Hutchison and bought the remainder in July 1995.

30. "Mr. Murdoch has a lot of beautiful dreams, but at this stage I don't think it will be possible in China for him to realize them." Statement of Li Kehan, deputy director of the Ministry of Radio, Film and Television, quoted in "China Snubs Murdoch's TV 'Dreams,'" *Financial Times*, August 15, 1996.

31. For information about these surveys and about STAR-TV generally, I have relied on portions of Lynch, ibid.

32. Murdoch was quoted as saying that "advances in the technology of telecommunications have proved an unambiguous threat to totalitarian regimes everywhere." Ibid.

33. In addition, in April 1995 CNN changed its satellite platform from a lower-powered INTELSAT satellite to a high-powered PanAmSat bird. Thus viewers with dishes the size of those now used to access STAR-TV also can watch CNN—although only in English.

34. In December 1997, MPT's China Telecom signed a deal with Orion Network Systems to provide international satellite links to multinational firms in both Hong Kong and the PRC. In Hong Kong it will compete with Hong Kong Telecom and Hutchison, while on the mainland it will benefit from MPT's existing monopoly on such services. Reported in *South China Morning Post*, December 9, 1997.

35. Upon Zou's scheduled retirement in March 1998, Vice Premier Wu Bannguo had been expected to succeed him in this role, but see the discussion of ministerial reorganization later in this chapter.

36. In fact, there are some indications that Li Peng initially had assigned the lead Internet role to MPT but changed that decision after a November 7 meeting of the State Council, which led to the policy enunciated in the February 4 decree. In an attempt to regain some control in this regard, MPT indicated yet another response to mitigate the dangers of the Internet. It announced that it was creating its own nationwide computer network, GNET, to be based on a series of intranational or regional networks that will be stitched together. This effort will be pursued jointly with the China Internet Corporation, which is controlled by Xinhua and five "prominent Hong Kong families." This network will interconnect with the Internet itself but will allow access only to "relevant international business information." Leaving aside the most obvious examples of pornography and political dissent, the reference to "relevant" business information illustrates the problematic challenge of such controls.

37. Reported by the Clarinet News Service on August 15, 1996.

38. Ibid.

39. In seeking to centralize and thus channel information to facilitate control, China may be taking a cue from Singapore in this regard. In September 1996 the Singapore minister of state for communications, trade, and industry, Goh Chee Wee, announced the creation in that country of the "Internetwork Hub" as the point of convergence for all Internet service providers, government, commercial, and other wireless data networks. Once the Hub is operable, he indicated, a company would need only one line to be linked to all available data networks.

40. Reported by Renée Schoof of the Associated Press and carried on the Internet service of the MSNBC network (msnbc.com/news/28162.asp) on September 13, 1996.

41. "China Cracks Down on Dissent in Cyberspace," *New York Times,* December 31, 1997, p. A3.

42. Ibid.

43. Ibid.

44. See the discussion in this regard in "NetNanny States," *The Economist,* September 17, 1996.

45. For example, as long as both sides of the communication path collaborate, contact can be maintained simply by avoiding the web sites most likely to be monitored and limited and constantly changing the pages used to communicate.

46. *Financial Times,* January 17, 1996. On June 17, in announcing a supplementary agreement on the enforcement of intellectual property protections, Acting U.S. Trade Representative Charlene Barshefsky cited this arrangement as "a massive IPR violation scheme." "It is designed to capture the benefits of U.S. software and U.S. data collection abilities without regard to the licensee." *The Economist,* June 22, 1996, p. 24. See also *New York Times,* June 18, 1996, pp. A1, A6.

47. By November 1996 the matter became a standoff. Reuters and Dow Jones apparently agreed to allow their services to pass through a Xinhua filter but have refused to pay a "fee" for this "service."

48. *New York Times,* June 26, 1996, p. A5. In this regard, Jiang Zemin has been quoted as referring to journalists as "engineers of human souls." Quoted in "Chinese Dissident Speaks Out on Press Freedom," *Financial Times,* August 1, 1996, p. 3. For a discussion of the interplay of science and dissent in the same connection, see Fang Lizhi and Perry Link, "The Hope for China," *New York Review of Books,* October 17, 1996, pp. 43–47.

49. Liu is regarded as one of the leaders of the Tiananmen protests. In referring to Beijing's new overture to the Democratic Party in Hong Kong, a Foreign Ministry spokesman quoted an old Chinese proverb: "A large forest may have many birds, and if a few want to sing, why not just let them sing?" Quoted in Richburg, "Walking Softly, but Carrying a Big Stick," *Washington Post,* national weekly edition, September 9–15, 1996, p. 18.

50. Reported on the Internet edition of the *South China Morning Post* (www.scmp.com), March 6, 1998.

51. Such separation, for example, was implemented in Taiwan in 1996, when Chung Hwa Telecom was separated from the Ministry of Communications and Transportation.

52. Interestingly, the Hong Kong government itself took a similar step in February 1998, when it announced "a rationalization exercise" combining the telecommunications and information technology responsibilities of the Economic Services Bureau and the Finance Bureau with those of the Broadcasting, Culture and Sport Bureau to create the new Information Technol-

ogy and Broadcasting Bureau. Reported on February 11, 1998, on the SAR government's web page (www.info.gov.hk/isd/news).

53. For a comprehensive view of China's imperatives, see The World Bank's detailed study, *China 2020* (Washington, D.C.: The World Bank, 1997).

54. For a contrary—at least far more cautious—view of the situation, see Milton Mueller and Zixiang Tan, *China in the Information Age: Telecommunications and the Dilemmas of Reform* CSIS-Center for Strategic and International Studies, Washington, D.C. (Praeger: Conn, 1997); and Arlsan Malik, "Can Tech Take China by Storm?," *Christian Science Monitor,* reprinted on the MSNBC home page, August 21, 1997. These authors assume that the government's authoritarian control will limit liberalization steps and outside access for years into the future. But see Ambassador Diana Lady Dougan's more positive assessment in the foreword to the Mueller and Tan study.

55. For an outstanding summary of U.S. interests in China's progress, see Michel C. Oksenberg, Michael D. Swaine and Daniel C. Lynch, *The Chinese Future* (Pacific Council on International Policy and the RAND Center for Asia-Pacific Policy: CA, 1997).

56. Quoted from *Selected Works of Deng Xiaoping* (Beijing: Foreign Languages Press, 1996), vol. 3, p. 360. Emphasis added.

# 8

# Foreign Involvement in China's Energy Sector

## TODD M. JOHNSON

THIS chapter examines the extent of foreign involvement in China's energy sectors since the late 1970s and the effect that such involvement has had on each sector, including energy policy and institutions. The general trend in the energy sector since 1980 has been toward greater openness and increased foreign participation. China's demand for foreign involvement in this sector can be explained primarily by economic self-interest—defined as the need by China for foreign technology and expertise and capital. The extent to which its behavior has deviated from this general trend since 1980 can be explained largely by nationalistic concerns (security and trade protection) and the absorptive capacity of domestic institutions. Because foreign technology and capital needs are increasing in some energy sectors, and new outward-oriented domestic energy institutions have been established, it is likely that foreign involvement in China's energy sectors will increase in the future.

China's demand for foreign involvement is only half of the equation. Since the mid-1970s, foreign interest and involvement in China has experienced wide swings, following changes in Chinese government policy, the policies of foreign companies' own governments toward China, and the commercial attractiveness of the specific sector. In some sectors competition among foreign companies has been intense, such as in the offshore oil industry between 1978 and 1986. Since the mid-1980s there has also been considerable foreign interest and involvement in China's rapidly expanding electric power sector, with a wide assortment of credits and soft loans provided by host governments. In other sectors, most notably nuclear power, until very recently export controls by leading technology suppliers have delayed the transfer of Western nuclear technologies to China and distanced the nation from important nuclear nonproliferation discussions.

## IMPORTANCE OF THE ENERGY SECTOR

China's need for foreign participation in its economy and its energy sector is enormous and is growing with each year that the country continues its economic reform program. While the pace of economic reform in China may appear slow to some in the West, reform has been remarkably steady over the past 15 years and probably long ago committed China to significant involvement with the outside world. In the energy sector the need for trade, internationally advanced technologies, and foreign expertise is becoming increasingly clear to Chinese policymakers. Without international involvement in the energy sector, the risks to China include (1) slower development of domestic reserves of energy, particularly oil and gas, resulting in increasing import dependence; (2) a slowdown in economic growth due to overall shortages of energy and, in particular, electric power; (3) the inability to maintain a low energy–gross domestic product (GDP) elasticity due to the insufficient transfer of advanced processes and energy-efficiency technology from abroad, thereby constraining economic growth; and (4) increasingly severe local and regional environmental problems due to the insufficient diversification away from coal and the slow adoption of clean coal technologies and pollution control equipment.

The risks to the rest of the world of letting China develop its energy industry with limited assistance from the outside are equally serious: (1) the increasing demand by China for imported supplies of energy, particularly Middle East oil, resulting in higher prices and growing energy security concerns for Japan and other Asian energy importers; (2) increasingly serious regional pollution problems affecting China's neighbors, such as acid rain and polluted international waters; (3) the rapid expansion of an entirely domestic nuclear power industry and the increased risk of a nuclear accident; and (4) unprecedented threats to global climate change from rising coal use and the inability to adopt energy-efficiency and renewable energy technologies on a large scale. The issue of lost trade opportunities to the United States and other countries has not been mentioned as one of the risks of letting China go it alone in developing its energy sector; however, the forgone economic benefits could indeed be enormous.

THE ENERGY REGIME

As with the case of banking and finance, there are few formal international regimes in the energy sector. China's participation is threefold. First, it is a member of the International Atomic Energy Agency (IAEA), which establishes standards for nuclear safety and protocols for restricting the transfer of weapons-grade nuclear materials. China joined the IAEA in 1984, when the country was aggressively seeking to acquire advanced nuclear technologies for its domestic nuclear energy program. Second, China has been an active participant in other important regimes that deal with energy at the regional and international levels, including multilateral lending agencies and development institutions. Since the early 1980s the World Bank and the Asian Development Bank (ADB) have been actively involved in China's energy sector, encouraging the transfer of advanced technologies and management practices by providing a source of foreign exchange financing and by requiring compliance with their lending practices, notably, international competition bidding for major contracts. Finally, there are also more informal regimes, such as the international norms that govern commercial transactions, within which China has had to operate.

The next section provides an overview of China's energy resources and a brief discussion of China's pre- and postreform energy policy. Then the chapter looks at foreign involvement in China's major energy sectors since 1980, focusing on the factors that have encouraged or impeded the transfer of foreign technology. The next section summarizes the effect of foreign involvement on China's energy industries, energy policy, and domestic institutions since 1980 and concludes with a brief discussion of the effect that China has had on international energy regimes. Then the chapter outlines those energy industries that are likely to have the greatest foreign participation in the future. Finally, the chapter offers some thoughts as to what China can do to attract foreign technology, and capital and how other countries can assist it and at the same time achieve their own commercial, strategic, and environmental objectives.

## Background: Energy Resources, Pricing, and Institutions

Foreign involvement in China's energy sector is integrally related to the growth of China's economy and the consequent demand for the nation to build up its energy production and supply infrastructure. Between 1980 and 1994 China's economy grew by an average of 9.5 percent per year, while primary energy output and electricity production increased by 4.4 and 8 percent, respectively.

China has abundant quantities of relatively high-quality coal. Proven reserves are estimated at about 300 billion tons, which at current consumption levels would last about 225 years. The huge reserves in Shanxi Province, which account for more than one-quarter of the country's total, are of particularly good quality: low ash content (usually less than 10 percent), low sulfur (less than 1 percent), low moisture, and high calorific value (7,000 kilocalories per kilogram or more). Despite the generally good quality of Chinese coal reserves, delivered coal often is of poor quality because of poor mining techniques and the lack of coal cleaning and sorting. While the average sulfur content of Chinese coal is relatively low (about 1.1 percent), the coal produced by certain mining areas (e.g., Chongqing) contains an average sulfur content of more than 4 percent.

In the case of oil, China emerged in the 1980s as one of the largest oil exporters in Asia but became a net oil importer in 1993 as a result of stagnating domestic oil production and the growing demand for road transport fuels (gasoline and diesel) and petrochemical feedstock (naphtha and fuel oil). China's reserves of oil and gas are much more modest than its coal reserves. Proven petroleum reserves are estimated at between 24 and 30 billion barrels, which would last 20 to 25 years at current consumption rates. As production at China's largest oil fields (Daqing, Shengli) has leveled off, hopes have been pinned on the Tarim Basin in Xinjiang Province, more than 1,800 miles from the major consumption areas in the east. Official natural gas reserves are estimated to be about 2 trillion cubic meters, with a reserve life of more than 100 years at current use rates. However, current natural gas production is very low, with gas accounting for only about 2 percent of China's energy supply (Table 8–1). Despite initially high expectations, there have been only modest discoveries of offshore oil and gas. In 1993 offshore oil production amounted to about 3 percent of total oil production.

China's hydroelectric resources are estimated at 380 gigawatts (GW), the largest in the world. So far about 45 GW of large-scale capacity has been constructed and a number of large-scale dams are currently under development. This includes the huge and controversial Three Gorges Dam project on the Yangtze River. If it is completed on schedule around 2010, it would be the largest hydroelectric dam in the world. Despite this rapid expansion of hydroelectric capacity in China since 1980, its contribution to the country's electric power needs has fallen because of the more rapid expansion of coal-fired power plants.

The energy potential of biomass (crop wastes and fuelwood) is also large and currently provides about one-quarter of China's total energy

Table 8–1.    China: Energy Production and Share by Fuel

|  | Coal | | Oil | | Gas | | Hydro | | Total |
|---|---|---|---|---|---|---|---|---|---|
|  | mtce[a] | % | mtce | % | mtce | % | mtce | % | mtce |
| 1980 | 443.0 | 69.5 | 151.4 | 23.7 | 19.0 | 3.0 | 24.0 | 3.8 | 637.4 |
| 1985 | 623.1 | 72.8 | 178.4 | 20.9 | 17.2 | 2.0 | 36.8 | 4.3 | 855.5 |
| 1990 | 771.4 | 74.2 | 197.6 | 19.0 | 20.4 | 2.0 | 49.9 | 4.8 | 1,039.2 |
| 1991 | 776.4 | 74.1 | 201.4 | 19.2 | 20.5 | 2.0 | 49.9 | 4.8 | 1,048.2 |
| 1992 | 796.1 | 74.2 | 203.0 | 18.9 | 21.0 | 2.0 | 52.6 | 4.9 | 1,072.7 |
| 1993 | 814.7 | 73.9 | 205.7 | 18.7 | 22.0 | 2.0 | 60.3 | 5.5 | 1,102.7 |
| 1994 | 865.4 | 74.2 | 210.9 | 18.1 | 22.0 | 1.9 | 66.7 | 5.7 | 1,165.6 |
| 1995 | 971.6 | 75.3 | 214.2 | 16.6 | 24.5 | 1.9 | 80.0 | 6.2 | 1,290.3 |
| 1996 | 997.3 | 75.2 | 225.5 | 17.0 | 26.5 | 2.0 | 76.9 | 5.8 | 1,326.2 |
| 1997[b] | 990.0 | 74.1 | 232.5 | 17.4 | 32.1 | 2.4 | 81.5 | 6.1 | 1,336.0 |

[a] mtce: million tons coal equivalent.
[b] preliminary.
*Sources: State Statistical Bureau, China Energy Statistical Yearbook,* (Beijing, China: State Statistical Press, 1995); *State Statistical Bureau, A Statistical Survey of China,* (Beijing, China: State Statistical Press, 1998).

supply. However, deforestation due to excessive fuelwood use has been a serious environmental problem; sustainable fuelwood production is estimated to be only about half of current use. Finally, with a capacity of 2.1 GW—about 1 percent of total installed capacity—nuclear power is currently a minor energy source in China; however, many Chinese energy experts anticipate a large expansion of nuclear capacity in the future.

ENERGY PRICING

Under the traditional system of central planning in the People's Republic of China, retail prices of energy and other key commodities were set by the central government. Consequently, end-use prices were well known in any locale; although they bore little relationship to production, transportation, and distribution costs. Since the early 1980s energy prices have been slowly but progressively decontrolled in China. As part of the World Bank–sponsored China Greenhouse Gas Study (1996), 21 industrial energy-efficiency case studies, representing a wide range of industries and locations throughout China, were carried out.[1] In each case the industries were paying market prices for their major energy supplies (coal and electricity). In 1996, coal prices in Shanghai and other coastal cities were the same as or higher than delivered prices in Japan ($40 per ton), with as much as 70 percent of the delivered cost of coal in coastal areas going to transportation and other transaction costs.[2] Coal prices are much lower ($20 per ton) in major coal-producing regions, such as Shanxi Province, reflecting the abundance of coal and relatively low production costs, the latter due in part to lax environmental and safety regulations. Electricity prices also exhibit a coastal-interior dichotomy, although for different reasons. In most coastal provinces, where new power capacity has expanded the fastest, electricity prices have been raised for cost-recovery purposes to levels approximating marginal costs. Average consumer prices of power in Zhejiang Province at the end of 1994 were around 50 fen per kilowatt-hour (kWh), compared with the long-run marginal cost of about 45 fen per kWh. A large proportion of electricity in inland provinces is still produced by plants built before 1980 that effectively have no capital costs, since they were built with nonrepayable central government funding. As a consequence, it has been more difficult to raise power tariffs to marginal cost levels in these areas. Although the average price paid to crude oil producers has been substantially below world market levels until very recently, the prices of most oil products (gasoline, diesel, fuel oil, liquefied petroleum gas) have been at or above world market levels for a number of years.[3] In 1994 the base price of crude oil was increased more than threefold, to a level approximating international levels.

## INSTITUTIONS

China's energy institutions have changed considerably since 1980. All of the major energy ministries—coal, oil, and electric power—established one or more affiliate companies to handle the increase in commercial transactions, including those with foreign companies. Many of these affiliate companies have become major national corporations, wielding considerable financial and political power. As will be discussed later, the government established some of these companies, including Sinochem (oil and petroleum product trade), Huaneng (power plant construction), and the China National Offshore Oil Corporation (CNOOC; offshore oil exploration and development) explicitly to handle transactions with foreign companies. The general trend in the energy sector—and in other sectors—has been toward smaller, centralized government agencies, reflecting the decline in central planning functions and involvement in day-to-day operations. Central affiliated companies have absorbed many of the former ministry staff. In the electric power industry the authority of regional and provincial power grids has increased tremendously since the mid-1980s because of the expansion of power capacity and the greater responsibility these grids have for raising funds and managing the operation of the system. The Ministry of Electric Power has been disbanded, with the State Power

Corporation handling commercial activities and the State Economic and Trade Commission responsible for regulatory functions for the power industry.

The power of the central energy agencies has declined considerably over the past 15 years. However, the central government, including the State Development and Planning Commission, is still very important in projects with major foreign involvement (joint ventures, foreign direct investment, or major foreign-supplied equipment) in part because of the need to raise foreign exchange for current purchases or to cover contract commitments in the future. Pending a fully functioning foreign exchange market in China, one of the responsibilities of the Ministry of Finance has been to balance foreign exchange resources with requirements.

## Foreign Involvement in China's Energy Sector since 1980

Since 1980 China's rapid economic growth has put tremendous pressure on the country's energy industries to expand production. Since that time coal production has nearly doubled and electricity output has more than tripled. By contrast, increases in petroleum and natural gas production since then have averaged just 2.4 and 1.2 percent per year. Beginning in the 1970s China's energy officials began looking abroad for solutions to expand domestic energy production and to increase efficiency. While the trend since 1980 has been toward greater foreign involvement in the energy sector (see Table 8–2), there were, and still remain, considerable barriers to the free flow of technology and capital to China's energy industries. Three key factors have determined the level of foreign involvement in each of China's energy sectors since 1980: foreign technology and capital needs, nationalism and protection, and institutional constraints.

### TECHNOLOGY AND CAPITAL NEEDS

Perhaps the most important determinant of foreign involvement in China's energy sector since 1980 has been the need for advanced technologies and expertise. While the country has become a major producer and exporter of much energy-production equipment, in many fields it still lacks the ability to produce equipment, and in sufficient quantity. Large capital equipment for the energy sector is still produced almost exclusively by state-owned enterprises (SOEs) in China, which has contributed to difficulties in terms of the quality of products, customer service, and the timeliness of supply.

**Table 8–2.  Foreign Investment in China's Energy Sector during the 1980s**

|  | Ministry of Petroleum | | Ministry of Coal | | Ministry of Electric Power | |
| --- | --- | --- | --- | --- | --- | --- |
|  | b yuan[a] | %[b] | b yuan | % | b yuan | % |
| 1981 | 0.10 | 3.6 | 0.43 | 17.4 | 0.12 | 3.2 |
| 1982 | 0.35 | 11.9 | 0.67 | 20.9 | 0.08 | 1.7 |
| 1983 | 0.05 | 1.7 | 0.60 | 13.8 | 0.25 | 4.3 |
| 1984 | 0.14 | 5.1 | 0.35 | 6.2 | 0.55 | 7.4 |
| 1985 | 0.61 | 19.0 | 0.03 | 0.6 | 0.64 | 6.4 |
| 1986 | 1.19 | 31.6 | 0.03 | 0.6 | 1.56 | 11.6 |
| 1987 | 1.10 | 28.8 | 0.07 | 1.2 | 0.86 | 5.6 |
| 1988 | 2.50 | 52.0 | 0.11 | 2.3 | 0.57 | 3.5 |
| 1989 | 2.93 | 43.2 | 0.31 | 5.0 | 2.23 | 11.5 |
| 1990 | 2.08 | 28.6 | 0.62 | 6.9 | 3.14 | 13.0 |

[a] Billion 1980 yuan.
[b] Percentage of total capital construction investment in the sector.
*Source:* For the survey of recent energy prices in China, see Jonathan E. Sinton, ed., *China Energy Databook* (Berkeley, Calif.: Lawrence Berkeley National Laboratories, 1996).

As many organizations in China have discovered over the past 15 years, it is not sufficient simply to buy advanced equipment from abroad. Although most organizations were hesitant initially to pay for foreign software, many have since learned that without training in the use and proper maintenance of hardware, the most sophisticated foreign technology cannot be utilized fully. Training is now a common component of advanced technology transfer and purchase agreements. At the same time, foreign expertise of the one-size-fits-all variety has not always been effective or practical in the Chinese context, as China has been quick to point out to international management consultants and to multilateral and bilateral aid and lending institutions.

Limited foreign exchange reserves in China and strict control over their use inhibited the purchase of foreign technologies for the energy sector during the 1980s. With the exception of offshore oil development and more recently with foreign independent power producers, foreign investment (as opposed to foreign technology purchases) has been limited in China's energy sector. Instead, foreign investment has been concentrated in small investments (i.e., the textile industry), where risks and the price of failure are lower and where part of the production can be sold abroad to earn foreign exchange. Prior to 1986 some 85 percent of capital needed for imported power equipment was provided through export credits.[4] China's dramatic increase in international trade over the past decade has made foreign exchange much more readily available, while domestic swap markets for foreign currency have increasingly meant that foreign exchange is no longer rationed by the central or provincial governments to the same extent as in the past. Today export credits are a much smaller percentage of the annual funding for foreign technology purchases, because of both the increased foreign technology needs and the increased availability of foreign exchange. China began raising capital for energy projects and other large infrastructure projects on international capital markets in the mid-1980s, although with limited success. It also has relied on loans from the World Bank, the ADB, and bilateral lending agencies, especially the Japanese Overseas Economic Cooperation Fund, for financing foreign technology purchases.

## Coal

China's coal industry has not been highly dependent on foreign technology for expanding production since 1980. This has to do with the sheer size of the domestic coal industry and the fact that China has a long history of coal production. Geology has been partly responsible for the dominance of underground (as opposed to opencast) coal mining in China; currently less than 10 percent of the nation's coal is from opencast mines.[5] While China is one of the world's leading producers of underground mining technology, most Chinese underground mines are so-called room-and-pillar mines, which are not as conducive to high-volume and mechanized mining. Major labor productivity gains have been made worldwide in underground long-wall mining technology over the past 20 years, and China has been interested in acquiring this type of technology. The country also has lagged in the development of large-scale equipment necessary for efficient opencast mining, and this has been a priority area for foreign technology acquisition since the late 1970s. As will be discussed, the coal industry in China has been slow to introduce the reforms necessary to attract either foreign or domestic investment.

Coal processing is a key area in which China has sought foreign technology since 1980. In large part the lack of coal processing has been due to historically low coal prices and a pricing structure that has paid little attention to fuel quality (measured by the consistency of the coal and the ash and sulfur content). Despite policy-related problems inhibiting the demands for coal processing, the Ministry of Coal and various mining administrations purchased a considerable amount of coal-processing technology from abroad during the 1980s, including coal-washing, handling, and preparation plants; coal gasification processes; and technology for capturing and treating coalbed methane.

*Oil and Gas Exploration and Development*
Given the rapid growth in China of petroleum products—gasoline and diesel fuel for road transport and petrochemicals for a wide variety of plastics and synthetic fibers—exploration and development of domestic oil resources is critically important. Lacking much of the technology for offshore oil development, China first invited Western oil companies to help find and develop offshore oil and gas resources in 1979. Throughout the 1980s foreign investment accounted for a significant portion of total capital construction investment in the petroleum industry, reaching more than 50 percent in 1988. (See Table 8.2.) During the 1980s some 45 foreign oil companies were involved in the search for Chinese offshore oil. Despite relatively good luck in finding oil and gas, most of the finds were small and not commercially viable. The failure to find significant quantities of oil offshore China has been a major disappointment to both Chinese and foreign oil companies. While interest by Western companies in offshore oil development in China has waned, there has been renewed interest through the opening up of onshore areas such as the Tarim Basin in Xinjiang to exploration contracts and production sharing agreements.[6] Overall, Western oil companies have had more success in oil equipment sales in China than in production-sharing arrangements. During the 1980s China purchased more than $1.4 billion worth of drilling and oil field equipment from the United States alone.

*Oil Refining*
One of the areas where a significant amount of foreign technology and expertise has flowed into China since 1980 has been in petroleum refining and petrochemicals. While China built up its refining industry during the 1960s and 1970s, since the early 1980s it has imported advanced equipment, particularly for more thorough processing of heavy oil to produce the light products in high demand by the transport and petrochemicals sectors. Sinopec was established as a national company in July 1983 to consolidate China's oil-refining industry. Sinopec immediately began constructing several new world-class petrochemical complexes, such as Jinling in Nanjing and Gaoqiao in Shanghai, and modernizing existing refineries in these and other cities, relying on foreign engineering, processes, and specialized equipment. In some cases complete processes were transferred. While there was some licensing of refining processes by foreign technology suppliers, there were few joint ventures. Financing for refinery upgrades and expansions was facilitated by the huge profits made by Sinopec and the growing export revenues of the oil industry as a whole. Sinopec earned substantial profits

as a result of the large differential in price it paid for crude (100 yuan per ton in 1985) compared with the value of refined products (about 390 yuan per ton in 1985) that it sold. The early and mid-1980s were also a time when China earned substantial foreign exchange revenues from crude oil and petroleum products sold on the international market.[7] Chinese energy exports, dominated by crude oil, accounted for as much as one-quarter of total gross export earnings between 1980 and 1985.[8]

### Electric Power

Since the late 1970s China has acquired the ability to produce sophisticated equipment for large-scale power boilers through joint-venture licensing and other arrangements. Economies of scale, through the use of larger units (300–600 megawatts [MW]), is one of the most important ways for China to improve overall energy efficiency and thus lower the demand for coal. From a technology perspective, China's domestic power equipment industry has faced two major problems. First, despite programs to transfer advanced power equipment production capabilities,[9] it will be several more years before China masters the production of 600 MW units, particularly the turbines. The second problem is production capacity. Electricity needs have been expanding so rapidly that China cannot produce sufficient quantities of such equipment; it therefore has imported technologies for which it has domestic production capabilities. China added between 10 and 15 GW of power per year between 1990 and 1996, and this trend is expected to continue. In 1994 major equipment (boilers and turbines) for 25 to 30 percent of installed power capacity had to be imported.[10]

### Nuclear Power

China has been quite successful at developing small-scale nuclear power technology; however, as plans for commercial-scale plants expanded during the 1980s, the country began looking overseas for technology suppliers and firms with nuclear power plant construction experience. While its foreign technology and capital needs for the nuclear power industry were high during the early 1980s, domestic and international political decisions played a major role in determining foreign involvement in the sector.

### Energy Efficiency

To date, most of the improvements in energy efficiency in China as a result of foreign participation have been passive. That is, most of the efficiency improvements have been embodied in technology that was purchased primarily not for energy-efficiency reasons. Nonetheless, the impact that such embodied technical progress has had on overall energy efficiency in China has been substantial and far outweighs dedicated energy-efficiency investments in terms of total energy savings. Many of the improvements have been in the industrial sector and involve increasing the scale of Chinese plants. Examples where larger-scale plants have resulted in significant energy savings and where foreign technologies have become a model for the respective industry include electric power, oil refining, petrochemicals, chemical fertilizer, and steelmaking. Improvements in the efficiency of widely used industrial and electrical equipment through joint ventures or other technology transfer programs also have been significant, especially in areas such as large-scale power boilers, household appliances (refrigerators, air conditioners), industrial motors, and lighting (compact fluorescents). However, for other equipment, there has been very little transfer of advanced foreign technologies—such as small coal-fired industrial boilers, which account for one-third of total Chinese coal consumption—partly because of the inability of foreign firms to export a portion of the production and earn foreign exchange.

*Renewable Energy*

To date, foreign involvement in China's small renewable energy market has been modest. While many energy-efficiency technologies and measures are financially viable under current conditions in China, renewable energy technologies in most applications are not. Although the country is something of a world leader in small-scale hydroelectric and biogas technologies, development of other high-potential renewables in China since 1980 has been minimal. Internationally, most renewable technologies have been developed with significant government subsidies or for small niche markets where they are currently commercial (e.g., solar photovoltaic [PV] for highway signs or isolated communication stations). Renewable energy technologies in China, including wind, solar PV, solar thermal, and geothermal, are much less advanced than the best-available technologies abroad. Bilateral assistance, primarily from Europe, has helped in the transfer of wind generator technology, which has been installed in Inner Mongolia and Fujian Province. There have also been some quasi-private, and not so successful, efforts to establish joint-venture solar PV production facilities in China.

## NATIONALISM AND PROTECTIONISM

National security concerns and protection of domestic industries have hindered the degree of foreign participation in China's energy sectors since 1980, particularly within the oil industry. There are a number of reasons for China's protectionism in the oil industry. First, most governments attach considerable strategic importance to maintaining access to supplies of petroleum. In the case of China, however, this sensitivity is heightened because of the exploitation of China's resources by other countries during the twentieth century: Germany in Shandong Province at the turn of the century, Japan in Manchuria in the 1930s, and the Soviet Union in northern China in the 1950s. Second, there are clear financial considerations in China's reluctance to open its oil sector. The central government has earned substantial revenues from the oil industry since China's first large field, Daqing, was discovered in the late 1950s. These financial rewards are a central consideration in the ongoing political debate within China over whether to open areas for joint-venture development, the percentage of foreign ownership of energy resources and production facilities, rates of return on foreign investments, and the degree of foreign access to the domestic market. At the same time China has demonstrated significant openness to the international community at several points, such as in the late 1970s and early 1990s, when it desired technical expertise or capital.

### The Politics of Nuclear Power

Since the early 1980s China actively has sought international assistance to help develop its nuclear power industry. The first projects were a small Chinese-designed nuclear power station outside of Shanghai (Qinshan) and a large turnkey nuclear power station in Guangdong, at Daya Bay. China was most interested in acquiring technologies directly from U.S. companies, since the United States was the industry leader. However, the Nuclear Non-Proliferation Act (NNPA) passed by the U.S. Congress in 1978 prohibited the sale of major items of equipment and nuclear materials by U.S. companies until a bilateral agreement on nuclear cooperation was in effect. Anticipating major nuclear power contracts from China, U.S. companies lobbied the Reagan administration heavily in the early 1980s to establish a cooperative agreement with China. The first government-to-government discussions of a U.S.-China agreement on nuclear cooperation were held in 1981; however, U.S. negotiators remained frustrated over continuing Chinese criticism of the NNPA and the fact that China had not yet joined the International Atomic Energy Agency. An agreement between the United States and China on nuclear cooperation finally was signed in 1985, a year after China joined the IAEA, although the agreement was never ratified by Congress. After several years of intense bargaining over contract terms, the Daya Bay contracts subsequently were awarded: to Framatome of France for the design of the plant and the two 900-MW reactors, and to

General Electric of the United Kingdom for the turbines. Key equipment for the domestically designed Qinshan power station was acquired from Japanese, German, and French companies. Because the supplying countries provided export credits for major imported nuclear equipment, it is unlikely that U.S. companies would have won these early nuclear contracts. The prospects of nuclear technology exports from the United States to China were again put on hold in 1989, with the suspension of military and high-technology exchanges between the two countries following the Tiananmen incident. Most recently, in October 1997 the United States again agreed to export nuclear technology to China, with the understanding that China would not assist Iran or Pakistan in the acquisition of sensitive nuclear technologies that could be used in weapons programs.

## INSTITUTIONAL CONSTRAINTS

What is mistaken abroad for foreign security concerns or protectionist policies often is merely the inability of Chinese institutions to interact effectively with foreign companies. On one hand, China's central government has maintained a number of restrictive policies on foreign involvement in the energy sector, such as limits on the share of foreign ownership, access to the domestic market for product sales, and unofficial limits on acceptable rates of return on foreign investment. On the other hand, many Chinese institutions have actively sought advanced technologies from abroad in many sectors but lacked adequate and appropriate legal, financial, and accounting systems and expertise necessary to carry out the contracts. Even as China has established basic laws and other systems, it has taken many more years to train the necessary personnel in these and other disciplines and for institutions to reform themselves sufficiently to understand and operate within new system boundaries. In the case of SOEs–which includes the bulk of China's energy industries—institutional reform has been especially troublesome. Continuing support for antiquated and inefficient SOEs is a remnant of the previous system of central planning and a political reality. State-owned enterprises still employ a large proportion of urban workers and are the providers of many social services, including employee health care, education, housing, and pension benefits.

While only a limited change in institutions is required to sell a truck to China, for large and complicated systems, such as an oil refinery or a power plant, usually a complete change in institutions and management processes must occur for the operation to be viable. Modern management systems are a critical component both of adopting new technology and of operating modern corporations. During the early 1980s most Chinese energy institutions were neither reformed enough nor sufficiently flexible to adopt, operate, and maintain complex foreign technologies and processes successfully. An additional constraint for joint-venture investments was that foreign companies usually demanded a major say in management decisions. The inability of SOEs to yield management control over asset use and personnel was, and still remains, a critical barrier to joint-venture investments in large and complicated investment projects in China; this inability must be changed if joint ventures or foreign direct investments are to expand in China in the future.[11]

Another factor limiting foreign involvement in China during the 1980s was that Chinese institutions were preoccupied with their own internal management reforms[12] that, apart from improvements in technology, were responsible for large productivity gains. In China's energy sector, large additions to production and improvements in efficiency were achieved during the 1980s as a result of policy reform; improvements included production increases in the coal and oil industries and efficiency gains in many existing electric power plants. Institutional changes will continue to have positive efficiency effects, particularly in the most unreformed energy sectors—onland oil and gas development, large state-owned coal mines, electric power transmission and distribution, and the transport of coal and petroleum.

At the same time, insufficient or inappropriate institutional capabilities should not be confused with the hard bargaining that typifies many commercial (and noncommercial) negotiations with Chinese counterparts. Sometimes Chinese hard bargaining pays off, and sometimes it does not. In some cases Chinese negotiators think the price of a transaction is too high, but in reality they are unfamiliar with the extent of costs and benefits. As noted earlier, many Chinese institutions were reluctant to pay for personnel training or foreign consultants. Many deals were delayed or canceled during the 1980s because of the foreign sellers' inability to obtain export credits or mutually agreeable barter arrangements, and this may have been part of the explanation for the unreasonable contract proposals put forward by Chinese institutions.

## Energy Efficiency

During the 1980s energy-efficiency projects in China were impeded not only by the underpricing of energy but also by an industrial organization system that rewarded increased production and paid little attention to cost reduction. Even today, when most industries in China face market prices for energy and electricity, enterprises are still slow to adopt energy-efficiency projects. Among the reasons energy-efficiency investments are not undertaken in China (and elsewhere) are the energy savings represent a small part of overall operating costs, technical and market risks are perceived as too high, and enterprises are concerned with other competitive issues, including developing new products and finding new markets.

*Private Power*

Since the mid-1980s China's electric power needs have increased dramatically, far outstripping the amount of financing available from multilateral development banks and bilateral aid. At the same time, China has had a difficult time attracting large amounts of capital from the private sector, as a result of unacceptable financial risks or perceived sovereign and political risks. While large numbers of independent power projects (IPPs) in China have not yet materialized, Gordon Wu and the Hopewell Company of Hong Kong have tested the waters. Hopewell has carried out two IPPs in China—Shajiao B and Shajiao C in Guangdong Province—under build-operate-transfer (BOT) contracts. Under these agreements, the plant is built and operated by Hopewell for a certain number of years in return for an agreed-upon payment schedule from the Chinese side. At the end of the contract—20 years for the Shajiao C plant—ownership of the plant reverts to China. Despite the fairly successful nature of both the Shajiao B and C plants, there has not been a wave of additional IPPs in China, pending clarification of a number of legal, contractual, and institutional issues for the nation's overall electric power sector. As one expert has noted, "the low success rate of power project negotiations mainly originates from the fundamental different view regarding investment risks between foreign investors and Chinese officials. While foreign investors perceive China as a high-risk region for business, and demand fast and high returns, the Chinese (especially the central government) consider China a low risk country . . . [and] thus refuse to grant approval to projects with high rates of return."[13] Although China has passed a new electricity law (April 1996) and the new State Power Corporation has been established (January 1997), exchange convertibility, power pricing, legal and contractual models, and acceptable rates of return all remain to be fully sorted out.

## COAL — A DIFFICULT SECTOR FOR FOREIGN INVOLVEMENT

*Joint-venture Investment*

The first large foreign-Chinese joint-venture investment that occurred in the coal sector was the Antaibao, or Pingshuo, opencast coal mine in Shanxi Province, involving Occidental Petroleum Corporation. One of China's major objectives for the Antaibao project was to acquire advanced opencast mining technologies from abroad. The project required many years to negotiate and involved China's highest-level leaders and the Bank of China. Once the contract was signed in 1985, it was another five years before any coal was produced. Financing of the Antaibao project was hampered by a major collapse in international coal prices during negotiations—between 1982 and 1986, international coal prices fell from $52 per ton to below $32 per ton. As an indication that technology transfer, and not increased domestic production, was the primary goal of the project, from conception, more than 90 percent of the mine's production was planned for export as a way for Occidental to earn foreign exchange. The project demonstrates the difficulties of joint-venture development in the coal sector, due to lack of management, ownership, pricing, and legal reforms in the sector in China. Occidental pulled out of the deal in 1991, shortly after the mine was completed.

*World Bank Activities in China's Coal Sector*
To date, the World Bank has been involved in only one coal-mining project in China, the Changcun coal mine in Shanxi Province, begun in 1985. The project involved the construction of three underground mine shafts (long-wall technology), a coal washery, related infrastructure, institutional strengthening, and personnel training. Compared with other energy projects in which the World Bank has been involved in China, the Changcun project has not been a stellar success. Management difficulties and disbursement problems resulted in a four-year delay in project completion.

Both Antaibao and Changcun illustrate the difficulty of foreign involvement in China's state-owned coal-mining sector. A fundamental problem for both projects was that the sector had yet to undertake key economic reforms related to resource ownership, management, and downstream transportation and marketing issues. The fact that the sector was not an attractive investment to Chinese investors is evidence that the difficulties for foreign companies were part of a systemic problem in the coal industry, not a problem exclusive to foreign involvement.

## The Impact of Foreign Involvement on China

### ENERGY POLICY

*Price and Investment Reform*
Many factors have contributed to the reform of energy prices in China. One of these factors is exposure to the international market. It is not

coincidental that the energy sectors in China that have experienced the most reform—petroleum and electric power—have been the ones most affected by international markets. For oil, the opportunity cost of forgone exports contributed to the reform of prices. As China became a major oil exporter in the early 1980s, the country quickly realized the cost of keeping domestic oil prices low; domestic petroleum products were soon decontrolled and in most cases have since followed international prices. In the electric power sector, tariff reform was a precondition for raising capital, affecting not only foreign-financed projects but entirely local ones as well. In order to attract financing for new power plants in Guangdong and elsewhere, electricity tariffs for new plants were decontrolled in 1985. The success achieved in Guangdong in self-financing electric power investments has been followed by other provinces in China, particularly those with an acute shortage of electricity.

In contrast to oil and power, the huge coal sector and the nascent natural gas industry always have been more insular. China's coal industry is not dependent on foreign technology or financing for its survival, and it has lagged behind the oil and power sectors in both pricing and management reforms. Nonetheless, to spur increases in coal production and productivity, coal prices were partially decontrolled in the early 1980s. In 1994 the central government began to reduce subsidies to the coal industry; this caused the industry to undertake serious efforts to reform its pricing and investment policies. The natural gas industry in China always has been regional and has not accounted for a significant percentage of the country's energy. The large ARCO offshore gas field, originally discovered near Hainan in 1982, was slow to be developed because of marginal economics, large financing requirements, and the necessity to sell most of its production to Hong Kong. Low domestic prices of natural gas were a primary impediment in developing the ARCO gas field and the reason why the domestic market ultimately received only a minor share of the gas. The reform of domestic natural gas prices has made considerable progress since 1990, as the demand for gas in the residential sector has increased and as gas utilities have found that they cannot cover their costs without significant increases in gas tariffs.

### Role of the Multilateral Banks

While energy projects account for a sizable portion of both World Bank and ADB lending to China, the conditions or rules of the game that govern multilateral bank lending in the energy sector are not dissimilar to those that would govern private-sector involvement; that is, prices and tariffs must be high enough to allow cost recovery. However, because investments by the multilateral banks generally are guaranteed by the central government, risks are lower than for the private sector. One condition that the multilateral banks do require of borrowers, including China, is that major contracts for goods and services must be open to international competitive bidding (ICB). While domestic protectionist and nationalist factions often oppose this condition, ICB has allowed China to acquire advanced foreign technologies with only minimal criticism from domestic protectionist camps and has itself become a model for competitive bidding for national infrastructure projects. This has resulted in lowering production costs and speeding project completion.

Some people have argued that the multilateral development banks, especially the World Bank, can have a significant impact on energy policies and investment plans in developing countries.[14] While the possibility for advancing the policy dialogue on tariff reform or private-sector development exists, the effect that the World Bank can have on a large country such as China is limited. Nevertheless, both the World Bank and the Chinese government (both central and local) often claim that the bank's policy conditionality and economic advice are of greater importance than is actually the case. Chinese officials sometimes use the World Bank as the "bad cop" in order to deflect the political fallout of unpopular reform measures, such as increases in energy tariffs. If a locality needs to blame the World Bank for the unpopular policy, the bank usually is happy to oblige, since policy reform (particularly increases in tariffs) often is a key to ensuring project success. It is clear, however, that policy reform does not come about simply as a condition of World Bank lending—there must be political will at both the national and the local levels, and the balance of policymaker opinion must be on the side of the policy reform.

## INSTITUTIONAL DEVELOPMENT

Over the past 15 years China has gained considerable expertise in dealing with the outside world. Existing domestic institutions have been transformed, new institutions have been created, and a new generation of officials with considerable foreign training and experience is emerging. All of these changes have led to more successful deals between China and foreign commercial interests and should allow future foreign participation in the energy sector to meet more closely China's significant technological and capital needs.

A number of institutions have been established in China since 1980 to facilitate foreign involvement in the country and its participation in international energy markets. Examples include Huaneng, CNOOC, and Sinochem.

The Huaneng International Power Development Company, established in 1985 primarily to convert power plants from oil to coal, has made use of both foreign technology and foreign capital for constructing thermal power plants in China. All of the equipment for the nine power project investments arranged by Huaneng in the 1980s made use of foreign technology (mostly 350-MW units). More than three-quarters of the cost of Huaneng plants in that decade was financed through export credits, with the remainder provided by commercial loans.

The China National Offshore Oil Corporation was established as a legal entity in the late 1970s for the purpose of signing contracts with foreign oil companies for offshore oil development. Together with its regional subsidiaries, CNOOC has been responsible for several rounds of offshore oil exploration and development bidding, signing contracts with 31 foreign companies in round one (1982) and another 20 companies in round two (1985). Between 1982 and 1992 foreign companies spent some $2.25 billion on oil exploration and $814 million on oil development in China.[15] In 1996 CNOOC signed an agreement with the China Petroleum Corporation (Taiwan) for joint oil exploration in the Taiwan Strait.

Sinochem, the China National Chemical Import-Export Corporation, was established to carry out foreign trade in chemicals, including crude oil and petroleum products, which was the most lucrative for China during the 1980s. Sinochem has established itself as a sophisticated oil trader in Asia, concluding purchase and sales agreements of crude and petroleum products throughout the world and establishing joint-processing agreements with Singapore and other refining centers.

*Power Industry*
The efficiency of China's power industry has improved considerably since the early 1980s as a result of foreign involvement. Cumulative foreign investment (including multilateral banks) in China's power industry between 1984 and 1992 was $12 billion, led by Hong Kong and the United States. U.S. sales of power equipment to China were $864 million in 1993 and more than $1 billion in both 1994 and 1995.[16] In addition to the transfer of production capabilities for advanced power systems, the recent flurry of interest by foreign independent power producers in China has hastened regulatory and management reforms in the country's power industry.

## CHINA'S IMPACT ON INTERNATIONAL REGIMES

China has had little impact on either the formal or the informal international regimes in the energy area. China's first commercial-scale nuclear power plant at Daya Bay began operation in 1993. There have been no reported difficulties for the IAEA in monitoring the operation of this plant. Since China joined the World Bank in 1980, it has been a model member and is currently the largest borrower, at around $3 billion per year (1997). As noted earlier, China has abided by World Bank procedures and has adopted the bank's procurement policies for many of its own domestic infrastructure projects.

According to industry experts, China has largely followed international norms for oil exploration and development and for refining contracts.[17] Difficulties with foreign companies in offshore gas development—such as the slowness to develop the large ARCO field—have been due primarily to China's inability to reform its natural gas pricing system. China has become an active participant in international energy markets since the late 1970s, trading crude oil, petroleum products, and coal. Despite a steep learning curve for Sinochem (and later other agencies) in becoming familiar with international energy markets, there is no evidence that China has had any deleterious impact on these markets.

## Prospects for the Future

China's economy certainly can continue to grow without additional foreign involvement in its energy sector or in other sectors where new technology can lower per-unit energy requirements dramatically. However, without additional foreign involvement, China cannot grow at the rate of the past decade. Oil import dependence will increase, and environmental degradation from coal burning will become more severe.

In addition to the economy's growth rate, other key factors that affect energy demand are the structure of consumer demand (and the consequent structure of production) and the technical efficiency with which goods and services are produced. Recent work by the World Bank and the Chinese government provide scenarios of future Chinese energy demand.[18] Under a high-growth scenario, real GDP increases about 8 percent per year between 1990 and 2020 (from $376 billion to $3,953 trillion in constant 1990 dollars), with per-capita GDP growing from $370 to around $2,600 (constant 1990 dollars), roughly equivalent to per-capita income in Mexico today. Assuming that the energy-efficiency improvements experienced in China since 1980 continue, the energy intensity of GDP in 2020 would fall to about one-third of the 1990 level. Primary energy use therefore would increase by about 4 percent per year in the high-GDP scenario between 1990 and 2020 (about half the rate of GDP growth), rising from 987 million tons coal equivalent (mtce) to 3,300 mtce.

Electric power production has grown slightly slower than GDP over the past decade, but Chinese officials hope that electricity generation can grow in line with GDP to the year 2000. By implication, China would need about 300 GW of installed capacity by the turn of the century, which would require it to add about 15 GW each year, equivalent to the total capacity of the Netherlands or Switzerland. Longer-term estimates are that electricity generation would need to rise about 6 percent a year between now and the year 2020 in order to sustain average GDP growth of 8 percent.

A threefold increase in energy use needed in the year 2020 to fuel China's economic expansion would require that the country rely heavily on coal. No other energy source could be expanded so fast in such a short period of time.[19] Although the nation possesses ample coal reserves, many Chinese energy experts feel that it will not be possible to produce and use 3 billion tons of coal by the year 2020, because of mining and transportation constraints and, most important, growing environmental consequences.

## ENERGY AND ELECTRIC POWER NEEDS AND OPTIONS

The U.S. Department of Energy (DOE) estimated in 1995 that China's total power financing needs between 1995 and 2000 are $90 billion and that the amount of foreign investment required is on the order of $25 billion. Given China's abundance of coal, coal-fired thermal power will provide the bulk of the country's additional electric power for the foreseeable future. What will become increasingly important for China's coal-fired power plants is the control of air pollutants (principally, fine particulates and sulfur), which will make less-polluting power technologies more attractive. However, even with the rapid expansion of other sources of electricity—hydro, nuclear, renewables— the percentage of China's power supplied by coal is unlikely to fall much over the next 20 years. Long lead times and high capital costs will pose difficulties for the expansion of both hydroelectric and nuclear power beyond levels currently planned. Many Chinese energy experts attach great importance to nuclear power; however, even if nuclear power expanded from the 2 GW today in China to over 87 GW by 2020—equivalent to the completion of ten 600-MW power plants each year after 2010—such power still would provide only 15 percent of China's electric power. The DOE has estimated that China's nuclear plant market could be between $6 and $8 billion by the year 2000, and $20 billion by 2010.

Increasingly, China will require coal processing (cleaning, sorting) and other, more sophisticated clean-coal technologies for both efficiency and environmental reasons. At present, many Chinese cities have serious air pollution problems as a result of inefficient coal burning. With the growth of the economy and limited supplies of alternative fuels, the situation is likely to get worse before it gets better. Many so-called clean-coal technologies have been developed in countries of the Organization for Economic Cooperation and Development (OECD) in response to stricter environmental regulations, such as coal gasification for power generation, postcombustion ash and sulfur removal technologies, and fluidized bed combustion. However, because of the generally higher cost of these technologies compared with the cost of natural gas, particularly for power generation, sales of clean-coal technologies in the West have been limited. Many Western companies thus are interested in selling their clean-coal technologies to China, where the demand is higher and growing, and the options in terms of alternative fuels are more limited. Until China's coal supply system improves, however, and market and regulatory signals provide incentives to coal suppliers to provide cleaner coal, the demand for more advanced processing technologies from abroad will not occur on a large scale.

In addition, in light of the rapid expansion of road transport since 1990, and the importance that China's leaders have attached to their nation's domestic automotive industry, many analysts foresee petroleum imports increasing significantly in the near future unless China makes major new discoveries of petroleum.[20] In the future natural gas development in China, especially onshore, is likely to accept greater foreign involvement, since the country needs additional gas for both energy diversification and environmental reasons. China has announced plans to expand its refining capacity to meet domestic demand for petroleum products, which could result in the expansion of existing refining capacity from 160 million tons (mt) per year (1993) to 215 mt per year by the year 2000, and perhaps as much as 320–370 mt per year by 2010.[21] China seems to have accepted the fact that it will have to import ever-increasing quantities of crude oil, since domestic oil production has not been able to keep up with domestic petroleum product demand. At the same time, China appears committed to expanding its refining capacity to meet domestic product demand, but this will require very different types of refining equipment—Chinese crudes are generally heavy, low-sulfur, and with a very high wax content, compared with Middle East crudes that are lighter and generally higher in sulfur.

## Renewables

Given China's need to find a cleaner alternative to coal, renewable energy technologies provide great long-term promise. Unlike the United States, Europe, or Japan, China will be adding significant quantities of electric power capacity over the coming decades to support the growth of the economy. Renewable energy increasingly will be the least-cost option for providing electricity to many people in remote and isolated areas. China has abundant sources of wind and solar energy that are becoming increasingly attractive in Inner Mongolia, Tibet, Xinjiang, Gansu, and Qinghai provinces. Both wind and solar PV should expand in China in the future if domestic manufacturing can help to lower costs and if an effective market for these technologies can be created and sustained, in part through effective fiscal and monetary policies. Because of the importance of renewables to China, the government needs to establish a large-scale and serious promotion program. Until recently, institutional responsibility for the development of renewable energy in China has been highly fragmented. While China can certainly benefit from the developments made abroad, it must have its own research and development program. Without continuing declines in production costs, which can be achieved only through domestic production, renewables will not be able to make a major contribution to China's energy supply.

## Energy Efficiency

Finally, although China can and will adopt more energy-efficient equipment and processes in the years to come, especially through joint-venture arrangements, the biggest potential for energy efficiency is in the widespread dissemination and adoption of fairly low-tech, higher-efficiency equipment, including small electric motors and pumps, steam traps, and insulation. Institutional innovations, including some from abroad, are likely to provide a larger stimulus to energy-efficiency improvements in China than pure technology transfer. The World Bank currently is working with the Chinese State Economic and Trade Commission to set up energy service companies (ESCOs) for undertaking energy-efficiency improvements. By taking on the financial and technical risk of energy-efficiency projects in return for a share of the energy savings, ESCOs can overcome many of the existing barriers to the adoption of energy-efficiency measures in China; however, they require rather sophisticated contracting arrangements. As Chinese electric power utilities become more market-oriented, and as incentives for reducing demand are integrated into utility regulation, more energy-efficiency projects will be undertaken in all sectors. Again, however, the solution is largely institutional rather than technical, and will require little in terms of foreign involvement.

## IMPROVING THE CLIMATE FOR FOREIGN INVOLVEMENT

The most effective way for China to improve the climate for foreign involvement is to continue the reform of its domestic economy. However, the Chinese government can take more specific measures to attract foreign involvement in its energy sector.

### Reform Antiquated State Industries
For efficiency and environmental reasons, China needs to reform many of its SOEs, including coal mines, oil fields, petroleum refineries, and power plants. Currently many of the most energy-inefficient and polluting firms in China are also the biggest money losers. Requiring SOEs to compete in the marketplace, reducing direct and indirect subsidies, and shutting down gross pollution violators would benefit not only China but foreign technology suppliers and investors.

### Reform Transportation System
Timely and affordable delivery of fuel to the plant is critical to power plant performance. Transportation problems have affected negotiations for IPPs and have created problems for coal shipments, such as from Antaibao. Introducing hard budget constraints, simplifying the complicated rules governing freight shipments, and introducing more competition into the transport system would help to reduce the relatively high costs of transport in China and allow more timely delivery of shipments. Not only would these reforms benefit foreign joint ventures in coal and power, but they would make China's coal sector even more competitive internationally.

### Extend Energy Price Reform
Although China has made considerable progress over the past decade in reforming energy prices, further reform is needed. Measures to further rationalize energy prices include nonpreferential tariffs for natural gas; improvements in the structure of electricity prices, including the elimination of subsidies and low in-plan prices for certain industrial consumers; and adoption of differential rates to indicate coal quality better. China also must guard against the potential for market-based

(still government-regulated) prices to become eroded through general price inflation. This will be of particular concern for those energy sources, such as electricity and natural gas, that are not directly traded internationally and that are government-regulated.

### Institute Financial Reform

The long-term solution to capital constraints for energy and other investment projects is for China to make its currency convertible. However, other financial reforms are also critical for foreign investment and for the long-term health of China's domestic economy. Ample capital available in international markets is poised to flow to Chinese electric utilities and other infrastructure projects once the risks of achieving modest returns can be assured. As noted earlier, both China and foreign investors are positioning themselves to get the best possible deal in anticipation of an expansion of private power development.

### Institute Free Entry and Competition

China needs to create a fair and competitive environment for all entrants. Competitive bidding on major projects lowers costs and reduces construction times. While directly negotiated deals such as the Shajiao B and C plants may have been important in demonstrating the concept of IPP in China, such sweetheart deals are no substitute for open competition.

### Reform Foreign Ownership and Control Rules

The inability or difficulty of foreign partners to hold majority stakes in joint ventures has been an impediment to foreign investment. Foreign companies often require management control over both personnel and asset use. Many of the negotiations for Chinese-foreign joint ventures during the 1980s and 1990s broke down over the lack of management authority by the foreign partner.

### Enforce Environmental Regulations

Many foreign technologies and processes currently deemed too expensive by China would be considerably more competitive if the country enforced its own environmental standards. Nonetheless, many localities in China already have made the decision to buy advanced foreign technologies, such as fluidized bed combustion boilers or pollution control equipment, as a way of limiting environmental impacts of coal burning. Such orders presumably would grow, as would joint ventures to produce less-polluting equipment in China, if environmental enforcement was tightened.

## STEPS TO INCREASE FOREIGN INVOLVEMENT

The long-term financial benefits of increased commercial activity in China by foreign companies are fairly obvious. However, increased foreign involvement in China's energy sector also can have important regional and global environmental benefits through the transfer of important technologies and expertise: pollution control, energy efficiency, and renewable energy technologies. In addition, strategic goals, such as energy security, can be achieved by increasing Chinese domestic energy supply and by involving China more integrally in international energy and technology markets.

### Support Institutional Reform

The most important way to increase foreign involvement in China is to encourage further reforms in China's economy, which in turn are likely to lead to reforms in the political arena as well. China should be encouraged to meet the conditions for membership in the World Trade Organization as soon as possible, and its entry should be backed by the United States and other advanced industrialized countries. Membership in the World Trade Organization (WTO) will help ensure China's compliance with international technology standards and protocols as well as the use and disposition of a vast array of hazardous chemical and other pollutants.

### Share Policy Experience

As China experiments with market mechanisms, there is a clear need for its policymakers to be aware of what policies have been used in other countries—both successfully and unsuccessfully—to address key energy and energy-related environmental issues. Policies for promoting energy efficiency and renewable energy technologies as well as energy-related environmental policies are of particular interest to China at the present time. Such information could be provided to Chinese policymakers through a range of public and private organizations.

### Targeted Export Credits

Since the United States currently provides very limited export credits to China, the following discussion is directed more to other developed, countries. While export credits have resulted in some foreign companies' obtaining an important foothold in their dealings with China, and China has received some very favorable contract terms on some projects, the overall benefits have been limited for both China and foreign companies. While such credits may have been needed in the 1980s, when foreign exchange was not abundant or readily obtainable by some organizations in China, such credits led to unrealistic expectations on the part of the Chinese for financing conventional (i.e., commercial) energy projects and have hampered competition in foreign technology supply. According to some analysts, the decline in the use of concessionary funds for power projects in China will help U.S. technology suppliers, since the United States has not matched the soft loans for China provided by other countries.[22] While some argue that the United States should provide export credits in order to compete with other countries that provide them, China's technology needs are so large that it cannot rely on export credits (or multilateral funds) to finance its technology purchases. The DOE estimates that China's capital needs in the energy sector will be between $200 and $300 billion for the period from 1996 to 2000, which is more than 100 times the annual amount of bilateral aid to China. Instead of providing concessional financing for commercial energy projects, export credits should be used more selectively to promote specific technologies that may not be able to gain an important foothold without support, but that have commercial and/or environmental importance in the future—again, energy efficiency, renewable energy, and pollution control technologies could all qualify on these grounds.

*Technical Assistance*

Finally, there are a number of ways in which the international community can support China while promoting regional and global objectives. China must be an active participant in international energy and environmental discussions and research of both a regional and a global nature. Providing the mechanism, where necessary, for China to attend such fora and participate in such research is important for informing Chinese policymakers as well as the international community. Assisting the country in long-term research and development on new energy-efficiency and renewable energy technologies can help accelerate commercial development. China has the potential to become a low-cost producer and export base for new technologies. Support for training Chinese personnel abroad, whether through academic exchanges or study tours, is an extremely important and low-cost way of influencing current and future Chinese energy policy.

# Notes

1. William A. Ward et al., "Energy Efficiency in China: Case Studies and Economic Analysis," *Issues and Options in Greenhouse Gas Emissions Control*, Subreport No. 4 (Washington, D.C.: The World Bank, December 1994).

2.  Xiaodong Wang, "China's Coal Sector—Moving to a Market Economy," report prepared for the China and Mongolia Department (Washington, D.C.: The World Bank, August 1996).

3.  For a survey of recent energy prices in China, see Jonathan E. Sinton, ed., *China Energy Datebook* (Berkeley, Calif.: Lawrence Berkeley National Laboratory, 1996).

4.  Todd M. Johnson, *China: Energy Sector Outlook,* The Economist Intelligence Unit, Report No. 1089 (London: The Economist Publications, 1987).

5.  The average depth of coal seams in China is 400 meters, compared with about 100 meters in the United States, where 60 percent of coal production comes from opencast mines.

6.  Some major oil companies, including British Petroleum, have given up their concessions in Xinjiang, given Chinese drilling failures in the more promising sections of the Tarim Basin. Pamela Yatsko, "Oh, Well: China's Tarim Basin Is Proving a Big Disappointment," *Far Eastern Economic Review,* September 19, 1996, p. 68.

7.  See Todd M. Johnson and David Fridley, "China's New Petroleum Export Policy," *Financial Times,* December 1985.

8.  Sinton, ed., *China Energy Datebook,* p. VII-11.

9.  In 1980, China negotiated a deal with Combustion Engineering (CE) and Westinghouse, both of the United States, to transfer the skills to produce large power boilers and turbines in China under license to CE and Westinghouse. In 1986, the first 600-MW boiler was produced in China at the Harbin Boiler Works.

10. World Bank, *China: Power Sector Reform: Toward Competition and Improved Performance* (Washington, D.C.: The World Bank, 1994).

11. One of the major constraints in a proposed joint-venture oil refinery expansion project in Guangdong Province reportedly has been the excessive number of staff members that the refinery employs and who had to be included in the management plan of the joint-venture company.

12. Such reforms included hardening of state loans, financial incentives for productivity gains, increases in prices of energy commodities, growing responsibility for profits and losses, and the ability to retain a portion of profits for reinvestment.

13. Feng Liu, "The Power Sector of Guangdong Province in China," paper prepared for the Nomura Research Institute, Ltd., Yokohama, Japan, April 1996, p. 1.

14. See, for instance, Michael Philips, who writes: "Through their economic advice, loan conditions, and investments in both energy-producing and energy-consuming sectors, these banks shape energy development and consumption in these [developing and east European] countries." "The

Least Cost Energy Path for Developing Countries: Energy Efficient Investments for the Multilateral Development Banks" (Washington, D.C.: International Institute for Energy Conservation, 1991).

15. U.S. Department of Energy, *China: Country Energy Profile* (Washington, D.C.: Energy Information Administration, February 1995).

16. Ibid.

17. Mikkal E. Herberg, Director, Emerging Markets, ARCO (New York: Council on Foreign Relations, July 18, 1996).

18. Todd M. Johnson et al., eds., *China: Issues and Options in Greenhouse Gas Emissions Control, Summary Report*, World Bank Discussion Paper No. 330, (Washington, D.C.: The World Bank, 1996); Junfeng Li et al., *Energy Demand in China: Overview Report*, Subreport No. 2, China GHG Study (Washington, D.C.: The World Bank, 1995).

19. In addition to a threefold increase in coal, the high-growth, business-as-usual scenario assumes that between 1990 and 2020 hydro will expand from 38 GW to 138 GW, nuclear will expand from 0 GW to 32 GW, and renewables will expand from 9 MW to 9,000 MW, while the unprecedented energy-efficiency improvements made in China during the 1980s—energy/GDP elasticity of 0.5—are maintained.

20. Some forecasts show that China may need to import more than 2 million barrels per day—100 million tons per year—of crude oil and petroleum products by the year 2005. L. Hussein and K. Wu, "China's Petroleum Product Balance Outlook: The Refining Industry Imperative" (Honolulu, Hawaii: The East-West Center, 1994).

21. P. Woodward and A. Flynn, "Looking Downstream," *China Business Review* (July–August 1994).

22. *China Business Review* (November–December 1993): 37.

# 9

# China and Environmental Protection

## LESTER ROSS

ENVIRONMENTAL protection in the international or global context
typically constitutes a type of soft or functional regime in which
one state's behavior does not present an overt threat to its neighbors. Rather, the principal danger arises from everyday activity of a general social or economic utility, which presents risks within the
originating state, to that state's neighbors, and possibly to the global
commons. Thus there is typically not an intent to cause harm or
encroach on neighboring territory; rather, it is the externalities of a given
activity that cause concern. Sovereignty issues become paramount when
transboundary externalities affect neighbors and/or the global commons. Certain international conventions, such as the Montreal Protocol
on Substances that Deplete the Ozone Layer (1987), that allow states to
impose trade sanctions against violators include enforcement mechanisms and therefore encourage participation by states like China.[1] Such
provisions are still relatively infrequent, however. There also are rare
cases on record in which a country has obtained judicial relief for environmental harms that originated in another country, but such issues are
overwhelmingly nonjusticiable.[2] International regimes typically provide
no effective avenue for judicial relief.

Despite the paucity of judicial avenues for dispute resolution, international environmental regimes have been established in increasing
numbers. This raises the issue of why states establish and participate in
such regimes and why they comply with the norms of such regimes
when the activity of member states is not well monitored.[3] Prominent
international relations theorists Robert Keohane, Peter Haas, and Marc

Levy argue that the key variable is "the degree of domestic environmentalist pressure in major industrialized democracies, not the decision making rules of the relevant international institution."[4] Moreover, even when violations are subject to an international regime, they are not necessarily readily subject to sanctions because (1) the regime relies on consensus; (2) the harm originates in the externality rather than the behavior itself; (3) sovereignty limits the reach of punishment; and (4) proof of causation is subject to considerable scientific uncertainty. As international legal specialists Abram Chayes and Antonia Handler Chayes and others have argued, this tends to place environmental issues within the ambit of cooperative or positive-sum regimes that are more suitable to a managerial or consensual style of diplomacy. In such cases, states are encouraged to adhere to international norms through suasion and appeals to their own best interests rather than fear of sanctions.[5]

For China, low income levels and restrictions on political participation limit the present potential for domestic environmentalist pressure. The questions, then, are whether and why China has become more participatory in international environmental regimes; whether the quality of China's participation varies by substantive area, the threat of sanctions, or other variables; and whether constructive engagement can shape China's participation.

## China: The Domestic Context

If international environmental issues are predominantly of the cooperative type, then the predisposition of the state is critical. If the state lacks, or is impervious to, knowledge concerning the existence of particular problems, their salience, or means for their resolution, the prospects for international cooperation are correspondingly reduced. If, conversely, the state internally acknowledges the existence of environmental problems and takes domestic action to resolve such problems, then the prospects for international progress through cooperation and enhancement of the state's environmental policymaking capacity are increased.

China began to manifest an awareness of environmental problems in the early 1970s, during the latter stages of the Cultural Revolution. This was at approximately the same time that the United Nations (U.N.) awarded the China seat to the People's Republic of China (PRC) and in the midst of the early stages of normalizing relations with the United States. Specifically, in 1971 China established a leading small group for environmental protection under the State Council to supervise China's preparations for the June 1972 United Nations Conference on the Human Environment (UNCHE) in Stockholm. Thus China's first high-level environmental policy body was established in direct and urgent response to an impending international conference, the planning for which had commenced in the United Nations in 1968, before the PRC had become a member. China did not play a particularly constructive role at UNCHE. Like developing countries in general, China assigned principal responsibility for pollution control to the advanced industrialized countries and defended the right of developing countries to exploit their own resources without external interference. China went further and attempted unsuccessfully to inject such tangential and divisive issues as the Vietnam War and nuclear testing in the UNCHE declaration. Although the declaration eventually was approved by consensus, in part to avoid a recorded vote, China publicly announced that it had not taken part in the voting.[6] In other words, China was a "laggard participant" in this international regime: it avoided international obligations by failing to sign treaty commitments or exhibiting a disdainful attitude with respect to compliance obligations.[7]

UNCHE is widely regarded as the origin of international environmental diplomacy. Importantly, it provided the impetus for China and other developing countries to create an environmental policy, notwithstanding their fear that advanced industrialized countries would make use of environmental concerns to curtail the economic potential of developing countries. In China, UNHCE also prompted the establishment of an environmental protection bureaucracy separate from the Ministry of Public Health, which previously had exercised responsibility for environmental protection with little effect. The establishment of the leading small group under the State Council was followed in 1974 by the establishment of the small Environmental Protection Office, also under the State Council. The two bodies since have evolved into the State Environmental Protection Administration (SEPA), now led by Xie Zhenhua. Xie is the first head of SEPA to have ministerial rank. Environmental policy arguably would have greater stature within China if SEPA were elevated to ministerial status. Nevertheless, the growth and elaboration of the country's environmental bureaucracy have been substantial, and it is rumored that SEPA eventually will be elevated to ministerial status in a later round of governmental restructuring.

Environmental regulation in China also can trace its origins to the early 1970s. Beginning in 1972 China stated the need to incorporate the environment in the national planning process, although not until the sixth Five-Year Plan (1980–1985) did environmental protection receive treatment in a separate chapter. China's first set of environmental regulations (excepting a few occupational safety and health norms adapted from Soviet models), "Some Regulations on Protecting the Environment," was promulgated in 1973. Environmental policy made slow progress during the next five years because of institutional weakness and the leadership succession crisis. Since the late 1970s, however, China has enacted or promulgated over a dozen environmental and related statutes, dozens of regulations, and about 400 standards. The legislative and regulatory processes in the National People's Congress and SEPA have also become relatively open to international advice, including the China Council for International Cooperation on Environment and Development, a high-level advisory body established in 1992, with many policies, such as discharge and emission permits, modeled after practice in the United States and other advanced industrialized countries.

Much of the impetus for expanding the scope, comprehensiveness, and stringency of environmental regulation is domestic. For example, the largest source of citizen complaints to environmental protection bureaus has been noise pollution, a purely domestic concern.[8] In response to such concern, the Law on Environmental Noise Pollution Prevention Control was enacted in 1996. However, even in such a domestic arena, international influences shape the policy process by diffusing scientific knowledge and expanding awareness of environmental harms, thereby strengthening SEPA and related agencies and fostering the emergence of a nascent environmental constituency. For example, Article 13 of the amended Water Pollution Prevention and Control Law (1996) provides that affected units and citizens may participate in the environmental impact assessment process; this opportunity for public participation was inspired in part by the applicable international convention. Spending on environmental protection also is scheduled to grow at a relatively fast pace that further signifies government recognition of the importance of environmental protection.[9]

With respect to international environmental regimes, it means that China resists the imposition of obligations that are deemed to be incompatible with its level of development and opposes initiatives in environmental diplomacy if they threaten to constrain its development potential or unjustifiably interfere in its internal affairs. Such a position was articulated in 1991 in advance of the United Nations Conference on Environment and Development (UNCED), when China convened a forum attended by some 41 developing countries that resulted in the promulgation of the Beijing Ministerial Declaration on Environment and Development. The declaration recognized the need for international cooperation to promote environmental protection and sustainable development but also demanded financial assistance and asserted both the right to development and opposition to interference in the internal affairs of developing countries.[10] It was rearticulated by President Jiang

Zemin in his address to the fourth National Environmental Protection Conference.[11]

Such formal policy suggests that China is more likely to be a leader in international environmental regimes that are not perceived to constrain its development potential and less likely to lead in those regimes that are perceived to impose such constraints. This further suggests that international organizations and other states may have to provide greater incentives or disincentives to elicit the desired behavior from China with respect to those obligations that are perceived to impose constraints on development. As discussed, however, there appears to be a long-term trend in China in support of environmental protection, in part because the nation believes that it is at risk from various environmental harms. If so, the current resistance to certain obligations would diminish over time through the diffusion of knowledge, rising incomes, and the growth of environmental awareness in China.

## International Agreements

International environmental regimes have increased in number and entered into force more rapidly since UNCHE and UNCED.[12] These trends have emerged primarily because of the heightened salience of environmental issues, a greater reliance on momentum-building processes involving framework conventions, and scientifically based accretions to broad agreements.[13]

Table 9–1 displays China's status with respect to international agreements that have a substantial relationship to environmental protection. Although not conclusive, the data suggest that China generally has become more willing to become a party to such agreements and to do so at an earlier date. Moreover, this tendency toward adherence to international obligations has become more pronounced in recent years as international environmental diplomacy has accelerated and as China's own capacity to participate has increased.

All of these agreements impinge to some extent on national sovereignty.[14] There is, however, significant variation in this regard. The Convention on Biodiversity imposes substantial constraints on development in selected, generally undeveloped areas in order to conserve biological diversity within and in some cases outside a jurisdiction, but it does not impose broad constraints on development in the economy as a whole. In this respect it is not surprising not only that China participated in the convention but also that Premier Li Peng prominently endorsed it in his address at UNCED and that China was the first major state (and fifth overall) to ratify the convention.

**Table 9-1. China's Status with Respect to International Environmental Agreements**

| Date of adoption | Date of entry into force | Amendment | Date of entry into force | Amendment | Date of entry into force | Action by China | Date of action by China | Reservations |
|---|---|---|---|---|---|---|---|---|
| 25-Oct-21 | 31-Aug-23 | | | | | | | |
| 8-Nov-33 | 14-Jan-36 | | | | | | | |
| 2-Dec-46 | 10-Nov-48 | 19-Nov-56 | 4-May-59 | | | accession | 24-Sep-80 | |
| 18-Oct-50 | 17-Jan-63 | | | | | | | |
| 6-Dec-51 | 3-Apr-52 | Nov-79 | 4-Apr-91 | | | | | |
| 12-May-54 | 26-Jul-58 | 11-Apr-62 | 18-May-67 28-Jun-67 | 21-Oct-69 | 20-Jan-78 | | | |
| 27-Feb-56 | 2-Jul-56 | 3-Nov-67 22-Jun-79 | 16-Aug-69 | 24-Nov-83 | 23-May-90 | | 6-Jun-90 | |
| 29-Apr-58 | 20-Mar-66 | | | | | accession | 11-Nov-70 | |
| 29-Apr-58 | 10-Jun-64 | | | | | | | |
| 29-Apr-58 | 30-Sep-62 | | | | | accession | 8-Jun-83 | |
| 1-Dec-59 | 23-Jun-61 | | | | | accession | 4-Oct-91 | |
| 3-Oct-91 | | | | | | accession | | |
| 14-Dec-59 | 19-Oct-60 | | | | | | | |
| 22-Jun-60 | 17-Jun-62 | | | | | | | |
| 29-Jul-60 | 1-Apr-68 | 28-Jan-64 | 1-Apr-68 | 16-Nov-82 | | | | |
| 2-Dec-61 | 10-Aug-68 | 10-Nov-72 | 19-Mar-91 | 23-Oct-78 | | | | |
| 5-Aug-63 | 10-Oct-63 | | | | | | | |
| 21-May-63 | 12-Nov-77 | | | | 8-Nov-81 | | | |
| 12-Sep-64 | 22-7-68 | 13-Aug-70 | 12-Nov-75 | | | accession | 12-Jan-84 | |
| 27-Jan-67 | 10-Oct-67 | | | | | | | |
| 23-Oct-69 | 24-Oct-71 | | | | | | | |
| 29-Nov-69 | 19-Jun-75 | 19-Nov-76 | 8-Apr-81 | 25-May-84 | | accession | 29-Apr-80 | |

*(continued on next page)*

Table 9-1. (Continued)

| Date of adoption | Date of entry into force | Amendment | Date of entry into force | Amendment | Date of entry into force | Action by China | Date of action by China | Reservations |
|---|---|---|---|---|---|---|---|---|
| 29-Nov-69 | 6-May-75 | | | | | accession | 4-May-90 | |
| 2-Feb-71 | 21-Dec-75 | 3-Dec-82 | 1-Oct-86 | | | accession | 31-Jul-92 | |
| 11-Feb-71 | 18-May-72 | | | | | accession | 28-Feb-91 | |
| 23-Jun-71 | 27-Jul-73 | | | | | | | |
| 17-Dec-71 | 15-Jul-75 | | | | | | | |
| 18-Dec-71 | 16-Oct-78 | 19-Nov-76 | | 25-May-84 | | | | |
| 10-Apr-72 | 26-Mar-75 | | | | | accession | 15-Nov-84 | |
| 1-Jun-72 | 11-Mar-78 | | | | | | | |
| 23-Nov-72 | 17-Dec-75 | | | | | accession | 12-Dec-85 | |
| 29-Dec-72 | 30-Aug-75 | | | | | accession | 14-Nov-85 | |
| 3-Mar-73 | 1-Jul-75 | 22-Jun-79 | 13-Apr-87 | 30-Apr-83 | | accession | 8-Jan-81 | |
| 2-Nov-73 | | 17-Feb-78 | 2-Oct-83 | 15-Mar-83 | | accession | 2-Oct-83 | |
| 2-Nov-73 | | | | 15-Mar-85 | | accession | 24-May-90 | |
| 4-Jun-74 | 6-May-78 | 1-Sep-89 | 26-Mar-90 | | | | | |
| 24-Jun-74 | 10-Jun-76 | | | | | | | |
| 18-May-77 | 5-Oct-78 | | | | | | | |
| 20-Jun-77 | 11-Jul-79 | | | | | | | |
| 23-Jun-79 | 1-Nov-83 | | | | | | | |
| 24-Oct-78 | 1-Jan-79 | | | | | | | |
| 13-Nov-79 | 16-Mar-83 | | | | | | | |
| 3-Mar-80 | 8-Feb-87 | | | | | accession; ratification | 10-Jan-89; 9-Feb-89 | |
| 20-May-80 | 7-Apr-82 | | | | | | | |
| 22-Jun-81 | 11-Aug-83 | | | | | | | |
| 3-Dec-82 | 1-Oct-86 | | | | | accession | 1-Jun-92 | |

| | | | | Action | Date | Note |
|---|---|---|---|---|---|---|
| 10-Dec-82 | | | | signatory | 10-Dec-82 | |
| | | | | ratification | 15-May-96 | declaration |
| 18-Nov-83 | 1-Apr-85 | | | accession | 2-Jul-86 | |
| 22-Mar-85 | 22-Sep-88 | | | accession | 11-Sep-89 | |
| | | | | | 10-Dec-89 | |
| 26-Jun-85 | 17-Feb-88 | | | signatory | 26-Sep-86 | |
| 26-Sep-86 | 26-Feb-87 | | | ratification | 10-Sep-87 | |
| | | | | | 11-Oct-87 | |
| 25-Feb-91 | | | | signatory | 26-Sep-86 | reservation |
| 26-Sep-86 | 27-Oct-86 | | | ratification | 10-Sep-87 | |
| | | | | | 11-Oct-87 | |
| 16-Sep-87 | 1-Jan-89 | 29-Jun-90 (adjust) | 29-Jun-90 (adjust) | signatory | 14-Jun-91 | |
| | | | | ratification | 12-Sep-91 | |
| | | | | accession | 11-Jan-90 | |
| 8-Jan-88 | 11-Nov-90 | 3-Jul-91 | 10-Aug-92 | signatory | 22-Mar-90 | |
| 2-Jun-88 | N/A | | | ratification | 17-Dec-91 | |
| 21-Sep-88 | 27-Apr-92 | | | | | |
| 22-Mar-89 | 5-May-92 | | | | | |
| 28-Apr-89 | N/A | | | signatory | 14-Jun-91 | |
| 29-Jun-90 | 10-Aug-92 | | | ratification | 10-Aug-92 | |
| 9-May-92 | | | | signatory | 11-Jun-92 | |
| | | | | ratification | 5-Jan-93 | |
| 5-Jun-92 | | | | signatory | 11-Jun-92 | |
| | | | | ratification | 5-Jan-93 | |
| 24-Nov-89 | 17-May-91 | | | | | |

China also has taken active measures to implement the convention. Even before it was adopted, the State Council organized the Coordinating Group on Establishing Biodiversity Convention, consisting of 13 ministries and agencies led by SEPA. By the end of 1993 China had adopted the China Biodiversity Conservation Action Plan, implementation of which commenced in 1994. Subsidiary action plans have been adopted, including the Forestry Action Plan under the Ministry of Forestry, the China Panda Migration Conservation Plan under the Ministry of Construction, and the China Agro-Biodiversity Action Plan under the Ministry of Agriculture. SEPA has been conducting a national survey of biodiversity under United Nations Environment Programme (UNEP) sponsorship since 1995. Nature reserves have been established at a rapid rate. By the end of 1995, 799 nature reserves with a total area of more than 175 million acres had been established, amounting to 7.19 percent of surface area.[15] Although the quality of management in such reserves is generally deficient, major efforts are under way to upgrade management and protect reserves against despoliation and encroachment. Of particular importance is the promulgation of the Regulations on Nature Reserves by the State Council in 1994. Under the regulations, management and administrative organizations with responsibility for nature reserves are authorized to accept foreign as well as domestic donations, providing a direct avenue for international influence at the administrative level, although, conversely, approval is required before foreign nationals can enter certain reserves. Penalties, including potential criminal responsibility, are provided for violations of the regulations, indicating a stiffening of resolve to protect the reserves.

By contrast, China has taken a less-prominent position with respect to the United Nations Framework Convention on Climate Change, which also was adopted at UNCED. Soon after its adoption on July 2, 1992, the State Committee on Environmental Protection directed the Office of the Climate Change Coordinating Group to prepare a draft analysis of the convention's impact on China. The office convened representatives of responsible agencies, notably the State Scientific and Technological Commission (SSTC), the former Ministry of Energy, SEPA, the China Meteorological Administration (CMA), and the Ministry of Foreign Affairs to draft a document analyzing China's obligations and assigned lead responsibility to different agencies with respect to the various components thereof. Importantly, lead responsibility was assigned to SSTC, SEPA, CMA, and the Chinese Academy of Sciences, not to the State Planning Commission, Ministry of Energy, or any other production agency, although these agencies played an important role.[16] China ratified the Framework Convention on the same date as the Biodiversity Convention, again becoming the first major state and fifth overall to ratify the convention. After ratification, CMA, rather than SEPA, was designated as the lead agency, with the Office of the Climate Change Coordinating Group placed under it.

Like most other states, China has moved more cautiously with respect to the Framework Convention than the Biodiversity Convention. China has participated in the UNEP/Global Environment Facility (GEF) project on greenhouse gases and sinks, completed a paper assessing the impact of climate change on the country using global circulation model results, and conducted various pilot studies, and is a participant in the UNDP project on least-cost emissions reduction.[17]

China is still in the process of preparing its National Action Plan on Climate Change. Legislative action has been uneven with respect to the Framework Convention. In 1995 China amended its Air Pollution Prevention and Control Law, originally enacted in 1987. The revised statute calls for coal washing and the designation of acid rain or sulfur dioxide control districts but generally contains no provisions or schedules to control greenhouse gas emissions. The Environmental and Resources Protection Committee of the National People's Congress took note of the international obligations that China had assumed under the Vienna Convention for the Protection of the Ozone Layer, the Montreal Protocol, and the Framework Convention when drafting the amendments to the Air Pollution Law.[18] On the whole, however, the statute falls short of satisfying such obligations. The Electric Power Law, also enacted in 1995, establishes a preference for clean and renewable fuels in electric power generation but similarly provides no schedules. The Law on the Prevention and Control of Pollution of the Environment by Solid Waste (1996) establishes controls on ash disposal, which would tend to discourage further the use of high-ash-content fuels. Furthermore, the Energy Conservation Law, which was enacted in late 1997 after a lengthy delay, is in many ways hortatory in nature and will require a great deal of preliminary work before its provisions can be operationalized.

China thus appears to have been more proactive with respect to the Convention on Biodiversity and more cautious under the Framework Convention. This does not necessarily mean that China has been obstructionist in the latter instance; rather it has been reluctant to take measures that go beyond the research or pilot project level or that imply the assumption of obligations. If and when obligations are established under the Framework Convention, it is likely that China will act to comply, as it generally has in the past.[19] It is less likely that the Chinese voluntarily will assume any obligations, although they may pursue conservation measures in order to conserve domestic resources and reduce imports as well as to reduce the domestic impact of pollution. Other measures may have to be taken, however, including the establishment of a more solid research foundation. The transfer of policy and a coordinating responsibility from CMA to the State Development and Planning Commission in 1998 may help in this respect, but SEPA leadership would be more significant.

## The Role of the Private Sector in International Environmental Regimes

The role of the private business sector in shaping international environmental policy is growing. Many companies have adopted corporate policies requiring compliance with all applicable regulatory requirements and sometimes demanded performance that exceeds such regulatory requirements. Moreover, corporations with international operations tend to impose such internal policies on a systemwide basis, regardless of location or enforcement, because the costs of adapting production and pollution control technologies to local regulatory requirements generally outweigh any cost savings. These companies also anticipate that regulatory requirements will become more stringent in less-developed countries, are averse to long-tailed Superfund-type and other environmental risks, and are wary of arousing public and investor concern over environmental liabilities. Companies such as Ciba-Geigy, ICI, Mobil, British Petroleum, and Showa Denko have adopted such internal policies on a worldwide basis.[20] In some cases, cognizant of the risks posed by investments in joint ventures like those encountered by Union Carbide at Bhopal, such companies insist on the right to exercise control over environmental matters in joint ventures disproportionate to the size of their ownership interests. In other instances, including potential investments in China, they have walked away from prospective deals because of environmental concerns.

Lenders in international transactions tend to impose strict contractual covenants on borrowers regardless of an investment's situs for their own reasons. Environmental liabilities jeopardize a borrower's repayment capability, a risk that has aroused great concern in the countries of the Organization for Economic Cooperation and Development (OECD) and that is magnified in nonrecourse and limited recourse lending characteristic of project finance and real estate credits. Lenders also are concerned about their own liability should they participate in management in a workout or foreclosure context, a concern that originated from domestic loans in the United States.[21] Loan covenants on environmental matters may be even more stringent when the lenders include multilateral development institutions and bilateral export credit agencies with more rigid loan (and where applicable, investment) approval procedures and, in the case of the World Bank, environmental guidelines with respect to project technology and environmental impact.[22]

As a result of China's economic reforms, which have increased the country's dependence on foreign trade, investment, and credit, it has become subject to external influence by the private sector. A prime example that is emerging in this regard involves standardization. China has long had a standard-setting process to promote commerce, science and technology, and social welfare. The Standardization Law was enacted in 1988, and in 1990 the Implementing Rules Concerning the Standardization Law were promulgated. The Standardization Law authorizes the formulation of standards for the safety and hygiene of industrial products. In Article 8, standardization is encouraged to protect people's health and safety, the rights of consumers, and the environment; promote resource efficiency; popularize scientific and technological advances; facilitate product interchangeability (Article 9); and promote economic and technological cooperation with foreign entities and foreign trade (Article 11). The production, sale, and import of nonconforming products and products that bear an improper appraisal symbol are punishable under law (Articles 20–22). Standards protecting human health and property are mandatory (Article 7). The Implementing Rules provide additional detail on the standard-setting and implementation process. Under these rules, the State Bureau of Quality and Technical Supervision (SBTS), as the administrative department in charge of standardization, metrology, and quality, supervises and coordinates the process. However, concerned departments of the State Council actually lead the drafting, examination, and approval of standards (Article 12). Thus SEPA coordinates standard-setting with respect to environmental matters, which increases its influence over the process relative to production ministries.

China also has established a process for encouraging and regularizing the adoption of international standards to promote technical exchanges, raise product quality, promote international trade, and meet domestic needs under its Procedures on Administering the Adoption of International Standards (for trial implementation).[23] Under the procedures, international standards can be adopted in whole or by reference. The Standardization Law further provides, in Article 4, that the state shall encourage the active adoption of international standards. As of August 1988 approximately 36 percent of all Chinese standards were adopted from international standards.[24]

China also is a member of the International Organization for Standardization (ISO), which has adopted the ISO 14000 series of environmental management standards.[25] ISO is an international organization headquartered in Geneva; it was established in 1946 but is not a United Nations specialized agency. Rather ISO is constituted by designated national standard-setting bodies. The nature of such bodies varies; for example, the British Standards Institute is a private organization; the American National Standards Institute (ANSI) is a private organization that operates in close coordination with government agencies and benefits from extensive technical support from the federal government; the French Association Française de Normalization is essentially a government agency; and China's SBTS is a government agency. At last count, ISO had 118 national standard-setting bodies as members, including 85 full members with voting power. Actions require a two-thirds vote, a supermajority that is, however, less demanding than a unanimity or consensus requirement. All OECD member countries have standard-setting bodies that are full members of ISO. Although China is a full member, most developing countries are nonmembers, correspondent members, or subscriber members.[26]

ISO issues two kinds of standards: specification standards, which facilitate commerce by normalizing product standards, and metastandards, which standardize procedures. For most of its history, ISO activity was confined to specification standards and highly technical metastandards. The value of such activity is readily apparent when one considers a product manufactured without the benefit of an international standard, such as electric plugs, which exhibit great variation among countries and sometimes even within a country. Nevertheless, such activity is highly technical and neither highly visible nor controversial.

The standard-setting process originates in technical committees, of which there are now about 200. If a technical committee does not yet exist, any national standard-setting body, existing technical committee, or other specified entity may propose the formation of a technical committee. Typically, the formation of a new technical committee commences with a report by ISO's senior policymaking body, the Technical Management Board (TMB), to ISO's governing body, the ISO Council. The technical committees are responsible for drafting new standards and revising existing standards for approval by the ISO Council, after which member standard-setting bodies determine whether to adopt such standards on a national basis.

ISO's character began to change in 1987 with adoption of the ISO 9000 series, the first series of soft metastandards, directed in this instance to quality management.[27] ISO 9000 was formulated by TC (Technical Committee) 176, charged with responsibility for quality management and quality assurance, and revised in 1994. The significance of the 9000 series included its impact on foreign trade. A rising number of companies in advanced industrialized countries decided to adhere to the standard, which entails certification by an accepted auditing agency that the company complies with the respective standard or standards. Such certification is conducted on a facility-by-facility basis and typically requires annual, biennial, or triennial audits.

As companies adopted ISO 9000, particularly ISO 9001, which governs design and manufacturing, they increasingly demanded that their suppliers also be certified. As such requirements diffused more widely, exporters in developing countries as well as suppliers in advanced industrialized countries were required to become certified if they were to maintain and expand their markets. Furthermore, many public procurement agencies—particularly in Europe, where the impetus for ISO 9000 had originated—increasingly required that bidders and their suppliers become ISO 9000–certified. Hong Kong, for example, will not accept bids on public contracts valued in excess of Hong Kong (HK) $10 million unless the bidder is ISO 9000–certified.[28]

Such diffusion of the ISO 9000 series also had an effect on accrediting agencies. Although certification may be and is commonly conducted by an auditing agency from the country where the facility is located, this is not an ISO requirement. Thus companies desirous of ISO 9000 certification, particularly in developing countries, may obtain certification from foreign auditing agencies, which may have greater acceptance than local certification. Many governments and, to the extent that they differ, standard-setting bodies encourage the development of a national accreditation industry.

China has endorsed ISO 9000 certification, and the process has become increasingly popular in the PRC. As SBTS Director Li Chuanqing has explained, ISO 9000 certification is promoted by the central government as a means to raise product, construction, and service quality; avoid the imposition of trade and technical barriers against Chinese exports; and raise the quality of enterprise management.[29] Standard GB/T 19001 was adopted in 1992 in conformance with ISO 9001. The China Council for the Quality System (ISO 9000) of the Export Manufacturers, established by the State Administration for the Inspection of Import and Export Commodities and 15 other government agencies and commissions,[30] encourages exporters to become ISO 9000–certified. Accrediting bodies have been established under the China National Accreditation of Certification Bodies, which determines if applicants merit the issuance of a Certificate of Conformity of Quality System Certification. As of year-end 1994, more than 120 state-owned and foreign-invested companies were reported to have been ISO 9000–certified.[31]

The ISO 14000 series reflects a comparable process. The TMB in 1991 created the joint Strategic Advisory Group on the Environment (SAGE) with the International Electrotechnical Commission (IEC),[32] reflecting the desire among some member bodies and ISO staff to explore whether and how ISO should respond to environmental issues. Such concern was heightened by the Business Council for Sustainable Development, an organization of international business leaders, which suggested that ISO play a role at the then impending UNCED to be held in Rio de Janeiro in 1992. SAGE convened four times between June 1991 and June 1993, with participants including businesspeople, consultants, academics, and government officials, as well as representatives of national standard-setting bodies. SAGE was asked to assess the need for international standardization with respect to sustained industrial development and environmental performance and/or management. At its third meeting, in October 1992, SAGE unanimously recommended that the TMB form a new ISO technical committee.

The TMB polled national standard-setting bodies on the proposal, and all 29 respondents voted in favor. ISO thereupon formed Technical Committee 207, with responsibility for standardization in environmental management and systems. TC 207 was directed to liaise with existing technical committees responsible for acoustics (TC 43), air quality (TC 146), water quality (TC 147), soil quality (TC 190), solid wastes (TC 200), and quality management and quality assurance (TC 176), as well as competent international industry and nongovernmental organizations (NGOs). TC 43, TC 146, TC 147, and TC 190 retained exclusive authority over testing methods for pollutants. TC 207 also was barred from drafting standards concerning pollution limits, environmental performance levels, or product standardization; rather it was directed to focus on environmental management tools and systems.

Like ISO activity in general, TC 207 was dominated by the advanced industrialized countries. Canada's national standard-setting body chaired the committee, and the six subcommittees were separately chaired by the counterpart bodies of Great Britain, the Netherlands, the United States, Australia, France, and Norway. Working groups convened by subcommittees to prepare working drafts similarly were chaired by individuals from advanced industrialized countries. Developing countries generally did not participate even in proportion to their overall membership in ISO.

The drafting process generally proceeds on a consensus basis, thereby providing veto power to any member. Working drafts that receive consensus proceed to formal reviews by the technical committee. In a two-stage process, this committee first issues Draft International Standards and then International Standards. In this instance, TC 207 was formed in 1993, and ISO 14001 (Environmental Management System—Specifications with Guidance for Use) was adopted as a Draft International Standard at Oslo in June 1995 and then as an International Standard at Rio de Janeiro in June 1996. Several other standards in the ISO 14000 series have been adopted; at least one has been returned for further consideration; and others remain at various stages in the drafting process. China, unlike most developing countries, has participated throughout the process, sending seven persons to the Oslo meeting and fourteen persons to the Rio de Janeiro meeting.

ISO 14001, the core standard in the series, establishes five requirements for certification:

1. The existence of an appropriate environmental policy for each facility, including commitments to continual improvement and prevention of pollution and to compliance with relevant environmental legislation and regulations and voluntary requirements, is documented and communicated to all employees for implementation and is available to the public.

2. Conformance assessments with respect to environmental objectives and legal and voluntary requirements.

3. Management systems to check compliance with the environmental policy statement.

4. Periodic internal audits and reports to top management.

5. A public declaration of ISO 14001 status.

ISO 14001 is the foundation of the ISO 14000 series but has been subject to criticism from several quarters, particularly environmental NGOs that did not recognize its potential significance until relatively late in the process and may have been handicapped in their ability to participate by the ISO structure, the complexity of the subject matter, and the logistics of attending many meetings held at various locations around the world over several years.[33] (Table 9–2 presents the complete ISO 14000 series in its current formulation.)

Environmental NGOs have criticized ISO 14000, particularly 14001, because it is a management rather than a performance standard. ISO 14000 focuses on management rather than compliance except with respect to a compliance commitment by management, and such a compliance commitment is bounded by applicable regulations and voluntary obligations. Thus a company and/or any of its facilities could be

**Table 9–2.    The ISO 14000 Series**

ORGANIZATION EVALUATION STANDARDS

| | |
|---|---|
| ISO 14001: | Environmental Management System—Specification with Guidance for Use |
| ISO 14004: | Environmental Management Systems—General Guidelines on Principles, Systems and Supporting Techniques |
| ISO 14010: | Guidelines for Environmental Auditing—General Principles on EA |
| ISO 14011/1: | Guidelines for Environmental Auditing—Audit Procedures<br>Part 1: Auditing of Environmental Management Systems |
| ISO 14012: | Guidelines for Environmental Auditing—Qualifications Criteria for Environmental Auditors |
| ISO 14013: | Management for Environmental Audit Programs (deleted from TC 207 Agenda—no further work scheduled) |
| ISO 14014: | Initial Reviews (deleted from TC 207 Agenda) |
| ISO 14015: | Environmental Site Assessments |
| ISO 14031: | Evaluation of the Environmental Performance of the Management System and Its Relationship to the Environment |
| ISO 1403X: | Evaluation of the Environmental Performance of the Operational System and Its Relationship to the Environment |

PRODUCTION EVALUATION STANDARDS

| | |
|---|---|
| ISO 14020: | Goals and Principles of All Environmental Labeling |
| ISO 14021: | Environmental Labels and Declarations (ELD) Self-declaration Environmental Claims—Terms and Definitions |
| ISO 14022: | ELD—Self-declaration Environmental Claims—Symbols |
| ISO 14023: | ELD—Self-declaration Environmental Claims—Testing & Verification |
| ISO 14024: | ELD—Environmental Labeling Type I Guiding Principles and Procedures |
| ISO 1402x: | ELD—Environmental Labeling Type III |
| ISO 14040: | Life Cycle Assessment—Principles and Practices |
| ISO 14041: | Life Cycle Assessment—Life Cycle Inventory Analysis |
| ISO 14042: | Life Cycle Assessment—Impact Assessment |
| ISO 14043: | Life Cycle Assessment—Interpretation |
| ISO 14050: | Terms and Definitions—Guide on the Principles for ISO/TC 207/SC6 Terminology |
| ISO 14060: | Guide for the Inclusion of Environmental Aspects in Product Standards (reassigned to ISO Guide 64—no longer a standard) |

ISO 14001–certified even though it does not comply with applicable standards, is subject to compliance obligations that are less stringent than international standards, or otherwise fails to provide adequate assurances with respect to environmental quality. Some industry leaders themselves have objected to ISO 14000 because it imposes an additional, quasi-regulatory burden and may benefit companies with weaker policies to implement.[34]

Such criticism is largely misplaced with respect to China, where the problem now is less due to a failure to adopt appropriate environmental legislation and regulations. Statutes, regulations, and standards are becoming increasingly numerous, comprehensive, and stringent. China also has increased the number of regulatory personnel to more than 80,000, with over 200,000 more employed in regulated industries and other sectors of society. Furthermore, although the standard-setting process is less open than that of the United States, where any interested party from industry, government, business, or NGOs may participate in a technical advisory group,[35] the process in China generally is open to input from experts as well as government officials and business.

Rather, to Chinese officials, the biggest problem is inadequate implementation or enforcement.[36] ISO 14001 and the entire ISO 14000 series can help in this regard by encouraging Chinese companies, directly and through pressure from purchasers of their products and services, to adopt environmental policies at the top management level, commit to complying with applicable regulatory requirements, dedicate resources to implement environmental management systems, and make a public declaration of their ISO 14001 status. Such measures establish benchmarks for environmental policy performance and require periodic, formal management review of environmental management systems. SEPA has established the Office of Environmental Management Systems to lead such work and has conducted trial certifications in five enterprises. At least one environmental management and consulting center has been established in part to conduct ISO 14000 certification. Such self-implementation can ease the burden on regulators and foster corporate cultures of compliance. SEPA and SBTS have jointly established the State Leading Committee on the Certification of China's Environmental Management Systems[37] to conducting educational activities, convene conferences on ISO 14000, and organize certifying agencies. China also convened an international conference on ISO in the fall of 1996 to increase awareness of certification.

In addition, China has taken measures to improve its environmental auditing practices, which is included in the ISO 14000 series. It has established a pilot program with UNEP and World Bank support to conduct cleaner production audits under the auspices of the China National Cleaner Production Center, a new entity established under the Chinese Research Academy of Environmental Sciences. This center may serve as a foundation for the establishment of an environmental audit service industry.[38]

Membership in the World Trade Organization (WTO) also will involve China in a set of commercially related environmental standards. The Final Agreement of the General Agreement on Tariffs and Trade (GATT, 1994), which is the foundation of the WTO, provides that international standards (voluntary guidelines approved by a recognized body such as ISO) are an important contribution to production efficiency and the conduct of international trade, and hence do not constitute impermissible trade barriers.[39] The WTO also allows that appropriate standards promulgated by other relevant international organizations (such as ISO) open for membership to WTO members may apply to sanitary and phytosanitary measures with respect to human, animal, and plant health not otherwise addressed by the Codex Alimentarius under the Food and Agriculture Organization (FAO), the World Health Organization (WHO), the International Office of Epizootics, or the International Plant Protection Convention.[40] Although the ISO 14000 series has not yet been determined to qualify as such standards under the WTO, it would appear that standards set by a national standard-setting body that conform to or are less stringent than ISO 14000 would not be deemed to be trade barriers. Therefore, failure to become ISO 14000–certified could constitute a basis for restricting imports from China.

In addition to standard-setting and international trade agreements, the private sector may influence policy through commercial contracts. Environmental risk management is now an accepted part of the basic credit process in most industrialized and traditional economies.[41] A borrower under a loan contract or indenture typically will be required to represent that it is in compliance with all applicable laws and regulations and covenant that it will comply with such requirements and indemnify the lender against all environmental liabilities. Indeed, under pressure from SEPA and others, the Chinese government has sought to harness the power of contractual obligations to induce borrowers to raise their environmental compliance. Under Article 24(2)(v) of the General Provisions on Loans (People's Bank of China 1996), China's banks are prohibited from extending credit for projects lacking environmental approvals.[42] Contractual provisions have relatively broader scope, which in principle apply not only to matters of compliance but also even to future liabilities, regardless of regulatory enforcement. To protect themselves against such liability, borrowers in theory seek to minimize their risk by implementing tighter controls and/or purchasing insurance coverage.

## Policy Implications

China is a ready participant in international environmental regimes and has procedures in place to establish policymaking bodies and coordinate various agencies in order to formulate positions and implement strategies with respect to such regimes. Yet it remains concerned lest such regimes infringe on its sovereignty and hamper its development potential. China is not a simple naysayer or violator of its international obligations, however. Rather, it has embarked on a long-term course to formulate and implement increasingly stringent environmental policies. Because of the country's importance with respect to the solution of global and regional problems, it is particularly important that China continue along such a track and further increase its participation in international environmental regimes on a positive basis. From this perspective, the following policy implications emerge.

### SANCTIONS

China's determination to develop its economy by safeguarding its access to export markets and continuing to be an attractive destination for foreign investment can make sanctions an effective incentive for participation and compliance. The Montreal Protocol[43] and the Convention on International Trade in Endangered Species of Wild Flora and Fauna (1973) as well as domestic legislation of importing countries such as the United States[44] contain provisions for such sanctions. As noted earlier, however, the scope of such sanctions is restricted, and they are difficult to apply under international environmental regimes. Private and quasi-private measures such as the standard-setting process provide a less-direct but broader means for discouraging nonconformist behavior by imposing trade barriers to substandard and otherwise nonconforming products. The ISO 14000 series creates new standards with the potential for restricting trade in products and services from noncertified facilities.[45] Except for certain labor standards and standards applicable to products derived from wildlife, international standards generally do not govern the process of manufacture (and would be of questionable enforceability under WTO) and in that sense do not address pollution arising in the manufacturing process. ISO 14000, however, has the potential to reduce environmental harms by addressing management systems and compliance policies.

## SCIENTIFIC AND TECHNOLOGICAL COOPERATION

China continues to maintain barriers to the free flow of information, as evidenced by the expulsion of foreign Greenpeace activists in 1996 and restrictions on the press. Nevertheless, information on scientific and technological matters is more widely available, and there are few barriers to receiving such information and acting upon it. The standard-setting process illustrates how novel ways of managing production and fostering compliance with government regulations on an autonomous basis can be diffused into China with minimal opposition, even though they may affect domestic policy implementation and raise compliance costs. Under such circumstances, maintaining and expanding scientific and technical exchanges would help to influence Chinese policymaking further in accordance with the norms and practices of international environmental regimes, without arousing ideological or nationalistic opposition.

## SHARING THE COSTS OF ENVIRONMENTAL PROTECTION

In R. H. Coase's classic treatment of externalities, equally efficient outcomes could be obtained regardless of whether the polluter or the victim assumes the burden of remedial action.[46] This seemingly amoral analysis of environmental problems may be ethically or politically objectionable if the quest is to apportion the costs of environmental pollution on the basis of culpability—for example, the polluter pays principle, to which China itself subscribes.[47] Foreign subsidies may appear morally more acceptable as well as Coasian-efficient when the issues are fundamentally nonjusticiable or the procedures for adjudicating disputes are so cumbersome as to be impractical, as typically is the case in international environmental regimes. This is particularly likely when the victim is both richer than the polluter and less tolerant of environmental harms. China has established the Trans-Century Green Project to solicit funds in this regard and claims to have received $3 billion in foreign financial support through this facility.[48] Such costs can be financed through external assistance and export credits on a bilateral basis, as Japan in particular,[49] the United States to a much lesser extent,[50] and other countries are doing, or multilaterally through the GEF and facilities like the Montreal Protocol Fund,[51] the scope of which has been expanded to include climate change and biodiversity to varying degrees. Therefore, if the United States and the world as a whole wish to foster environmental protection in China, they should be prepared not only to share knowledge with China but also to provide training on a subsidized basis to enhance that country's technical capacity and otherwise provide funds to ease the financial burden of environmental protections.[52] As others have noted, the United States can do more in this regard by relaxing cold war restrictions on the involvement of the Agency for International Development (AID) and the United States–Asia Environmental Partnership in China.[53] Such programs also can provide support for exporters of environmental goods and services.[54] This implication does not necessarily provide any direct solace to poorer victims, however. To the extent that Chinese externalities harm poorer neighbors such as Laos, Myanmar, and Vietnam, it is unlikely that such countries could help to finance China's costs of environmental protection. However, China's commitment to compliance not just with national environmental regulations but also with bilateral and multilateral environmental agreements and the environmental requirements of multilateral development banks in the Tumen River Economic Development Area and relevant areas of Northeast Asia indicates a determination to cooperate with its neighbors on behalf of environmentally responsible economic developments.[55] Furthermore, this recommendation does not call for the issuance of blank checks but rather for providing carefully targeted assistance to achieve the goals of international environmental regimes with direct benefit to the donor[56] while gradually weaning China away from such subsidies as its economy develops.

## PREVENTING FREE RIDING AND EXTORTION

Although the preceding policy implication may be attractive to China because of its cost-sharing promise, it presents potential free-rider and extortion problems and is subject to budgetary limitations. With respect to free riding, China like any other polluter could act with impunity in the face of problems affecting its neighbors or the global commons in the expectation that richer countries or the world as a whole would then take corrective measures. In terms of extortion, a polluter could threaten its neighbors or the global commons unless payments were made to induce better behavior. China would be in an excellent position to make such threats because of its size and strategic importance. As we have seen, China has demanded that developed countries make larger financial contributions and reductions in pollution in order to resolve global environmental problems, as in the control of ozone-depleting substances. However, such behavior does not appear to constitute a tendency to free ride but rather reflects a demand for cost sharing and additional time to develop its own economy, a perspective that has been reflected in certain international environmental agreements.[57] In other words, China generally has not denied the existence of particular environmental problems, challenged the merits of consensual solutions to such problems, or refused to contribute to their resolution, but it has disputed the amount and terms of its contributions. Evidence against any proclivity to extortion may be found in China's general tendency to become party to international agreements, the paucity of reservations in Chinese accession and ratification instruments with respect to environmental agreements, and domestic environmental statutes that contain express treaty supremacy provisions. China has, in fact, criticized the United States and other countries on environmental grounds for exporting harmful products to it; China consequently tightened controls on the import of waste products.[58] One American has been convicted of violating customs regulations with respect to the importation of waste products, and several cargoes have been rejected.[59]

To address this issue from a different perspective, China over time has attached greater importance to environmental protection in its domestic policy. While the pace and breadth of China's policy changes in this regard are far from sufficient, they constitute substantial progress and are occurring at an earlier stage of economic development than generally has been the case in advanced industrialized countries. This is partly a matter of self-interest, because China itself typically is the biggest and most proximate victim of its own behavior.[60] Part of the explanation is the diffusion of knowledge. To the extent that environmental quality is a universal value rooted in scientific knowledge, the Chinese elite, government, and, less directly, population at large have become more supportive of environmental protection programs and more accepting of some restrictions to their behavior.[61] There is even some evidence that certain Chinese leaders would prefer to create a highly sanitary and environmentally clean, albeit politically controlled, society like Singapore.[62] Of course, some of China's environmental loadings will continue to increase as the population and economy expand, and new environmental concerns will emerge. International NGOs can monitor China's compliance with international environmental agreements, providing critical and even embarrassing information that can further spur compliance in a manner that neither domestic environmentalists nor the Environmental and Resources Protection Committee of the National People's Congress (NPC) can accomplish at present.[63] On the whole, enhancing communication with China through both official and unofficial channels is likely to raise environmental consciousness and reduce any tendency toward free riding or extortion.

## INFLUENCING CHINA'S ENVIRONMENTAL DIPLOMATS

As Samuel Kim has observed in Chapter 2, China's U.N. diplomacy and, by extension, its participation in international regimes generally has been characterized by a high degree of passivity or aloofness. Because of China's size, such conduct may impede the negotiation of international agreements and preserve the status quo at the expense of environmental quality. Although other countries do not have direct influence over Chinese foreign policy, the technical nature of environmental issues provides some opportunity to shape the perspective of Chinese diplomats. Specifically, some members of China's diplomatic teams involved in environmental issues are seconded from SEPA and other agencies, such as the State Administration of Oceanography, that tend to be more favorably disposed to environmental protection than the Ministry of Foreign Affairs. In some cases, too, these agencies occupy lead positions in negotiations; for example, SEPA shared coordinating responsibility with the Ministry of Foreign Affairs with respect to the Agenda 21 negotiations. SEPA also generally welcomes international attention to enhance its own influence within China's government. Senior SEPA officials have indicated interest in training programs in international relations to enhance their capabilities and to increase SEPA's leverage at home against rival agencies. Such programs are likely to be most effective when sponsored by multilaterals or NGOs. However, the United States could take a modest step in this regard by preparing an international training module on environmental diplomacy.[64]

If such training programs can be established or expanded, it may be possible to influence both individual diplomats and, indirectly, China's positions on environmental issues. Examples that may be susceptible to such influence is the transfer of nuclear technology to other countries and tests of nuclear devices for ostensibly peaceful purposes.

## FOREIGN INVESTMENT

In addition to opportunities in the environmental industry itself,[65] many transnational businesses already recognize the necessity and even the desirability of establishing and adhering to high standards of environmental compliance. Their motivation is a product of heightened environmental awareness, risk aversion, public- and investor-relations consciousness, increased pressure to disclose material environmental facts to the investing public, and competitive pressures. One way that transnational businesses can influence China is by insisting that their facilities there adhere to the same high standards that they impose elsewhere. Another way may be to impose an ISO 14000 certification requirement on their suppliers, which will encourage Chinese businesses to become certified in order to qualify as vendors of goods and services. This is particularly important to the extent that China's current problems are due to implementational shortcomings as opposed to statutory and regulatory deficiencies. Furthermore, as foreign investment has increased, many foreign investors themselves have become more aware of the compliance burdens imposed by the current Chinese regulatory regime. For example, some American companies, particularly concerned about potential long-tail Superfund-style liability, have been storing their toxic and hazardous wastes on-site or disposing of them very carefully even before enactment of the Solid Waste Law and pending implementing regulations thereunder. As the amount of foreign investment increases, the growing market for waste treatment and disposal services is encouraging the establishment of appropriate facilities that will be available to domestic as well as foreign-invested enterprises. To foster such private-sector involvement, foreign companies should continue to share information on an informal basis and work with their Chinese counterparts through business associations to address common problems, raise each other's consciousness, and, not incidentally, prevent Chinese companies from acquiring competitive regulatory advantages.

# Notes

1.  Michel Oksenberg and Elizabeth Economy, "China: Implementation under Economic Growth and Market Reform," November 1995 draft.

2.  The North American Agreement on Environmental Cooperation among the United States, Canada, and Mexico is an exception. Adopted as part of the NAFTA accord, this agreement provides that one party may make a submission to the commission that another party is failing to enforce its own environmental laws, and also requires that each party provide private judicial remedies for environmental harms. See International Court of the Environment Foundation, *The Global Environmental Crisis: The Need for An International Court of the Environment* (Florence, Italy: Giunti Gruppo Editoriale, 1996).

3.  U.S. General Accounting Office, *International Environment: International Agreements Are Not Well Monitored* (Washington, D.C.: January 1992).

4.  Robert O. Keohane, Peter M. Haas, and Marc A. Levy, "The Effectiveness of International Environmental Institutions," in Haas, Keohane, and Levy, eds., *Institutions for the Earth: Sources of Effective International Environmental Protection* (Cambridge, Mass.: The MIT Press, 1993), p. 14.

5.  Abram Chayes and Antonia Handler Chayes, *The New Sovereignty: Compliance with International Regulatory Agreements* (Cambridge, Mass.: Harvard University Press, 1995), pp. 6–8.

6.  Lynton Keith Caldwell, *International Environmental Policy: Emergence and Dimensions* (Durham, N.C.: Duke University Press, 1984); *Peking Review,*

June 23, 1972, p. 8; Lester Ross, *Environmental Policy in China* (Bloomington, Ind.: Indiana University Press, 1988), p. 137.

7. Keohane, Haas and Levy, "Effectiveness of International Environmental Institutions," p. 16, classify states into four categories: *laggards,* which (1) avoid international obligations or (2) accept such obligations but fail to comply with them; and *leaders,* which (3) comply with such obligations or (4) lead others to exceed such obligations and assume additional obligations.

8. "Noise Pollution Law on the Way in China," *China Environment News,* September 15, 1996, p. 1.

9. These and other accomplishments in this regard are recited in "White Paper on China's Environmental Protection," *People's Daily,* June 5, 1996, pp. 1 ff. Spending is projected to increase to 1.5 percent of GDP by 2000, up from 0.7 to 0.8 percent at present. Ma Chenguang, "Plan for Greener Future," *China Daily,* December 16, 1995, p. 1.

10. Li Peng, "Protecting the Environment Is a Major Task Facing China," in Lester Ross and Mitchell A. Silk, eds., *Environmental Law and Policy in the People's Republic of China* (Westport, Conn.: Greenwood Press, 1987), pp. 35–43.

11. Jiang Zemin, "Speech at the Fourth National Environmental Protection Conference," *People's Daily,* overseas ed., July 19, 1996, p. 1.

12. Peter M. Haas with Jan Sundgren, "Evolving International Environmental Law: Changing Practices of National Sovereignty," in Nazli Choucri, ed., *Global Accord: Environmental Challenges and International Responses* (Cambridge, Mass.: MIT Press, 1993), pp. 405, 410–411.

13. Haas with Sundgren, pp. 416–417.

14. Principle 21, United Nations Conference on the Human Environment.

15. "Priority Given to Animal, Plant Sanctuaries," *China Daily,* June 5, 1996, p. 4.

16. Office of the State Climate Change Coordinating Small Group, "Conditions for Developing Follow-on Work to the Framework Convention on Climate Change," December 20, 1992, in State Committee on Environmental Protection, ed., *Compendium of Documents of the State Committee on Environmental Protection* (Beijing: China Environmental Science Press, 1992), vol. 2, p. 569.

17. Jan Fuglestvedt et al., "A Review of Country Case Studies on Climate Change," *Global Environment Facility Working Paper,* No. 7, (Washington, D.C.: 1994), p. 30.

18. Lin Zongtang, "Explanation of the 'Air Pollution Prevention and Control Law of the People's Republic of China (Revised Draft)'" (October 21, 1994), in *Gazette of the National People's Congress of the People's Republic of China* (1995), p. 547.

19.    Oksenberg and Economy, "China."

20.    United Nations Conference on Trade and Development (UNCTAD), *Self-regulation of Environmental Management* (Geneva: United Nations, 1996); Sir David Simon, The British Petroleum Company, "Corporate Responsibility, Profitability & the Public Good," paper presented at the World Bank/International Monetary Fund annual meeting seminar program 1996, Washington, D.C., September 28, 1996. The Clinton administration has encouraged U.S. businesses to adopt and implement voluntary codes of conduct for doing business around the world, including such areas as environmental protection and environmental practices. *Model Business Principles*, May 26, 1995.

21.    See especially *United States* v. *Fleet Factors*, 901 F.2d 1550 (11th Cir. 1990); Jaret Seiberg, "Banks Learn Cleanup Liability Fears the Hard Way," *American Banker*, June 6, 1995, p. 3. Lender concerns were alleviated in part by the Asset Conservation, Lender Liability, and Deposit Insurance Protection Act of 1996, enacted into law as Title 11, Subtitle E, of the FY 1997 Defense Appropriations Act. The new law exempts lenders from the definition of "owner or operator" from Superfund liability so long as the lender does not "participate in the management" of the property prior to foreclosure. Fiduciary liability also is limited under the new law. U.S. Cong. Conf. Rpt. 104–863, September 28, 1996.

22.    World Bank, *Operational Manual*, Part 4; *Industrial Pollution Prevention & Abatement Handbook* (preliminary version, July 1995); Export-Import Bank of the United States, *Environmental Procedures and Guidelines*, Washington, D.C., April 2, 1996.

23.    State Economic Commission, State Science and Technology Commission and State Administration of Standards 1982. The scope of international standards provided includes (1) international standards set by (a) international standard-setting organizations, namely the International Organization for Standardization and the International Electrotechnical Commission, and (b) U.N. agencies such as the International Telecommunications Union and standards established by international agreement; and (2) advanced foreign standards set by (a) regional standard-setting organizations such as the European Committee for Standardization, (b) national standard-setting bodies in advanced industrialized countries such as the United States and (c) internationally recognized standard-setting organizations such as the American Society for Testing and Materials, the American Petroleum Institute, and Underwriters' Laboratories.

24.    "Editor's Note to Standardization Law," *China Law and Practice* 3, No. 2: 54.

25.    This section draws heavily on UNCTAD, *ISO 14000: International Environmental Management Systems Standards: Five Key Questions for Developing Country Officials* (Geneva: United Nations, 1996 draft).

26.    Correspondent members are organizations with observer status that do not qualify as national standard-setting bodies. Subscriber members are

national standard-setting organizations from small countries and have limited participation rights.

27. For more on ISO 9000, see Robert W. Peach, ed., *The ISO 9000 Handbook* (Fairfax, Va.: CEEM Information Services, 1992).

28. *International Environmental Systems Update*, 3, No. 4 (1996), p. 20.

29. Ma Zhiping, "Revised ISO 9000 Series Discussed," *China Daily*, April 22, 1995, p. 2.

30. Announcement No. 1, 1995, *China Daily*, April 26, 1995, p. 3. The SBTS has its own mandate to verify that products satisfy quality standards. "Products Must Attain Standards of Quality," *China Daily*, September 28, 1995, p. 4.

31. Qiu Qi, "100 Chinese Firms Aim for ISO Quality Standard," *China Daily*, May 29, 1995, p. 5.

32. Established in 1906, the IEC sets international standards for electrical equipment and electronic products. China is a member of the IEC. Vice Premier Wu Bangguo has stated in an address to an IEC advisory body that China must adopt international standards and raise product quality to be successful in international markets. Ma Zhiping, "Experts Discuss Standardization," *China Daily*, May 23, 1995, p. 2.

33. See, for example, Daniel C. Esty, *Greening the GATT: Trade, Environment and the Future* (Washington, D.C.: Institute for International Economics, 1994), p. 173 n. 30. ("ISO procedures have only limited opportunities for public involvement. More disturbingly, the only representatives at many meetings are invited business representatives from the industry to be regulated.")

34. "ISO 14001 Should Not Be Required by Law or Regulation, Attorney Says," *BNA: Daily Executive Report*, February 14, 1996, p. A-23. The United States and other countries have charged that China itself uses standards and certification practices as trade barriers. JayEtta Z. Hecker, "International Trade: Challenges and Opportunities for U.S. Business in China," Testimony before the House Committee on Banking and Financial Services, (July 29, 1996, U.S. General Accounting Office GAO/T-NSIAD-96-214).

35. U.S. Environmental Protection Agency, *ISO 14000: International Environmental Management Standards* (Washington, D.C.: EPA, 1995).

36. Oksenberg and Economy, "China."

37. "Our Country Develops Environmental Management Systems Standards and Certification," *People's Daily*, overseas ed., July 13, 1996, p. 5.

38. NEPA, China National Cleaner Production Center, *United Nations Environment Programme Industry and Environment*, and World Bank, *Cleaner Production in China: A Story of Successful Cooperation* (Paris: United Nations, 1996).

39. *Agreement on Technical Barriers to Trade*, MTN/FA II-A1A-6, p. 1.

40. *Agreement on the Application of Sanitary and Phytosanitary Measures*, MTN/FA II-AIA-4, Annex A.

41. United Nations Environment Programme, *UNEP Global Survey: Environmental Policies and Practices of the Financial Services Sector* (Nairobi: United Nations, 1996), p. 9.

42. See also Decisions Regarding Certain Problems in Environmental Protection, State Council August 3, 1996, Sec. 3.

43. See Oksenberg and Economy, "China."

44. U.S. sanctions under the Pelly Amendment to the Fishermen's Protective Act of 1967, 22 U.S.C. § 1978, were applied against Taiwan in 1994 and lifted on September 11, 1996. Chinese regulations to curb illegal international trade in endangered species are being drafted by the Endangered Species Import and Export Managing Office under the State Council. Chen Chunmei, "State Curbs Illicit Wildlife Trade," *China Daily*, May 17, 1996, p. 2.

45. Stephen L. Kass, "ISO Plans Uniform Standards," *National Law Journal*, November 6, 1995, p. C4 ("ISO 14000 sponsors can have considerable confidence that their efforts will survive challenges under both the Uruguay Round agreements and NAFTA.").

46. R. H. Coase, "The Problem of Social Cost," *Journal of Law and Economics* 3, No. 1 (1960): 30–34; Robert D. Cooter, "Economic Theories of Legal Liability," *Journal of Economic Perspectives* 5, (1991): 16–21.

47. Decisions Regarding Certain Problems, Sec. 7.

48. Liu Yinglang, "'Green' Fund Increasing," *China Daily*, November 24, 1995, p. 1.

49. Peter Evans, "Japan's Green Aid," *China Business Review* 21, No. 4 (July–August 1994): 39.

50. Vanessa Lide Whitcomb, "A Cleaner Tiger," *China Business Review* 21, No. 4 (July–August 1994): 44.

51. Instrument for the Establishment of the Restructured Global Environment Facility (September 1994). On the U.S. decision to fund the Montreal Protocol Fund under pressure from other countries, see Richard J. Smith, "The Ozone Layer and Beyond—Towards a Global Environmental Diplomacy," paper presented to the American Chemical Society, August 24, 1994. China was among the few developing countries participating in the establishment of GEF to support the principle that all participants should contribute to the core fund, regardless of their level of development. Helen Sjöberg, "From Idea to Reality: The Creation of the Global Environment Facility," *Global Environment Facility Working Paper* No. 10 (Washington, D.C.: GEF, 1994), p. 30. China's contribution is in the minimum amount of 4 million SDRs.

52. Chayes and Chayes, *The New Sovereignty*.

53. David M. Lampton, "Chinese Security Objectives and U.S. Interests in Policy," Testimony before the House Committee on National Security, March 20, 1996. 104th Cong., 2d Sess.

54. Other examples are the Environmental Trade Working Group, co-chaired by the Department of Commerce and Environmental Protection Agency, and the Office of Environmental Technologies Exports within the Department of Commerce. Trade Promotion Coordinating Committee Environmental Trade Working Group, *China: Environmental Technologies Export Market Plan* (Washington, D.C.: U.S. Department of Commerce, International Trade Administration, 1996).

55. Framework Agreement for Environmental Protection Governing the Tumen River Economic Development Area and Northeast Asia, December 19, 1995; Memorandum of Understanding on Environmental Principles Governing the Tumen River Economic Development Area and Northeast Asia, May 30, 1995.

56. See also Oksenberg and Economy, "China."

57. Article 4(2) of the Framework Convention establishes different commitments for developed country parties and other parties.

58. Law on the Prevention and Control of Pollution of the Environment by Solid Waste (1995), Articles 24–25; Notice Regarding Strictly Controlling the Transmission of Hazardous Wastes into China from Abroad, State Council Office November 7, 1995; Notice Regarding Strictly Controlling the Transmission of Hazardous Wastes into China from Abroad [91] Huanguanzi No. 098, NEPA and General Administration of Customs, March 7, 1991; "Emergency Meeting Lays Down Garbage Law," *China Daily*, May 30, 1996, p. 2.

59. Seth Faison, "China Convicts American as Trash Smuggler," *New York Times*, January 14, 1997, p. A3.

60. NEPA, State Planning Commission, United Nations Development Programme, and World Bank, *China: Issues and Options in Greenhouse Gas Emissions Control*, Summary Report (Washington, D.C.: World Bank, 1994), p. 56. One study estimates that pollution costs amount to 3 percent of gross national product. "Quantified Index Set 1992 Pollution Losses at 100b," *China Environment News*, November 15, 1996, p. 3.

61. Yufan Hao, "Environmental Protection and Chinese Foreign Policy," in Thomas W. Robinson, ed., *The Foreign Relations of China's Environmental Policy* (Washington, D.C.: American Enterprise Institute, 1992), pp. 157–158.

62. Jasper Becker, "Journey through Jiang's Utopia," *South China Morning Post International Weekly*, February 3, 1996, p. 7 (describing Zhangjiagang County).

63. Oksenberg and Economy, "China."

64. United States Environmental Protection Agency, Washington, D.C.—Office of International Activities, *International Training Modules: Information Catalogue*, 1996.

65. E.g., Sun Hong, "Foreign Investment Sought for Ecology Protection," *China Daily*, August 7, 1995, p. B8.

# Appendix A

## Chinese Nuclear and Conventional Weapons

### JAMES MULVENON

### Doctrine and Capabilities

Since mid-1985 the doctrine, strategy, and tactics of the People's Liberation Army (PLA) have focused on combating "local, limited wars" (*jubu zhanzheng*) around China's periphery.[1] Specifically, the PLA might fight (1) small-scale conflicts restricted to contested border territory, (2) conflicts over territorial seas and islands, (3) surprise air attacks, (4) defenses against deliberately limited attacks into Chinese territory, and (5) punitive counterattacks launched by Chinese into enemy territory to "oppose invasion, protect sovereignty, or to uphold justice and dispel threats."[2] This doctrine represented a fundamental paradigm shift in war preparation (*zhanbei*) from the earlier threat of an "early, major, and nuclear war" with either of the superpowers, the probability of which was perceived to be declining throughout the 1980s. It also called into question the efficacy of the Maoist doctrine of "people's war," which had guided Chinese military strategy since the revolutionary era.

China's current military doctrine, by contrast, emphasizes "active peripheral defense" (more akin to a traditional notion of positional warfare) and rapid power projection. One key element of this new strategy is technology, which, as illustrated by the 1991 Gulf war, effectively nullifies China's traditional advantage in manpower. To rectify this situation, the Chinese have placed a high priority on the development of air and naval electronic warfare systems, improved missile and aircraft guidance systems, precision-guided munitions, the construction of communications and early-warning satellites, and in-flight refueling technology. The second key element is speed, in terms of both reaction to enemy moves and offensive assaults. This emphasis on mobility is largely a reaction to the increasing influence of technology on the modern battlefield. The Chinese perceive that modern technology allows the aggressor to seize the initiative in the opening phases of the battle, doubling the importance of a speedy counterattack. To this end, the Chinese have paid great attention to the development of rapid reaction units (also known as fist units, or *quantou*).

Translating these theoretical changes in military doctrine to capabilities, however, is constrained by China's budgetary situation and by a variety of internal organizational, process, and attitudinal problems. High rates of inflation largely nullified the large increases in the Chinese defense budget in the late 1980s and early 1990s, limiting the ability of the military leadership to develop or purchase modern weapons systems. China's military research and development, manufacturing, and organizational structure is plagued by a variety of problems that likely will hinder the full implementation of its military modernization program for many years. These include excessive adherence to self-reliance as a guiding principle; a lack of horizontal integration; separation from the civilian commercial sector; a lack of skilled experts, managers, and labor; poor infrastructure; and technology absorption problems.[3]

## Nuclear Weapons

Chinese nuclear doctrine has been a fertile subject of debate among Western analysts. Some describe China's past nuclear strategy as a policy of "minimum deterrence."[4] "Minimum deterrence" hinges on the belief that China's limited number of nuclear warheads are a credible deterrent because they can inflict what is perceived to be unacceptable damage on a handful of enemy cities with a simple, undifferentiated countervalue second strike ("city busting"). "Minimum deterrence," therefore, ignores the qualitative and quantitative disparities between the Chinese and enemy arsenals, gambling that the potential loss of even one city is enough to deter the adversary from escalatory action.

However, Iain Johnston has identified a potential new nuclear doctrine, known as "limited deterrence" (*you xian wei she*), in the writings of Chinese strategists. "Limited deterrence" relies on a limited flexible response capability, which in turn requires "sufficient counterforce and countervalue tactical, theater and strategic nuclear forces to deter the escalation of conventional or nuclear war."[5] If this deterrence fails, then "limited deterrence" dictates that this capability should be sufficient to control escalation and to compel the enemy to back down. This doctrine is essentially similar to the Kennedy-era doctrine of flexible response, which posits a range of strategic and substrategic capabilities to deter any level of nuclear conflict and in a nuclear war to contain escalatory pressures. This doctrine requires a nuclear force capable of hitting a range of countervalue and counterforce targets, including enemy strategic nuclear missiles, conventional military bases and troop concentrations, transport hubs, and command-and-control centers. Realistically, "limited deterrence" requires a much larger and more technologically advanced arsenal than the Chinese currently have; thus it is possible that Chinese deterrence theorists may be using their abstract framework as a justification for a renewed nuclear arms buildup. This potential nuclear buildup causes concern among observers.

Although China does not now have the capability to prosecute a limited deterrence strategy, such a doctrine might provide a possible guidepost for the direction of the nation's future nuclear force modernization. The nuclear arsenal of the People's Republic (PRC) is much more comparable to the arsenals of nuclear powers such as France and Great Britain than to the massive stockpiles of the United States or the former Soviet Union. (Even if START II is ratified, the ratio will still be 10 to 1.) The PRC has roughly 300 strategic missiles, with ranges up to 14,500 kilometers. Currently land-based missiles are the strongest leg of the Chinese strategic triad. Developed during the 1960s and 1970s, this family of missiles are designated *Dong Feng*, or "East Wind": DF-3, DF-4, DF-5A (known in the West as CSS-2, CSS-3, and CSS-4). The DF-3, a single-stage, liquid-propellant intermediate-range ballistic missile (IRBM), was China's first indigenously designed ballistic missile and was built originally to target U.S. forces in the Philippines, although now it may be targeted against population centers in central or eastern Russia and possibly India. The DF-4 is a multiple-stage, liquid-fuel missile that can reach U.S. forces on Guam but is now deployed in China's western provinces and is capable of hitting Moscow. In mid-1981 the Chinese deployed the DF-5, which was the first genuine Chinese intercontinental ballistic missile (ICBM) capable of hitting targets in the continental United States. Its improved follow-on, the DF-5A, has a longer range (8,000 miles) and an even more destructive payload (4–5 megatons), and currently is deployed in hardened underground silos.[6]

Most reports suggest that this force is technologically obsolete and capable of effective attacks against only large, soft countervalue targets, such as metropolitan cities. The warheads are far too large for tactical warfighting purposes, and the entire supporting system of command, control, communications, and intelligence (C[3]I), including early warning, attack assessment, and battle management, is either obsolete or nonexistent.[7] As a result, most analysts believe that China's missile, submarine,

**Table A1–1.   Estimated Chinese Nuclear Force, 1998**

| Designation (US) | Type[a] | Number | Range (km) | Payload | CEP[b] |
|---|---|---|---|---|---|
| DF-3/3A (CSS-2) | IRBM | 50–60 | 310 | 2/1–3 MT | 2–3.5m |
| DF-4 (CSS-3) | IRBM | 10–20 | 5,500–6,300 | 3 MT | 2–5m |
| DF-5/5A (CSS-4) | ICBM | 4–7 | 11,000–14,500 | 3/4-5 MT | 2–5m |
| DF-11/M-11 (CSS-7) | SRBM | ? | 300 | ? | 150–300m |
| DF-15/M-9 (CSS-6) | SRBM | ? | 500–600 | 250KT | 600m |
| DF-21 (CSS-5) | MRBM | 10–36 | 1,700–2,000 | 200–500 KT | 1.5–3m |
| JL-1 (CSS-N-3) | SLBM | 12 | 1,700–2,000 | 200–500 KT | 2–5km |
| DF-31 | ICBM | planned | 8,000 | ? | ? |
| DF-41 | ICBM | planned | 12,000–13,500 | ? | ? |
| JL-2 | SLBM | planned | 8,000 | ? | ? |

[a]IRBM: intermediate range ballistic missile. SRBM: short-range ballistic missile. SLBM: submarine launched ballistic missile. ICBM: intercontinental ballistic missile.
[b]Circular error probable.

bomber, and C[3]I capabilities could be destroyed entirely or damaged seriously by an opponent's first strike. Although the Chinese might be able to launch a second strike against large cities, it is unclear that they would be able to attack targets of opportunity or launch coordinated strikes.[8]

To remedy this situation, the Chinese have embarked on a multifaceted nuclear modernization program. The overall objective is to "improve the survivability of the missile forces by reducing the prelaunchtime period, to find less vulnerable basing modes, and to make general improvements in accuracy, range, guidance, and control."[9] As with conventional modernizations, Beijing's progress has been very slow, and many years pass between the first test of a new ballistic missile, submarine, or bomber and its operational deployment.[10] One of the highest priorities has been the development of solid-fuel, mobile missiles to replace their volatile liquid-fuel counterparts, a transition that would enhance operational flexibility by reducing launch preparation time.[11] Five major solid-fuel programs have received attention in the West: the DF-11, DF-15, DF-21, DF-31, and DF-41. The DF-11 and DF-15 (known more commonly in the West by their export designations of M-11 andd M-9, respectively) are short-range ballistic missiles that are solid fuel and nuclear-capable. The ranges of these missiles limit their operational radius to China's immediate neighbors, but their accuracy, as witnessed in the Sino-Taiwan tensions of 1995–1996, makes them a potent coercive weapon. China deployed the DF-21 medium-range ballistic missile (MRBM) in 1988, and at present approximately 10 to 36 missiles are based in northwest and southwest China. The

DF-31 and DF-41 solid-fueled mobile ICBMs are still being developed, but early reports suggest that when are deployed (in the late 1990s), they will have an effective range of 8,000 and 12,000 to 13,500 kilometers, respectively. Both the DF-31 and the DF-41 will be missiles launched from transporter-erector launchers (TEL), a mobile capacity that neither Washington nor Moscow currently possesses.

A second priority for China's strategic forces has been the development of a MIRV (multiple, independently targetable reentry vehicle) capability. Some analysts have speculated that China's continued nuclear testing and stalling maneuvers during the Comprehensive Test Ban Treaty (CTBT) negotiations were a function of its desire to develop the miniaturized warheads necessary for MIRVing their ICBMs.[12] A third priority has been expansion of the remaining two legs of the strategic triad: air- and sea-launched missiles. China already has deployed the solid-fueled Julang-1 (CSS-N-3) submarine-launched ballistic missile (SLBM) (essentially the same missile as the DF-21) in its lone operational Xia-class strategic submarine ballistic nuclear (SSBN), but problems with the nuclear power plants on the boats and solid-fuel technology in the missiles has prevented any advances. The second-generation SLBM, designated JL-2, will be a sea-launched version of the DF-31 with a range of nearly 8,000 kilometers. Deployment of this missile, which would require the parallel development of a new class of SSBN, likely would cause the Chinese to rethink their traditional reliance on the land-based leg of the triad. Efforts to improve the Chinese bomber force have met with similar technological impediments and have resulted in a deemphasis on air-delivered weapons. Finally, the Chinese have made initial efforts to upgrade their C[3]I capabilities (also known as "strategic conventional technologies"[13]) through the importation of advanced communication technologies, such as fiber optics, and microwave equipment.

Overall, the Chinese nuclear force is improving steadily, although force modernization will continue to encounter serious technological difficulties. If the writings of Chinese theorists are any indication of long-term doctrinal change, however, the PRC nuclear force might pose a long-term challenge to the present nuclear status quo, particularly if START II and other similar trends continue to reduce the arsenals of the United States and the former Soviet Union.

## Conventional Weapons

### NAVAL DOCTRINE AND MODERNIZATION

The Chinese see the eventual development of a blue-water (*yuanyong-fangyu*) navy as essential to the nation's long-term interests, since a strong navy can both protect China's maritime economic interests (i.e., the coastal Special Economic Zones) and serve "as the principal instrument for realizing China's aspiration to be an independent international power."[14] Throughout the history of the PRC, the PLA Navy (PLAN) served only a coastal defense (*jinhaifangyu*), or brown-water, role, because of both its technological limitations and the dictates of Soviet naval strategy. In the post–cold war era, however, the PLAN has taken on a significant, perhaps even leading, role as the front line of China's green-water "offshore active defense" (*jinyangfangyu*).

To facilitate the transition from coastal to offshore defense, since the mid-1980s the PLAN has added several new principal surface ships to its fleets, including two new classes: the Luhu-class destroyer and the Jiangwei III–class missile frigate. These two vessels reflect a growing improvement in the quality of Chinese shipbuilding, possessing significant missile capabilities (including Silkworm surface-to-surface missiles [SSMs], surface-to-air missiles [SAMs], and antimissile systems), sophisticated radar and fire-control systems (primarily imported systems), improved antisubmarine warfare (ASW) capabilities, and electronic countermeasures. The other destroyers and frigates of the principal surface fleet (Luda, Jianghu, and Chengdu class), however, are still largely suited to the earlier coastal defense mission. Designed for antisurface warfare, the ships are armed with SSMs and guns, but their short-range SAMs are poorly placed for air defense. Command and control, radar, fire-control, and ASW systems are all primitive by modern standards. The remainder of the Chinese fleet is made up of nearly 1,000 patrol and mine countermeasure craft, again largely suited to the coastal defense mission. Like the principal vessels, these smaller craft have adequate offensive capability (200 have SSMs and the rest are armed with torpedoes) but have very limited air defense capability. Finally, the PLAN theoretically has 54 amphibious landing craft, capable of transporting 6,100 troops and 350 tanks. Short of a reverse Dunkirk, the PLAN does not offer a significant amphibious threat to any theater except perhaps the small islands of Spratlys or those islands nestled between China and Taiwan. If the PLAN decides to develop a potent amphibious force, it will represent a major technological breakthrough, enabling the Chinese to project sufficient force to threaten an adversary's homeland (i.e., Taiwan).[15] Table A1–2 presents the estimated PLAN force structure.

Of particular interest to Western analysts is China's submarine fleet, which has undergone some lurching changes since the late 1970s but portends a future "sea denial" capability (i.e., interdiction of trade movements or sea lines of communication) that, if attained, would radically alter the naval status quo in East Asia.[16] Currently the PLAN has only

**Table A1–2.    Estimated PLAN Force Structure, 1998**

| Type[a] | Class | Current | Recent | Planned |
|---|---|---|---|---|
| Destroyer (DDG) | Luhu | 1 | 1 | 3 |
| Destroyer (DDG) | Luda III | 2 | 2 | 14 |
| Destroyer (DDG) | Luda II | 2 | — | — |
| Destroyer (DDG) | Luda | 13 | — | — |
| Missile frigate (FFG) | Jiangwei | 4 | 4 | 2 |
| Missile frigate (FFG) | Jianghu I/II/III | 30 | ? | ? |
| Missile frigate (FFG) | Chengdu | 4 | — | — |
| SSBN | Xia | 1 | 1 | ? |
| SSN | Han | 5 | — | 1–5 |
| Submarine | Song | 1 | 0 | ? |
| Submarine | Kilo | 2 | 4 | 18 |
| Submarine | Improved Ming | 13 | 10 | ? |
| Submarine | Modified Romeo | 36 | 1 | ? |

[a] DDG: guided missile destroyer; FFG: guided missile frigate.

one SSBN, the Xia class, the product of a long and disorganized indigenous program.[17] While it successfully launched an SLBM in 1988, the Xia is reputed to be extremely vulnerable to acoustic detection and attack by modern ASW systems. Given these limitations and the fact that three to five hulls are required for the maintenance of one constantly patrolling submarine, the Xia currently has limited strategic value.[18] Additionally, there have been persistent reports of power-plant difficulties with the Xia, preventing the continuation of line and prompting some in the Chinese military leadership to call for a completely new class of SSBNs. China's five Han-class nuclear-powered attack submarines (SSNs) suffer from similar problems as the Xia, since they were developed from the same basic technology. Presently, the exact role of the Han-class submarines is unclear; they have been used for area ASW support in support of the SSBN and for antisurface operations. The remaining 43 diesel submarines, a mixture of Ming (type 035) and obsolete ex-Soviet "Romeo" class (type 033) boats, are being improved slowly (in the case of the Ming) or replaced by the new Song class (Wuhan-C), which contains a mixture of advanced Russian, French, and Israeli technologies, and the four recently imported Kilo-class submarines from Russia.[19] The Kilos are relatively advanced boats in comparison to the rest of the fleet and are extremely well suited to green-water operations.[20] Furthermore, the crews of these boats are being trained by the Russians at the Submarine Academy in St. Petersburg.

In the long term, one can deduce from the statements of Chinese officials that the PRC is interested in building a world-class navy, complete with aircraft carrier battle groups and a full ballistic missile submarine capability. It must be emphasized, however, that these two goals are far from realization, for budgetary, technological, and organizational reasons. For example, even if the Chinese were to purchase a foreign aircraft carrier, they do not now have the capability to outfit its hull with the proper electronics systems (neither the Ukrainians nor the Spanish, both mentioned as possible suppliers, will sell China a fully equipped vessel), nor do they have the wherewithal to purchase or construct the accompanying ships necessary for a functioning carrier battle group. Because of these and other limitations, many experts believe that the Chinese would not be able to acquire a carrier before the middle of the 21st century. It is clear, however, that the possession of a "breakthrough" capability such as a carrier battle group would alter the balance of power in East Asia, permitting China to overcome a major geographical impediment (the Pacific Ocean) and project force throughout the region. Second, as discussed earlier, technological problems continue to hamper the development of further SSBNs, although the addition of the Kilos makes the Chinese diesel submarine force a growing concern for the U.S. Navy.[21]

Overall, the projected addition of increasingly sophisticated vessels and the explicit desire on the part of the Chinese leadership to build a blue-water navy poses a significant potential long-term threat to the naval status quo in East Asia.

## AIR FORCE DOCTRINE AND MODERNIZATION

As with naval doctrine, airpower doctrine received little attention during the strategic dominance of Maoist "people's war," since defensive guerrilla operations did not require projection of air or sea power. Until very recently the People's Liberation Army Air Force (PLAAF) had little or no experience with offensive counterair operations, close air support of ground units, battlefield interdiction, and sophisticated airborne command and control systems.[22] Chinese airpower strategy continued to improve incrementally until the American coalition's success in the 1991 Gulf war forced a major overhaul of PLAAF doctrine. In particular, the Chinese military leadership was impressed by the complete battlefield dominance exercised by coalition air forces, and the extent to which those aircraft easily destroyed Iraq's largely Soviet- and Chinese-origin air defenses and ground equipment. These lessons have not resulted in a real doctrinal evolution, however, primarily because of the tremendous technological constraints upon the force itself. Currently the

**Table A1–3.    Estimated PLAAF Force Structure, 1998**

| Type | Class (Russian) | Current | Recent | Planned |
|------|-----------------|---------|--------|---------|
| Fighter | Su-27 | 50 | 24 | 272 |
| Fighter | F/J-10 | 0 | — | ? |
| Fighter | F/J-8 | 100 | 12/year | — |
| Fighter | F/J-7 (Mig-21) | 500 | 40/year | — |
| Fighter | F/J-6 (Mig-19) | 3,000 | — | — |
| Fighter | F/J-5 (Mig-17) | 400 | — | — |
| Medium Bomber | H-6 (Tu-16) | 120 | 4/year | — |
| Light Bomber | H-5 | 300+ | — | — |
| Transport | (IL-76) | 10 | 25 | ? |

PLAAF is largely limited to an air defense role, since most, if not all, of its aircraft have a tightly proscribed combat radius.

The PLAAF itself is the third-largest air force in the world, with almost 5,000 combat aircraft. The vast majority of these planes, however, are obsolete models of MiG-17, MiG-19, and MiG-21 fighters (known to the Chinese as the J-5, J-6, and J-7, and to Westerners as the F-5, F-6, and F-7, respectively) as well as the Soviet Tu-16 bomber (H-6), all based on 1950s and 1960s technology. The PLAAF also operates a small number (about 100) of the more advanced and indigenously produced J-8 fighters. The J-8, however, continues to be plagued by engine and fuel consumption problems and poor weapons systems, and is emblematic of China's inability to design, manufacture, or even reverse-engineer an advanced indigenous fighter.[23] Table A3–3 presents the estimated PLAAF force structure.

As a result, the PLAAF has turned to the import market for assistance. China has already purchased 26 Su-27s from Russia and secured agreements on another 24 in December 1995, with a coproduction deal for hundreds more near completion. The Su-27 greatly enhances China's air capability, providing the PLAAF with an all-weather, counterair fighter with an integrated fire-control system, look-down/shoot-down radar, and in-flight refueling capability. The planes are armed with AA-10 ALAMO and AA-11 ARCHER air-to-air missiles, and its Chinese pilots were sent to a 12- to 18-month training course in Russia beginning in June 1991. While the addition of these advanced fighter aircraft would, on the surface, appear to vastly improve the capabilities of the Chinese air force and its ability to project military power, the "Iraq scenario" must be kept in mind. In the 1991 Gulf war Saddam Hussein chose to send his most advanced Soviet aircraft to Iran rather than sacrifice them to the destruction of the U.S. attack. Indeed, the political cost of losing a number of these very expensive planes, because of the inadequacies of the PLAAF's other logistic and support systems, may be too high a price for the PLAAF to bear until the more primitive systems achieve some semblance of technological parity with more advanced air forces in the region.

Three other air-related acquisitions deserve mention, because they are deemed to be "breakthrough" technologies and therefore pose a potentially destabilizing threat to the regional balance of power and U.S. security. The first is long-range transport and lift capability. The Chinese have acquired ten IL-76 MAINSTAYs, the Russian equivalent of the U.S. C-141 Starlighter. The IL-76 can carry 40 tons of payload 3,100 miles in six hours. This type of airlift capability is potentially destabilizing because it would symbolize a desire for extended strategic reach and possibly be a precursor to some greater and more sustainable form of force projection; enable its possessors to mount at least some limited projection operations, involving ground troops, with the intent of holding and occupying territory; and enable its possessors to sustain military operations in a more concentrated way at a greater distance from home.[24] These planes also can be converted to air-refueling tankers as well as airborne warning and control aircraft (AWAC), which are the second and third air-related "breakthrough" technologies.

The Chinese already have begun to experiment with air-to-air refueling, allegedly converting up to five new B-6 Badger bombers into tankers with technology acquired from Iran, Pakistan, or Israel.[25] Such capabilities would allow the Chinese to augment their force projection by extending the range of tactical aircraft for a longer operational reach and increasing the tempo of operations and warfighting efficiency.[26] For instance, these tankers could extend the combat radius of China's J-8 fighter from 431 miles to 632 miles, enabling China to conduct missions over the South China Sea, near Taiwan, along the Sino-Indian border, and over the East China Sea. It is believed that the PLAAF will have a fleet of dedicated tankers early in the next century.[27] A similar type of "force multiplier" technology is airborne warning and control aircraft. Currently the Chinese have no airborne early-warning (AEW) craft, which exacerbates the fact that ground-based radars cannot provide adequate surveillance of China's vast territory. There have been unconfirmed reports that the Russians have retooled some of China's IL-76s into AWACs planes, but there is no evidence that these have been deployed.

In the long term, therefore, the PLAAF may pose a threat to regional neighbors, but the extent of that threat is mitigated by serious and seemingly endemic impediments to modernization of the force. Short of a wholesale importation of a new air force, which contains within it dilemmas of equal magnitude, the PLAAF will continue to struggle well into the next century.

It is clear from statements of the leadership in Beijing and the military's selective force modernizations that the Chinese intend to play a major, if not commanding, role in their hemisphere. If current trends continue, China's conventional armed forces 20 years from now will be smaller, better trained, better equipped, and capable of significant force projection beyond their borders. At the same time, it could be argued that certain elements of the Chinese military are progressing faster than others. Some experts believe that, as a result of the tensions over Taiwan in 1995–1996, China's weapons programs likely will place a particular emphasis on acquiring capabilities designed to strengthen the credibility of Beijing's military options against the island and to deter the United States from deploying aircraft carriers in an effort to counter such options. Specific conventional military systems relevant to such capabilities include large amphibious landing craft, especially those capable of traversing wide, shallow mudflats as are found on the west coast of Taiwan; medium-range fighter/interceptors; short- and medium-range ballistic missiles; conventional attack submarines; improved $C^3I$ and carrier detection systems; and long-range, stand-off, antiship weapons, including cruise missiles and anticarrier torpedoes.[28]

However, attainment of Chinese objectives in these and other areas faces enormous obstacles, as mentioned. Nontheless, the greatest near-term threat will originate in China's naval modernizations, both because of the PLAN's relative success in blending indigenous systems with imported hardware and the fact that "the East Asian region is a maritime theater."[29]

# Notes

1. Paul H. B. Godwin, "Force Projection and China's National Military Strategy," in C. Dennison Lane, Mark Weisenbloom, and Dimon Liu, eds., *Chinese Military Modernization*, (Washington, D.C.: AEI Press, 1996), pp. 69–99.

2. Ibid., p. 4.

3. This list is drawn from John Frankenstein and Bates Gill, "Current and Future Challenges of Chinese Defense Industries: Organization, Acquisitions, and Modernization," paper presented at the CAPS/CAPP Conference on the PLA Towards 2000, July 13–15, 1995, Hong Kong, p. 7.

4. For an elucidation of this thesis, see John Wilson Lewis and Hua Di, "China's Ballistic Missile Programs: Technologies, Strategies, Goals," *International Security* 17, No. 2 (Fall 1992): 5–36.

5. Alastair Iain Johnston, "China's New 'Old Thinking': The Concept of Limited Deterrence," *International Security* 20, No. 3 (Winter 1995–96): 5–6.

6. John Caldwell and Alexander Lennon, "China's Nuclear Modernization Program," *Strategic Review* (Fall 1995): 28.

7. Dingli Shen, "The Current Status of Chinese Nuclear Forces and Nuclear Policies," paper released by the Princeton University Center for Energy and Environment Studies, 1990, p. 11.

8. Alastair Iain Johnston, "Prospects for Chinese Nuclear Force Modernization: Limited Deterrence versus Multilateral Arms Control," *China Quarterly* (June 1996): 17.

9. Robert Norris, Andrew Burrows, and Richard Fieldhouse, *Nuclear Weapons Databook, Volume Five: British, French, and Chinese Nuclear Weapons* (Boulder, Colo.: Westview Press, 1994), p. 372.

10. Dunbar Lockwood, "The Status of U.S., Russian, and Chinese Nuclear Forces in Northeast Asia," *Arms Control Today* (November 1994): 23.

11. Caldwell and Lennon, "China's Nuclear Modernization Program," p. 30.

12. It is significant that the Chinese already have successfully launched multiple satellites from a single ICBM booster, but they have not yet shown the capacity to deploy small, long-range solid-propellant rockets with sufficient throw-weight for MIRVing.

13. Ashley Tellis, "Military Technology Acquisition and Regional Stability in East Asia," in Jonathan Pollack and Hyun-Dong Kim, eds., *East Asia's Potential for Instability and Crisis* (Santa Monica, Calif.: RAND Center for Asia-Pacific Policy and The Sejong Institute, 1995), pp. 55–57.

14. Alexander Chien-cheng Huang, "The Chinese Navy's Offshore Active Defense Strategy: Conceptualization and Implications," *Naval War College Review* (Summer 1994): 7–32.

15. Tellis, "Military Technology Acquisition," p. 67.

16. Ibid., p. 68.

17. For a detailed, if somewhat "official," version of the Xia's story, see John Wilson Lewis and Xue Litai, *China's Strategic Seapower: The Politics of Force Modernization in the Nuclear Age* (Stanford, Calif.: Stanford University Press, 1994).

18. John Downing, "China's Evolving Maritime Strategy Part 1: Restructuring Begins," *Jane's Intelligence Review* (March 1996): 129–33.

19. For more information on the Song-class boats, see "China Continues Ming Submarine Production," *Jane's Defense Weekly*, September 16, 1995, p. 16.

20. For information on the Kilo-class boats, see "Submarine Force Priority for China's Modernization Plan," *Jane's Defense Weekly*, November 19, 1994, p. 2.

21. It is a common misperception that diesel boats are somehow noisier than their nuclear counterparts. In many cases, the exact opposite is true; some would even argue that the diesel boats have an advantage in coastal and green-water operations.

22.    Kenneth Allen, Glenn Krumel, and Jonathan D. Pollack, *China's Air Force Enters the 21st Century* (Santa Monica, Calif.: RAND Corporation/Project Air Force, 1995), p. 103.

23.    For an excellent, highly detailed analysis of China's largely unsuccessful attempts to modernize its fighter force, see ibid.

24.    Tellis, "Military Technology Acquisition," p. 62.

25.    Bill Gertz, "Chinese Arms Buildup Increases Attack Range: Refueling Tankers Vital to Arsenal," *Washington Times*, March 12, 1996, p. 1. For reports of foreign involvement in the development of a Chinese air-refueling capability, see Nicholas Kristof, "Experts Fret over the Reach of China's Air Force," *New York Times*, August 23, 1992.

26.    Tellis, "Military Technology Acquisition," p. 62.

27.    Allen et al., *China's Air Force*, pp. 170–171.

28.    This paragraph is taken from Michael D. Swaine, "Chinese Military Modernization: Motives, Objectives, and Requirements," in *China's Economic Future: Challenges to U.S. Policy (Study Papers)*, submitted to the Joint Economic Committee, 104th Congress of the United States, 2d session, August 1996, pp. 320–338, Washington., D.C., U.S. Government Printing Office.

29.    Tellis, "Military Technology Acquisition," p. 58.

# Appendix B

# Major Chinese Arms Control Organizations

## KIRSTEN SPEIDEL

Figure A2–1 depicts the key organizations that collectively contain a small but growing community of arms control specialists; it is not an attempt to provide a definitive guide to the arms control policymaking hierarchy in China. Indeed, little is known about the exact chain of command in arms control and disarmament decision making except that primary responsibility for the general parameters of policy most likely resides at the highest levels of the government and military apparats, while specific bargaining positions and strategies are worked out in an interagency process involving the Ministry of Foreign Affairs Arms Control and Disarmament Department, the relevant organs in the General Staff Department system, and technical specialists in the Commission on Science, Technology, and Industry for National Defense (COSTIND) and the nuclear weapons and missile communities.

Each of the institutes and organizations presented in the figure houses some arms control experts; however, the majority of these specialists may be found in the Ministry of Foreign Affairs (particularly the new Arms Control and Disarmament Department [formerly the fourth division in the International Organizations Department]); the Arms Control and Disarmament Program within the China Defense Science and Technology Information Center under the PLA General Equipment Department (formerly under COSTIND); institutes in the nuclear weapons laboratory system, such as the China Academy of Engineering Physics (CAEP) and its Beijing affiliate, the Institute of Applied Physics and Computational Mathematics (IAPCM); institutes in the

**Figure A2-1  China's Weapons of Mass Destruction Arms Control Community**

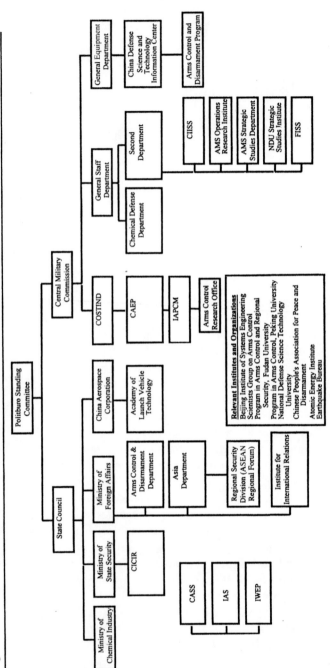

*Source:* Information for the organizational chart was drawn largely from: Alastair Iain Johnston of Harvard University and the following three pieces by Johnston, "China and Arms Control: Emerging Issues and Interest in the 1980s," *Aurora Papers* 3, The Canadian Centre for Arms Control and Disarmament, (January 1986); "Learning versus Adaptation: Explaining Change in Chinese Arms Control Policy in the 1980s and 1990s,"*China Journal,* (January 1996); "China's New 'Old Thinking': The Concept of Limited Deterrence," *International Security* 20, No. 3 (Winter 1995–96): 5–42; and Banning Garrett and Bonnie Glaser, "Chinese Perspectives on Nuclear Arms Control," *International Security* 20, No. 3 (Winter 1995–96): 43–78. Additional assistance was provided by John Frankenstein of Hong Kong University, Bates Gill of the Stockholm International Peace Research Institute, and Harlan Jencks of Lawrence Livermore National Laboratory. At the time of writing, it is unclear whether the CAEP and IAPCM will remain under COSTIND or will be moved over to the General Equipment Department.

missile program, such as the China Academy of Launch Vehicle Technology; and those in the Second Subdepartment and the Chemical Defense Subdepartment of the General Staff Department. Other important institutes containing arms control experts include the Institute of American Studies (IAS) and the Institute for World Economics and Politics (IWEP), both within the China Academy of Social Sciences (CASS); the China Institute of Contemporary International Relations (CICIR); the Ministry of Chemical Industry; National Defense University's (NDU) Strategic Studies Institute; the Second Office of the Academy of Military Science's Strategy Department; and the Earthquake Bureau (seismology). Many of these bodies have been represented at different times, depending on the issue, on the delegation to the Chinese mission at the U.N. Conference on Disarmament in Geneva, which has become a training ground of sorts for Chinese arms control experts. However, since 1980, when China first began to participate formally in the Conference on Disarmament, the bulk of these delegates have been from the Ministry of Foreign Affairs and the General Staff Department.

Initially, lines of authority and communication within China's arms control community were primarily vertical in nature; only within the last ten years have horizontal linkages become more apparent among the various relevant organizations. Conferences bringing together arms control specialists from their respective institutions are now held quite frequently. Within the technical arms control community in Beijing there is a specialist group composed of scientists and experts from several COSTIND institutes, from the CAEP and IAPCM, and from the General Staff Department that holds regular seminars to discuss different arms control topics. COSTIND's Arms Control and Disarmament Program apparently was established, in part, to coordinate the flow of technical information to the Ministry of Foreign Affairs and other sections of China's security apparatus. This body is also responsible for setting up the arms control seminars within COSTIND and across other units with arms control responsibilities.

Chinese arms control experts also have established ties with specialists and organizations in the West that deal with arms control matters. Such organizations include Stanford University's Center for International Security Arms Control, the Stockholm International Peace Research Institute, the U.S. Natural Resources Defense Council, the Union of Concerned Scientists, the Federation of American Scientists, the Stimson Center, and the Nonproliferation Program at the Monterey Institute of International Studies. Chinese arms control experts also have participated in seminars organized by the International School on Disarmament and Research on Conflicts, based in Rome.

# About the Authors

ELIZABETH ECONOMY is the Fellow for China and Deputy Director of the Asia Studies Program at the Council on Foreign Relations. She currently directs Council projects on Asia and the environment and U.S.-China relations. She also cochairs the Woodrow Wilson Center working group on China and the Environment. Her most recent publications include *The Internationalization of Environmental Protection*, with Miranda Schreurs, and an American Academy of Arts and Sciences occasional paper, *Reforms and Resources: The Implications for State Capacity in the People's Republic of China*. Dr. Economy also has served as a consultant to the MacArthur Foundation and the U.S. government on issues related to China and the environment.

TODD M. JOHNSON is an environmental economist with the World Bank. Previously he was executive director of an economics education and research program in China at the National Academy of Sciences and coordinated the China Energy Study at the East-West Center. Mr. Johnson's most recent publications include *Clear Water, Blue Skies: China's Environment in the New Century* (coauthor) and "Development of China's Energy Sector: Reform, Efficiency, and Environmental Impacts."

ALASTAIR IAIN JOHNSTON is John L. Loeb Associate Professor of the Social Sciences at Harvard University. He is the author of *Cultural Realism: Strategic Culture and Grand Strategy in Chinese History* and has written articles and book chapters on China's multilateral diplomacy, the ASEAN Regional Forum, foreign policy learning, strategic culture, and normative structures in international relations. Currently, he is working on a book on socialization in international institutions.

SAMUEL S. KIM is Adjunct Professor of Political Science and Senior Research Associate at the East Asian Institute of Columbia University. He is the author or editor of over a dozen books on Chinese foreign policy and world order studies. His articles have appeared in leading professional journals on China and international relations, including the

*American Journal of International Law, China Quarterly, International Interactions, International Journal, International Organization, Journal of Chinese Law, Journal of Peace Research, World Politics,* and *World Policy Journal.*

NICHOLAS R. LARDY is a Senior Fellow in the Foreign Policy Studies program at the Brookings Institution and the Frederick Frank Adjunct Professor of International Trade and Finance at the Yale School of Management. Previously he was Director of the Henry M. Jackson School of International Studies at the University of Washington. He has written and edited numerous articles and books on the Chinese economy and is a member of the editorial boards of *The China Quarterly,* the *Journal of Asian Business,* and the *China Economic Review.*

JAMES MULVENON is Associate Political Scientist at the RAND Corporation in Washington D.C. specializing in Chinese military affairs.

ANDREW J. NATHAN is Professor of Political Science and former Director of the East Asian Institute at Columbia University. He is chairman of the Advisory Committee of Human Rights Watch's Asia Division. His books include *Chinese Democracy, Human Rights in Contemporary China* (coauthor), *China's Crisis, The Great Wall and the Empty Fortress* (coauthor) and *China's Transition.*

MICHEL OKSENBERG is a Senior Fellow at the Asia Pacific Research Center at Stanford University, where he is also Professor of Political Science. He was on the faculty of Stanford University, Columbia University, and the University of Michigan, where he was also Director of the Center for Chinese Studies. He has served as a staff member of the National Security Council in Washington, D.C., with special responsibility for China and Indochina. He also has served as President of the East-West Center in Honolulu. His most recent publications include *The Chinese Future* and *Living with China.*

MARGARET M. PEARSON is Associate Professor of Government and Politics at the University of Maryland. Focusing her research on China's role in the world economy and foreign business in China, she has published two books: *Joint Ventures in the People's Republic of China* and *China's New Business Elite.* Her most recent research is on China's accession bid to the World Trade Organization.

LESTER ROSS is an attorney in the Beijing office of Paul, Weiss, Rifkind, Wharton & Garrison, where he focuses on foreign investment, international banking and finance, project finance, and corporate and environmental law matters. Mr. Ross has extensive experience representing foreign banks and corporations in their strategic expansion in the United States. He is author of *Environmental Policy in China* and coauthor of *Environmental Law and Policy in the People's Republic of China.*

KIRSTEN SPEIDEL is Instructor in Mandarin Chinese at Swarthmore College, Department of Modern Languages and Literature.

MICHAEL D. SWAINE is a Senior Political Scientist in International Studies at RAND and Research Director of the RAND Center for Asia-Pacific Policy (CAPP). Previously he was a consultant in the business sector, a Postdoctoral Fellow at the Center for Chinese Studies, University of California, Berkeley, and a research associate at Harvard University. His recent writings include *The Role of the Chinese Military in National Security Policymaking* (revised edition) and *China: Domestic Change and Foreign Policy.*

FREDERICK S. TIPSON is Director of Regulatory Affairs in Hong Kong Telecom (HKT). Before joining HKT, he was an International Public Affairs Vice President with AT&T. He joined AT&T in 1984 as an attorney for the International Communications Services group. From 1988 to 1991 Dr. Tipson was Regional Director for Government Affairs in AT&T Asia/Pacific Inc. in Hong Kong. He has been Counsel to the Foreign Relations Committee of the U.S. Senate, first as Minority Counsel under Jacob K. Javits of New York and then as Chief Counsel under Charles H. Percy of Illinois. He recently contributed an article to *Foreign Affairs* entitled "Culture Clash-ification."

# Index

Printed in the United States
803500003B

9 780876 092255